Performing Political Identity:
The Democrat Party in Southern Thailand

PERFORMING POLITICAL IDENTITY: THE DEMOCRAT PARTY IN SOUTHERN THAILAND

Marc Askew

SILKWORM BOOKS

ISBN 978-974-9511-38-1

First published in 2008 by
Silkworm Books
6 Sukkasem Road, T. Suthep, Chiang Mai 50200, Thailand
<info@silkwormbooks.com>
www.silkwormbooks.com

Typeset and cover design by Silk Type
Cover photograph and all other photographs by Marc Askew

Printed in Thailand by O.S. Printing House, Bangkok

5 4 3 2 1

CONTENTS

LIST OF MAPS, PLATES, AND TABLES

Maps

Plates

Tables

NOTE ON TRANSLITERATION AND SPELLING OF THAI NAMES

In the transliteration of Thai words and names, I have used the Royal Institute (Ratchabundittayasathan) romanization guidelines to the fullest extent possible. Where Thai authors' names or those of well-known public figures are commonly spelled using different romanization systems in published material, I have generally conformed to these spellings if they are consistent (e.g., Chuan Leekpai, instead of Likphai, as it would be according to the RI System). The ordering of Thai authors in the bibliography follows customary Thai practice of listing by personal name rather than surname. The Thai term *phuak* will not be italicized after it has been defined because it occurs so frequently throughout the book.

PREFACE AND ACKNOWLEDGMENTS

This book is about the Democrat Party political machine in southern Thailand and how it successfully mobilized an electorate against an unprecedented threat to its long-standing regional dominance during the years 2003–05. This account of campaigns, candidates, and voters in Songkhla Province shows how the southern Democrats' successful defense against Thaksin Shinawatra's nationally dominant Thai Rak Thai (TRT) Party in successive elections during 2004 and 2005 was achieved not through the blandishments of money (though this was judiciously used), but primarily through the rhetorical and symbolic seduction of ordinary voters and the astute management of allegiances among key followers. "Seduction" is perhaps not the precise metaphor to describe the Democrats' methods of securing majority voter support because most ordinary voters in Songkhla Province, as with those in most of the southern region, have been willing victims in the conquest, as shown in every national election in the region since September 1992. In early 2003, when TRT leaders were confidently proclaiming their intention to conquer this one remaining Democrat Party electoral base, a Bangkok journalist with a gift for simile remarked, "If you likened people in the south to a woman, she would be the most faithful type."[1] Rather than "seduction," then, the people-party relationship might be better described as a marriage that is periodically rekindled by romance and ardent expressions of fidelity.

Above all, the people-party relationship is rekindled in the powerful and emotive dramas of the southern Democrats' election campaigns and their central ritual and rhetorical arenas, the political rallies. Democrat Party rallies in the south are festivals of loyalty. They persuasively project categories of the ideal southern citizen and the ideal democratically infused political party, and they pit this symbolic political community against demonic and dictatorial enemies bent on "eating the country" (*kin mueang*). Although skillfully performed myths sustain the party's public potency for voters, it is the deeply embedded constellation of *phuak*—tightly knit coteries bound together by mutual interests—that form the party's pragmatic infrastructure of middle-ranking supporters, whose allegiance to Democrat politicians and the party needs constant cultivation through various forms of support. Added to the Democrats' mythic potency and its pragmatic phuak-based organizational strength is a campaigning formula that relies on undermining enemies through scandal and rumor, a method which remains effective because of the party's capacity to elicit high levels of popular trust. Southern civil society activists bemoan the Democrat Party's hegemony in the region as an unscrupulous exploitation of "southern political culture," a set of ideal categories and practices (centering on everyday idioms of loyalty and trust), which they have progressively constructed in scholarship and which they yearn to harness as the basis of their own model of people-based politics. Against the Democrats' multi-level arsenal, the party's opponents in the south have so far been unable to compete successfully, despite their strenuous efforts to assemble their own phuak and project electoral claims founded on local development imperatives and their own public repute.

Southern Democrat politicians and their key supporters in the constituency branches are masters of the political game. Yet southern voters are not the simple "cultural dupes" of the party's orators and myths as their opponents complain, certainly no more than the northeasterners who have enthusiastically embraced Thakin's TRT populism as a sign of tangible commitment to bettering their lives and "working" for their votes. Nor are southern voters narrowly parochial in embracing the Democrat Party as, "the party of the south." Rather, in the vision of moral politics generated and reinforced by the party's leading icons (preeminently Chuan Leekpai), voters perform a region-based nationalism that exalts the Democrat Party as a political organization which represents the very best of themselves in the service of the country. "Southern Thais" are, in fact, a diverse group (comprising urbanites and rural dwellers, Sino-Thais, ethnic Thais, and Muslims) and their articulation of allegiance to the Democrat Party is varied in emphasis and sophistication. Yet, their views are united in perceiving the Democrat Party as a trustworthy institution. Old Democrat Party stalwarts are honest enough to admit to the corruption within the ranks of the party's politicians, although as one of them confided to me, "We know that many [in the party] are rotten, but where else are we going to go?," meaning that there is no other comparable party in the country to commit one's trust. Since Thaksin Shinawatra's election victory in 2001, many southern Democrat voters have been willing to accept that his leadership and government was marked by decisiveness and useful practical policies, while also conceding that the Democrats have been hesitant and slow when in power. Yet, when in 2005 they were faced with the choice of endorsing Thaksin's triumphant performance-based government or opposing his governing methods as urged by the Democrat Party fraternity, they chose the latter, based on a normative view of the political order that upholds political morality as an irreducible principle.

From mid-2003 until early 2005, I was in Songkhla Province for three separate periods totaling some eleven months, also returning during 2006 and 2007, after the elections described in this book. I spent this time badgering national and local politicians, talking with aspirant and failed candidates, listening to the gossip and chat of political party members, journalists, and ordinary voters, and attending meetings and political rallies in towns and villages across the province. In short, I "hung around with a purpose," as a close colleague has aptly described the habits and preferred methods of anthropologists. As an anthropological investigation of electoral politics, this book is unashamedly detailed in its portrayal of events and people, but through this detail and the election narratives of its key chapters, the book's aim is to explore a number of key themes in political life in the south and in Thailand generally. It is about the meaning of political representation and the nature of political solidarities as they are expressed in the performative uses of language, political symbolization, and the pragmatic mobilization of alliances and loyalties, viewed from the vantage point of one of the south's largest provinces and most prominent strongholds of the Democrat Party.

At one level, this book can be read as a detailed account of political campaigning and a delineation of candidates and supporters (a rarity in Thai political studies) in a key period of Thailand's political life, a period that has been indelibly marked by Thaksin's controversial attempts to restructure the nature of electoral politics and governance, and by resistance to this project. The conflicts generated in this period are still being played out following Thaksin's ousting by military coup-makers in September 2006. In Songkhla, the contest between Thaksin's TRT and the Democrat Party took place under the frightening shadow of an escalating insurgency in the province's southern districts, which was extending from its epicenter in Songkhla's neighboring provinces of Pattani, Yala, and Narathiwat. This ongoing insurgency had a critical effect on local representations of the political struggle against Thaksin's rule and his party. While this context is critically important to understand the character of the electoral contests of 2004–05 in the south, at the same time the book is also an ethnographic analysis of Thailand's electoral politics as a symbolic and thus culturally informed process. The accounts in this book describe the ways that people express their understandings of political contestation, judge candidates according to key values and categories (concerning morality, loyalty, trust, and identification), enact political interests, and manipulate cultural codes to legitimize these actions in political arenas at various levels.

Throughout the course of the research behind this book, I have benefited greatly from the assistance of individuals and institutions. First, I must acknowledge the invaluable assistance of King Prajadhipok's Institute, which provided funding support until the end of 2004. My thanks go particularly to Thawilwadee Bureekul of KPI for her encouragement and support. Thanks also to Sathithorn Thananitichod of KPI, who provided important practical assistance in numerous ways. At various stages in researching and writing this book, I benefited greatly from the advice and ideas of Thai and Western academic specialists and colleagues, including Anek Laothamatas, Anusorn Limanee, Pasuk Phongpaichit, Yot Santasombat, Suraphong Sothanasathian, Pitch Phongsawat, Chris Baker, Michael Herzfeld, Duncan McCargo, Michael Montesano, and Michael Nelson. In Songkhla, I benefited greatly from discussions with Wichai Kanchanasuwon of the Prince of Songkhla University (Hat Yai Campus). Thanks also to Southern Thai folklore specialists Akhom Detthongkham, Sutthiwong Phongphaibun, and Charun Yuthong, who generously gave me the time to discuss their ideas and writings on southern Thai society. Special thanks to my colleagues Monica Minnegal and Peter Dwyer of the Anthropology Program, University of Melbourne, who continually challenged me to clarify my own assumptions, and to Chandra Jayasuriya for the maps.

Without the cooperation of key political figures across the party political spectrum in Songkhla and beyond, the research for this book would have been impossible. I am grateful to a number of senior politicians of the Thai Rak Thai Party for permitting me to interview them, including Suranand Vejjajiva (official TRT spokesman) and Wira Musikaphong (then TRT coordinator for Songkhla and Phatthalung Provinces). In Songkhla Province, I was fortunate to gain access to politicians at all levels, together with provincial and municipal officials and journalists. The many people with whom I conducted formal interviews are indicated in endnotes connected to the text (unless, where indicated, they remain anonymous for various reasons), and I thank them all. In particular, thanks to Rungarun Dansap, formerly *rong palat thesaban* of Ban Phlu Municipality, with whom I first became acquainted before the commencement of this project, and who has maintained a keen interest throughout. My particular thanks to the former Mayor of Hat Yai, Khreng Suwannawong and to his daughter Patthama, who kindly allowed me time for interviews at a particularly stressful time in their family's political life. My grateful thanks to Khun Sathian Manirot, director of Songkhla's Provincial Election Commission (PEC) during 2003, and to his successor Khun Phaithun Chehair, who during 2004–05 allowed me access to election documentation and confided to me with great frankness his views and knowledge of electoral malpractices in the south. I am also indebted to Lt.-Colonel Mongkon Bunchum and to Captain Chawalit Kalabaheti, chairmen of constituency-based PEC committees in the province. Particular thanks go to a key local informant who assisted my investigation into vote-buying practices in Constituency "X" and who, by request, remains anonymous.

Above all, I must express deep appreciation here to the Democrat MPs of Songkhla and to their *phuak* members who good-naturedly tolerated my pestering questions and my frequent presence in their homes, at numerous party activities, and rallies. They include Niphon Bunyamani, Phrai Phatthano, Lapsak Lapharotkit, Thawon Senniam, Wirat Kalayasiri, Wichit Suwit, and his son Naracha Suwit. I am grateful also to Nawaphon Bunyamani and Atsawin Suwit, who shared their views and information on provincial election campaigns. Particular thanks to former Songkhla Democrat MP Sawai Phatthano, who, though handicapped with illness, honored me with time for an interview about his life, political experience, and views on the political contests. Numerous Democrat Party branch office-bearers welcomed me to party activities and gave me time for interviews and discussion. Particular thanks to Thamanun Selimin (formerly chairman of DP Constituency 2) and to Nirut Mai-on (former Democrat Party branch advisor, Constituency 2), and to Chiap and her cheerful band of women party activists, the stalwart foot soldiers of Songkhla's Democrat Party. Special thanks to Police Sergeant Chum, Phrai Phatthano's affable bodyguard, and to Don, the equally humorous assistant of Niphon Bunyanani, with whom I spent many a jocular (and informative) evening. Of Thai Rak Thai and other party candidates, their key organizers and supporters, I gratefully acknowledge for their cooperation and frankly confided views Niran Kaenyakun, Surasak Mani, Chamlaeng Mongkhonnitphakun, Seri Nuanpheng, Seri Pathumwan, Manop Pathumthong, Thip Phromphet, and Sanya Watcharaphon. Local journalists and newspaper editors were generous with their time and sharing of information and journalists' gossip. They include Samrit Bunrat (owner, *Samila Times*), Wichan Chuaichuchai (then chief editor, *Samila Times*), Prasan Suksai (manager, *Focus Phak Tai*), Piyachot Intharaniwat (then senior journalist, *Focus Phak Tai*), and Samatcha Nilaphatama (then journalist, *Focus Phak Tai*). There were many more men and women who shared ideas and information, allowed me to listen-in on their conversations, and welcomed me to attend events and meet with their friends and phuak (women have "friends," men have phuak). Their names are too numerous to list here, but their hospitality, understanding, and tolerance were indispensable to my undertaking. Through these people, I have tried to make sense of the political worlds and understandings of actors at different levels of Songkhla's political landscape. The usual caveat applies that all flaws in interpretation and errors of fact in this book are to be attributed to me alone.

Note

1. Sukanya, "Gift-Bearing TRT."

Part I

Introduction: Culture Myths and a Political Heartland

CHAPTER 1

Making Sense of Difference: The Democrats and the Electricity Pole

IN SONGKHLA, as in most of southern Thailand, there is a popular saying among Democrat Party supporters: "The Democrats could send electricity poles (*sao faifa*) to stand as candidates for parliament and we would still vote for them." This metaphor condenses the ideal that voters' commitment and trust in the collective entity of "the party" overshadows any judgment about the eligibility of individual parliamentary candidates. It is an assertion of difference against the character of other political contenders and their parties, both in the region and the rest of Thailand. Non-Democrat politicians are invariably portrayed as weak in their fundamental commitment to party and ideology (*udomkan*), and their parties are dismissed in standard Democrat Party polemics as short-term or expedient vehicles for opportunists. Against these sham parties—lacking *udomkan*, driven by vested interests (*phonprayot*) and sustained by money power—shines the virtuous and iconic Democrat Party, conspicuous as the oldest political party in the country, with heroic leaders who are evoked as exemplars of courage, constancy, and sacrifice for the public weal against the ever-lurking demon of "dictatorship" (*phadetkan*).

More often than the aphorism of the electricity pole that affirms the virtue of stubborn collective allegiance, popular attachment to the Democrat Party is expressed by supporters in visceral metaphors of blood and emotion, or in culturally normative sayings that highlight shared ideals of group solidarity and trust. As one female party member in Hat Yai expressed her bond with the Democrat Party, "It's not about *liking* the party—it's about *love*" (*khwam rak*). Or as Manun, a Muslim party member and key vote canvasser affirmed in masculine tones, "*Mai thing phak, mai thing phuak*," which roughly translates as, "You don't abandon your party and you don't abandon your in-group." The word *phuak* (a tightly knit coterie, band, or group) is as emotively powerful as it is flexible, with normatively positive as well as pejorative and descriptive uses. Unconditional loyalty to one's phuak is an ideal that is frequently contradicted in everyday life and also among political players in the south, but it is constantly enunciated in the symbolic language of loyalty shared by Songkhla's Democrat Party supporters. As with all the emotion-charged rhetoric surrounding the Democrats and the south, however, the metaphor of the electricity pole and its associated popular expressions of affection and commitment belie the complex mix of machine politics and myth that sustains the Democrat Party ascendancy in Thailand's southern provinces.

It is not often acknowledged that the most strident detractors of the southern Democrats are also southerners, who depict the party's regional dominance and popularity as the product of a cynical confidence trick played on southern voters by wily Democrat orators and their self-serving crony groups (or phuak, here used in the negative sense). To these detractors, Democrat politicians are not the heroes and icons of southern virtue as they project themselves to be, but liars, hypocrites, and villains (see plate 1.1). This view is condensed in a crude popular saying prevalent in Thailand and the south, which parodies the moral posturing of leading Democrat politicians: "Pretending to be sad, telling a story full of lies, and screwing your friend's wife" (*Ti na sao, lao khwam thet, yet mia phuean*).[1] In Songkhla Province, political rivals of the Democrats and civil society advocates alike deplore the party's symbolic hegemony and yearn for a different kind of politics—the former advocate tangible development achievements (*phon ngan*) as an index of political eligibility, while the latter seek wider popular participation outside the stifling control of Democrat phuak-based groups. Their critiques, however, have not substantially affected the durability of a symbolically suffused party-people relationship that has been harnessed successfully by Democrat orators and canvassers to mobilize voter support in every national election in the region since the early 1990s.

...ผู้แทนฯเมืองใต้
ไม่โกงกิน..ไม่ขี้เมา..และไม่เอาเมียเพื่อน...เฮื้อกๆๆ

1.1 The southern Democrat politician as hypocrite and trickster. This cartoon caption reads, "Doesn't cheat, isn't a drunkard, and doesn't take his friend's wife, ha!" Note the pointed finger echoing a nang talung *puppet character. (Source: Journal of Southern Thai Studies)*

As depicted in detail in this book, in the national election of 2005, the southern Democrats delivered a humiliating region-based rebuff to the nationally dominant Thai Rak Thai (Thais Love Thais) Party (TRT). This was a striking contrast to a nationwide trend of overwhelming TRT triumph and Democrat Party defeat in the rest of the country (conspicuously in Bangkok, the Democrats' original base, and in the northeast). The election results in the south reaffirmed a region-based party dominance that had been in place for over a decade, but had been strong even before then. What is the basis for such a striking anomaly in Thailand's contemporary political landscape?

The south's prominence as a Democrat Party stronghold from the early 1990s has attracted frequent comment from scholars, journalists, Democrat politicians, and their opponents (who are often renegade Democrats). But though popular, journalistic, and academic explanations for the south-Democrat link abound, they are commonly highly generalized, often reductionist, and usually superficial, stressing factors such as the distinctiveness of "southern Thai culture" and its shaping of popular political values, or alternatively the southern Democrats' calculated exploitation of idioms of regional pride for electoral purposes. With the exception of a few Thai postgraduate students who have bravely attempted to explore the Democrat-south relationship (mainly by surveys, the standard instrument in Thailand's social science research practice[2]), Thai and Western academics alike have been content with broad-brush explanations. As Duncan McCargo has rightly observed in an important review of the literature and arguments on southern Thai politics, the lineaments of this electoral nexus have never been explored in any detail, in particular the popular meaning of the Democrat Party to southern voters.[3] This book represents one attempt to explore this nexus.

In the wake of the Democrats' successful defense of their southern heartland in 2005, the southern Democrats claimed that this had demonstrated again that a distinctive "political culture of southern people" (*watthanatham thang kanmueang khong chao tai*) was consistent with key features of their party's traditional opposition to *phadetkan* and the misuse of power (*amnat*). Songkhla's academics commonly evoked primordial categories of cultural or ideological distinctiveness in the south to explain the TRT defeat. In this book, however, I am not concerned with proving or disproving the existence of southern Thai uniqueness. The construct of "southern Thai political culture" is a fabrication, but a fabrication that has important uses and meanings for different constituencies of actors on the political stage. Constructs like "southern Thai culture," and other affirmations of "southern-ness" become real for people in the moment of their assertion because they are statements of difference that define and shape a symbolic political community. My interest in this book is to explore the nature of these *assertions of difference*, their symbolic uses in political campaigns, and why they are important to various actors.

As Frederick G. Bailey reminds us, political competition is won by those contestants—comprising leaders, their core teams, and followers—who command and deploy superior resources within the terms of the game, and adapt their tactics to unbalance their opponents and exploit weaknesses.[4] In Songkhla in 2004, and again in 2005, the Democrats won the decisive majority of votes by skillfully managing a range of critical resources available to them through experience and by virtue of their long political incumbency. This Democrat arsenal included powerful symbolic capital represented by the emotive imagery of sacred *udomkan*, exemplary leaders and heroic voters, critical levels of group support through phuak alliances, and the hard-nosed instrumental techniques of fomenting rumor and scandal to discredit opponents. This book tells the story of how those resources were deployed and why they were effective.

EXPLORING THE DEMOCRAT ASCENDANCY

This book is an anthropological investigation of electoral politics in southern Thailand focusing on the dynamics underlying the regional political ascendancy of the Democrat Party. This ascendancy is a phenomenon much remarked upon, but never fully explored. This book emphasizes both the symbolic and structural—as well as the organizational and tactical—dimensions of political group formation and contestation as I encountered them during the period of 2003–05. This was a particularly stirring and significant period in Thailand's political history. During these years, the beleaguered Democrats were mounting a desperate defense of their voting heartland against Thaksin Shinawatra and his Thai Rak Thai Party, who appeared poised to transform the very nature of electoral politics and governance in the country.[5] The book explores the meaning of political representation and allegiance as expressed in the performative uses of language and in the symbols deployed by key actors in election campaigns. It is equally an inquiry into the structuring of political solidarities and the pragmatic mobilization of alliances and loyalties through kin groups and the bonds of phuak. These are viewed from the vantage point of one of the region's largest provinces and most prominent strongholds of the Democrat Party. More broadly though, the book aims to show the importance of symbols and language in Thai political life, and how the manipulation and assimilation of symbols and ideal categories express the imperative need to affirm (and gain) trust and legitimize power in moral terms.

As with all anthropology, the accounts in this book reflect the conviction that big questions can be explored by means of intensive examination of small, or particular, places and groups. My focus is on the detailed description and interpretation of events, the composition of groups, and the understandings of individuals within those groups, derived largely from my own direct engagements with people and events, whether through interview, conversation, or observation. I deliberately focus on the constituency-level cut-and-thrust of political campaigning and political group mobilization. The campaigns reflect strategies emanating from the contesting parties' national "centers," and this is acknowledged in the book, but my main concern is to describe and interpret the rough-and-tumble of national political competition as it was played out in the constituencies, which is where the votes must be won in Thai election contests.

This excursion into Songkhla's political world began in mid-2003, prompted by a cluster of closely related questions. First, how does the Democrat Party assure its solid electoral dominance in the south, and what is the basis of the party's popularity? Second, and, intimately connected to these questions, would this dominance and popularity endure the assault of Thaksin Shinawatra's TRT Party in the coming 2005 elections? Since Thaksin's first stunning election win in 2001, the Democrat Party had been in crisis—relegated to opposition status and with no answer to TRT's policy and populist dominated marketing strategies. In early 2003, Chuan Leekpai, the southern Democrat icon and former prime minister, stood down from party leadership. With no hope of gaining government in the next elections, the Democrats in the south were handicapped because they could not campaign, as they had done in 2001, on the prospect of Chuan becoming prime minister. At a national level, with TRT riding high and proclaiming endless successes with its "CEO"-style leader, the departure of Chuan from the Democrat helm brought into even greater relief the party's chronic policy weaknesses and lack of a competitive national image.[6] In 2003, the TRT Party was already predicting that its populist-based and media-driven electoral marketing approach to elections would prevail over the Democrats' remaining voting base in the south. This political environment was an opportune time to try to discover how the Democrat Party worked in the south, and indeed whether it would survive the coming electoral onslaught.

My focus on Songkhla Province as an exemplar of the "Democrat South" was prompted by political developments there. During 2003–04, a set of important and interlinked local and national electoral contests unfolded in this province, events which offered a prime opportunity to observe the mobilization of political groups and the links between local and national politics. Most decisively, early in 2004, Songkhla Province became the site for the only national by-election to be staged in the Democrat-dominated southern region for the period 2001–05 between national elections. It was to be a critical test of strength both for the TRT governing party and for the Democrats. Shortly after this, an historic municipal election was held in the city of Hat Yai. The 2004 by-election, in fact, was determined by the decision of a local Democrat MP in 2003 to step down and run in the Hat Yai mayoral election, a decision with significance consequences for the campaigns. The political atmosphere of Songkhla was enlivened by these events, which were staged just prior to the scheduled nationwide Provincial Administrative Organization (PAO) elections for March 2004. The PAO contests were viewed as an important preliminary in laying down support networks for the forthcoming national election campaigns of February 2005. Thus in Songkhla, over the space of a few months in early 2004, there followed in rapid succession a by-election, a city election, and a provincial election, all of which prefigured the alliances and tensions that emerged later in the national election. These events determined my choice to explore political competitions in Songkhla

Province, but Songkhla is nevertheless a reasonable exemplar of the Democrat-dominated Buddhist-majority and Thai-speaking south, which encompasses most of the peninsula's fourteen provinces (with the exception of the three largely Malay-speaking Muslim-majority border provinces, which feature rather different political dynamics and allegiance patterns).[7]

Two interacting dimensions inform this portrayal of Songkhla's political world and the dynamics underlying the reproduction of the Democrat Party electoral ascendancy. First, the symbolic: that is, the fabrication of the political community through the staging of emotionally powerful rhetorical performances, seen most dramatically in election rallies. Second, the pragmatic: i.e., the organization of alliances and interests forged between closely knit groups of political actors at all levels, commonly known as phuak, which, aside from acting to benefit their own members in various ways, serve as critical intermediaries between the party and electorate in the process of vote canvassing. Both of these dimensions (rhetorical performance of symbols and the solidarities of phuak formation and reproduction) are culturally informed processes combining functional and expressive imperatives—that is, they *do* something towards a political goal and they *symbolize* and therefore *mean* something for the actors in the process. They are critical political resources among competitors, who engage in the active manipulation of the cultural symbols and categories that people recognize and commonly attach to ideas of loyalty, morality, and credentials for leadership, even if these ideals are often breached in practice, as they are in all cultures.

What I describe as the "Democrat ascendancy" in Thailand's south is not a permanent and inert state of affairs. It needs to be continually nurtured because it is constantly challenge by enemies. This electoral ascendancy, based on both symbolic legitimacy and organizational strength, needs to be reproduced and reaffirmed at all levels—district, municipal, provincial, and national—against the claims of rival political groups that persistently contest this ascendancy. An understanding of Democrat dominance can not be comprehended without equal attention to the Democrats' local opponents and their own supporting groups. It is perhaps ironic that many rivals to the Democrats were once themselves former members or key supporters of the party. Personifying these opponents vividly as undemocratic—and in the case of TRT, demonic—"others" was one of the primary symbolic means through which the Democrats, lacking a coherent party image in the rest of the country, mobilized support in their southern constituencies during the period 2003–05.

THE SOCIODRAMA OF ELECTIONS: PERFORMANCE AND LANGUAGE

This book explores the contours of the Democrat Party ascendancy in southern Thailand in the dynamic setting of election contests. My interest, like that of a relatively small number of anthropologists who have concerned themselves with election campaigns, is to describe and interpret the ways in which key political actors (groups and individuals) "perform" symbolically what is at stake in the electoral arena—how they demonstrate their own political eligibility against their opponents' claims—by crafting language, rhetoric, and rituals towards galvanizing identification and political loyalty among audiences and voters. In this view, politics can be viewed as "sociodrama," and the symbolic competition that is central to this process invariably involves the manipulation of cultural categories, for the obvious purposes of claiming legitimacy and undermining opponents' claims.[8]

Election events offer unique opportunities for undertaking a symbolic analysis of political practice and its meanings. They are particular moments, or rather clusters of interacting moments, when networks and groups are activated and become visible. The groups involved and constituted through this competitive interaction are developed and perceived in culturally specific ways. As F. G. Bailey highlights, "Each culture has its own set of rules for political manipulation, its own language of political wisdom and political action."[9] At the same time, election contests are dramatic punctuations in the flow of everyday public life. They are moments when roles and values are articulated more sharply than they are in periods between such dramas. I have approached election events in Songkhla Province as examples of what Victor Turner describes as, "potent processes of social action."[10] In

Thailand, as elsewhere across the world, election events push usually dormant values and political positions into prominence in public and everyday life—parties and candidates mobilize their policies and rhetoric in the media and at rallies, canvassers tour neighborhoods, and ordinary people discuss issues and gossip about candidates. People, in short, are impelled to position themselves in various ways and consider loyalties, allegiance, and identity. It is during these intense moments that cultural idioms and categories make their appearance in a range of forms that are accessible to ethnographic observation, interview, and talk.

In Thailand, in the discourses surrounding Democrat Party identification with southerners—whether it be in everyday articulations or in the highly choreographed dramaturgical settings of party rallies—categorical statements of regional cultural identity are always prominent. These evocations are rhetorical performances that serve to mark the boundaries between "us" (Democrats) and "them" (non-Democrats), even though much of these apparently distinctive southern cultural values (e.g., loyalty to kin, phuak, and personal honor) appear to be pervasive throughout Thailand. Some might suggest that the question of southern Thai political exceptionalism demands a comparative empirical demonstration to confirm that southern Thais (a diverse group, in ethno-religious terms, in fact) are distinct in their political values and practices from the Thais of other regions of the country. This is a virtually impossible task, certainly from the standpoint of conducting detailed constituency and site-based field investigations. But in any case, it is more meaningful to ask, why does it seem necessary to many southern Democrat voters to appear—or demonstrate themselves to be—distinctive in the context of national political contests? In terms of political identity, "southern Thainess" is a rhetorical and symbol construct that asserts boundaries. Like the powerful constructs of community identity discussed by the anthropologist Anthony Cohen, "southern Thainess" is an idealization that becomes politically meaningful to ordinary people when their moral ideals (however partially adhered to in everyday life and political practice) are perceived to be threatened by "outsiders;" it is a collective identity that becomes tangible and coherent when symbols are convincingly assembled and performed before people, helping them make sense of their political world and affiliations.[11]

The "performative" dimensions of politics are treated in this book not only in the ways that the Democrat Party—its politicians and key supporters, such as party branch officials and members—presents itself to the electorate. Performances are also visible in interactions between political actors and supporters, and the ways that political eligibility is expressed in meaningful language that encompasses loyalty to one's phuak and kin groups, determinations of leadership qualities, public virtues, and obligations. They find expression in powerful terms such as *barami* (morally infused repute generated by good deeds), *kwangkhwang* (well connected, expansive, generous) and *chai nakleng* (having "the heart of a *nakleng*"), the qualities of boldness, courage, generosity, loyalty, self-sacrifice, and truthfulness. In the south, as elsewhere in Thailand, politicians' evocation of ideal moral qualities jostle with modern and global categories of political eligibility (i.e., worthiness for election to public office) that stress vision (*wisaithat*), having policies (*nayobai*), transparency (*khwam prongsai*), and ability based on education (*kan sueksa*), particularly internationally gained qualifications. Thamora Fishel proposes that in Thailand, notions of progress and rationality inform one key moral discourse of power that coexists dynamically with an older personalist and patronage-centered moral discourse.[12]

It is in the enactment of this language in election dramas that we see the play of symbols in politics and the manipulation of cultural categories.

THE POLITICAL USES OF "CULTURE"—IDIOMS AND IDENTIFICATION

The reader will probably by now be thinking that I am playing fast-and-loose with the idea of culture here: on the one hand, treating it as a fabrication by political organizations, yet also seeing it as bedrock of meaningful categories used by people to position themselves as voters or supporters. Let me briefly clarify my usage here without boring the reader with a tedious recounting of the theoretical ping-pong that still surrounds the use of these words in the academic world. The expression "political culture" as well as the term "culture" are widely and very loosely used in the media as well as state and specialists' discourses, referring to specific as well as general phenomena (e.g., "culture of rumor," "culture of violence"). "Political culture" is essentially a normative construct (it defines what should, or shouldn't be), and even when used descriptively, can easily slip into value-laden use. It is inseparable from ideologies of political development (either state or non-state centered), as represented, for example, in discourses of "Thai-style democracy."[13] In this book I use the term "political culture" in a specific way to refer directly to the idealized constructs of political groupings that have explicit collective agendas, whether they are the Democrat Party, civil society activists, or the state. "Political culture" is still commonly used by academics of various stripes to refer to those values and norms that are commonly applied by societies in the political realm, but I do not accept this separation between "political values" and the broader cultural scheme of symbols. I refer to these schemes of everyday values simply as "cultural" (not "political culture"), leaving "political culture" to stand for ideological categories.

There are, of course, recognizable patterns and idioms in Thai society, as in others. They serve to give coherence and justification to people as they act in the world, relate to others, and identify themselves. These are fabrications that we can collectively call "culture"—a system of symbols mobilized by people to comprehend and anticipate their actions and those of others. Symbols are the stock in-trade of our everyday life.[14] Yet while such symbols and values can be itemized by ordinary people as well as academics in their efforts to represent themselves and their societies, symbolic production is dynamic. The anthropologist Robert Murphy gave one of the most succinct and appropriate depictions of the relationship between people and their cultural categories when he pointed out that, "Man does not live *by* them; he lives *with* them."[15] In this book, I will talk far more about symbols and "idioms" than about some monolithic *thing* called "culture." I do this to highlight how symbols and categories, though critically important in helping people order their worlds, have to be actively manipulated (by them and others), so as to manage the relationships and understandings necessary to the task of political positioning—these are relationships and understandings of critical issues such as loyalty, trust, and affiliation, whether among active followers of candidates or among ordinary voters. In Thailand, in the interactional settings of villages and neighborhoods, anthropologists have highlighted the role of rhetoric and the uses of normative categories in peoples' negotiation of loyalties, obligations, and in the justification of self-interest.[16] Election competition, as will be shown in this book, brings many of these categories into intense play, both publicly and privately. We will see in various accounts in this book how such hallowed qualities such as *barami* (merit-filled repute) can be rhetorically inverted by contestants to depict amoral and self-interested power and influence (*itthiphon*) in their rivals. One man's *barami* is, literally, another's *itthiphon*. We will see how the value of phuak loyalty, universally evoked as a quintessential southern virtue, is often subverted and contradicted in practice, yet the normative *ideal* of such loyalty still retains its importance.

Though I have described "southern Thai culture" and particularly "southern Thai political culture" as fabrications, I am not denying that there are tangible features of regional dialect, diet, customs, and entertainment traditions that mark the "*khon tai*." Many of these traditional customs are now quite attenuated in the wake of social and economic change, as Wattana Sugunnasil has recently highlighted, while others, such as the *nang talung* puppet performances are being self-consciously publicized by various segments of the region's middle class in efforts to revive local traditions.[17] Despite the obvious existence of these distinctive characteristics, however, the evocation of regional distinctions to form the political entity of "southern Thai political culture" generates a moral, cultural, and ideological construct of quite a different order to everyday objectifications of difference. In southern Thailand, as everywhere else in the country, a strong value is attached by people to local identification with birthplace—usually expressed as "*ban rao*," an identification that is frequently evoked in order to claim legitimacy and eligibility for political office. In this book, I describe this, following others, as "localism" (not to be confused with the "localism" used by many writers now to depict anti-globalization and community-focused development movements). Students of elections in Thailand have rightly noted the importance of local identification as an emotional bond and a symbolic construct that is universally drawn upon by political contenders as well as voters in their evaluations. The idea of the "*ban*" (village, home) is an ideal construct of a social order, and such a locality, like a person, can lose face. Aiming to bringing honor to a district is a standard claim of political candidates.[18] Protecting "local face" was one of the lynchpins sustaining the legitimacy of Hat Yai's long serving mayor, Khreng Suwannawong, whose rise and demise is documented in chapter 4. Delivering speeches in regional dialect is a standard feature of politicians' performative repertoires—it is an affirmation of local bonds and identification with place, rhetorically unifying speakers with their audiences as an intimate community. Though the use of dialect is particularly conspicuous among Democrat politicians in the south, its use by politicians in Thailand is hardly exclusive to this region alone. In Songkhla, the Democrats' opponents were just as determined to affirm local loyalty in regional dialect. The contests, as will be seen, were between the strength of different calls to the emotive bonds and allegiances of "us" and "our." As Andrew Walker notes in a recent study of election contests in a district of northern Thailand, local attachment is itself quite a malleable idea that changes in importance depending on candidates and the level of the election contest.[19]

Through symbols attaching themselves to place and to trustful relationships, people in southern Thailand, as elsewhere, constantly objectify their identities in order to position themselves in certain situations, individually and collectively. Southerners claim that they are distinctive because they are highly conscious of their honor, and are incorruptible, plain speaking and truthful, unconditionally loyal to phuak, and that they are canny political analysts. In turn, to make themselves "legible," politicians attempt to harness and magnify the power of these symbols and identifications at multiple levels. In the rhetorical evocation of these multiple levels of fictive kin, locality, and political bonds, southern Democrat Party politicians are highly skilled, and none more so than Chuan Leekpai. The following example, taken from an impromptu speech given by Chuan in Hat Yai during August 2006, helps to illustrate the rhetorical union of many layers of identification. Speaking after a merit-making ceremony at Hat Yai's

Khok Suea monastery, Chuan intoned before an adoring audience about his party and the south:

> We won completely in the southern region—because southern people don't sell themselves. The party is morally indebted to the people [*chaoban*] They [Thai Rak Thai] give money, but southern people don't want money. This is a characteristic of people of our home [*khon ban rao*] . . . A national leader must serve people equally in all regions. Thaksin has said that he will help only those people in provinces that have voted for him. Of the regions paying tax, Bangkok pays the highest tax. Second in line is the south, then comes the north, and then the northeast. If the government is to represent all the people, then it has to help people in all regions.

Chuan's brief address was finely tuned to condense a range of identifications, loyalties, and moral qualities at different registers. He began with a statement of virtue that was an explicit contrast between the morality of the ideal southern Thai person (*khon tai*) and the immorality of selling votes, explicitly equated with prostitution in the phrase "*mai khai tua*" (selling one's self). The first "we" was an inclusive reference to the Democrat Party as a political community. Chuan then personified the party (*phak*) by evoking its moral indebtedness to voters in the expression, "*pen ni bunkhun*," which affirmed an intimate bond of reciprocal obligation. The second "we" coupled with the emotive "our home" (*ban rao*) fused the identity of the Democrats with southerners, and Chuan himself with the audience. The next passage contrasted Thaksin's mercenary partiality with the ideal of a national leader serving everyone, while it also highlighted the wealth of the south (second only to Bangkok), literally presenting the region as nobly sacrificing its income for the nation. The use of the term *chaoban* (literally, "villager") was a rhetorical device that leveled the party and the people as equals, affiliated by intimate connections to a fictive village, despite the fact that there were educated middle-class urbanites in his audience. By exploiting powerful moral idioms that prevail in everyday discourse, together with localist identification, Democrat Party oratory, as exampled here, takes such everyday fabrication of identity to another level in constructing the ideal southerner as a political actor in a national arena.

POLITICAL FIELDS AND THE CAST OF PLAYERS

The periodic dramas of election campaigns and the vivid rhetorical performances of the Democrats galvanize an emotively powerful imagined political community among voters. But the Democrat ascendancy in Songkhla is also sustained by carefully managed alliances and solidarities among political actors at numerous levels, alliances that are sustained as much by mutual self-interest and ambition as high-flown political ideals. Songkhla's political world comprises competitors for power and office in a number of political "fields," i.e., competition at provincial, municipal and sub-district (*tambon*) levels. Without an infrastructure of support built on these groups, groups that maintain their own ambitions, the Democrats could not sustain solidarities needed for national political competition. In Thailand, as the small number of scholars who have closely studied election contests demonstrate (and Thai political commentators implicitly accept), the dynamics of national political competition cannot be fully understood without acknowledging the critical role of these overlapping and competing political groups.[20] So too in Songkhla, political aspirants and supporters are generated and nurtured from the ranks of local politicians. The contests described in this book include municipal and provincial level struggles. Through these, we see how political alliances at various levels were brought into alignment and tension, and how the Democrat-affiliated phuak and their opponents exerted a critical influence in local politics, which in turn configured the political groups that were mobilized against each other in the national election. Phuak groups are critical to the structuring of political support.

Throughout the narrative accounts of election contests in this book, the reader will encounter a host of people and names. Their various roles in the dramatic game of political competition in Songkhla should be fairly obvious in these accounts. Nonetheless, it is worth clarifying the positions and roles of these various people and their overlapping political fields, as introduced above. We can view them in a scheme that delineates "leaders" (the key individual election contenders), "teams" (their groups of key organizers and vote canvassers), "supporters" (those providing symbolic and material backing), and the voters themselves.[21] We can also treat the local and national press as other key actors, playing a role in interpreting the campaigns and candidates and being used in various ways by contestants themselves to establish or change the public narratives of the contests. It will become clear that the national level players rely on the assistance of "teams" comprised of people who are themselves "leaders" in provincial, municipal, *tambon* and village level political fields. Conversely, in provincial and local contests, the national-level players change their roles to become "supporters" of these "leaders" of teams in the provincial and local political fields. As will be seen, this symbiotic process of political support is not without tension, conflict, and fractures between groups. In fact, as shown in this book, in Songkhla during 2003–05, there was a clear element of comedy, farce, and irony in the whole process, with once staunchly loyal phuak members splitting away to become fervent enemies of former bosom companions, and faithful party followers being backstabbed by hard-nosed political operatives (in both the Democrat and TRT camps).

In the national level political contests in Songkhla, the individual players in the competitive drama of election contests can be grouped as follows:

Incumbent Democrat MPs and newly endorsed candidates. The Democrats held the high ground in the contests of 2004–05. They had won all eight parliamentary seats in 2001, continuing their electoral dominance in the province since 1992. From 2004 to 2005, this group of candidates included the well-established members with firm phuak and branch support, as well as newly endorsed candidates. Songkhla's Democrat MPS have extremely varied records of parliamentary and administrative performance (several are clearly mediocre, though others have strong records), but they have always been assured of winning because of the strength of popular support for the party in the province.

Challengers to the Democrats. Whatever the party banner they adopt, rivals to the Democrats are habitually lumped into the category of "non-Democrats" (*mai pen Prachathipat*) by the Democrats, highlighting the strength of Democrat supremacy and the marginality of their competitors. In 2004–05, however, these challengers included strong candidates with good credentials. There was a variety of other contenders, among whose ranks were the province's habitual "political losers" who came forward regularly under different party banners, and suffered defeat just as regularly. Among the Democrats' enemies were many renegade Democrats (both former parliamentarians and party branch officials), as well as ambitious province-level politicians. The strongest of these rivals sought and gained endorsement as TRT candidates, while the others had to be content with running for the less prominent parties (Chat Thai and Mahachon).

Teams. Indispensable to these contenders were the various "teams" that provided the canvassing and local infrastructural base for contestants' campaigns. In the case of the Democrats, these were the party branch activists, many of whom were *tambon* and provincial-level politicians, while their rivals also drew heavily on local and provincial-level politicians and their associated phuak. Lending key assistance to the rival candidates (via their key lieutenants) were the *kamnan* (*tambon* chiefs) and *phuyaiban* (village headmen), who in their localities utilized their own kin and phuak links to mobilize canvassing power. These team members were animated by varied motivations, ranging from unadulterated personal loyalty and political ideals, to stark mercenary concerns.

Supporters. All of Songkhla's national-level contenders needed to draw on supporters of various capacities. The weaker candidates standing against the Democrats were handicapped by both limited funds and small teams. Though some Democrat candidates relied primarily on the party's limited funds, some had their own substantial private funds derived from business activities. The TRT candidates were advantaged by substantial outlays of money from their party's central coffers, supplemented in some cases by considerable assistance from wealthy friends who were established national politicians or government ministers. For the Democrats, disadvantages in material support were offset by the power of symbolic support from the key figures in the national leadership, particularly the revered former leader Chuan Leekpai.

Voters. The ordinary voters of Songkhla (that is, those not actively involved in teams) are, as in Thailand generally, a varied group, ranging from educated middle-class urbanites to humble rural folk. Their responses to, and interest in, the political contests varied, as did their way of expressing and perceiving what the parties stood for. Overwhelmingly, their strongest voting loyalty was with the Democrats, a habit which the TRT candidates sought to break by appealing to other schemes of eligibility. Nonetheless, both major parties made appeals to bonds of kin and personal admiration in efforts to win people's votes, and the voting result for TRT in at least one constituency was to highlight the effectiveness of these appeals.

The Press. Aside from these key actors, the local and national press also played a role in framing the terms of the contests in Songkhla Province. The local press had a limited circulation beyond the major towns and market centers, but was a forum for candidates to gain publicity through interviews and statements. More significant, local newspapers gave detailed coverage to various scandals and speculation, partly reflecting popular rumor, but partly provoking it as well. In all the elections covered in this book (i.e., the national, municipal, and provincial contests), scandals were reported and fanned in the local press. In Songkhla, the Democrats demonstrated a high level of skill in fomenting scandals and speculation against TRT, then referring to national press reports as authoritative confirmations during their rallies.

PHUAK: A MALLEABLE FORM, A VARIABLE NORM

As a normatively charged idiom of group identification and loyalty (both negative and positive) and as a structural pattern of group formation, the phuak is one of the most important elements in Thai social organization and group consciousness. Though it has not been given adequate importance in formal (Western or Thai) models of Thai sociality, phuak is so widely accepted in Thailand that it is rarely mentioned in scholarship. Among Western commentators, only recently has the phuak been explicitly highlighted as critical in political organization, by political sociologist Michael Nelson.[22] In the mid-1970s, the Thai anthropologist Akin Rabhibadana paid attention to phuak as an important idiom of group loyalty in a focused urban ethnography, but his insights were never mainstreamed into academics' schemes of Thai social relations, which remained dependent on the idea of patron-clientage.[23] Three decades after Akin's emphasis on the role of phuak idioms, anthropologists' and political scientists' portrayals of group formation are still dominated by a stress on the vertical linkages and "asymmetrical exchanges" of patronage rather than more horizontally arranged group loyalties, as Withaya Suracharitthanarak has rightly pointed out.[24]

In common Thai usage, the term phuak and the frequently used compound words *phakphuak* (company of friends, accomplices, followers) and *phuakphong* (band, gang of friends) have many descriptive and emotive applications, and this makes it difficult to find any term in English that conveys their multiple subjective and descriptive meanings and registers. In Thai grammar and speech, the word phuak is used as a plural noun classifier referring to self- and other-connected groups (e.g., *phuak rao*, us; *phuak khao*, them). It is also used in a very neutral descriptive sense to classify collectivities of things and people (e.g., *phuak khru*, teachers). But the word also refers to a particular type of bonded or purposive social collectivity. Phuak finds itself translated in many ways in English, ranging from "group," through to "band," "gang," and most negatively, "clique."[25] Importantly, the moral and emotional connotations of phuak usage vary according to whether the phuak is self-related or other-related. Universally, one's own phuak (my gang, my band, my buddies, my group) has positive resonance, highlighting intimacy and fellowship. By contrast, the phuak morphs into something sinister when somebody else is gaining advantage by their own phuak associations—"*len phak len phuak*" (literally, "to play with one's phuak") connotes self-interested cronyism. At a basic level, phuak can describe the fellowship bonds between students who share the same class at school, or people who work together in the same unit or institution. The universal use of the term *phuak* in everyday life underlines the importance of achieving intimate relationships of trust at all levels of Thai society, often expressed in the term *khwam phukphan* (or closeness). *Phuak* therefore has a highly inclusive resonance when articulated by members of a phuak. The tendency in English language use to apply the term "clique" as a mono-dimensional structural definition of phuak reflects the difficulty in incorporating what, in fact, is both a flexible norm and a flexible structure into a social scientific model of group formation in Thai society.

It is possible that the significance and structural manifestations of phuak vary between the regions of Thailand. Southern Thai scholars argue that bonds of friendship and group allegiance expressed in terms such as *phuk dong*, *phuk kloe* (strong brotherhood and camaraderie bonds), as well as *phakphuak* are of central significance in southern Thai culture. There are, however, equivalent expressions of intimate bonding relations elsewhere, such as *phuk siao* and *siaokan* in the Lao-speaking communities of northeastern Thailand.[26] In Songkhla, loyalty to one's phuak is a quality that helps to define a worthy person and an admirable leader. This value was expressed well by a speaker delivering an election speech supporting the leader of a team running for the Kho Hong Tambon Administrative Organization (TAO), on the eastern fringe of Hat Yai, "Tell your *phakphuak* and *phi nong* to vote for Kamnan Khran (Thawirat). He is always truthful (*chingchai talot*), he loves his phuak, and loves his *phong* (*rak phuak rak phong*)." To "*rak phuak*" is a strongly positive value, and although it is an ideal that is frequently contradicted in real life by ruptured friendships and shattered phuak, it remains an important paradigm in the south. Thais from other regions often refer to the strength of phuak bonds among southerners, though as a term identifying group membership and allegiance it is universally used throughout the country.

Given its universal significance in social life, it is hardly surprising that phuak support is fundamental in political activity at all levels in Thailand. In his studies of national and provincial level politics in Chachoengsao Province in Central Thailand, Michael Nelson has argued that the *phakphuak* is one of the fundamental units (together with family lineages) of political group formation. I would agree with his assessment, although in national electoral politics in the south the existence of a durable Democrat Party organizational structure means that there is a complex relationship between phuak and party, a feature that is absent in Chachoengsao, where there has never been enduring party-linked voting traditions or support networks. Nelson defines *phakphuak* variously as "informal local political groups," "local political groups," or "cliques."[27] Although phuak are employed in political activities to forge alliances and to build networks for vote canvassing, they are often multifunctional and flexible groups. It is probably better to refer to those phuak that are shaped primarily by political activity as "political phuak," whose members are drawn from other general or "social phuak" connections into more purposive formations. Even here, however, the boundaries between the political and general function of these phuak are blurred in the often diffuse types of mutual assistance shared among members. This is the case in the Democrat phuak in Songkhla, which comprise both politicians (national and local) and others who regularly play a role in supporting the fortunes of phuak members in their political activities and beyond. Moreover, it is common for politically active individuals to identify and express loyalty to their political phuak while still maintaining bonds with close friends they also call "phuak," but who happen to belong to opposing political phuak. Much of the highly detailed and sensitive information on vote buying presented in this book, in fact, derives from information flows circulating among these crosscutting social and political phuak groups.

There is an ambiguity about the phuak as a formation—certainly in its political manifestations—because, while membership connotes a subjective sense of fellowship and an ethos of equality among phuak members, in structural terms the politically orientated phuak have recognized leaders and core members. Phuak are often held together by relations of obligation and exchange that can closely resemble patron-clientage, so that when support and material resources cease flowing among members, phuak can split, though it is not always a simple question of money. Thus, for example, Surasak Mani, one of Songkhla's TRT candidates, was proud of the mutual loyalty of his own phuak of local politicians who helped each other's political endeavors: "Where one goes, we all go," he intoned, in late 2003. A year later, one of his phuak decided to run as a candidate for the Chat Thai Party and was thereafter shunned by Surasak's phuak because, as one of them explained, "He passed over the head (*kham hua*) of Surasak."

Structurally, then, the phuak is an elusive and variable formation. At a basic level, such as among school friends or close work colleagues, a phuak may be highly egalitarian in its membership composition, but in other cases phuak include elements of hierarchy and dependence on leaders, and this is the case with political phuak, because of their larger size and the need for resources. As such, they begin to resemble Lucien Hanks' "Entourage and Circle" model of Thai patronage relations, which portrays sets of interlinked vertical patron-client clusters ramifying into numerous "circles," though Hanks never spoke of these "circles" as phuak, or referred to Thai expressions for them.[28]

In Songkhla, there is a strong ideology of unconditional loyalty surrounding intra-phuak relations, affirmed in expressions such as "*ao phuak wai kon*" (the phuak comes first). Yet the phuak is also a fragile formation. Political phuak need constant nurturing through support to affirm the bonds and obligations between members, particularly by core members who command more resources. This is the case among the Democrat phuak, where, as shown in one case in this book, phuak members can split away if they feel betrayed or when there is a clash of interests. Yet, despite this volatility, the phuak idiom has powerful normative resonance. This moral duality of the phuak idiom pervaded the language surrounding the election contests in Songkhla among key political actors and voters alike. "Phuak" was used to decry exclusive and self-serving cabals. The morally positive, inclusive sense of phuakness was evoked just as frequently, connected with images and familiar superlatives of loyalty, leadership, sacrifice to locality, and southern Thai-ness. Democrat supporters condemned Thaksin for his cronyism (*len phak len phuak*), but the resonance of the term *phuak* took on a glow when associated with the Democrats. One woman vendor had no idea that she voted for the Democrats, she knew them only as "Chuan's phuak." As a concrete political coalition forged by mutual loyalties and interests, the constellation of Democrat-affiliated phuak in Songkhla is one of the party's most critical resources for perpetuating the Democrat ascendancy.

PATRONAGE AND THE MORAL ECONOMY OF OBLIGATION

As a system of concrete transactions with an accompanying range of culturally endorsed expectations and moral justifications, patronage takes numerous forms in southern Thai society and politics, as it does throughout Thailand. In formal terms, patronage as a system is described in Thai as *rabop uppatham*, though this arcane usage is generally restricted to academics and journalists (and politicians, when they are denigrating the practices of opponents).[29] During my time in Songkhla, young local news reporters fresh out of university courses on political development habitually made distinctions in their columns between styles of *tambon* politics based on *uppatham* (standing for "traditional" patronage-based political campaigning) and *wisaithat* (vision, standing for "modern" policy-based campaigning). The reality, however, was far more untidy, as we will see exemplified in Phrai Phatthano's Democrat-supported campaign for the Hat Yai mayoralty, where he based his legitimacy on both inherited family prestige based on his fathers' good works (*barami*) in combination with a modern imagery of "transparent" and "reforming" governance. Ordinary people, predictably, do not express the patronage relationship that obligates them to benefactors in such abstract terms as *uppatham*, but in immediate and everyday expressions of morality and personalism such as "helping" (*chuai*), or "returning merit" (*topthaen bunkhun*, or its Malay equivalent, *balas budi*).

In its classic scholarly formulation, the traditional Thai system of patron-clientage (the core of social organization in the pre-modern period) has been defined in terms of personal, vertical (i.e., hierarchical), "dyadic" (between individuals), and diffuse relationships between people of differing resources, embodied in the social form of "entourages" (*boriwan*), comprising dependents (*luknong*) and their acknowledged superiors and patrons (*luk phi*, *phi liang*).[30] Scholars of Thai politics (in common with anthropologists) argue that these once morally suffused patron-client links have been comprehensively undermined by capitalism, whereby largely money-based and exploitative transactions have replaced the face-to-face character and the generality of older patron-client relations, though such money-based ties are still cloaked by politicians in the older cultural idiom of patron-client bonds ("culture" is thus mystified for ideological purposes). Adopting a Marxist model of social change under capitalism, scholars have argued that a particular system of political patronage has developed based on the essentially commodified relationships now prevailing in contemporary Thai society. They suggest that this manipulation of cultural idioms is exemplified by the vote-seeking practices of constituency politicians in their electorates, who build reputations through donations (notably to temples) and participation in traditional ceremonies (funerals and weddings, in particular). The stark cash nexus informing political loyalties is highlighted by these scholars through reference to the primarily money-based ties that link vote-canvasser networks, where the personalized relations of "traditional" patron-clientage are apparently absent.[31] This, however, is a highly simplified rendering of a more variable reality in the social organization of Thai electoral politics, as Anyarat Chattharakul has emphasized in a recent study of canvassing networks in a Bangkok constituency, which shows the critical importance of personal ties in voter mobilization. A wide range of patronage relations persists at various scales, encompassing individuals as well as communities, and often mediated by very personalized relations that are framed by common cultural expressions and justifications. Depictions of cultural norms as instruments of political manipulation used by elites in modern Thai capitalist society, though valid, tend to romanticize the pre-modern Thai patron-client system and downplay the self-interest, manipulation, and exploitation that have long been a central feature of traditional Thai social relations.[32]

In Songkhla, patronage relations are manifested in a continuum extending from starkly utilitarian transactions to highly personalized and enduring relationships. For example, the utilitarian expression of political patronage is shown in the way that one TRT candidate, a *nai amphoe* (district head) approached a resident of the constituency with a request to act as his vote canvasser in exchange for his promise to use his bureaucratic connections to transfer her husband, an army sergeant, to a more convenient post. By comparison, a more personalist and long-term form of the patronage relationship is shown in the support given by a prominent Democrat MP to one of his long-standing vote canvassers, who requested assistance in paying a hospital bill for his wife who had been injured in a traffic accident. Patronage is not only an individualized relationship; it has important collective dimensions, with accompanying expectations of generalized reciprocation. The ties forged by patronage are expressed in the moral idiom of paternalism and the identification of leaders with localities and local pride. This has been well exemplified by Yoshinori Nishizaki, who demonstrates the popular moral basis for the legitimacy of the controversial political strongman, Banhan Silpa-acha, in Suphanburi Province.[33] Similarly, Khreng Suwannawong's legitimacy claims as Mayor of Hat Yai, and popular recognition of these, were built on his accumulated good works for the city of Hat Yai and the sense of obligation that flowed from this accumulated *barami*. Even Hat Yai's Democrat supporters who rallied behind Phrai Phatthano to oust Khreng's son expressed strong feelings of respect and obligation to "Uncle Khreng" as a civic patron.

The language that legitimizes relations of patronage is part of a wider set of personalized and morally infused idioms of exchange and obligation that pervade social relations and discourse in Songkhla as elsewhere, idioms that evoke communal and kin ties as much as hierarchical benevolence-respect bonds.[34] It is hardly surprising that Democrat politicians take advantage of these idioms as much as their opponents in evoking the relationship between the party and its loyal voters, as expressed in Chuan's phrase, quoted earlier, about the party's moral indebtedness to the people. Whether or not we regard it as an ideological manipulation by political operators, the moral economy of merit and its emotive language play a potent role in articulating widely accepted notions of political legitimacy. In the game of political morality, the Democrat Party in the south enjoys prominence, because the party itself is widely perceived as a collective moral entity with collective merit and *barami*. As frequently expressed by Democrat supporters in Songkhla, the party and the people are bound by a history of mutual indebtedness (*mi bunkhun tokan*).

SONGKHLA: A DEMOCRAT PROVINCE

Southern Thailand is a region that is notable for its peninsular geography, its economy founded on rubber and fisheries, and its ethnic diversity.[35] There is a high degree of variation between sub-regions and no single province can absolutely typify "the south," though broad economic indicators confirm the general view that the region's fourteen provinces enjoy a relatively higher standard-of-living than the north and northeast of the country (see table 1.1). This does, however, mask differences between and within provinces in levels of economic prosperity (see table 1.2). Songkhla occupies Thailand's lower south, with its southernmost province boundary abutting the Malaysian state of Kedah. It shares boundaries with four other provinces: Satun to its west, Phatthalung to the north, and the Muslim majority Malay-speaking border provinces of Yala and Pattani to its southeast. It is the highest rubber-producing province of the south with a large population of rubber-growing smallholder farmers, but its coastal districts are based on fishing. Songkhla is the second largest province in the south in terms of population size, hosting a large rural population as well as the biggest urban center of the whole region, Hat Yai, which is the acknowledged business metropolis of the south. In the south at a regional level, Hat Yai has functioned much as Bangkok has for the nation, attracting migrants in search of opportunity. Its business elite, in common with the south's other towns, is primarily of Chinese descent. Manufacturing (primarily seafood processing) is prominent in Songkhla's economy, largely concentrated around its two largest urban centers of Hat Yai and Songkhla on its coast. Commerce, manufacturing, and extensive rubber production is the foundation for Songkhla's position as the second most prosperous province in the south, together with a lucrative tourist industry which, until the major outbreak of insurgent-driven violence in the border provinces from 2004, drew millions of visitors from Malaysia and Singapore.[36]

TABLE 1.1

Thailand: Gross Regional Product (GRP) Per Capita, 2003

Region	GRP (in baht)
Bangkok and Vicinity	230,997
Central	148,371
North	47,371
Northeast	30,860
South	69,450

Source: NESDB (www.nesdb.go.th/econSocial/macro/grp-data/).

TABLE 1.2

Southern Provinces: Population and Gross Provincial Product (GPP) Per Capita, 2000/03

Province	Population	GPP (in baht)
Chumphon	446,206	62,022
Krabi	336,210	80,639
Nakhon Si Thammarat	1,519,811	58,620
Narathiwat	662,350	38,533
Phangnga	234,188	83,999
Pattani	595,985	57,621
Phuket	249,446	172,932
Phatthalung	498,471	40,266
Ranong	161,210	65,960
Satun	247,875	67,600
Songkhla	1,255,662	92,614
Surat Thani	869,410	81,137
Trang	595,110	6,691
Yala	415,537	52,737

Source: NESDB (www.nesdb.go.th/econSocial/macro/GPP-data/).

Like all of Thailand's provinces, Songkhla is an administrative artifact. Though anchored on the historical core of the old port-based *mueang* of "Singhora," the *changwat* boundaries emerged under King

Chulalongkorn's project of the late nineteenth century to centralize, modernize, map, and discipline Siam's political territory. The former *mueang* of Songkhla was gazetted as a province within the *monthon* (territorial division) of Nakhon Si Thammarat in 1896, and its once hereditary governor was subsequently replaced by a centrally appointed bureaucrat.[37] Though a Buddhist-majority space before and after these administrative reforms, Songkhla had always encompassed a diverse ethnic population, with a significant Muslim minority occupying its coast and the rim of its saltwater lake. Prior to the appointment of a Chinese tax-farmer as the *mueang*'s governor in the early nineteenth century, the multi-ethnic principality of Songkhla was ruled by a Muslim nobleman, Suleiman, who governed at the behest of Nakhon Si Thammarat.[38] Many of Songkhla's Thai-speaking Muslims (in the districts surrounding the old port city and Songkhla's lake region) trace their ancestry to the period of Suleiman, but in the southeastern districts the linguistic, religious, and political heritage of Muslims is linked with the former sultanate of Pattani.[39] Punished in the late eighteenth century for resisting Siam's suzerainty, the political space of the Malay Muslim sultanate of Pattani on the edge of Singora was periodically subdivided to ensure greater control by the Siamese state and by the early twentieth century, this space was organized into the three provinces of Narathiwat, Pattani, and Yala. Later, the thinly settled Malay-dominated districts of Thepha and Sabayoi were sliced from Pattani Province and incorporated into the administrative space of Songkhla Province, no doubt to bolster Songkhla's continuing role as a buffer zone against a restive Muslim periphery (see map 1.2).

Songkha Province hosts a diverse economy and population, and to that extent, it represents in concentrated form much of the diversity of the peninsula itself. Politically, the province also exemplifies the ethno-religious diversity of the Democrat-dominated south, a heartland which extends from Chumphon in the north down to Songkhla (see map 1.1). For purposes of comparison we can broadly distinguish Songkhla and the other provinces comprising the "Democrat south" as the "Buddhist-majority south" (with the exception of Thai-speaking Muslim-majority Satun) to differentiate this region from the three Malay-majority border provinces with their rather distinctive political affiliations (until recently

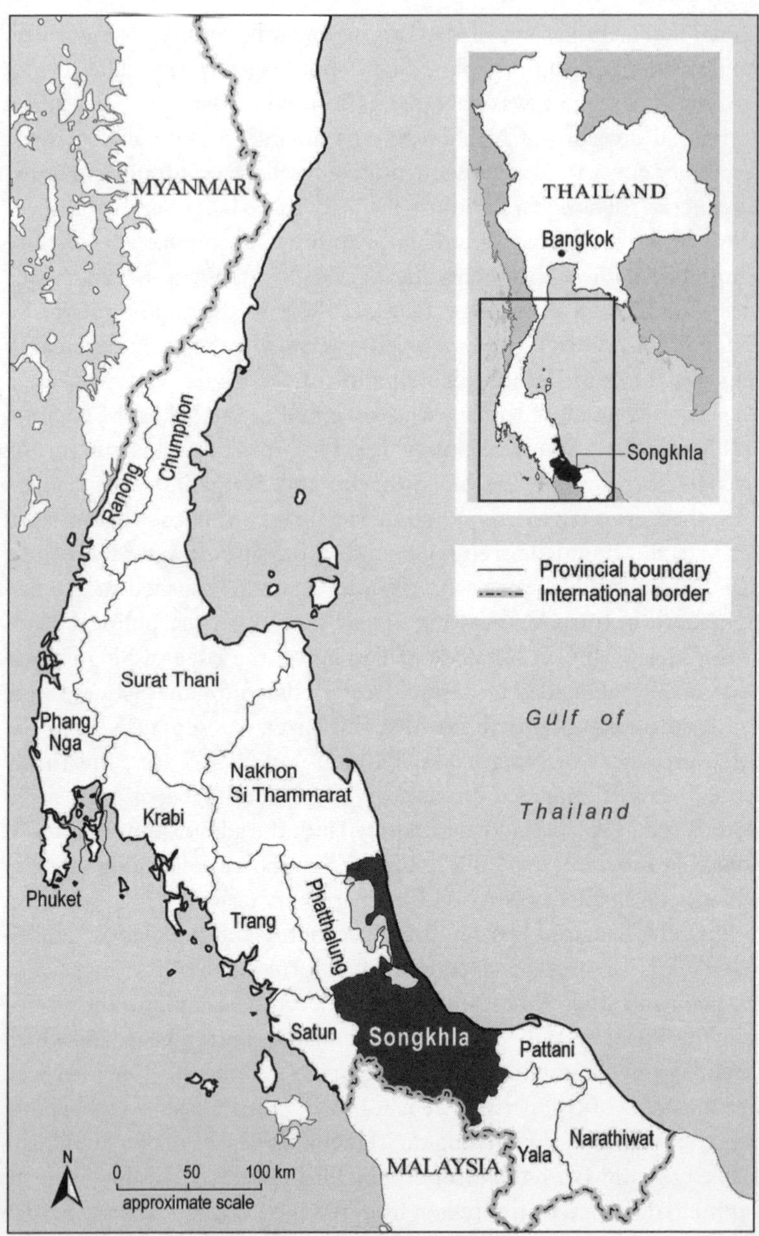

Map 1.1 Songkhla and the provinces of southern Thailand

Map 1.2 The administrative districts (amphoe) *of Songkhla Province*

at least). Nevertheless, Muslims actually form a substantial group in Songkhla's population. In its proportion of Muslim residents, Songkhla stands midway between the Muslim-majority border provinces on its southeastern border and its overwhelmingly Buddhist-majority northern neighbor, Phatthalung (see map 1.1). An estimated 23 percent of the province's population are Muslim, primarily of Malay descent, though not in terms of language loyalty. The primary language of many Songkhla Muslims is the southern Thai-dialect, which reflects a long history of coexistence and integration. They are distributed in varying concentrations across the province. Muslims in the districts (*amphoe*) of the northern and central parts of the province make up 15–25 percent of the population, while the southeastern districts close to Pattani and Yala (Chana, Thepha, and Sabayoi) host higher proportions of Muslims, representing between 50–60 percent (see table 1.3 for province-wide figures). In these latter areas, especially the districts of Thepha and Sabayoi, Malay-speaking Muslims predominate in varying proportions, though most are fluent in southern and central Thai dialects, in strong contrast to many of their neighbors in the three adjacent Muslim-majority border provinces. One of the parliamentary constituencies treated in this book (Constituency 8) covers part of this Muslim-majority sub-region of Songkhla (see map 1.3).

TABLE 1.3

Religious Adherence: Songkhla and Adjacent Provinces (%), 2000/03

Province	Buddhist	Muslim	Other	Unknown/ Unspecified
Songkhla	76.35	23.08	0.15	0.40
Narathiwat	16.55	83.13	0.05	0.25
Phatthalung	87.93	11.05	0.12	0.40
Pattani	17.83	81.26	0.10	0.79
Satun	31.79	67.55	0.17	0.46
Yala	28.79	70.58	0.22	0.36

Source: NSO, Population and Housing Census 2000, Narathiwat, Yala, and Pattani, updated 2003.

THE DEMOCRAT PARTY IN SONGKHLA

The pattern of Democrat Party representation in Songkhla has followed broad trends in the south generally. They are trends that, until 1992, have reflected the peaks and troughs in the national party's inner politics and its electoral fortunes in the changing political conditions of the nation. Since 1946, Songkhla voters have returned Democrat Party politicians to parliament, but it was not until 1975—when they won four out of five seats—that they became a dominant presence in the province. In this turbulent period of Thailand's brief parliamentary experiment before its quashing by military coup, the Democrats gained popular endorsement by being associated with anti-militarism. The nationwide boost in Democrat electoral fortunes in 1976 was registered in the south and in Songkhla, where the party was again returned with four out of five MPS.

Following the return of the military to power in 1976, the party's electoral fortunes fluctuated at the national level, but in Songkhla, and in all elections that followed (except March 1992), the Democrats were returned with at least four members, representing more than half the number of MPS in the province. During most of the 1980–88 period of General Prem Tinsulanonda's benevolent parliamentary dictatorship (the period of so-called "half-way democracy"), the party gained strength in the south and elsewhere, although it suffered reverses at the end of this period owing to a damaging party split in January 1988. In the July 1986 national election, the Democrats of Songkhla captured all seven seats in the province. In 1988, the first contests held under a fully parliamentary regime, they still held five of these seats, despite the severe effects of the recent party rift. The Democrats of Songkhla enjoyed an advantage during the Prem years, not only because the party shared coalition governments, but also because Prem, though an unelected prime minister, enjoyed strong local support because of his Songkhla origins. The figure of Prem is still evoked by party orators in Songkhla as a revered ancestor figure embodying ideal leadership virtues comparable to the key virtues of the Democrat Party—truthfulness and honesty—even though he has had no formal affiliation with the Democrat Party.

In the election of March 1992, conducted under the shadow of Suchinda Khraprayun's coup, the Songkhla Democrats managed to retain three of seven seats, equaled in numbers by MPS of the New Aspiration Party (NAP), formed by General Chavalit Yongchaiyudh in 1990. But six months later, in the new national polls that followed the downfall of Suchinda, Songkhla's Democrats captured all seven seats in the province, benefiting from the symbolic leadership of southerner Chuan Leekpai and popular identification with the Democrats as a party of democratic reform. The September 1992 election gave the southern Democrats 80 percent of the region's constituencies and provided nearly half of the party's seats in the national parliament. Songkhla reflected the regional trend with all its seats being gained by the Democrats. In the three elections that followed in 1995, 1996, and 2001, Songkhla's Democrats retained their hold on all the province's constituencies, which were expanded to eight single-member constituencies before the 2001 contest (see map 1.3).

The Democrat Party in Songkhla has maintained a continuing presence in the province for over three decades, and during most of this period, even before the advent of Chuan's leadership, Democrat MPS have outnumbered representatives from other parties. In contrast to the Democrats' permanent presence and steady electoral success, candidates and MPS for other political parties in Songkhla have experienced varied fortunes. An exception should, however, be noted in the case of the highly regarded Songkhla MP, Anan Rueangkun. First returned as an independent candidate in 1968, Anan later joined Kukrit Pramoj's Social Action Party (SAP) and was re-elected by the province's voters continuously to 1988. After Anan's death, however, no SAP candidate was able to gain election to replace Anan, not even his son. The characteristic volatility of most of the non-Democrat parties in Songkhla has constrained their ability to maintain a sustained local presence or continuous association with voters for long.

The success of the Democrats under Chuan Leekpai in September 1992 certainly marked a critical turning point for the party and its popular identification with southerners. This, however, was built on existing foundations of electoral strength and continuity established nearly a decade-and-a-half earlier. In the years following September

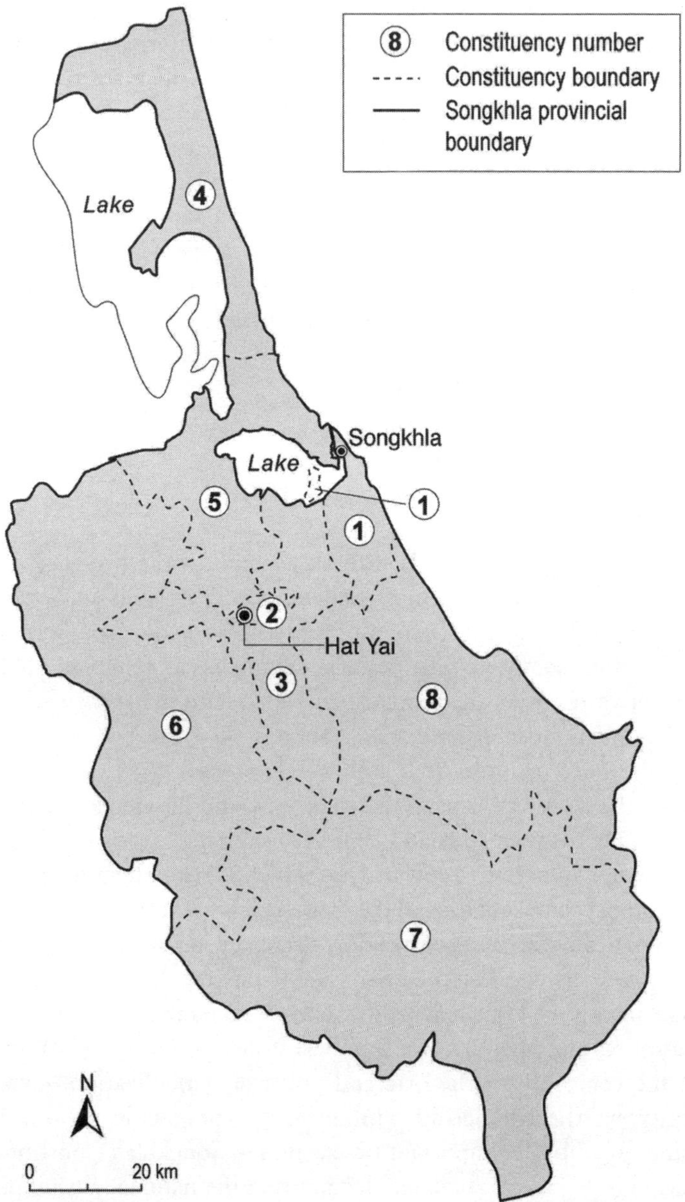

Map 1.3 Songkhla Province and its eight single-member national electoral constituencies (used in 2001 and 2005 elections)

1992, the Songkhla Democrats, like their counterparts throughout the south, benefited from their participation in government and enjoyed an unparalleled continuity and dominance of representation in the province. They consolidated their constituency-based phuak networks, expanded the number of party members, consolidated their branch structures, and forged a symbolic bond with voters that proved an effective defense against the new TRT assailants in 2001. As the 2005 elections approached, they faced a renewed challenge from a greatly strengthened TRT Party which controlled the government, and under Thaksin Shinawatra appeared to have transformed the terms of electoral politics in the nation.

SUMMARY OF CHAPTERS

The book begins (chapter 2) with an account of the presence of the Democrat Party in the south and its configurations in Songkhla Province, including a discussion of representations of "southern Thai culture" and "southern Thai political culture" as a prelude to the later substantive chapters that explore the connections between identity, culture, and political party symbolization in Songkhla.

In the core chapters that follow (chapters 3–9), I describe and analyze the election events, political groups, and the election outcomes in Songkhla between 2004 and 2005. These chapters are organized as a combination of narrative and analysis, which also highlight the national and regional context of each of the contests. I present the election events here as narrative in a deliberate effort to convey the highly charged local atmosphere surrounding the events and to portray the pulse of political action among the key participants. In these accounts, I include detailed description and analysis of a number of key political performances, and the centrality of rhetoric and political symbolization. Chapter 3 describes the competing symbolism and pragmatic organization behind the critically important by-election in Songkhla's Constituency 3 staged in February 2004, an election that the nationally triumphant TRT government hoped would provide an opportunity to break open the Democrat monopoly as a prelude to a full assault in the following year's national election. Voters rallied to the Democrats in a contest symbolized by the party as a competition between good and evil. The account highlights the significance of the Democrats' call on southern political virtue, and the successful portrayal by Democrat party orators of the government party as the antithesis of true Democratic political virtues, as exemplified in the figure of the revered former leader and southerner, Chuan Leekpai.

Chapter 4 changes the register to local politics with an account of the mayoral election for Hat Yai City, followed by an examination in chapter 5 of the province's PAO elections for president and councilor positions. As elsewhere in the country, these elections in early 2004 were the first to include direct elections of municipal and provincial executives. In Songkhla, both of these campaigns were intimately tied to the fortunes of Democrat Party political networks. In both elections, the victorious candidates owed their success to the mobilization of local Democrat constellations of phuak. As highlighted in the PAO elections, however, there were also divisions and conflicts among Democrat phuak which had implications for vote canvassing and candidate alignments in the approaching national election.

Chapters 6–7 focus on the 2005 national election in Songkhla Province, where the Democrats, in common with their compatriots throughout the region, faced a major challenge to preserve the Democrat heartland against the considerably more powerful national electoral force of the TRT Party. These accounts show the critically important role of Democrat political symbolism in countering the efforts of rival party candidates, and orators' assiduous skill in using the prevailing southern border unrest to de-legitimize the TRT Party in the eyes of many voters, particularly Muslims. Chapter 8 exposes the equally critical role of phuak, canvasser networks, and vote buying in the election contests, and illustrates how in Constituency "X" the TRT candidate's vote-buying efforts were undermined by his Democrat rival's judicious outbidding and spread of rumors that undermined TRTS efforts, despite their greater financial resources. Constituency "X" is a deliberately disguised Songkhla constituency used to protect my informants. Chapter 9 reviews the verdicts made, both nationally and locally, about the factors responsible for the Democrats' regional victory in the overall context of the party's national failure against TRT in 2005. The final substantive chapter (chapter 10) draws together and expands upon points made in the narrative chapters. It presents an analysis that focuses on the character of the Democrat political ascendancy as a dynamic product of two intersecting dimensions: the "poetic" (cultural idioms of loyalty and trust that inform popular party loyalties and solidarity) and the "pragmatic" (bonds of phuak, patronage, and family). The epilogue looks briefly at the fortunes of the Democrat Party at national and provincial levels in the years since the critical 2005 national election, particularly the party's revived fortunes that followed in the wake of Thaksin Shinawatra's overthrow by military-led coup in September 2006.

CHAPTER 2

Constructing a Democrat South: Claiming "Political Culture" and Territory

TWO EMPIRICALLY dubious but symbolically potent primordial images inform representations of the bond between the south and Thailand's Democrat Party. In Democrat rhetoric and much southern popular folklore, the Democrat south is a union between two primal entities: a revered political party that has, since its inception, championed democratic processes against the ever-present forces of corruption and amoral power; and a southern citizenship culturally endowed with a hereditary sensibility that shuns authoritarianism and money politics, and recognizes the virtues of political loyalty. Both of these representations are contradicted by more complex realities, but they are constructions that have powerful resonance. Here, I briefly examine arguments surrounding the role and mythic character of the Democrat Party and outline the emergence of its electoral heartland in the south. I then consider how southern Thai folklore scholarship has played its own part in objectifying local norms and cultural practices as "southern Thai culture" with a distinct "political culture." While these scholars and associated civil society activists ground their aspirations for a truly people-based politics in a primordial "community culture" of southerners, they have been unable to compete with the Democrat Party's overtures to voters that are based on a similar primordial ideal of "southern Thainess."

THE DEMOCRAT PARTY IN THAILAND: FLAWED SURVIVOR, HEROIC WARRIOR

The Democrat Party is the great survivor in Thailand's fraught history of parliamentary politics. Often brilliant in opposition, but usually mediocre and cautious in government, the Democrat Party's history is as flawed as it is heroic. The party's publicity habitually stresses a number of enduring features that distinguish the party as an organization and as an idea. As an organization founded in 1946, it is indisputably the oldest political organization in a country where political parties have been notoriously short lived. Party propaganda claims that this longevity is itself a vindication of the party's authenticity as a "real" party, exemplified by an administrative structure based on genuine elective office for its members, and a system of constituency branches that allow for full participation by party office-bearers and members. Indeed, the party is held to be the very symbol and embodiment of true democratic ideals and practice in Thailand.[1]

The party's longevity reinforces a claim to the enduring relevance of the party's *udomkan* (poorly translated into English as "ideology"), which represents the essence of liberal democratic ideals that the party has bravely championed in the eternal task of defending and promoting constitutional democracy against its enemies. Official Democrat Party literature and the party's leaders frequently invoke the party's *udomkan* as the enduring core that sustains the party's identity and its heroic political stance against imposters that are bent on "eating the country" (*kin mueang*). Although the Pali-derived term "*udomkan*" is conventionally glossed as the equivalent to Western concepts of "ideology," in the context of its usage and in relation to the specific components of the Democrat Party's formally itemized *udomkan* elements, there is little to distinguish *udomkan* from "principles" (*lakkan*), "ideals" (*udomkhati*), or even "policies" (*nayobai*). This vagueness in the use of *udomkan* reflects its ambiguous status in Thai political language more generally.[2] The party's itemized *udomkan* reflects very clearly the historical and political environment that shaped its formative years as a party upholding constitutionalism (a conservative, royalist version). This set of statements refers more to a moral stance and commitment to upholding parliamentary government than any distinctive social vision or theory. The party's founding principles proclaimed commitment to honest representation, adherence to parliamentary government and elective principles (in both internal party as well as national government), broad support for the decentralization of power, and vehement opposition to military dictatorship.[3]

Democrat claims to consistent adherence to founding principles are contradicted by its historical performance. The party has been wracked by damaging splits and defections that highlight divergences in political ideology and interest within the party. Moreover, the party's identity as a democratic political actor has been shaped more by political conditions than its own consistencies, while success in gaining government has been at the behest of opportunities created by others. Only a year after the foundation of the party under Khuang Aphaiwong, the Democrats supported Phibun Songkhram's military coup in 1947 against the socialist-inclined government of Pridi Banomyong. Khuang accepted the prime ministership and the Democrats were returned by election in 1948, but they were soon ejected from government by the junta. It was after this, and particularly during elections in 1957, that the party gained its reputation as an opponent of dictatorship, achieving strong support in Bangkok, though it was essentially conservative in orientation (particularly when compared to the Socialist Front, with its core among northeastern politicians). When parliament was restored in the late 1960s after a decade in abeyance under military rule, the Democrats gained strong electoral support (especially in Bangkok) and assumed the role of a "loyal opposition" until 1971, when the military prime minister, General Thanom Kittikhachon, dissolved the troublesome parliament.[4]

The fall of the military junta in 1973, following concerted student protest, was followed by a new constitution and elections in 1975, which saw Democrat popularity soar in the electorates in both Bangkok and the provinces, including the south. The Democrats won the largest number of seats among numerous contesting parties that year, but Seni Pramoj's coalition government ruled for only eight days before falling foul of a no-confidence vote. In the next election of early 1976, the Democrats made strong electoral gains and Seni became prime minister again. But his rule was brief. The Democrat-led coalition government was toppled by military coup in October, following a brutal crackdown on protesting students in an atmosphere of anti-communist paranoia fomented by the military and conservative nationalists.

The polarizing politics of the mid-1970s was reflected in a severe split within the party's ranks between old royalist conservatives epitomized by Samak Sunthonwet, an arch nationalist and anti-communist, and a new breed of "progressives" represented, among others, by the young Chuan Leekpai and his fellow southerner Surin Masdit. Samak was active in organizing the nationalist Village Scout movement against student protesters, while the progressive members of the cabinet supported student demands that the returned former junta leader Thanom be expelled from the country. Chuan and his colleagues also played a part in the removal of two conservative Democrats from Seni's cabinet but, branded as communists, they were compelled to resign following demonstrations by Village Scouts. Leading student radicals shunned the Democrats as impotent.[5] Neither Seni nor the progressive Democrats could do anything to prevent the massacre of students on October 6, 1976, or the coup that rapidly succeeded it. That the party could host politicians of such divergent positions, ranging from arch reactionaries to liberal reformers, says much about its ideological flabbiness at this time, even given the unprecedented circumstances of these years.[6]

Arguably, it has been compromise more than principle that has marked the Democrat Party's political record. Thus, during the 1980s, under Prem Tinsulanonda's "semi-democracy," the Democrats willingly accepted cabinet positions and participated in his plural party system of guided democracy. Over the party's history, the *udomkan* so repeatedly invoked in its self-proclamations has done little to keep the party together in the face of leadership squabbles and battles over ministerial portfolios. The most crippling party split happened in 1988, when forty disaffected Democrat MPs (the so-called "January 10 Group" led by party secretary-general Wira Musikaphong) opposed the party leader Pichai Rattakun and voted against a government-sponsored copyright bill, prompting Prime Minister Prem Tinsulanonda to dissolve parliament and call new elections. The subsequent rupture in the party's ranks caused Democrat electoral support to plummet in the July election of that year (see table 2.1)

Most commentators argue that the Democrat Party's performance when in government during the 1990s was mixed at best, while election successes were the result of opportune positioning and good luck more than determined initiative, clear party policies, or a coherent political image. The Democrats' electoral success in September 1992 following the popular protests against Suchinda Khraprayun's junta were gained by the party's identification as "angels" against the parties of "devils" that supported the junta. As one critic noted, they reaped the electoral benefits "even though they had contributed almost nothing to bringing the junta down."[7] Street fighting is not the party's forte—the party's role, as proclaimed by Chuan Leekpai, has been parliamentary contestation, not engagement in social movements, as shown in his indifference to farmers' assemblies, such as the Assembly of the Poor. During the first Chuan-led government, eagerly awaited reforms were slow in coming. In addition, the party's well-cultivated image of integrity and propriety was seriously besmirched by a scandal involving southern Democrat MPS and their illegal peddling in land earmarked for the poor. Fanned by a hostile news media, the scandal brought down Chuan's first government (Suthep Thueaksuban, a prominent Surat Thani MP, was implicated).[8] While Chuan's reputation as a clean-handed and self-sacrificing leader remained high, his inability to control his party was patently clear. An opponent of the Democrats in Songkhla expressed this view to me in culturally resonant moral terms: "The party is like a monastery with a pure abbot who can't control his rotten monks."

The Democrats returned as the leaders of a coalition government in late 1997, after the collapse of the inept administration of Chavalit Yongchaiyudh following the onset of the economic crisis. During the 1990s, there were attempts to renovate the party's image and bolster its key personnel with experienced technocrats and economists. The Bangkok electorate responded positively to these initiatives, as reflected in the expansion of the Democrats' metropolitan electoral base in 1996. Chuan's second administration stressed professional expertise and modernity, but it was unable to respond to the exigencies of the economic crisis decisively enough, or shake off the nationalist-evoked claim that it was obediently following the dictates of the IMF economic restructuring program. By 2000, when Chuan's government fell, it had few resources available to compete with the emerging TRT Party, which marshaled the symbolic force of a millionaire business leader, snappy slogans, and a mission to save the country.

Despite its flaws and shortcomings, the Democrat Party can claim to possess distinctive organizational characteristics and traditions. Since Khuang Aphaiwong, the party has been headed by highly talented and widely respected figures. It is not surprising that in 2006, the sixtieth anniversary of the party, the Democrats marked the occasion by sponsoring the republication of Seni Pramoj's reminiscences.[9] From its inception, the party placed a premium on oratory, public speaking, and expertise in argument, and though there are many lackluster speakers in the parliamentary party, its best are unrivaled by other parties. The party prides itself on producing parliamentary performers with enviable skills of oratory.[10] The party has also been distinctive for the large number of lawyers among its MPs.

Despite the damaging splits that have marred it history, the Democrats remain the only enduring political organization with a fully elective basis for office holding at all levels. Moreover, unlike the bulk of Thailand's political parties, in the past and present, it is not owned by any individual or group. In the early 1980s, the Thai scholar Kramon Thongthammachat voiced a common view when he noted that, "Thai political parties, with the exception of the Democrat Party, are not real political parties mainly because they have built few extra-parliamentary organizations and commanded little popular following. In addition, they have not become institutionalized."[11] During the 1990s, this situation changed following the resumption to full parliamentary government. With the exception of the Democrat Party, however, most were the creations of individual patrons or small groups. Most Thai political parties have not functioned to advocate or represent coherent ideological positions. They have characteristically comprised pragmatic groupings of phuak and kin-based factions who move to other parties when resources are not sufficient, making parties subject to frequent transformation, dissolution, and change in parliamentary membership.[12]

By the 1990s, a number of parties had emerged which did depart from these characteristics and shared some features that the Democrats had previously claimed as exclusive to them. For example, the National Aspiration Party of Chavalit Yongchaiyudh (formed in 1990) proclaimed a platform of broad reconciliation and aspired towards a mass bureaucratic model with large membership and constituency-based branches. The Palang Tham (Power of Truth) Party of Chamlong Srimueang advanced an identity based on anti-corruption and Buddhist-inspired social reform that attracted enthusiastic support in Bangkok in the early 1990s, at the expense of the Democrats, until it lost much of its impetus when Chamlong departed. In the late 1990s, Duncan McCargo critically reviewed the Western-centered paradigm of the real, or "authentic" political party to Thailand, noting that it had been based on a model of the "mass bureaucratic party" now outmoded in the West, where "electoral professional parties" had become a dominant form. Nevertheless, he admitted that the Democrat Party most closely approximated the "authentic" model in Thailand, while also highlighting that the Democrats lacked any clear political direction or distinctive identity. Writing of trends in political party development in Thailand, he further suggested that there was an indication that "electoral professional parties" were developing. These are parties focused around the marketing of party leaders and party policies, rather than party membership, branches, and constituency-centered activity. Despite this trend, he suggested, it was likely that the "old style faction bosses" would still be used to deliver up-country votes to the national parties.[13] This point was remarkably prescient, because Thaksin's new TRT party was based precisely on a combination of marketing and provincial machine politics—a combination that decisively routed the Democrats in Thailand's election of 2001 in every region but the south.

DEMOCRAT PARTY REPRESENTATION IN THAILAND'S SOUTH

From its inception in 1946, the Democrat Party has maintained a presence in the south, with four southern parliamentarians (including

Thai-Buddhist, Muslim, and Sino-Thai) among its thirty-five founding members, including one in Songkhla. In the second national election of 1957, the party won eight seats in southern constituencies, compared with eleven in Bangkok, though the north gained most Democrat seats. In the 1969 election, held after the restoration of party politics, the Democrats swept all twenty-one Bangkok seats and the south remained stable with nine seats, a figure that represented less than a third of all southern parliamentary seats. Democrat representation in the south was unremarkable in this period when compared with Bangkok and the northern constituencies, but a concentration of support for the party in the south began to reveal itself during Thailand's brief efflorescence of parliamentary democracy in the mid-1970s.[14]

In 1975, Democrat representation in the south increased to fifteen seats, now roughly equaling the party's strength in the north, northeast, and central regions, with the southern Democrat MPs now holding half of all parliamentary constituencies in their region. In 1976, this increased to the extent that 80 percent of MPs returned by southern electorates were Democrats. In that year, southern Democrats outnumbered MPs returned from every other region, including Bangkok, which up to that time had been the acknowledged stronghold of the party. Since 1975—and despite fluctuations in electoral support in the south until the early 1990s—southerners have been the single largest regional group among the party's MPs (with the exception of 1986).[15] It was only from the early 1990s, however, that the Democrats gained a near hegemonic electoral hold in the south and became the dominant element in the national party. This development coincided with the elevation of the southern Democrat Chuan Leekpai to the party's leadership—proudly welcomed by southerners—and to the political crisis of 1991–92, which saw the Democrats gain increased popular support through aligning themselves with other "angelic" parties against the military coup makers and their supporting parties. In Songkhla, for example, the Suchinda-aligned Chat Thai Party, which had been returned in the March elections, was shunned by voters in September, and its MP, Nikon Chamnong, who had first gained election for the party in Songkhla in 1988, never ran for office in his home province again.

The Democrats emerged from the critical September 1992 elections as the largest party, with southern voters returning thirty-six of the Democrats' seventy-nine MPs. Chuan Leekpai headed the ruling coalition until 1995, when the land scandal brought his coalition government down. But this did not dent southern electoral support; in fact, the party made greater gains in the elections of 1995 and 1996, by which time the Democrats held all but five of over fifty southern constituencies. The other southern seats were stubbornly held by the Muslim "*Wadah*" (unity) faction politicians of the National Aspiration Party in the three Muslim-majority border provinces of Narathiwat, Pattani, and Yala.

TABLE 2.1

Democrat Party MPs Returned to Parliament (by region), 1957–2001

Election Date	Bangkok	Central	South	North	Northeast	Total	Total MPs
Feb. 1957	4	1	6	17	12	40	160
Dec. 1957	11	4	8	13	3	39	160
Feb. 1969	21	4	9	13	8	55	219
Jan. 1975	23	12	15	17	5	72	269
Apr. 1976	28	17	29	15	24	114	279
Apr. 1979	1	3	15	7	9	35	301
Apr. 1983	8	2	25	8	13	56	324
Jul. 1986	16	10	36	10	28	100	347
Jul. 1988	5	4	16	6	17	48	357
Mar. 1992	1	-	26	5	12	44	360
Sep. 1992	9	9	36	8	17	79	360
Jul. 1995	7	7	46	12	14	86	391
Nov. 1996	29	14	47	21	12	123	393
Jan. 2001*	9	18	48	18	5	130	500

*Includes thirty-two party-list MPs. Source: Democrat Party. In 2002, the Democrat Party gained an additional constituency seat following the dissolution of another party, increasing total constituency seats from 97 to 98.

In regions outside the south, Democrat Party representation fluctuated considerably during the 1992–96 period, and the Bangkok electorates, formerly the main core of Democrat support to the mid-1970s, proved to be volatile in their voting preferences (see table 2.1). Thus, while the Democrats were returned in November 1996 with renewed strength in Bangkok, and also enjoyed gains in the northern and central constituencies, these seats were swept away in the 2001 polls by the upsurge of popularity for the new Thai Rak Thai Party. In sharp contrast to these political trends, the southern constituencies returned Democrat parliamentarians as regularly as they had before. After the party's comprehensive drubbing by the new electoral machine of TRT in the 2001 polls, Democrat Party strength across the country was reduced from 123 to 97 seats in an expanded parliament of five hundred MPs. For a party whose popularity had been eroded everywhere else by the TRT's electoral onslaught, the Democrats' forty-eight southern seats represented a critical bastion of support (see table 2.2).

The 2001 contest was fought under the novel conditions established by the reformist 1997 constitution, which for the first time established single-member constituencies and a twin system of voting based on direct elections at the constituency level and proportional voting by

2.1 A phalanx of Songkhla Democrat MPs with the new party leader (Sept. 2003). From left: Phrai Phatthano, Thawon Senniam, Banyat Banthatthan (DP leader), Niphon Bunyamani, Chuea Ratchasi.

party-list ballots. These, together with more stringent rules preventing last minute "party-hopping," established conditions that favored the emergence of TRT as an electoral marketing machine. Some pundits saw the 2001 results as signaling the emergence of truly ideological and policy-based politics, built around larger parties, with governments assured greater stability though reduction of multi-party coalitions. The stunning rise of TRT, however, was based as much on the harnessing of older-style provincial machine-based factions, the use of money, and the subversion of constitutional provisions and the electoral law as any legal and normative-driven structural shift.[16] Following TRT's triumph and its subsequent absorption of a number of other parties in 2002 (including NAP), the political map of Thailand was substantially redrawn. Yet, despite these radical changes in electoral geography, the persisting strength of the Democrats in the south stood out in clear and anomalous relief. As one prominent political columnist remarked, "The Democrats have had a southern base for twenty-five years, and other parties in the past have been regionally biased. But never has the electoral map been sliced quite so starkly."[17]

TABLE 2.2

2001 National Election Results: Distribution of Seats by Party and Region

Party	Bangkok	Center	North	South	NE	Const'y	Partylist	Total
TRT	29	47	54	1	69	200	48	248
Democrat	8	19	16	48	6	97	31	128
Chat Thai	-	21	3	-	11	35	6	41
NAP	-	3	1	5	19	28	8	36
Chat Phatthana	-	4	2	-	16	22	7	29
Seritham	-	-	-	-	14	14	-	14
Ratsadon	-	1	-	-	1	2	-	2
T. Thai	-	-	-	-	1	1	-	1
S. Action	-	-	-	-	-	1	-	1
Total	37	95	76	54	138	400	100	500

Source: Election Commission of Thailand

CONSTRUCTING "SOUTHERN THAI CULTURE"

Pointing to the phenomenon of "localism" (*thongthin niyom*) and "regionalism" (*phumiphak niyom*) in Thai society in the mid-1990s, the prominent historian and public intellectual Nithi Ieosiwong argued that it could be interpreted not so much as a product of spontaneous popular cultural identification, but more a result of policies enacted by the Thai state involving the establishment of region-based centers of scholarship, museums, and tourist promotion organizations that aimed to "regulate difference" within the body of the Thai nation. He further argued that this *phumiphak niyom* was being actively fabricated by political parties in their efforts to gain popular support. To Nithi then, the increasing trend in the 1990s towards regional identification in its various guises was a construct of the state and opportunistic political parties.[18] This reflected his own anxieties that the non-linear and people-centered historiography that he championed was being co-opted and commodified, and that scholars were becoming part of this process. Southern folklore scholars, though motivated by their own concerns to recover lost (or preserve declining) popular traditions have participated in state-initiated processes of classifying cultural identities. Their methods and approaches have tended to perpetuate and encourage fixed and stereotypical attributes to the people that they study. Whatever their motivations, they have played a role in constructing and labeling a "southern Thai culture." In the process of fabricating a distinctive culture and "political culture," there has emerged a struggle to claim this entity as a ground of action—between civil society–oriented southern scholars who deem the entity to be an authentic people's culture, and Democrat politicians who promote themselves and the party as its unique political expression. To their great disillusion, scholars and development activists have found that the Democrats continue to beat them in this struggle.

"Southern Thai Culture"

The school of Southern Thai folklore scholarship was spearheaded by the now-prominent scholar Suthiwong Phongphaibun, who founded a research institute in Songkhla (a division of the Prince of

Songkhla University) in the early 1980s. Suthiwong's major project, the ten-volume *Encyclopedia of Southern Thai Culture* (first published in 1986, then expanded and republished in 1999 in eighteen volumes), embodies the key characteristic of this folklore approach, with its major emphasis on compilation and cataloguing. One of the early projects of Suthiwong's center was research into "the worldview of the Thai people of the south" (*Lokathat Thai Phak Tai*). This approach to "worldview" represents the didactic and positivist dispositions of Thai scholars then and now, aiming to classify Thai "cultural knowledge" under the sociological rubric of "Thai worldview."[19]

This research outlined a number of key characteristics that these folklorists considered distinctive of southern Thais, and this work is still cited as an authoritative text by those writing on "southern Thai culture." Drawing on popular songs, poems, and sayings (*suphasit*) as their primary evidence, they proposed that the southern worldview was a direct product of a distinctive environmental, social, and political history. Communities, they claimed, had developed relatively autonomously without dependence on elites and centers of state authority, and the natural abundance of the peninsula explained relatively low levels of out-migration from the region. The basic values and customs that developed under these conditions in the past were, despite economic change, still adhered to strongly, they argued. Southern Thais, they claim, esteem livelihoods based on intelligence and mental skills (*sati panya*) as well as government service (*kan rapratchakan*) because these bestow both honor (*mi kiat*) and a more comfortable life (*sabai kwa*) than other occupations. Evidence for this enduring value was adduced from the *nang talung* shadow puppet plays, where the hero has always been a person of high intelligence, and from traditional songs that highlight the preferences of young women for *kharatchakan* as marriage partners. Southern people esteem artists and performers highly. In the past, particular importance was placed on the *nora* dance performers and masters of *nang talung*. These scholars highlight the prestige of the performing arts by citing a custom in Trang Province where fathers would test the suitability of prospective sons-in-law by posing two questions: "Can you perform the *nora*?" and "Can you steal buffaloes?" If the young man could not answer both questions in the affirmative, then the father would refuse permission to marry his daughter. Ability to perform both of these skills signified a man's capacity for self-reliance and skill. In this catalogue of attributes, a number of other features stand out, including a high valuation of women's virtue, a jealous protection of personal and family honor (*saksi*), and an acute consciousness of rights and independence (*huang sitthi seriphap*).

In addition, they emphasize distinctive modes of speech, models of leadership and group loyalty. Southern Thais value truthfulness (*khwam chingchai*) and directness in speech (*trong pai trong ma*). They argue here that the high importance placed on directness and truthfulness by southern Thais has a direct bearing on the positive values given to the qualities of the "*nakleng*." *Nakleng* here refers both to individual *nakleng* who occupy a key social role as "tough guys" in traditional rural communities as well as to shared dispositions and behaviors among southern Thais more broadly. "Honesty," "directness," and "courage" are highly valued qualities, so much so, in fact, that people of the central region view southern Thais as rough, tough, and aggressive people (*kaorao*, *khaeng*, *kradang*). Of the specific character of the *nakleng* as a social type, they quote aphorisms and songs that highlight the boldness, self-confidence, and courage of tough men who can treat anyone's home as their own and carry weapons with impunity. Here, the ambiguity of the *nakleng* role stands out, both as a local hero and protector as well as a criminal and dangerous person. Southern Thais embrace a love of and loyalty towards their phuak (*rak phuak rak phong*), which is another valued quality associated with the *nakleng*. Phuak and *phakphuak* encompass bonds with relatives, friends, and associates, and might be translated in sociological terms as "in-group." To love one's phuak is to be loyal to phuak members at all costs and to offer support and help whenever necessary, whatever the costs.

Since the appearance of *Lokathat Thai Phak Tai* in 1984, further studies have been produced in book form and also as articles in the *Journal of Southern Thai Studies* (*Warasan Thaksinkhadi*). These have elaborated on the themes of the distinctive historical and cultural characteristics of people of the region. While varying in specific focus, scholars' writings have tended to reinforce the key points highlighted in the 1980s. For example, Somchettana Muni, writing on bandit groups in southern Thai history, stresses a popular heritage of resistance to state interference and strong sub-group loyalties in communities of the south.[20] Two major works by Akhom Detthongkham from Nakhon Si Thammarat's Rajabhat College stand out. Akhom's first major work (published first in 2000 and reprinted three times), explored the bull trainers (*hua chueak*) of Nakhon Si Thammarat Province. In this ethnographically based study (a rarity in southern Thai studies), Akhom portrayed this group of competitive bull trainers as exemplars of southern Thai masculine culture, and he interpreted bullfighting contests and the symbolism surrounding them as metaphors of this southern masculine culture. The bull keepers were straightforward in their speaking, suspicious of strangers, and ruthless opponents who would often resort to extreme tactics to win bullfights. He highlighted the prominence of ruthless masculine competition by citing statistics of murders in Nakhon Si Thammarat, showing that in this province murders were the highest in the whole country.[21]

Akhom's book stimulated a controversy over the public image of southerners, with a number of prominent southerners and Democrat politicians (including the Mayor of Nakhon Si Thammarat) charging that Akhom had insulted southern people's honor by branding them as pitiless and violent.[22] Paradoxically, Akhom had touched a raw nerve among local public figures by employing the very southern-style honesty in his writing that was embodied by the bull trainers in his research. In a sense, he had betrayed the "cultural intimacy" of his southern community with his imaginative scholarly rigor.[23] But his critics had overlooked the fact that Akhom had also highlighted the significance of social bonds among southerners in his portrait. Extreme hatred and resentment expressed by his Nakhon Si Thammarat bull keepers was simply the intimate twin of the highly valued and equally extreme southern ideal of true loyalty, "Whoever you love, you love truly; conversely, whoever you hate, you hate completely."[24] Fearing for his life, Akhom went into hiding for a time until his mentor Suthiwong Phaiboon arranged for a public seminar to defuse the criticism. Ironically, Akhom himself is a staunch Democrat supporter, an admirer of the *nakleng* tradition, and an enthusiastic trainer of fighting bulls.[25]

Akhom's second major work, published in 2001, explored the historical foundations of social loyalties in the south. He affirmed the cultural importance of *phuk dong*, *phuk kloe* (camaraderie and kinship bonds) and *uppatham* (patronage) in the Songkhla Lake region through case studies of events and families in the past.[26]

Folklorists' portrayals of southerners have been generated from key assumptions embedded in their approach. In presenting the "southern Thai worldview," they have maintained an undifferentiated and static notion of "southern Thais"—their archetypal "southern Thai" is a rural (and Buddhist) villager. They rely on archetypes in popular literature that float in an undefined "past time" that somehow informs the present. As Duncan McCargo has pointed out, links between the past and the present are rarely delineated to demonstrate the dynamics of continuity.[27] Even more critically perhaps, despite their affirmation of southern distinctiveness, they provide little confirmation (beyond assertion) that the "distinctive" cultural features of southerners—such as the prominence of family loyalties, the phenomena of phuak, and patronage processes—are more marked than other regions of Thailand. The possibility that their own folklore paradigms affirming southern Thai distinctiveness are constructs emerging from institutional imperatives (as Nithi suggested) is understandably never considered. From the mid-1990s, major projects funded by the Thailand Research Fund began exploring ethnic and religious diversity (the Chinese, Muslims and Buddhists) and varied folk traditions, and Suthiwong himself wrote about the Muslims of the Malay-speaking region of the Lower South.[28] But though the ideas of diversity and "dynamics" were being introduced, southern folklore studies was firmly wedded to the promotion of local development through "community culture" and saw an underlying unity in the south as an environmental space. In their own view, these scholars were attempting to subvert monolithic state-centered models of development and firmly embrace what now is identified as a "localist" ideological movement. Their studies had a highly didactic purpose. As emphasized by Suthiwong in an introduction to a major compilation of these studies, the effort was to "compile the structures that make up cultures and geographic areas," with a view to affirming "local culture" as the basis for development.[29]

"Southern Thai Political Culture"—A Disputed Ground

The notion of a distinctive southern Thai "political culture," in its scholarly guise, has been part of the broader folklorist project to categorize the region. It is hardly surprising, however, that the timing of these efforts coincided with the rise of the Democrat Party to government under Chuan Leekpai and the electoral hegemony of that party in the region. This chafed with many southern scholars' own commitments to an alternative "people-centered" politics. Since the turbulent days of 1992, many of these scholars have been actively engaged in civil society politics, which was particularly strong in Songkhla Province. A broad coalition of groups among NGOs and middle class professionals gained strength during the 1990s, joining to lobby against environmental degradation, support various rural communities, and push for democratic reforms outside the old model of parliamentary and party-bound politics. Some of the most prominent were based at the Institute of Southern Thai Studies (ISTS) in Songkhla.[30] Despite their efforts to promote consciousness of people's culture simultaneously with alternative politics, by the late 1990s these scholars were dismayed and disappointed to find that their precious regional people's culture had been hijacked by the Democrat Party.

In 1999, an explicit treatment of "southern Thai political culture" appeared as a special issue of the *Journal of Southern Thai Studies*. The essays in this volume reveal southern folklore scholars' ambivalence towards the dominant characteristics that they have identified as the region's "political culture." On the one hand, they stress that these characteristics are rooted in the conditions of a commonly experienced history and environment and that they spring from ordinary people, but they are deeply pessimistic about the prospects for the emergence of a truly participatory politics among ordinary southerners. The editor of the issue, Charun Yuthong of ISTS, defines "political culture" (*watthanatham thang kanmueang*) as a sub-set of a culture that is shown in patterns of beliefs, feelings, and consciousness regarding power, conflict, and leadership. This definition followed the classification scheme designed over three decades earlier by political scientists Gabriel Almond and Sydney Verba for use in comparative quantitative surveys of political development. Charun's judgment is that southern Thais' political attitudes are rooted in a traditional outlook, notwithstanding the transformation of Thailand's political system to law-governed electoral democracy. He claims that this outlook, as revealed in people's contemporary electoral preferences, is dominated by traditional orientations of faith (*sattha*) and trustful belief (*khwam chuea*) that focus on the individual qualities of representatives (*tua bukkhon*) and that are strongly shaped by loyalties to family (*yat phi nong*) and tightly knit in-groups (*phakphuak*).[31] In a second essay, Charun goes on to list the accepted attributes of the southern Thai "world view," including the high value placed on individual freedom, tolerance, and opposition to heavy-handed authority, and the embrace of *nakleng* ideals of courage, directness, and skill. He adds to these a reference to the influence of traditions of the *nang talung* shadow puppet performances and characters in reinforcing and reflecting widely held values of truthfulness as ideal qualities of leaders, the need to "care for one's speech" (*raksa khamphut*), and admiration of skilled oratory. In keeping with the folklore approach, links between the past and present are not established, but simply asserted, and Charun's "southern people" appear to be unchanged ethnic Thai villagers. There is no acknowledgment here of the industrialized post-peasantry, particularly prominent in Songkhla Province, or the predominantly Sino-Thai middle classes of the south's urban areas, exemplified in the burgeoning southern metropolis of Hat Yai.

Charun's discussion of "southern political culture" weaves between the descriptive and the normative, bringing into relief a number of contradictions. He echoes a general view in claiming that southern Thais are more interested in political affairs than Thais of other regions, attributing this, as others have, to a long historical experience of relative autonomy from central authority and the self-dependence of southern communities. But Charun concludes his essay by referring to his own local research that highlights a general lack of understanding of national political affairs among his southerners. Ordinary southerners, he argues, show a lack of understanding of politics that is based on principles (*udomkhati*) or real ideology/principles (*udomkan*). Southerners in general, he asserts, lack political education and focus upon "the person" (*tua bukkhon*) in their politics, and not policies (*nayobai*). For Charun, the "political culture" of ordinary southerners is not amenable to his preferred form of participatory politics (*kan suanruam*), and because of this, he deems the political culture of the south to be the most backward (*la lang*) in the world.[32]

In addressing the characteristics of southern political culture in the contemporary period, the contributors could not escape the obvious fact of the electoral dominance and widespread popularity of the Democrat Party in the south. Charun's editorial introduction had already adopted a critical judgment of the "backwardness" of southern political attitudes, and a number of essays pointed to the Democrat Party as the institution responsible for reinforcing this culture. Criticism of Democrat politicians and the party was, however, muted because open criticism by southern scholars would have attracted condemnation from prominent Democrats, particularly at this time, when Chuan Leekpai was prime minister. In an essay on "The Worldview of Chuan Leekpai," Charun presented information from a range of press interviews and other commentaries about the Democrat leader, careful to avoid directly commenting on this revered southern figure himself. He cleverly ends his piece with a quote from the prominent Thai social critic Sulak Sivaraksa, stating that despite Chuan's reputation as an incorruptible "good person" dedicated to parliamentary democracy, he has not had the boldness to confront the bureaucracy, and thus he has not been a decisive national leader. Moreover, he had acquiesced to the rule of dictatorial military regimes in the past. Charun concludes from Sulak's statements that although Chuan presents an image of a remarkable politician, he, in fact, shows characteristics of being a typical politician in his pragmatic adaptability.[33]

The final essay in the ISTS volume by Sathaphon Sisatchang (a scholar from Phuket), advances a candid portrait of the symbolic dynamics underling the Democrat Party's electoral dominance, though it is based entirely on his opinions and not on any research. Referring to the significance of family loyalties and bonds of camaraderie (*phuk dong, phuk kloe*) in southern society, the writer stresses that political candidates' electoral successes are based strongly on family and phuak support, which could be seen in the character of *hua khanaen* groups (vote canvassers) during elections. He notes that the strength of this *yat phi nong* and *phakphuak* factor is evident in the example of Chuan Leekpai's own support base in Trang Province, a base that revolves around his mother's extended family and its own phuak networks. He continues by highlighting the prevalence of patronage and benevolence (*uppatham*) in the south. Patronage, he claims, plays a critical role among politicians in the building of their repute (*barami*), which is employed as a symbolic resource in securing voting bases (*than siang*) in elections. Patronage among these politicians (clearly he is referring to the incumbent Democrats) ranges from practical assistance in arranging civil service promotions for their supporters, to material and symbolic patronage of important local rituals such as funeral ceremonies. All could be grouped under the pervasive system of *uppatham*, which generates the multiple obligations that are regularly harvested in the form of votes by politicians at election time. Political popularity is also based on image building (*kan sangphap*), which relies on the construction by "an old party in the south" (clearly the Democrats) of a collective sense of *barami* that is spread by the party in its claims to achievements (such as increases in rubber prices) and the party's self-promotion in reified terms as a perpetually honest and truthful organization (*suesat chingchai*). Through a generalized *uppatham* linked to a collective as well as personalized *barami*, political parties (again a clear reference to the Democrat Party) could build a strong current (*krasae*) of support in the region. Loyalties and feelings of obligation grounded in traditional values and long-established patterns of social relations are the principal base of southern Thai politics, argues Sathaphon. It is this system, he concludes, that made southern Thai politics a "politics of belief" ("*kanmueang baep 'phro chuea'*"), rather than a "politics of truth" ("*kanmueang baep 'phro thaeching'*"). To Sathaphon, this *uppatham*-based system made southern Thai politics "backward," showing that the history and culture of the region imposed limits on political change. He concludes with the plaintive questions: "What can be done? Who can answer this if southern Thais don't answer?"[34]

A problem for the folklore scholars was clearly evident. If an alternative participatory politics was to be grounded in local culture, what was to be done if this admirable local culture helped to perpetuate the dominance of the Democrat Party, whose very electoral success was apparently based on the persistence (and apparently the manipulation) of this culture? In a later paper, Charun Yuthong was more explicitly critical of the Democrat Party in the south, proposing that the party had appropriated an existing local cultural identification to its own political ends—it was exploiting a predominant "politics of belief" for electoral purposes, but doing nothing to undertake practical development for communities. The only way that Charun could avoid concluding that his innately wise *chaoban* were complicit in this ideological hegemony was to suggest that the Democrats were the manipulators of local culture, not the *chaoban*.[35] Charun's pronouncement here was an admission that folklore scholars committed to community development and people-based democracy had lost the battle with the Democrats to shape and control "southern Thai culture" as a political instrument. Charun trenchantly expressed his bitterness about the Democrat Party's dominance in the south in a volume of poetry, which he prepared for publication in the months prior to the 2001 national election. The volume included several rhymes with biting criticisms of the Democrats. One of them, entitled, "Tasteless Soup, Electricity Poles—the Floor Rag" concluded with the lines, "The constant rubbing of feet makes the floor rag stink, can't you see they tread on us from morning to night? Our honor is in whose hands? Aren't there any southern Thais better than this?"[36] Charun's book was published under a pseudonym by a group of his colleagues in November 2000 during the election campaign period. Fearing a hostile local backlash, however, he decided against the book's distribution until after the polling.[37]

Southern folklore scholars have played a part in codifying dominant customs and norms into what they portray as a distinctive regional culture. This entity with its component traditions (such as banditry and resistance, for example) is portrayed as a timeless, primordial, and collective essence. Their claims to its historical continuities, however, are empirically weak, though as McCargo notes, the popular cultural and historical images that they have uncovered and mapped should themselves not be discounted as playing a role in shaping political understandings.[38] They have identified important embedded practices and meaningful idioms that indisputably inform the contemporary life of that diverse group labeled as "southern Thai," but, at the same time, they have constructed an image of an ideal political community that conforms to their own political imperative of people-based development. Though most ordinary southerners never read their specialist publications, some of these scholars are regularly called upon by the local and national media to comment on local issues and elections. Charun Yuthong, in particular, still makes efforts to propagate civil society ideals in his writings and, albeit indirectly, continues to critique the Democrat Party hegemony. Following the 2001 elections, Charun wrote political reformist columns for *Focus Phak Tai*, with one series provocatively entitled, "Party or Phuak?" Though he did not explicitly attack the Democrat Party in these columns, his critique was obvious in his blanket dismissal of all Thai political parties as inauthentic, since they did not respond to the true wishes of "the people."[39]

It is not surprising that critiques by academics and others of political regionalism should have emerged in the mid-1990s.[40] After the ignominious collapse of Chuan's first government in the wake of a land scandal sparked by his own politicians, the southern Democrats fought the 1995 election campaign on the twin pillars of protecting southern honor and demonizing opponents for their massive vote buying. This campaign was effective, allowing them to expand their number of seats in the south, while by contrast Democrat support collapsed in Bangkok. The critiques of the southern folklore scholars reflect the impact of the 1995 election campaign and the Democrats' continued election victories in the south throughout the decade. Ironically, perhaps, the center of their scholarship and publication is Songkhla Province, where the Democrat Party enjoys an enviable degree of popularity. Moreover, the Democrat Party in Songkhla displays a continuing capacity to harness politically an ideal construct of "southern Thai culture" commensurate with the strength of its other political resources.

Part II

A Wall in the South: The First Battle

CHAPTER 3

"A Beautiful Political Culture": The Democrats Defend Southern Virtue

IN FEBRUARY 2004, the national political spotlight fell on Songkhla Province as the country's two major political parties prepared to run in a by-election for Constituency 3. Staged just a year before the impending national elections, this contest was made necessary by Phrai Phatthano, the sitting Democrat MP, who in the previous August had declared he was standing down from national politics to run for mayor of Hat Yai in the elections scheduled for early 2004. Nationally, this was not a good time for the hapless opposition Democrats to be pitted against the TRT electoral juggernaut, though in retrospect following their convincing by-election victory, it would be viewed as a propitious opportunity for the display of Democrat strength against Thaksin's party. It was especially significant because it was the only national by-election held in the south in the period between the national election of 2001, which swept Thaksin to power, and the next scheduled election of 2005. With the south as the only remaining Democrat base after their 2001 rout, the contest assumed critical significance for their survival and what was left of their credibility. Just as ominous for the Democrats was that the election was to be fought without Chuan Leekpai as the party's official leader.

The contest for Constituency 3 was conducted in an atmosphere of intense excitement, generated by the presence of nationally prominent politicians and by the powerful symbolic dimensions of the struggle, where two competing models of political legitimacy clashed. It was fought in the shadow of escalating violence, which had broken out in early January 2004 in the Muslim-majority provinces bordering Songkhla, a situation that the Democrat national leadership blamed on Prime Minister Thaksin's ignorance of conditions in the south and his wrong-headed methods of administration. While intermittent insurgent-style raids had taken place in the three border provinces during 2001–02, Thaksin had not treated them as acts of separatist-inspired militancy. Instead, he dissolved the long-standing Southern Border Provinces Administrative Center in 2002, claiming that disorder in the region was the result of gangsters and "influence" groups, not Muslim secessionists. His government, therefore, was taken by surprise on January 4, 2004, when insurgents raided a military camp and armory in Narathiwat Province, killing four soldiers and confiscating over 300 assault weapons. Later that month, the public was stunned by news of the gruesome beheadings of Buddhist monks in Pattani. By the eve of the Songkhla by-election, there was widespread fear and confusion among people in the province, added to which was the tangible economic effect of these incidents in reducing the tourist numbers from Malaysia and Singapore to Hat Yai and the border towns.[1] Commenting on the intense atmosphere, local journalists remarked that never before had so many leading Democrat Party politicians or TRT government ministers descended on Hat Yai and Songkhla Province.[2] Hat Yai and its surroundings were further enlivened by the overlapping campaigns of the teams competing for the city and provincial elections. The conduct of the two parties' campaigns and their underlying patterns of organization revealed significant contrasts and exposed the multifaceted strengths of local Democrat organization and popular loyalties, despite some notable advantages enjoyed by the government party.

Songkhla's Constituency 3 by-election struggle through the period of campaign preparation and organization extended from late 2003 to election day, on February 22, 2004. Considerable backstage maneuvering took place within the rival parties in their efforts to secure candidates, and there were strong contrasts between their modes of organization, both of which disadvantaged the TRT campaign. I place primary stress, however, on rhetorical performance and language as a vital dimension of the election. This contest was a powerful social drama, where an unfolding set of political performances of the rival parties contested the meaning of the competition. On their home turf and marshalling their full symbolic resources in the person of the iconic Chuan Leekpai and other leaders, the Democrats held the high ground. They successfully undercut the TRT message of development benefits and efficient government by portraying the contest as a moral struggle between the forces of political virtue and the amoral forces of authoritarianism and money politics.

In rhetorically shaping the narrative of the election as a moral struggle against Thaksin's evil parliamentary dictatorship, Democrat Party organizers and orators mobilized a range of familiar and culturally resonant symbols among the electorate to evoke the relationship between their party and the southern people as a communal compact. At the Democrat election rallies, eagerly anticipated and enthusiastically attended, orators evoked politicians, party, and voters as an intimate fellowship upholding the political values of loyalty, integrity, and incorruptibility. The rallies, functioning as familiar communal rituals, were the Democrats' most powerful vehicle of persuasion. More than the detailed content of speeches that addressed specific policy issues, the oratory aimed to express unity among a symbolic fellowship that drew its potent strength from an idealized image of southern political virtue. In turn, this regionally embodied political virtue was portrayed as intimately aligned with the party's sacred essence of "*udomkan*," an essence that was at the heart of the party's own creation myth and its centrality in the nation's birth of democracy.

THE NATIONAL AND LOCAL STAKES

What made the Songkhla contest of early 2004 critically important for the two rival parties was its location and timing. This was to be the only national-level election held in the Democrat stronghold of the south since the Thai Rak Thai Party had swept the national polls in 2001. TRT had taken seats in all of the regions except the south. Here, the

Democrats held on to forty-eight of fifty-four seats, and completely dominated representation in eleven of the region's fourteen provinces, leaving six seats held by the Muslim *Wadah* faction in the Muslim-majority border provinces as the only outpost of non-Democrat support. During 2003, by-elections were held in the central region (Nonthaburi) and in the northeast (Sisaket), where TRT won convincingly over the weakly organized Democrat Party.[3] Not surprisingly, these by-election results were proclaimed by TRT as a clear vindication of its populist policies and public confidence in Prime Minister Thaksin Shinawatra's decisive "CEO" leadership style. The south, however, presented a much tougher challenge for the ruling party. TRT had been probing the south throughout 2003, when Thaksin and his ministers toured the provinces to announce the launch of a number of major projects that were clearly aimed to generate popular support for the next national elections. Thaksin and his government retinue visited Songkhla several times that year, announcing plans to develop Songkhla as a national center of rubber research and production, and to redevelop the Songkhla Lake region. On the basis of TRT and other opinion polls that confirmed widespread support for the government's 30-baht hospital insurance scheme and its 1-million baht village development fund program, TRT spokespeople confidently proclaimed that the party's popularity had increased in the south, and that it would win twenty seats there in the upcoming national elections.[4] For the TRT, Songkhla's by-election presented a prime opportunity to begin the process of breaking open the Democrats' southern electoral base, and to test its candidate selection and electioneering methods before its major assault on the region in 2005.

Songkhla's Constituency 3 was one of the eight single-member constituencies of Songkhla Province established during the national electoral boundary redistributions of 2000 (the constitution of 2007 has since mandated larger multi-member constituencies). The constituency incorporated eleven sub-districts (*tambon*) extending from the suburban fringes of Songkhla's main urban center of Hat Yai (the largest city in the south) to village-based rural districts populated by both Buddhists and Muslims. Most of these *tambon* fall within the boundaries of the administrative district (*amphoe*) of Hat Yai, which is distinct from the municipal boundaries of Hat Yai City, which formed a separate constituency (see map 1.3). This area was the solid political territory of the Democrat Party, and had been since the 1970s when Sawai Phatthano, a native of Hat Yai, won the election. Sawai was repeatedly returned as a constituency MP for twenty years until he retired in 1995. After this, his son Phrai inherited the Democrat Party mantle.

For the Democrats, the successful defense of this Songkhla seat was imperative at national, regional, and provincial levels. Nationally, they needed a victory to assert their status as a meaningful parliamentary opposition party and an effective political vehicle for emerging public criticisms of the Thaksin administration. They needed to validate in concrete electoral form the force of their principled opposition to what they portrayed as Thaksin's authoritarian and nepotistic governing style, the corruption of his business cronies, and the party's control over the news media. In addition, the Democrats had focused criticism on the incompetence of ministers in the management of the bird influenza epidemic and treatment of the southern border provinces, where violence was escalating. Interior minister Wan Muhamad Nor Matha ("Wan Noor," member of the *Wadah* faction) was a key target for the Democrat attack on Thaksin's claims that the government was ruling the country efficiently. A win in this by-election was important to boost the flagging morale of the party and demonstrate support prior to the important Bangkok governor election (scheduled for August). In Bangkok, the Democrats had chosen a new and attractive candidate, Aphirak Kosayodhin, in an effort to recapture the metropolitan vote, which it had lost in 2001. Since the south was the party's only clear base of support, the Democrats had to protect the region at all costs so as to preserve their prestige. This was also a test of the party's support under its new leader, Banyat Banthatthan, elected early in 2003 to replace the revered Chuan Leekpai. Some commentators speculated that the retirement of Chuan Leekpai had removed the key iconic factor underlying popular voter support and identification with the Democrats in the south. Chuan's resignation from leadership, they reasoned, would now allow other parties to have a greater chance to displace the Democrats from their strongholds, including Songkhla Province, where the party had firmly held all parliamentary seats since 1992.[5]

The burden of proving continued party strength in its southern heartland fell on the Songkhla's Democrat MPS—particularly Thawon Senniam, director of the party's affairs in the province—who were keenly aware that if Constituency 3 fell to TRT, it would prove to be an ominous prelude to further losses in the region. Moreover, Thawon had a personal stake in the matter, because it was his protégé Wirat Kanlayasiri who had been chosen as the new Democrat candidate to replace the retiring Phrai Phatthano. Other political ambitions were at stake in the election results at the local level. For Phrai Phatthano, campaigning for the Hat Yai mayoralty, and for Nawaphon Bunyamani, running for the leadership of the Songkhla PAO, a Democrat victory was essential for maintaining their electoral appeal and reputations, which were tied to Democrat Party affiliation.

A SCRAMBLE FOR CANDIDATES: PATRONAGE, AMBITION, AND RIVALRY

Although the role of the individual party candidates was overshadowed by the national dimensions of the by-election, the selection of suitable candidates to run for the Democrats and TRT was still important. The two parties employed contrasting methods of choosing their candidates, and ultimately TRT undermined its own efforts by adhering to a method that proved deeply offensive to one of the strongest political aspirants. As a result of TRT's slight on his dignity, this local politician redirected votes from his supporters to the Democrats.

With the resignation of Phrai Phatthano, the Democrats of Songkhla faced the challenge of choosing a replacement for a popular sitting member. Phrai Phatthano's *barami* was strongly reinforced by widespread local respect and affection for his father Sawai Phatthano. Constituency 3 has the strongest level of Democrat Party support in Songkhla. In 2001, Phrai won the seat for the Democrats with the highest absolute number of votes and the highest winning Democrat margin for the whole province (54,682), convincingly defeating his TRT opponent, Thawisak Thawirat (11,375). Although Thawisak claimed repute and support through membership in the extensive and locally influential Thawirat-Suwannawong clan, in the 2001 election he attracted little more than 14 percent of all Constituency 3 votes (compared with Phrai's 62 percent).

According to Democrat Party procedure, prospective candidates were to be chosen by vote conducted among local standing MPS and party branch chairmen. The process of nominating members was generally mediated through sponsors of candidates among leading Democrat politicians of the province. In this process, personal networks and patronage play an important role, although there are standard criteria that must be considered in the final selection, in particular, factors that include party membership and the service and experience of the prospective candidate. There was some speculation about the identity of the replacement for Phrai. However, it was clear that the Phatthano family believed that it had the first option to nominate Phrai's replacement. During September, informants in the news media indicated that proposed candidates for the Democrats included Phrai's younger brother Phruek.[6] In an interview with me in that same month, Phrai's father, Sawai, stated confidently that his younger son Phruek would replace his elder brother, emphasizing as he said this that aside from Phruek's good character and formal qualifications for politics, "*trakun* plays an important role here, and it is more important than Democrat Party identity."[7] Phruek was a Democrat member and had assisted his brother in campaigning. However, the press noted that Phruek had not been actively involved in politics or the constituency for some time and this could count against him. Moreover, the same journalist noted that by promoting a family member to succeed him, Phrai would be vulnerable to charges of dynastic arrogance, which was the main ground of his own attack against the Suwannawong family in the Hat Yai mayoral contest.[8]

Attention also turned to Sunthon Pathumthong, a relative of Phrai by marriage, and a former long-serving district head (*nai amphoe*) of Amphoe Hat Yai who had long been a Democrat Party member and supporter of Phrai and his father. Around Hat Yai, Sunthon had a reputation as a popular district head and he had used his influence to the advantage of the Democrats during many elections. In short, he was regarded as a suitable candidate to stand for Constituency 3 because he was one of the Democrat *phakphuak*. Sunthon's support for the Democrats in the 2001 elections had been recognized by TRT and this led to his transfer from Hat Yai after TRT won government and gained control of the powerful Ministry of the Interior. As a punishment, Sunthon was posted to a smaller *amphoe* in Phangnga Province and his scheduled promotion to a higher rank (province permanent-secretary) was deliberately delayed. Despite Sunthon's former record of support, however, the Democrats of Songkhla found that by late 2003, Sunthon was shifting his political allegiance towards TRT and had actually been approached indirectly by prominent members of the party to consider standing as a TRT candidate in the same by-election![9] Sunthon's wife later revealed that Sunthon had given consideration to the invitation from senior party figures to nominate him for the Democrat candidacy in Constituency 3, but, in addition to his growing disillusionment with the party itself, Sunthon was aware that there was a factional struggle within the Songkhla Democrat ranks, and that Thawon Senniam was pushing strongly for the appointment of his protégé Wirat Kalayasiri. Under these circumstances, Sunthon was not prepared to risk a failure that would compromise his political prospects, and so withdrew his application.[10]

Wirat Kalayasiri was a strong candidate who had the backing of the prominent Democrat parliamentarian Thawon Senniam, an MP for Songkhla's Constituency 6. Wirat is a lawyer, a long-standing Democrat Party member, and for several years had served as private secretary to Thawon and also as chairman of the Constituency 6 party branch. Wirat had also formerly served as a provincial councilor (*so cho*). A native of Bang Klam District located outside Constituency 3, Wirat was not well known among people of the constituency outside the active Democrat Party membership. Nevertheless, he could show a record of loyal service, with political experience both at branch level and in parliament, in addition to his professional qualifications. With strong backing from Thawon, Wirat was proposed as a suitable candidate. In mid-October, a committee of the Songkhla MPS forwarded the names of Sunthon and Wirat to Bangkok for selection by the Democrat Party leadership. Some sources suggested that Phruek Phatthano was also formally nominated by the province-level Democrat committee. However, this was not the case and, in fact, only Sunthon and Wirat were proposed. The discovery of Suthon's move towards TRT and his withdrawal in late October left Wirat as the only feasible choice, and his candidature was confirmed by party headquarters by the end of that month.[11]

The TRT Party's procedure for selecting candidates appeared simple and efficient and in keeping with their corporate approach to electoral politics. Candidate selection was presented as an essentially market-driven process, and evaluation was based on the results of a secret polling of prospective candidates' popularity in constituencies. An inner circle of prominent party members close to Prime Minister Thaksin was in charge of final confirmation of these selections. In reality, however, the process was more complicated, because it clashed with the political patronage practiced by prominent party members who were charged with electoral organization in the south. TRT's Election Committee for the Southern Region (*kammakan amnuai kan lueaktang phak tai*) was responsible for coordinating TRT efforts in the south in preparation for the 2005 election. All were southerners. Wan Noor was in general charge, with responsibilities for specific clusters of provinces divided among TRT politicians of southern origin, chosen for their specific connections to particular provinces.

Wira Musikaphong was in charge of electoral preparation for Songkhla and Phatthalung. Formerly a prominent Democrat Party politician, Wira was a leading figure behind the "January 10" schism of 1987. Since then he had failed to win election to any seat in the south against his old party. In 2001, Wira unsuccessfully ran for Songkhla's Constituency 5 under the New Aspiration Party. When NAP was absorbed into TRT in 2002, Wira followed his fellow NAP members into the ranks of the government party, taking the position of assistant to Wan Noor in the Interior Ministry. However, sponsorship of prospective TRT candidates was not solely in the hands of Wira, because Wan Noor was also active in contacting networks of TRT supporters in Songkhla and neighboring provinces. In addition, members of Thaksin's inner circle were also approached by aspiring candidates from Songkhla. The task was a delicate one of cultivating and considering potential candidates, but at the same time withholding final commitments, pending the secret polls to determine the respective level of support for nominees. In Songkhla, this vertically oriented mixture of patronage and marketing science was far from effective in the timely choice of a candidate, and in the end proved to be detrimental to TRT efforts.

In the period September–October, there were at least five people jockeying for sponsorship as the TRT candidate for Constituency 3. Among them was Chamlaeng Mongkhonnitphakun, a renegade Democrat who had in 2001 stood unsuccessfully under the banner of the NAP. Chamlaeng, who had won only 2,723 votes in that election, failed to gain support from TRT. Another was Akrawit Laparotakit, son of the prominent businessman Bunloet Laparotakit, head of the Hat Yai–based automobile conglomerate "Ban Suzuki." Bunloet had many connections with TRT businessmen and key politicians. Akrawit was proposed as a candidate by Thaksin's younger sister Yaowapha Wongsawat, a key member of the prime minister's inner circle. In 2001, Akrawit had hoped to stand for TRT in Constituency 2 (Hat Yai City), but he faced opposition from his uncle Lapsak Laparotakit, the sitting Democrat member, and he had stood down in order to avoid internal family conflict. In 2003, he failed again, this time because a poll showed that there was insufficient local support for him in Constituency 3. Wan Noor then proposed Sunthon Pathumthong whose interest in standing for TRT had been cultivated both by his brother (who was close to Phumtham Wetyachai of Thaksin's inner group) and his wife, a teacher who had been close to Wan Noor since his time as a college lecturer.[12] However, although he was willing to run, Sunthon was unable to stand in the election because he had neglected to resign from the Democrats after becoming a TRT member. The regulations of the Election Commission of Thailand (ECT) stipulated that ninety days were required to elapse between the change of party membership and the election date. Sunthon was the favored candidate among TRT's inner circle until a month before the election date, when his disqualification was discovered, but this was not known by other aspiring TRT candidates or their party sponsors.[13]

A highly eligible nominee for candidature was Niran Kaenyakun, a motivated and ambitious provincial councilor with over ten years experience of local politics and strong voting support based on kin and phuak networks in his home *tambon* of Nam Noi (in the northeast of the constituency), as well as support from close supporters among provincial councilors. When I spoke to Niran in late October 2003, he was confident that he was the best candidate for TRT and would easily poll the best results of any of the other available contenders. His main supporter in the TRT hierarchy was Wira Musikaphong.[14] Around the same time, the local Hat Yai press released the news (evidently leaked by Niran or Wira) that TRT had confirmed Niran's selection by Thaksin's inner circle, and pointed out that it was too late for further polling owing to the imperative need for campaign preparation.[15] Soon after this, Wira formally introduced Niran to the public as the party candidate when TRT's Election Coordinating Center opened on the outskirts of Hat Yai.

But in mid-January 2004, after candidate registration and election dates were announced by the ECT, disaster struck for Niran. He discovered on a trip to TRT headquarters in Bangkok that Thawisak Thawirat had been chosen by the TRT party center after a last-minute secret poll had been conducted on the instructions of inner-circle member and TRT heavyweight Phumtham Wetyachai. It was typical of TRT's top-down, vertical, and ultimately fragmented management style that Niran was not informed of the decision. TRT paid a high price for its selection of Thawisak. Niran was angry with the party, while Wira himself, as TRT campaign director for the election, was deeply embarrassed.[16] Seri Nuanpheng, a friend of Niran's, tried to persuade him to bide his time and seek selection as TRT candidate for Constituency 2 in the next national elections, but Niran would not be placated, and resigned from the party in a fit of pique.[17] Other friends close to Niran pointed out that because of the insult he was going to direct votes away from TRT during the by-election.

Speaking of the Niran debacle just before the by-election, Wira pointed out that the TRT method of selection might be effective in other regions of the country, but it was certainly not appropriate in the context of southern Thailand, where personal honor was cherished. Wira had emphasized to TRT Party leaders that the use of the secret poll and top-down candidate selection method would have deeply negative consequences for efforts to build TRT party strength in the south because:

> In the south when someone is deeply disappointed they will nurture this hurt [*chepchai*] and resentment for a long time and as a result people will withdraw their cooperation in elections. Also, southern Thai people uphold pride in the region and are loyal to *phuak*—methods like this will create disunity.[18]

Another consequence of this flawed selection process was that the late choice of Thawisak—who had disappeared from public view since his earlier defeat at the 2001 polls—meant that he was given the short time of less than a month to re-introduce himself to the electorate as a serious political contender. Local TRT campaign coordinator Seri Nuanpheng felt that he was seriously handicapped in campaign preparation because he was ignorant of the candidate's identity until TRT's late announcement.[19]

THE CAMPAIGNS: ORGANIZING AND CANVASSING

The public process of electioneering began, according to legal stipulation, after candidate registration with the province-level ECT commenced on January 26. Thawisak, who was chosen by TRT after this date, needed to register later. With the election date set for February 22, there was little over three weeks available for formal campaigning. As expected, the contest involved just two parties, unlike the previous general election, when the NAP (now absorbed into TRT) had fielded Chamlaeng Mongkhonnitphakun in the constituency.

In organizational terms, the Democrats enjoyed a considerable advantage over their rivals. The party already had an established system for coordinating provincial and sub-regional party activities throughout the south, whereby senior-level MPs were allocated responsibilities. In this division of labor, Thawon Senniam, who also happened to be the sponsor of Wirat, was responsible for overall party management in Songkhla Province. There was already a high level of cooperation between party MPs and branch officials in Songkhla and its neighboring provinces of Phatthalung and Satun.[20] Among them were Democrat personalities well known among people in Constituency 3, such as

3.1 TRT election billboard for Thawisak Thawirat. The proclamation at bottom reads, "A true child of ours asks for the chance of just one year to make a difference."

Thanin Chaisamut, a Muslim MP of Satun Province who was a skilled and popular orator. Party members of these constituencies already knew each other through past campaigns and the various ongoing party activities that were a feature of Democrat life in the province.

The Democrat campaign headquarters were established at the home and constituency offices of Thawon Senniam situated at the junction of his own constituency and Constituency 3 on the main road connecting Hat Yai's airport to the city. The headquarters featured a complex of shophouses and a large open meeting hall, which doubled as an eating area. It was here where stocks of billboards, brochures, and candidates' cards were stored and distributed, where the party faithful were addressed, food supplied, formal and informal meetings and discussion held, and where prominent national party leaders were welcomed. It was also a venue for the inspection of voters' rolls and press conferences where Thawon hosted gatherings of the national and local press for announcements. Thawon's home during the three weeks of the campaign was a hive of activity where hundreds of ordinary members from neighboring party branches, friends, and volunteers gathered to exchange rumors and information, and to mount the pick-up trucks used to carry canvassing cavalcades through the constituency. Members and MPs from at least five of Songkhla's constituency branches converged on Thawon's home to help in the campaign. Phrai Phatthano also pledged his support to assist the campaign for Wirat, even though his main effort was to campaign for the forthcoming Hat Yai elections. Key members of the Constituency 3 Democrat Party branch had followed Phrai and were standing as candidates in his "*Thim Hat Yai Prongsai*" ("Team Transparent Hat Yai"), but other branch members were directed to help canvass in Wirat's campaign.

As a matter of policy, the TRT Party, unlike the Democrats, placed no importance on party branches, and none existed in Songkhla Province. A number of prominent figures in local politics were members of TRT, or otherwise known to support TRT, but since the elections of 2001 all public political activity under the TRT banner had subsided.[21] Such communication that did take place was restricted to contact between individuals and the party center in Bangkok, or occasional personal meetings with Wira Musikaphong or Wan Noor when they visited the province. Centers of support for TRT were dispersed, and prior to the by-election preparations there was no local organizational base to coordinate party-based activity of a character equivalent to the Democrats, and there was no tradition of continuous political activity that could generate group coherence. In contrast to the pattern of Democrat organization, which could draw on long-standing horizontal linkages and party loyalties, the TRT system was reliant on re-activating non-Democrat groups based on phuak and family bonds. So, when Wira set up the TRT coordination center in January 2004, he was forced to draw on his own scattered patronage-based and personal connections, and to activate support from among the various non-Democrat phuak and family-based alliances scattered throughout the constituency.

Key figures among these non-Democrat groups included Seri Nuanpheng, the former long-serving mayor of Ban Phlu Municipality (on the southern fringes of Hat Yai) and a TRT member who harbored deep resentment against the Democrat Party phuak, which had ousted him from his mayoralty (see also chapter 4); Kamnan Chop, a *nakleng*-style phuak leader and former chairman of Tambon Khuan Lang (a semi-rural sub-district encompassing the southern suburbs of Hat Yai); and Aphichat Sangkhachat, former chairman of Tambon Khlong Hae (north of Hat Yai), recently an unsuccessful political contender for the presidency of the adjoining Tambon Kho Hong (on the eastern fringes of Hat Yai). Apichat had cut his political teeth in Bangkok as a twice-serving president of the Ramkhamhaeng University Student's Association, and he enjoyed strong connections with the TRT party center as well as province-wide prominence through his chairmanship of the Songkhla Tambon Organization Assembly. Aside from his local phuak support, Aphichat was a close friend of Thawisak Thawirat and Wirachai Suwannawong, both former TRT contenders in 2001. In addition to these leading figures, a number of local politicians at *tambon* level among the outlying rural districts came forward to act as principal vote canvassers (*hua khanaen lak*).

In general, the public electioneering of both parties followed a similar form and sequence that is typical of political campaigning in Thailand. However, the proceedings were charged with a greater intensity because of the presence of leading national politicians (including Thaksin himself) and the staging of large rallies featuring party heavyweights. The atmosphere was further enlivened by the wide circulation of rumors and scandals focusing on the misuse by TRT of state power in electioneering and widespread vote buying. In the first week, large billboards and posters were attached to electricity polls and buildings, while pick-up trucks adorned with pictures and slogans of the candidates circulated neighborhoods accompanied by amplified music and recorded statements promoting the parties.

Ordinary people as well as active supporters of both parties were acutely aware that the role of the individual candidates would be minimal in this contest—it was above all a confrontation of strength between two contrasting party "*krasae*" (tides/currents). As one

Democrat supporter pointed out, "This election is different from the last one here; now the *krasae* of TRT is much stronger after three years in government. TRT is claiming success with its 30-baht hospital scheme and its village funds, and Thaksin says that he is responsible for the increase in rubber prices."

The first campaign cards distributed by TRT featured a portrait of Thawisak with a small inset picture of Prime Minister Thaksin above him, accompanied by TRT's original progressive and populist slogan: "*Khit mai tham mai phuea Thai thuk khon*" (Think New, Do New—For All the Thai People). By the second week, new TRT cards and posters appeared showing Thawisak garlanded with flowers, with Thaksin standing next to him wearing a benevolent, visionary expression. A quotation attributed to Thaksin was printed above that stressed Thawisak's local eligibility and his status as an assistant of Thaksin, reading, "Strengthen your hearts and choose Thawisak, a child of Hat Yai, to come and help me work." Wirat's posters did not mention his local birthplace (he was, after all, born outside the constituency), but rather evoked the foundational Democrat Party loyalties of the electorate in a simple slogan, "*Phak khong rao, khon khong rao*" (Our Party, Our Person).

SCANDAL, RUMORS, AND VOTE BUYING

Democrat members were confident that ordinary voter's love and deep-rooted attachment (*khwam phukphan*) to the Democrats would assure a victory. However, by the second week of the campaign, fears were increasing that this local advantage was being eroded by TRT's extensive vote buying and the government's use of officials to intimidate and pressure voters. On February 17 and 18, national newspapers were quoting statements from Songkhla-based election officials that they had received news of TRT *hua khanaen* distributing 3,000 baht to each family in return for votes. Songkhla MP Winai Senniam (brother of Thawon and Democrat by-election campaign committee member) told journalists that he had been personally informed that government ministers were distributing money directly to village headmen in a hotel in Hat Yai. Numerous government ministers descended on Hat Yai from Bangkok and gathered at a number of closely guarded hotels. Word was that the TRT had established a division of labor whereby each minister was responsible for one of the constituency's eleven *tambon* to arrange vote buying and other forms of voter persuasion. At the neighborhood level, young people supposedly were given free mobile phone SIM cards by canvassers in exchange for their votes for Thawisak. Throughout the campaign, the Democrats kept up a barrage of press releases claiming TRT's abuse of government power and its comprehensive vote-buying efforts.[22]

As local non-Democrats in Songkhla frequently point out, the Democrats are highly skilled at fostering rumors in order to demonize and de-legitimize their political opponents. Nonetheless, and despite public denials of Democrat claims by prominent TRT ministers such as Wan Noor, information provided to me by various informants through the constituency indicates that vote buying and the pressure applied on civil servants to canvass for TRT was real and substantial. In an interview conducted just prior to polling day, a prominent school headmaster and highly respected member of the Songkhla Teacher's Council confessed that, although he was a supporter of TRT policies, he was disgusted at the news from fellow colleagues that they had been directly instructed at a hotel-based "conference" by ministry officials to support the government party.[23]

Villagers gave me a variety of accounts of local *hua khanaen* payments and vote buying. Kamnan Chop of Tambon Khuan Lang was said to have received a free Toyota van in return for his support to TRT in canvassing. It was also said that some fifty of these vans were being distributed to principal *hua khanaen* throughout the constituency. In Khuan Lang, a group of village headmen in Kamnan Chop's phuak acted as local *hua khanaen* for TRT, and had apparently tried to arrange for advanced voting for groups of villagers so as to confirm their promises to vote for Thawisak after receiving payments of 300 baht each. In the rural *tambon* of Khu Tao, the chairman of the Tambon Administrative Organization (TAO) promised residents of his home and neighboring village (Villages 3 and 4) that if TRT won the election, projected road upgrading in the locality would be rapidly completed.

In the neighboring Muslim village (Village 8), it was known that a prominent local-born Muslim police general was a TRT supporter and was applying pressure on villagers to vote TRT through his younger brother—a *nakleng* and vice president of the Khu Tao's TAO. In Village 8, it was reported that TRT *hua khanaen* had kept the identity cards of at least one hundred villagers as insurance for their votes for TRT after payment. A close friend, Sombun, a taxi driver, confided to me that he had driven a police captain to this same village. The captain, a friend of his, told him that he had been "instructed" by his superiors to canvass for TRT votes. There was an edge of fear when villagers in Khu Tao related these stories, and as one of them said, "The Democrats have *phakphuak* and good friends here, but TRT doesn't know anyone, so they are sending in outsiders—this is scary." In Thung Yai, another rural *tambon*, the *kamnan* informed me on the day of the by-election that over the past two days he had received telephone calls from local villagers telling him that TRT canvassers had been offering 300–500 baht for each vote. He had no hard evidence, but he believed the stories to be true. He noted that during the campaign period, many police officers had traveled through his *tambon*. "People here don't trust the police—they're not neutral," he said.

To the Democrat members and volunteers who gathered at Thawon Senniam's home each day, their confidence in the deep popular loyalties to the party throughout Constituency 3 was tempered by a fear that TRT's use of "money power" (*amnat nguen*) and "state power" (*amnat rat*) would undermine support. According to a number of party branch officials, the rural people were the most vulnerable to offers of money for votes, because "they have no *udomkan*"—that cherished binding force of the Democrats. Thawon Senniam highlighted what was at stake in the by-election when he addressed local party workers and Democrat supporters from Bangkok at his home on February 20, with the words: "This election will show that the strongest political culture in the country cannot be broken." In strategic terms, the challenge for the Democrats was to maximize their home-ground advantage and deploy to their best advantage the Democrats' most powerful symbolic resources.

THE DEMOCRAT BIG GUNS AND CAVALCADES OF LOYALTY

In the daily campaigning, which progressively grew in intensity from the second week of electioneering, the Democrats used these resources to the full. Their key symbolic resource was the former leader Chuan Leekpai, who accompanied election cavalcades throughout the constituency and walked through suburban streets and villages to universal welcome. Chuan was accompanied by prominent members of the parliamentary party, including his highly popular protégé, the handsome and urbane Bangkokian, Abhisit Vejjajiva. In the space of two weeks, it was said that Chuan visited at least half of the communities of the constituency. Even local Democrat Party branch members were astounded to witness the affectionate embraces given to Chuan and Abhisit by women in the constituency. Against Chuan's powerful iconic role as the embodiment of the moral and regional status of the Democrats, TRT had no competitor. The best that TRT could do before their scheduled large rally at the close of the campaign was stage a number of small rallies where Wan Noor and Wira were the featured speakers. Wan Noor also attended Friday prayers at a number of mosques around Hat Yai. But according to one prominent Muslim Democrat Party branch chairman, Wan Noor's high personal status among the Muslims of the constituency had been compromised by the escalating violence in the Muslim border provinces and his apparent inability to solve the problems.

Aside from the person of Chuan himself, the Democrat cavalcades were distinguished by their festive character and fraternal evocation of Democrat loyalty and identification with the south. On the day before the election, convoys of pickup trucks crowded with members wearing blue or white party jackets—from Songkhla as well as Bangkok—left Thawon's home to circulate through the constituency (see plate 3.2). The trucks were adorned with large billboards and members held aloft the party's sky-blue flags emblazoned with the distinctive emblem of the party's patron deity, Mae Thorani. I accompanied one of these pickup truck cavalcades on its final three-hour circuit of the constituency. Throughout the tour, the truck broadcast recorded exhortations stressing Wirat Kalayasiri's sterling qualities as a loyal and virtuous party member with wide political experience, as well as the party's traditional standing as a morally upright and southern political institution. The following excerpt from a truck broadcast on this day expressed the key Democrat message pronouncing the grounds of its political eligibility:

> Brothers and sisters of the *tambon* of Amphoe Hat Yai, Constituency 3, in the name of the Democrat Party, the party that has stood with the south for a long time . . . the party that has *udomkan* . . . the party that provides the qualification for candidates who have quality and ability to follow the principle that, "The party chooses the person—the people choose the party."
>
> Now the party puts forward a good person, a person of knowledge and ability to be the representative of Constituency 3—that is Mr. Wirat Kalayasiri. He is prepared for this position in many ways, having ability and political experience. He has served the Democrat Party for fifteen years, so that now he takes the opportunity to serve as the representative of the brothers and sisters of Constituency 3, according to the principles of politics that are transparent and honest, whether that be in solving problems, or promoting development and progress.
>
> Mothers and fathers, brothers and sisters that we respect—the Democrat Party that is the symbol of the southern people, the blood in the heart of the Democrats, offers you Mr. Wirat Kalayasiri, a good person of Constituency 3, to serve you from now on in the place of Phrai Phatthano.

This convoy of five trucks sped along the main roads, with party members cheerfully waving to passersby and other vehicle drivers. In the back roads, the convoy slowed down and members called out the voting number and name of the party (No. 1). The trucks stopped where there were markets or clusters of houses to allow members to dismount and hand out brochures, and were welcomed everywhere by smiling residents from their doorsteps or on the streets. As the convoy proceeded, a number of the Bangkok-based members began to craft their slogans based on resident responses. At the beginning of the tour, their calls had been, "*Boe nueng la khrap, khun Wirat boe nueng la khrap*" (Number One, Mr. Wirat), or "*Boe nueng, Prachathipat la khrap*" (Number One, Democrat Party). However, among the group in my truck, local residents responded by referring to "*Phak Nai Chuan*" (the party of Chuan Leekpai), so members in my truck began to focus their own appeals on Chuan Leekpai with short slogans like, "*Chop Prachathipat, rak nai Chuan, lueak boe nueng*" (If you like the Democrats and love Chuan, then vote Number One), or "*Lueak nai hua Chuan, boe nueng*" (Vote for Leader Chuan, Number One). In response to these calls, some local residents happily shouted, "*Dai laeo, lueak Nai Chuan laeo*" (We've already chosen Chuan). Despite the fears expressed among themselves, the overwhelmingly positive reception given to these festive Democrat cavalcades generated confidence among members that this publicly expressed support would be translated into votes at the polling booths.

3.2 The Democrat Party election cavalcade. Shown as it prepares to leave the campaign headquarters of Thawon Senniam on the final day of campaigning for the by-election.

PERFORMING PARTY IDENTITIES: THE RALLIES

The highlights of the campaigns were several large rallies that had been advertised in advance by handbills and local press announcements. They were held a few days before polling day, scheduled for Sunday, February 22. Both parties placed considerable importance on these major rallies, where, aside from final appearances of the candidates, the claims of the respective parties to eligibility would be articulated by party leaders. Aside from the major arguments and issues presented, the atmosphere, speaking styles, rhetoric, and audiences revealed strong contrasts.

The Thaksin Rally—Authority, Deference, and the Delivery of Central Policy

The TRT rally held on Thursday, February 19, derived its public importance largely because of the presence of Prime Minister Thaksin Shinawatra, although his ministerial colleagues were advertised as an essential supporting cast. The site for the TRT rally was at the entrance to Hat Yai Municipal Park. It is a monumental space featuring a large concrete forecourt below a statue of King Rama V. The TRT platform was a huge stage featuring two stacks of twenty-four loudspeakers. Large posters of Thaksin served as a backdrop to the stage along with a banner that read:

In just three years we have proven clearly
that we have followed every promise
thinking more, doing more
for all Thais throughout the kingdom

The TRT rally had been advertised to begin at 4:30 p.m., but by this time neither audience nor principal government party representatives had yet arrived. Instead, the area was crowded with scores of police officers and soldiers, with only a few small groups of sound technicians and journalists scattered among this swathe of noticeably tense official guardians. At around 5:15 p.m. the first speaker mounted the platform, by which time several hundred listeners had arrived. No seats had been provided, so new arrivals either stood on the edges of the concrete space or sat cross-legged in groups. The standing groups appeared to have been comprised largely of civil servants in standard grey and blue outfits, and office workers. Those sitting were mainly rural people, both Muslim and Thai Buddhists. Over the next hour, the audience increased, but not enough to fill the large space in the center of the concrete square. The curiously muted atmosphere that dominated the occasion seemed to be explained not only by the formality and starkness of the space itself, but by the fact that large numbers of people among the audience did not know each other and were not, in fact, residents of the constituency, nor were they from Songkhla Province. My own inspection of the car park showed that many people had been brought to Hat Yai in over a dozen tour buses from the southern provinces of Phatthalung and Nakhon Si Thammarat.

It was clear from the talk among people in the crowd that they were looking forward to catching sight of Thaksin Shinawatra, but this atmosphere of anticipation was overlain with one of subservience, which was reinforced when Wira Musikaphong mounted the podium and appealed to the audience to move into the center of the square so as not to disappoint the prime minister when he gazed out onto the crowd. This rally was clearly intended to be a spectacle of support for TRT, designed for media reporting and to impress the constituency's voters with a spectacle of "local" support for TRT before polling day. Notably, the hundreds of visitors brought from other provinces were not formally acknowledged by the speakers. Instead, the crowd was addressed as "people of Songkhla Constituency 3 and neighboring *tambon*." I was to learn later from a network of tuk-tuk driver informants that during that afternoon local TRT *hua khanaen* were giving tuk-tuk drivers 500 baht each for transporting friends and neighbors to the rally.

It was noticeable at this TRT final rally that none of the speakers who mounted the podium to give the customary preliminary warm-up speeches in advance of the party heavyweights were prominent Songkhla public figures. In fact, although the first speaker gave his address in the southern Thai dialect, he was a local politician from Nakhon Si Thammarat. Wira Musikaphong, who announced himself as the host of the event (*chaophap*), was the only principal speaker who could claim a Songkhla birthplace, but he had never represented a

Songkhla constituency, and was not widely known among ordinary people in Hat Yai and its surroundings. Wira cited his long experience in government as the basis of his authority to judge the achievements of the TRT government, though he carefully avoided mentioning that all his experience in government had been gained when he was a Democrat Party MP nearly twenty years earlier, and that he had failed to gain election to any southern constituency since leading the "January 10" defectors out of the party in 1987.

Three interconnected themes dominated the speeches, including the final speech made by Thaksin: de-legitimizing the Democrat Party, both as the party of southerners and as an effective party alternative; the importance of the by-election, despite the fact that the government's tenure would run for only one year; and most importantly, the success of the TRT government's policies and achievements.

The first theme was pursued in a rather delicate manner at this rally, for it involved de-coupling the status of Chuan Leekpai from the identity of the Democrat Party. TRT could not afford to alienate Songkhla residents by insulting the revered figure of Chuan. The first speaker made an attempt to attack the Chuan-based image of the Democrats by arguing that the Democrats were no longer the party of the south because Chuan had stood down as party leader in April 2003. Not only that, but Chuan had supported his Bangkok protégé Abhisit Vejjajiva as successor, and the elected leader was Banyat Banthatthan, who, although a long-serving southern Democrat, was supported by the faction of the morally dubious powerbroker Sanan Kachonprasat, who was Central Thai (with a strong electoral power base in the northern province of Phichit). Banyat was thus the creature of a non-southern political leader. Moreover, he claimed, all eight of Songkhla's Democrat MPs had opposed Chuan's protégé Abhisit in the party leadership contest and voted for Banyat.[24] Thus, the Democrats were no longer eligible as a worthy party of the south, both because Chuan had stepped down and because the Songkhla Democrats had been disloyal to Chuan. Another speaker pointed out that the Democrats were misleading the voters in this by-election by telling voters that a vote for the Democrats was a vote for Chuan to become prime minister—they were misusing the name of Chuan Leekpai to take advantage of simple villagers.

TRT was introduced as the party of a "new era" (*yukmai*), a party that emphasized policy and performance, with a decisive and committed leader. Wira intoned in a strong southern Thai accent, that, "In all my thirty years experience in politics, there has never been anyone whose work has achieved success to equal Thaksin Shinawatra." TRT had acted decisively and quickly on its election commitments to implement programs to relieve rural indebtedness. This contrasted starkly with the Democrats who had not followed through on any policy when in government, and when in opposition could only complain and criticize. The Nakhon Si Thammarat orator, who mounted the stage several times between the main speakers during the evening, pointed to Phrai Phatthano's resignation as indicating that Democrat politicians were deserting the opposition party because it had no future. He criticized the Democrat campaign slogan, "Our Party, Our Person," by pointing out, that here was a party with no policies and no desire to change, unlike TRT, which already had demonstrated its success with many innovative projects. Furthermore, although they claimed to be the party of the south, the Democrats had not done anything to increase the price of rubber, nor had they ever had a policy for attacking the drug trade, and nor had they ever promoted development projects for the south, such as the TRT policy for redeveloping the Songkhla Lake region.

As for the significance of the by-election, it was pointed out that even though the government had only one year of its term remaining, electing Thawisak as TRT representative for this constituency was a chance to test how effectively TRT could perform for Songkhla Province. Anticipating the major Democrat rally scheduled for the next day, Wira signaled the seriousness of this election while simultaneously warning listeners against being seduced by the renowned rhetorical skills of the Democrats. This election, he stressed, was not like a Miss Thailand contest where voters made decisions on beauty and style, this was about concrete policies and, therefore, voters needed to evaluate the parties according to their achievements (*phon ngan*).

Thaksin's arrival at the rally, surrounded by police and journalists, distracted all attention away from the speakers for some time. Accompanied by Thawisak, he squatted down and talked to a group of Muslim women, while he and the candidate were both adorned by garlands that had been distributed by party officials in advance. It was now approaching 8:00 p.m., and Thaksin with his police retinue moved to the rear of the speaking platform, which by now seated over thirty prominent government ministers and MPS clad in white TRT jackets. Wan Noor addressed the crowd briefly, emphasizing that TRT was committed to *khunnatham* (virtue), *nayobai* (policy), and *phon ngan* (results, achievements). To Wan Noor the contrasts between the two parties were easy to make. TRT proposed policies and carried them out, while the Democrats couldn't say anything that wasn't abusive (*mai mi arai cha phut mak wa da*) and had no results to demonstrate. Thawisak was then introduced to the audience. Thawisak received his garlands with the deferential demeanor befitting a young candidate before his powerful sponsors. Meanwhile, the speaker denounced Wirat Kalayasiri as Thawon Senniam's purse carrier, noting that Wirat had failed in his last attempt to gain election for the Songkhla PAO, and that he was not a truly local person, being born in Bang Klam, which lay outside the constituency. The Democrats, he declaimed, had insulted Hat Yai people by presenting Wirat as candidate. A smiling Thawisak then took the podium and spoke for less than two minutes, enough time to stress the importance of the by-election and to point out that he was born in Hat Yai. Thaksin then took the podium. Thawisak, holding a single red rose and wearing a beatific smile, stood humbly next to the prime minister as he spoke.

Thaksin's speech reiterated the three key themes of this rally in his characteristically declarative and confident style that rhetorically condensed his governments policy objectives to products of his own personal will. In all of his declarations, it was not "my government," but "I." He began with a number of barbed comments that aimed to dismiss the distinctive reputation of the Democrats in the south as formidable orators. He began by saying, "We won't talk until 2:00 a.m. and make your bladders burst like the Democrats." Then, more humbly, "I've never been good at abuse (*phom da mai khoi keng*)," because his parents taught him to always maintain good manners (*marayat*). Referring to the next day's major Democrat rally, he noted with a casual smile, "Tomorrow there will be another festival of abuse directed at me, but I've had my fill of abuse."

Thaksin went on to assert his leadership and policy commitment to the country, bringing the consequences of electors' choices into stark relief, "I will not allow poverty to continue in this country . . . if you want to be poor then vote Democrat." He then summarized the well-known policies of the government and their success over the past three years, stressing that TRT has achieved more in its three years in government than the Democrats had ever achieved in over fifty years. He next signaled his desire to develop the south and personally oversee the progress of development projects, emphasizing his commitment to the region by noting that, "I am not a person from the south but my name is "Thaksin" (a name meaning "south"). To undertake this work, he needed a representative in the south to communicate with the government, and Thawisak was the representative needed for Thaksin to carry out his "work." Smiling kindly, he turned to Thawisak and said, "Non is like my younger brother." Thaksin then added, in a tone of appeal that appears to have been calculated to reduce any residual sense of obligation that electors may have felt towards the incumbent Democrats, "After all, we only want *one* constituency in Songkhla, so we can demonstrate how we work . . . there will still be seven constituencies that are not ours."

He concluded with a final triumphant jibe at the Democrats, "The Democrats will be in opposition for another twenty years—and even *then* they won't have any policies." The election was about "helping each other." That is, by returning Thawisak to parliament, Songkhla Province would benefit from the largesse of the TRT government by receiving more development funds and projects. Thaksin personally promised listeners that TRT was not engaged in vote buying in the campaign. He concluded, "Tomorrow the Democrats are bringing their army (*kongthap*) and I know what they are going to say, therefore don't change your minds."

The TRT rally had been marked by a use of language and a reiteration of key words that discounted "politics" as empty argument and abuse (*da*) and upheld the stabilizing resonance of the word "administration" (*kan borihan*) and the intrinsic practical appeal of "development" (*kan phatthana*). Government and politics were about "work," not "talk," and what was at stake was the material development of the province as against the prospect of voting for a party that had no possibility of bringing development to the district because it was in opposition, a fact which in itself confirmed the Democrat Party's impotence. Notably, however, none of the speeches dealt with the critical issue of the unease of southern Muslims that they were being singled out in the government's anti-terrorism policies. Nor did they acknowledge the widespread fears among villagers that the violence afflicting the adjacent provinces of Pattani and Yala would spread into Songkhla Province and threaten personal security, or the increasingly negative impact that the border violence was having on Hat Yai's important tourist economy.

The TRT rally audience numbered at its height an estimated five thousand people. That it had been necessary to transport a significant proportion of the audience from elsewhere highlighted TRT's anxiety that it could not compete with the popularity of the Democrats, whose strength was measured by the appeal of its rallies. News reporters pointed out that at least a thousand members of the crowd were soldiers and police, aside from the substantial numbers of people brought in from other provinces, as clearly indicated by the presence of numerous inter-provincial tour buses.[25] The TRT rally broke up a little after 9:00 p.m. Its atmosphere was subdued and the behavior of the audience deferential.

The Democrats Perform: A Moral Community and Its Enemies

The final Democrat appearance was held the day after Thaksin's rally, on Friday, February 20, with a markedly distinct use of rhetoric, atmosphere, and relationship between speakers and audience. It was marked by a level of collective intimacy that was completely absent from Thaksin's rally.[26] The venue was a deep rectangular grass field opposite Hat Yai's busy "Big C" department store, located to the north of the city in the suburban area of *tambon* Khlong Hae (see plate 3.3). This was a strategic choice, for the field was accessible to Friday shoppers and public transport. As was customary, and in contrast to the TRT rally, Democrat organizers set up plastic chairs for the audience, a measure that not only ensured comfort for elderly people and families, but also served as a method that could be used for calculating attendance. On this occasion, some three thousand chairs were set up, but they only occupied around two-thirds of the field. The area was full to capacity and the standing audience was overflowing onto the pavement by 6:30 p.m. The audience was diverse, including Buddhists and Muslims, family groups with children, elderly people and groups of young men, mostly informally dressed. Food vendors selling drinks and snacks plied an active trade on the pavement. Reporters estimated that the crowd numbered around ten thousand people.[27] The speaking platform was substantially smaller than the TRT stand, featuring only eight seats and twelve amplifier speakers. This was not simply an expression of the party's limited financial resources; it was as much an expression of a Democrat Party tradition where those MPS and party officials not engaged in speaking sit or stand near the audience, enabling them to interact with party members and the public. The contrast with the TRT hierarchical ordering of space and proximity between politicians and the public was striking.

Beginning with local Democrat Party officials, and gaining momentum and force with an accumulating array of the party's

3.3 The crowd assembling in the early stages of the final Democrat rally for the Constituency 3 by-election.

politicians and prominent leaders, the speeches portrayed the election contest in terms of political and moral contrasts: between the Democrats as a party of the common people and TRT as a party of rich capitalists; between the Democrats as a party of principle and TRT as a party of opportunism; between Democrat representatives as self-sacrificing people of professional competence with legal training and TRT as a party of profit-oriented businessmen-politicians who owed their election to vote buying, and perpetuated their power by restricting press freedoms and abusing state power. The contest was evoked as a critical struggle to uphold principle against amoral power. The first announcer stressed to listeners that the contest was not a competition between Wirat and Non (Thawisak's nickname), but between Wirat and Thaksin. It was not simply a contest in this single constituency of Songkhla Province, but a vital struggle to protect principled and honest politics, which the Democrat Party embodied, against money and state power that threatened to destroy democracy itself. An old man sitting next to me—who had been a party member since 1987—emphasized the by-election's significance by saying, "This election here will be an example to the north, the central and northeastern regions, because here in the south our *udomkan* is high."

The Democrat Party slogan "*Phak khong rao—khon khong rao*," was made tangible by the language of inclusion, fraternity, and familiarity. The warm-up speakers announced to the growing crowd that people had come this evening to meet, "Than Chuan" and "Than Banyat," leaders of a party that had built its repute (*barami*) over a long time among the southern people. They used the warming and inclusive possessive pronoun "our" (*rao*) to affirm the mutual identity between party and people. Chuan and Banyat were "our Chuan and Banyat" (*Than Chuan lae Than Banyat khong rao*), and the party was "our Democrat Party" (*Phak Prachathipat khong rao*). By contrast, TRT was an alien presence. The difference was cleverly evoked by the second party speaker who spoke of the TRT rally held the previous evening, "Last night, TRT held their rally. I thought that it might have finished at midnight, but they closed the rally at just 8 p.m.! Perhaps the prime minister was scared of being killed?" After the laughter subsided following this remark, he went on to argue that Thaksin's brief visit showed how little real interest the leader of TRT held for the south—why didn't he stay longer to try and solve the problems of violence in the border provinces?

The Democrat meeting was contrasted with the atmosphere surrounding Thaksin's rally of the night before:

> At our rally tonight we Democrats don't have to have policemen standing around holding guns, or soldiers, and you don't have to line up to have your identity cards checked. Brothers and sisters can come and listen to the Democrats with easy hearts (*doi khwam sabai chai*). We Democrat people (*chao Prachathipat*) welcome everyone to come and listen to the speeches—you can go and eat, then come back at your convenience—and we're going to speak for a long time—we will finish at about 2 a.m.!

This announcement about the duration of the rally was a proud affirmation of a long-held tradition that identified the Democrats as formidable orators and distinguished their rallies as popular events for southerners. Further, it was explained that rallies such as this were necessary because the TRT government controlled the newspapers and television broadcasts; thus, face-to-face meetings such as this were the only way that the party could communicate the truth to the people. The preliminary speeches established the key themes for the speakers that followed, i.e., honorable and well-qualified Democrat representatives such as Wirat needed to enter parliament for the opposition in order to scrutinize the government's activities; TRT and Thaksin were the causes of the problems facing the country, including the bird flu epidemic, border troubles, and increasing indebtedness; Thaksin and his cronies were enriching themselves at the expense of the people through company monopolies (e.g., mobile telephones); and Thaksin's style of government ignored legal processes and concentrated power. The only choice was to elect Wirat as a member of the party that embodied trustworthiness and moral uprightness.

After nearly an hour of preliminary speeches by branch officials, Democrat parliamentarians mounted the podium, beginning with Narit Thanarat, a Muslim MP for Phatthalung, followed by Churin Laksanawisit, a deputy leader of the party and former minister in

Chuan Leekpai's previous governments. During this time, more Democrat politicians began entering the grounds and were greeted by the crowd with affectionate shouts and loud clapping, as if they were a home football team. Great distraction was caused by the entrance of two prominent young Democrats from Bangkok, deputy party leader Abhisit and his colleague Aphirak Kosayodhin, the newly selected party candidate for the forthcoming Bangkok City governor elections. Churin good-humoredly invited the women in the crowd to admire the two men's good looks, but the women needed no encouragement from the podium. Both men wended their way slowly through the audience from the rear of the field. Swamped by well-wishers—mainly women—it took them some twenty minutes to reach the speaking platform. Like all large Democrat rallies in the south, this was a ritual for narrating the history of the party, renewing collective loyalties between the Democrats and southerners, and affirming the identity of the party as a heroic force for protecting political righteousness against the abuses of authoritarianism.

Narit Thanarat of Phatthalung devoted his speech to the people-party bond in the south and its fusion into a distinctive "political culture of the south" (*watthanatham thang kanmueang khong phak tai*) in the following terms:

> In this campaign for the election of Wirat Kalayasiri, we have used the method of the rally (*wethi prasai*)—there is no other method that the Democrats use. The Democrats have used this method continuously since the party was founded. This particular election time is an occasion of great concern, but the Democrat Party has experience in the field of political fighting for fifty-seven years. We believe that today, Hat Yai people are still with us; but state power is being used in the south and will be used in other parts of the country in the future. If the power of the state gains victory this time, the people will be the losers. The election rally of the south—of the Democrats—involves standing before brothers and sisters at election times, speaking of the true issues and giving information for brothers and sisters to make decisions, each time. Brothers and sisters have made their decisions alongside the Democrats always. This time it's the same, and what I've said—standing

> before brothers and sisters, addressing the true issues and providing information—is the political culture of the south. We [the Democrats] have always nurtured and maintained the political culture of the south. This time, brothers and sisters, is another occasion when we wait for the views from the hearts of the Hat Yai people. Will they take care of this political culture, one that is admirable and beautiful, or not?

Although this was clearly an appeal to southern pride, it was not narrowly parochial. Rather, it was an affirmation that this "political culture," so widely cherished in the south, was consistent with the *udomkan* of the Democrats at a national level. The enthusiastic welcome given by the crowd to the Bangkok Democrats and other prominent non-southern party personalities, such as Sanan Kachonprasat, demonstrated clearly that they viewed themselves as a part of a wider Democrat community, albeit a special part of this community.

Churin Laksanawisit complemented Narit's speech by commenting on the TRT rally of the previous evening, reporting to the audience that he had been told by journalists that five thousand people attended the TRT rally, and two thousand of these listeners were police and military guards. He then countered the charges made by TRT speakers that the Democrats had no policies and had done nothing for the south, using examples of the free medical care program for elderly people first introduced under Chuan's Democrat government. Churin gave examples of sports complexes built in Songkhla Province during his term as sports minister in Chuan's government, and commented to the laughing crowd that the Democrats had even been responsible for establishing Thaksin University (Southern University) in the city of Songkhla. He concluded with an assessment of the critical importance of the by-election. In a triad of powerfully delivered phrases, he argued that, *if* TRT won this by-election from the Democrats, then TRT's hope to win twenty seats in the south was possible; *if* TRT won the election, then Thaksin's aim to win four hundred seats in the next general election and to establish a one-party government was possible; and *if* TRT won this seat, which was the most powerful support base of the Democrats, it would show that the Democrats were unable to take care of their constituencies in Songkhla Province. This was a rallying cry for the defense of the Democrat heartland. The failure or success of this defensive effort would play a large part in determining the political future of the country, because the next general elections were crucial. If Thaksin gained four hundred seats, then according to the constitution, the opposition—with only a hundred seats—could not mount censure motions and debates against the prime minister. In fact, he pointed out, with no powers to censure even government ministers, an opposition party with only a hundred seats would be equivalent to having no opposition in parliament at all. If TRT gained four hundred seats in the forthcoming elections, it was the same as giving the country to Thaksin. Right now, the Democrats held 129 seats, following the resignation of Phrai Phatthano. Every seat was vital for the party, and he thus appealed to voters to return Wirat to Constituency 3 as a replacement for Phrai Phatthano. "Don't take any notice of TRT's appeal for you to experiment by giving them one of the eight Songkhla Democrat seats," Churin cried. "You don't have to taste TRT noodle soup, because you know that Democrat noodle soup is much tastier—and don't even *try* TRT noodle soup; it's got Borax [an abrasive powder] in it!" (loud cheering and clapping followed).

When Thaksin dismissed Democrat rallies as long-winded affairs that served only to make people's bladders burst, he betrayed an ignorance of the many-layered functions of southern Democrat rallies as political rituals. And, when Wira Musikaphong proclaimed that all the Democrats could do was talk, not act, he was ignoring the fact (as he well knew) that for the Democrats, words themselves could be put to many uses in rhetorical performance. The Democrat rally was not only an event where specific government policies were critiqued; it was simultaneously a familiar ritual aiming to renew trust and intimacy among people and the party. This was achieved by assembling the whole pantheon of the party's well-known politicians and deploying their various skills to reinforce the legitimacy of the Democrat opposition to the TRT government, in particular to attack the leadership and personality of Thaksin. Collectively, these speakers presented the face of the Democrat Party to the audience. Aside from the common use of the southern Thai dialect, the speakers all varied with regard to their personalities and body language, their style of verbal delivery, and the content of their addresses. This in itself was important, because it served to impart a rhythm and vitality to the rally, where careful political criticism, humor, and moral outrage alternated and reinforced each other.

The complementary variety of Democrat orators was displayed clearly by the last three of the rally's speakers and was used to great effect. Trairong Suwankhiri, a well-known Songkhla Democrat and senior party member (now party-list MP), adopted his well-known pose of comic mock bewilderment modeled on the irreverent *nang talung* shadow puppet character of "*Ai Theng*," who is commonly given the role as the voice of the simple but perceptive southern villager poking fun at powerful and self-important figures. Trairong opened his speech with a self-deprecating admission calculated to identify with his audience, "I've been in politics since before I could even speak Central Thai—actually, I *still* can't speak it" [loud laughter followed]. In a thick rural accent, punctuated with bursts of very fast passages to give dramatic effect, Trairong devoted the main topic of his speech to the Thaksin government's inefficient handling of the bird flu epidemic. His address was peppered with mockery of Thaksin in common peasant language, which drew roars of laughter and clapping. "*Na khiang*" ("chopping-board face," referring to Thaksin's square-shaped face) was alone responsible for messing up the country (*tham prathet chiphai*), "I told you, brothers and sisters, three years ago 'don't vote for chopping-board face.' The southern people believed me, but people from the other regions did not!"

Trairong was followed by Surin Phitsuwan, the prominent Muslim Democrat of Nakhon Si Thammarat, who addressed himself in particular to the Muslims in the audience. Standing with one hand in his pocket, and beginning in measured tones that gradually rose to a crescendo of volume, Surin denounced Thaksin's overweening pride and arrogance as sinful to both Buddhism and Islam. The continuing problem of the violence in the Muslim border provinces was, he claimed, a direct result of the prime minister pretending to be God. Surin portrayed Thaksin as an embodiment of "*phadetkan*" (authoritarianism, dictatorship), the traditional enemy and moral antithesis of the Democrats. It was critical, therefore, to support the Democrats as the parliamentary opposition:

> There *has* to be a limit to power. You *have* to be able to examine and criticize. You can't just "think it yourself and do it yourself" [a play on the TRT slogan, "Think New, Do New"]. That's not democracy, that's authoritarianism! The *southern people* cannot accept this. *Songkhla* people cannot accept this. *People of Constituency 3* cannot accept this!

The highlight of the rally was the eagerly awaited appearance of Chuan Leekpai. Though the audience had listened attentively to a speech by the new party leader Banyat Banthatthan earlier in the evening, there was no question that Chuan was still their hero and the symbol of the Democrats. Chuan's softly spoken, intimate, and anecdotal oratorical style contrasts markedly with the explosive force and high drama of Trairong, Surin, and other renowned speakers.[28] His speech and demeanor on the platform are consistent with a carefully cultivated public persona that projects modesty, integrity, piety, and dedication to the party and the country. On this evening, he opened his speech with one of his standard fraternal pronouncements, "*Phom pen huang phi nong*" (I am worried/concerned about my brothers and sisters). He quoted statements from the crowds of students he had met at Hat Yai University and villagers at Tambon Khu Tao who told him that, "We would surely win." But he also told stories that indicated a high level of vote buying by TRT opponents. He related an amusing case of a Hat Yai tuk-tuk driver he had just encountered at a petrol station, who complained to Chuan that he had missed out receiving 300 baht from TRT *hua khanaen* at the previous night's rally.

Chuan's anecdotes all led up to the key theme of the truthfulness and trustworthiness of the Democrats, "All these stories are true and we [the Democrats] have always spoken the truth because we follow the dictates of honesty." He reinforced this with a statement in Pali from the Buddhist scriptures. Therefore, he continued, he must counter the criticisms of TRT opponents, and point out the contradictions in their criticisms. For instance, during the elections in the northeast, the Democrats were criticized by TRT for being a party of the south and favoring that region in development projects, yet in the present campaign, they were attacked by TRT for doing nothing for the south. Under the Chuan government, all regions were treated equally, and he gave the example of the four-lane highway system introduced under the Democrat government that ran through all regions.

Chuan's inclusive language contrasted strikingly with Thaksin's self-oriented pronouncements of the previous evening. He personalized the Democrat government by naming its ministers (most of them sitting behind him on the platform), and constantly reinforced the collective identity of the party with the expressions of "our party" and "your party," which echoed the main slogan of the campaign.

Chuan accused Thaksin's government of untruthfulness in not admitting the true situation in the country. This was demonstrated by the disastrous state of the three border provinces. He conveyed the insecurity and violence in the border provinces through stories conveyed to him by ordinary people he had met. Speaking of the murders of monks to highlight the gravity of the violence, Chuan stressed that Thailand had never met a situation like this before. He spoke of the importance of the king and queen in visiting the south and engendering trust between Muslims and officials. Under Democrat governments, disorder and separatism in these provinces had gradually subsided, because they had stressed consultation by means of the long-established Southern Border Provinces Administrative Center (SBPAC). But what had happened to create the upsurge of violence and who was responsible? If the violent events were caused by external factors beyond the control of the government, he would not assign blame. However, it was clear that the prime minister had created these problems since coming to power because of his own mistakes. Thaksin had declared that there were no more problems in the border provinces and they could be solved in a few months; he therefore dissolved the SBPAC in 2002, destroying the good work of decades. Chuan then drew his points together by centering on the key issue, which was Thaksin's disrespect for Democratic processes. Thaksin had used the electoral system to come to power, but once in power had ignored democracy. The contrast between TRT and the democratic system, embodied by the Democrat Party, was thus made vividly clear by Chuan through reference to the violence and everyday insecurity prevailing in Songkhla's neighboring provinces.

This final Democrat rally before polling day ran until after 1:00 a.m. the next morning. It epitomized the character of large Democrat rallies in the south as communal rituals evoking popular loyalty to a trusted institution, serving to renew solidarity by means of rhetorical performances of well-known party personalities. Evoking southern pride, the speakers also portrayed the voters of Constituency 3 as part of a wider national Democrat community, who were charged with the heroic task of defending the system of democracy against its enemies.

VOTES AND VERDICTS

Beginning around 8:00 p.m. on the evening of polling day, thousands of people began to gather at the vote-counting center for Constituency 3, a technical school on the fringes of Hat Yai. Press reports later estimated the number of onlookers at about five thousand. The vote counting itself was slow, and only began at 9:45 p.m., following the arrival of all ballot boxes from the 182 polling booths of the constituency's eleven sub-districts. Although Democrat Party members were quietly confident of victory, they were annoyed that the prime minister had commented on ITV television before the vote counting that TRT would win by several thousand votes. In private, the TRT campaign director Wira Musikaphong had been more circumspect, but at the very least, he hoped that Songkhla's by-election would serve to demonstrate an increase in TRT popularity in the south. A few days prior to polling day, Wira was confident that even if TRT lost, the party would nevertheless attract at least thirty thousand votes from this electorate of nearly a hundred thousand listed voters.[29] The vote counting was slow. TRT officials triumphantly proclaimed that their exit polls during the day showed Thawisak leading the Democrat Wirat by 10 percent (55 to 45 percent), but they were gravely wrong.[30] At midnight, the final count was still not complete, but it was clear by this time that the Democrats had won the by-election. When Wan Noor showed up at the counting station with his entourage, the Democrats were already clearly in the lead, and the party's jubilant supporters shouted defiantly to Wan Noor as he left the area, "That'll teach you [TRT] what happens when you try and eat the country! (*kin mueang*)"

The final tally showed an impressive victory for the Democrats, with a winning margin of some twenty-five thousand votes. The voting figures showed Democrat candidate Wirat Kalayasiri victorious with 51,936 votes, trailed by Thawisak Thawirat for TRT with just 26,636 votes, several thousand short of his campaign director's target. A comparison of these results with each party's votes gained in Constituency 3 in the previous national election of 2001 showed a slight fall in Democrat votes and an increase of over fifteen thousand votes for TRT. In this by-election, 66.6 percent of qualified voters had cast ballots, while in 2001 the proportion had been 77.1 percent, which may have had the effect of lowering Democrat vote levels. TRT had possibly attracted votes in 2001 that had been cast for the New Aspiration Party, although NAP had gained only 2,723 votes in 2001. A few days after the poll, Thaksin claimed that the increase in votes for TRT (11,375 in 2001 to 26,636 in the 2004 by-election) was a significant advance for the party's fortunes in the south.[31]

Songkhla's by-election results were interpreted by the Democrats and the national press as highly significant at a number of levels. Not surprisingly, Thaksin and TRT spokespeople were much less prepared to publicly accept that any "lesson" had been learned at all. For the Democrats, who had the most to lose by a defeat, the victory in Songkhla was a vindication of their criticisms of the Thaksin administration. It was certainly a morale boost for the new party leader Banyat, who claimed that the TRT defeat was a warning that TRT could not gain its hoped-for four hundred seat parliamentary majority.[32] For his part, Thaksin denied that the TRT loss would reduce his party's chances of gaining four hundred seats at the next national elections.[33] The defeat in Songkhla, however, did lead TRT managers to reduce their expectations for future victories in the south, and they publicly downgraded their declared target of twenty seats down to fifteen.[34] Political commentators in Thailand's major national newspapers saw the Songkhla by-election results as signaling a critical check on TRT's hitherto successful populist policy marketing. In Constituency 3, the voters had not been persuaded by TRT's much-applauded achievements, nor had they been impressed sufficiently by Thaksin's apparent success in raising rubber prices to 40 baht per kilogram.[35]

Above all, national-level press commentators were struck by the persistence of Democrat strength in the south, despite judgments over the past years that TRT had helped to transform the nature of politics towards policy-orientated electoral choice (see plate 3.4). Many claimed that the by-election exposed the distinctive character of southern loyalties and the particular features of a southern "political culture." The TRT *krasae* that appeared to be sweeping the country was not as strong as had been assumed, and Songkhla was an example of the fact that the south was still a Democrat bastion that resisted this *krasae*.[36] Although not a southerner himself, senior Democrat and former party Secretary-General Sanan Kachonprasat pointed to the political impact of southern pride when he suggested that Thaksin had antagonized voters during his Hat Yai rally by telling them to vote for TRT if they wanted to be rich, but choose the Democrats if they wanted to remain poor. This, he claimed, was interpreted as an insult, and other news commentaries concurred.[37] The results showed that Songkhla voters would still return Democrat candidates despite TRT's deployment of

3.4 The cartoonist Arun's depiction of the effect of the Democrat rebuff on Thaksin's TRT Party in the Songkhla by-election. (Source: Nation, *February 25, 2004)*

considerable sums of money. Thawon Senniam proudly announced to journalists that, "Money can't buy southerners."[38] Clearly, the intense national press coverage of the by-election results was being used by Democrat national leadership to highlight the party's popularity and TRT's flaws. Thaksin's rebuff in Songkhla presented a field day for newspaper cartoonists (see plate 3.4)

Yet even more neutral national commentators saw the results as a reflection of what they defined as distinctive regional "cultural" factors at play in voter decisions. These columnists pointed out that all of TRT's strongest points at a national level had been turned into weak points in the south. Thaksin's popularity, the use of money, influence of state officials, the use of government funds, and TRT policies had all failed before the critical non-economic factor of voters' feeling of "*mansai*" (intense resentment) towards TRT's assumption that it could win with promises of riches. TRT's Western-orientated approach, epitomized by its polling techniques to monitor voter preference, would never fathom the significance of this "cultural" factor.[39] The week before the election, the Hat Yai-based *Samila Times* weekly paper ran a full-page article entitled, "The Results of the Constituency 3 Election Will Show the Political Culture of the South." Drawing on an interview with a prominent local university academic (Dr. Wichai Kanchanasuwan), the article highlighted the salient characteristics of "southern political culture" as comprising a high level of popular interest in politics, but above all it was characterized by a strong loyalty to phuak that could not be shifted by even the most highly developed policy alternatives. Dr. Wichai pointed out that it was this love of phuak, exemplified in the persistence of an old and familiar party and its networks, which was likely to lead to a Democrat victory in the by-election.[40]

Reflecting on the Songkhla by-election results a week later, *Focus Phak Tai* journalists judged that the most critical factor assuring the Democrat victory was the popularity of Chuan Leekpai and his active role in the vote canvassing.[41] This judgment was also made by major national weekly news magazines. *Nation Sutsapda* ran a two-page analysis with the heading, "Today the Democrats Are in Debt to Chuan's *Barami*," while *Siam Rat Sapdawichan* entitled its by-election analysis, "Chuan Leekpai's *Barami* Sends Wirat to the Stars."[42] While press commentators and politicians read various meanings into the by-election results and attributed primary causes to the voting, the Democrat Party's exit polls suggested that a number of factors were at play in shaping the views of ordinary voters, from immediate campaign-related features to broader issues. These polls showed that 76.3 percent of the sampled voters were unhappy with the government's handling of the southern border province disturbances, while 40 percent were critical of the apparent government cover-up of the bird influenza issue. Notably, 30 percent of the voters interviewed admitted they had voted Democrat because of Chuan Leekpai.[43]

The TRT defeat exposed a number of critical weaknesses in its organizing methods in the south. Reflecting on the TRT by-election defeat a year later, Thawisak's campaign organizer, Seri Nuanpheng, expressed a concern that TRT could not compete in the south unless the party established branches that could ensure the continuing presence and identity of the party as well as coordination among leading supporters. "To be successful in the south," he pointed out, "a political party has to stand permanently, not simply appear during elections, and then disappear again till the next elections." Seri had emphasized this point to Thaksin personally, but nothing was done, because the party relied on vertical organization. After the by-election, leading TRT supporters in Constituency 3 went their separate ways, and continued to rely on separate communications with the party center. The top-down, poll-based TRT method of selecting the candidate was also subject to criticism, and one newspaper suggested that TRT should not have selected Thawisak at all, because he had already been defeated in the same constituency by the Democrats in 2001.[44] Others highlighted how the last-minute dumping of Niran Kaenyakun for Thawisak revealed persistent internal TRT conflicts between the Muslim "*Wadah*" faction of Wan Noor and the "*Wang Bua Ban*" group led by Thaksin's sister.[45] Wira Musikaphong confessed prior to the by-election that the distinctive character of political contestation in the south required that TRT candidates needed to be trained in public oratory; otherwise, they would be handicapped when competing against the Democrats. He believed that a school should be established for training southern TRT candidates in oratory.[46] These points, made by southern TRT organizers, highlighted the distinctive characteristics of the south as a political arena, but the national elections in the following year would show that the party center had little interest in investing effort to build a party presence through local branches, or tailoring campaigning and organizational patterns to suit southern conditions.

At the local level, the Democrat victory proved to be critically important for a number of key political actors and for the party itself. As previously mentioned, the campaign for Wirat overlapped with the campaigns for both the Hat Yai and PAO contests. The Democrat by-election victory proved to be indispensable to Phrai Phatthano's efforts to unseat the ruling dynasty of Khreng Suwanawong in the Hat Yai elections. Phrai had calibrated the timing of the resignation as a sitting Democrat member of Constituency 3 to take full advantage of the enthusiasm generated in the by-election campaign and presence of popular party leaders in Hat Yai. His prestige as a national politician was tied to his family's Democrat identity, and he needed the support of Democrat networks and the renewed force of the party's *krasae* to overcome the inertia of local support for the reigning Suwanawong family. The Democrat by-election campaign and victory was also critical for the fortunes of Nawaphon Bunyamani in his efforts to win the Songkhla PAO elections scheduled for March. Contesting the position of PAO president against the popular and long-serving incumbent Worawit Khaothong, Nawaphon needed to harness the support of his elder brother, the Democrat MP Niphon, together with the province's Democrat phuak as well as the national party. In turn, the success of Phrai and Nawaphon were important in maintaining the grassroots strength of Democrat networks and the party's *krasae* in preparation for the next year's national elections. Party affiliation was to be a decisive factor in both local contests.

A HEARTLAND UNITED

The Democrat repulse of TRT in the Songkhla by-election exposed a critical miscalculation by TRT pundits, as well as most local TRT campaign organizers, and also some Songkhla academics. In my discussions and interviews with them, there had been much talk about how Thaksin's "new" politics based on business management and result-oriented policy campaigning would attract the younger generation of educated voters in Hat Yai's suburbs. Hat Yai's bookshops were full of hagiographic books on Thaksin and business management texts endorsed by the prime minister. The ties of southerners to the Democrats were the mark of an older generation, they asserted, and educated southern youngsters would break out of the emotional web of loyalty binding their elders and instead vote with their "heads," not with their "hearts." The by-election result dramatically defied these assumptions. Middle-class and farming families in Constituency 3 responded equally to the Democrats' damning indictments of Thaksin as a dictator, a business monopolist, and an enemy of true democracy. The fully charged rallies and the presence of Chuan had palpably reinforced the idea that election choices were moral choices about allocating power, not simply decisions about the efficient delivery of policy. The victory affirmed the continuing potency of Democrat political theater.

Part III

Riding the Tide: Local Politics and Democrat *Krasae*

CHAPTER 4

The Struggle for Hat Yai: Localism, Lineage, and the Loyalty Game

IN THE GAME of political competition, as F. G. Bailey reminds us, victory often goes to those who can act in ways unforeseen by their opponents; ways that are unanticipated in the "rules" of the game.[1] This was demonstrated dramatically in the Hat Yai municipal election in early 2004. Here, the "rules" changed at both the level of legal regulation and in the sense of long-established convention. They changed in the regulatory sense because from 2004 direct election of mayors was now mandated by law, and elections were to be monitored by the Provincial Election Commission, and not by the municipal authorities, as previously. But in Hat Yai, there was another rule, in the sense of an established convention, which was enforced by the long-standing mayor's local political machine. This convention had effectively kept national parties out of Hat Yai's municipal contests. This all changed in 2003–04, however, when the character of local political competition was transformed by the entry of Phrai Phatthano, a mayoral candidate who brought the symbolic and pragmatic resources of the regionally ascendant Democrat Party into the contest with decisive effect.

Hat Yai's councilor and mayoral elections of February 29, 2004, were held a week after the national parliamentary by-election that enlivened not only the districts of Constituency 3 that encircled Hat Yai, but also excited Hat Yai's largely Democrat-voting population. The Hat Yai mayoral contest of 2004 was unprecedented in the history of the city, in terms of both its intensity and its final result, which saw the unseating of the long-entrenched Suwannawong family and its allies. It was the first time in Hat Yai's history that national-level political party allegiances were comprehensively and explicitly mobilized in support of a contesting group. Although the national Democrat Party leadership stopped short of official endorsement of Phrai as a party candidate, the party's heavyweights were firmly behind Phrai's campaign, as were Democrat branch members in the city and province. The party provided the decisive symbolic and canvassing support necessary for Phrai to subvert successfully the localized political capital and networks of Prasong Suwannawong and his father's embedded support groups.

At the height of his power in the early 1990s, Hat Yai's long-serving mayor Khreng Suwannawong proudly told journalists that he had never allied himself with any national political party because his loyalty to serving the city overrode all other considerations. Local administration was a distinctive sphere, he asserted, where national political organization and alignment had no place. In the past, some parties had signaled intentions to challenge Khreng's ruling team. Khreng had effectively warned them off his turf with the confident knowledge that his political terrain was unassailable under a well-nurtured political machine and a symbolic legitimacy founded on his image as a self-sacrificing and practical civic leader, with an intimate knowledge of the problems and needs of the city's people. He repeated the same credo of independence from political parties to me in early 2004, but his tone was one of desperation rather than triumph, because now the formidable Democrat Party was battering at the gates of his formerly impregnable local citadel.[2]

The tendency for families (*trakun*) to perpetuate dynastic rule over urban centers has not been unique to Hat Yai alone; it is a general pattern found in other cities of the south and elsewhere in Thailand. The pattern reflects the centrality of prestige and patronage as key foundations of governance and electoral legitimacy, the disinterest of many town dwellers in voting, and the prevalence of fraud under weakly enforced electoral law.[3] Struggles to unseat these families have been particularly difficult for opposing groups, and it has usually been major public controversies or weaknesses in succession transition that have provided the conditions for opponents to topple these families. For decades, some mayors had passed on power in their towns to wives and sons, but Khreng Suwannawong's thirty-year tenure was the record for an individual incumbent in Thailand. Ironically, while Khreng depicted the Democrat challenge as an unprincipled invasion and an instrument of unnatural discord in the community, he was, in fact, the major culprit provoking this political transformation by arranging for the mayoralty to be passed to his son Prasong following his own resignation in 2002. Against a rising discontent among Hat Yai's residents that was cleverly harnessed by the Democrat politician Phrai Phatthano, Khreng's son Prasong was unable to perpetuate his family inheritance. He was defeated in Hat Yai's election showdown in February 2004, primarily because he could not control the narrative of the election in the face of the symbolic resources mobilized against him.

As with provincial politics, municipal politics in Thailand has always been connected with national politics in various ways, though

4.1 Khreng Suwannawong

only in the metropolis of Bangkok is party-based competition fully institutionalized. In the past, successful town mayors have used their office as a stepping-stone for entry into national politics. So too, national politicians have endorsed various teams in municipal elections, and drawn on the prestige of their parties to aid friends and protégés. In 1995, for example, the rising young star of the Democrats, Abhisit Vejjajiva, assisted the brother of one of Petchaburi's Democrat MPs in his campaign to oust the ruling Bunthong family. The campaign rhetoric of the challenging team was dominated by the standard Democrat mantra condemning "dictatorship." Despite Abhisit's symbolic support, however, this effort failed to dislodge the locally dominant Bunthong family machine.[4] During 2003, there was no guarantee that party-backed candidates would be able to defeat locally prominent ruling groups, as evidenced in mid-2003, where in Pathum Thani and Samut Prakan the challenging TRT-backed teams had been trounced by incumbent teams of locally entrenched power elites.[5] The conditions surrounding the Hat Yai contest were very different, however, because of its location in the Democrat Party heartland, the circumstances surrounding the challenge to the Suwannawongs, and, critically, the involvement of the Democrat leadership and the effect of the party's victory in the previous week's by-election.

The following account of the Hat Yai election focuses on the ways that the two main contesting groups (Phrai and his Democrat-supported team "Transparent Hat Yai," and Prasong Suwannawong and his father's "Old Team") constructed powerful symbolic claims to leadership eligibility before Hat Yai's voters while also employing various pragmatic tactics of persuasion. Hat Yai's mayoral contest can be read as a struggle for power and legitimacy that involved a number of interacting dynamics and agendas among key political actors at different levels. It was a family turf war as well as a local conflict over models of city government that had long been contained and muffled by Khreng's patrimonial regime. It also involved a strategic mobilization by the challenger of local Democrat Party support networks that were necessary to compete with Khreng's entrenched power, and a concomitant deployment of symbolic capital of a scope that dwarfed the prosaic issues of local government. At regional and national levels,

Phrai's campaign was supported by the Democrats' national leadership as part of its own agenda to shore up electoral support in the face of the danger of TRT expansion into the south.

Days after securing the party's victory in the by-election, the Democrats' "big army" (*kongthap yai*) returned to Hat Yai with the revered Chuan Leekpai and gave their blessings to Phrai's cause, endorsing his attack on the Suwannawongs as a local version of their great morally righteous crusade against entrenched power, corruption, and dictatorship. In Phrai's campaign, his opponent Prasong Suwannawong was never considered or represented as the main opponent, and Prasong's policies were not discussed—what was being attacked was a system, dramatized as the antithesis of political virtue, and crystallized in the alleged dynastic pretensions of Prasong's father Khreng.

THE FATAL SPARK

In December 2001, nearly two years after he and his *Thim Kao* ("The Old Team") were returned to power for their sixth consecutive term, Khreng Suwannawong, now age seventy-five, announced his retirement as mayor of Hat Yai. He had held the mayoralty for over thirty years and was nationally renowned as the longest-serving mayor in the country. Officially, at least, he left the choice of successor to his team's councilors who commanded twenty-three of the council's twenty-four seats and were led by his elder brother and staunch lieutenant Khran Suwannawong. In February 2002, this rubber-stamp majority voted unanimously for Khreng's eldest son Prasong to be the new mayor.[6] Prasong Suwannawong, known locally as "Palat Oi," possessed the experience and qualifications that seemed to suit an executive position. Aged forty-four, he held a law degree and a master's degree in public administration, together with experience as a local government official, having previously worked as *palat* (district chief clerk) in three *amphoe* of Songkhla Province. After a faltering start—losing in a by-election in 1992—he finally gained election to the Hat Yai council in 1993 and gained quick promotion to *thesamontri* (councilor with portfolio) with

Khreng's encouragement. Notwithstanding his formal credentials and the technical legality of Prasong's appointment, however, what stood out for critics in Hat Yai was the clear nepotism behind the move, achieved by virtue of a rubber-stamp council that featured only one opposition member.[7]

Prasong's appointment catalyzed opposition among a number of disgruntled groups in the city (including former councilors), who privately denounced it as an arrogant act of phuak favoritism. To outsiders, the core of Khreng's *Thim Kao* that dominated the municipal council was a self-serving phuak, since it comprised not only Khreng's relatives but also his close associates within the city's elite, including some prominent Sino-Thai businesspeople. They had become accustomed to ruling Hat Yai, facing largely token opposition in the four-yearly municipal elections. Despite rumbles of dissatisfaction with Prasong's appointment, there were good reasons for *Thim Kao* members to feel confidence in their choice, because Prasong's public legitimacy rested on the formidable reputation that his father had established as a benevolent administrator of the city. Khreng's electoral dominance had been assured by a system of patronage-based machine politics that was effective so long as voter turnout was kept at traditionally low levels (never more than 45 percent), and the educated middle classes of the city remained uninterested or disillusioned with municipal elections.

In late 2003, when Phrai Phatthano announced that he would resign as Democrat MP for Constituency 3 and run for mayor against Khreng's son in the next municipal election, he crossed an unspoken boundary separating the spheres of political influence of the Phatthano and Suwannawong families. Both of these prestigious families were related by blood in a wider family constellation that had long presided over the political life of Hat Yai and its environs. The Phatthano family, a distant branch of the Thawirat-Suwannawong kin network, had enjoyed a singular prominence in Hat Yai since Sawai Phatthano entered national politics as a Democrat Party MP in the mid-1970s. Phrai, Sawai's eldest son, easily won election to his father's seat in 1995. Thereafter, Phrai enjoyed a high popularity and esteem, based on his own abilities as a Democrat representative as well as the accumulated *barami* of his father and the widespread local respect for his mother, who had long been an energetic advocate for the family. The Phatthano family's repute was intimately linked to its record of loyalty and service to the Democrat Party. Paralleling the dominance of the Phatthanos in national politics, the Suwannawongs had exercised dominance in the sphere of municipal politics. From 1972, the mayoralty of Hat Yai was under the control of Khreng Suwannawong, with the support of the closely related and extensive Thawirat family and allies from the Chinese business elite. The history of the Suwannawong-Thawirat kin group was inseparable from the history of Hat Yai itself, and Prasong's appointment as mayor in 2002 represented a clear effort to perpetuate this link.

In the national elections of 2001, two younger members of the Thawirat and Suwannawong families had come forward as TRT party candidates, one of them the son of Khran Suwannawong, Khreng's brother and his right-hand man in the municipal council. They had both suffered defeats at the hands of reigning Democrat MPs, including Phrai, who had easily defeated Thawisak Thawirat in Constituency 3. It could be said, then, that it was the Thawirats and Suwannawongs, not the Phatthanos, who had been the first to trespass the boundaries marking a long-established family-based division of political labor. Khreng himself had always professed an independence from any formal connection with national political parties, but members of the Suwannawong-Thawirat kindred were increasingly aligned with TRT political interests, and this was again displayed in the February by-election when Thawisak Thawirat ran in Constituency 3 for the second time, having been selected by TRT on the basis of his dense network of kin support. In this context, for a Suwannawong to argue that the field of local politics should be kept free from party identification verged on hypocrisy, though Prasong continued with his father's refrain of heroic localism as the foundation of his campaign. With the entry of an experienced and locally prominent Democrat politician into this terrain, the folksy appeal of Khreng's village-style localism was to be overwhelmed by more powerful symbolic claims to allegiance. On the pragmatic level of campaigning, the old tried and trusted methods of Khreng's machine—threats and other persuasions—were undermined by the wily Democrats, whose techniques were based on carefully cultivated rumors and scandals, as well as the energetic vote canvassing of ordinary Democrat supporters.

HEGEMONY AND ITS DISCONTENTS: THE SUWANNAWONG INHERITANCE

Hat Yai is the largest city in southern Thailand, with a population approaching 190,000 people.[8] It is a commercial city whose growth and status as the principal marketing, trading, and tourist hub of the lower south is based on its strategic position straddling trade routes between Bangkok and Malaysia, and the enterprise of its Chinese business elite. The establishment of a railway connection with Bangkok in 1917, together with later junction lines connecting with Malaya stimulated the growth of the town's market, helped along by donations of land from the railway contractor, "Chia Ki Si," who was granted a title by the king ("*Khun Niphatchinnakon*"). By 1928, the growing market area was elevated to the status of a Sanitary District (*sukhaphiban*) within the *amphoe* of Hat Yai, and Khun Niphat was appointed as one of its committee members. [9] Hat Yai's economy and population progressively grew thereafter, with its importance acknowledged by elevation to municipal status in 1935 (*thesaban tambon*), and thence to *mueang* (township) status in 1949, with a corresponding expansion in its boundaries. By this time, Hat Yai had outgrown the town of Songkhla, the province's administrative capital on the coast. Over the next two decades, the mayors of Hat Yai (elected from among the councilors) were businessmen of Chinese origin.

It would seem incongruous that the administration and politics of this bustling business center should, from the 1970s, be dominated by an ethnic Thai family of village origins. This phenomenon, however, is not entirely unusual, and reflects a characteristic historical pattern of reciprocity between Chinese business interests and ethnic Thai administrators. The Thai and the Chinese have administered Hat Yai in a collaborative partnership of mutual benefit centering on the parallel progress of the city and the welfare of its population. Sino-Thai businesspeople shared elective office as councilors with prominent ethnic Thais and contested elections in alliance with them. Khreng Suwannawong gained his first experience in local administration as an assistant to his famous uncle, Won Thawirat, a renowned *kamnan* of Kho Hong Sub-district, with a reputation as an influential *nakleng* with a knack for solving problems and getting things done.[10] Khreng, who then made a living as a cattle dealer, had no official position, but he helped his uncle out of respectful loyalty. Khreng remembers Kamnan Won fondly as a role model on which he based his own practice of personalistic leadership, founded on *kan sang khwam pen tham* (building justice), *kan sang khwam di* (building goodness), and the personal qualities of *khwam chueathue* (trustworthiness), and *khunnatham* (virtue). These culturally grounded virtues that defined the good *nakleng* formed the basis of Khreng's model of governance as a system of relationships founded on reciprocity, respect, and harmony. When elections were announced for Hat Yai's council in 1957, Khreng was persuaded to stand as a candidate, largely, he admits, because he was known to have "many phuak," an indicator of his wide kin network and a popularity born of his active practical role in local affairs.[11]

In 1972, Khreng was chosen by his fellow city councilors to replace the Sino-Thai mayor Wichian Kowithaya, who had fallen seriously ill. Over the next twenty-six years, from 1974 to 2000, six municipal elections were conducted, with Khreng and his allies (comprising both Thai and Sino-Thai councilors) winning all of them convincingly, albeit based on very low levels of voter turnout. Khreng has never claimed to be an expert in urban policy or administration. He defines himself as a "practical person" (*phu patibat*), not a theorist, who has learned his administrative skills through experience and the advice of elders and friends. He administered the city and maintained his position through this long period by exercising a range of practical and personal leadership skills, which incorporated an intimate knowledge of the city, an ability to cultivate personal relationships with central government officials, a capacity to maintain mutually beneficial networks within the city's elite, and an adaptive ability to harness the expertise of both groups to further the development of Hat Yai. He assured the reproduction of his power base by developing a strong electoral machine founded on personal and patrimonial rule, and a symbolic legitimacy based on accumulated *barami* that flowed from his public service and commitment to the city.

Late in 1992, Khreng (then aged sixty-two) received the royal decoration The Order of the Crown of Thailand, First Class (*Prathamaphon*

Mongkut Thai) in recognition of his public service, the first municipal mayor to be awarded the honor. To mark his award, an illustrated souvenir volume was prepared by councilors and province officials to commemorate his achievements in a life of civic service spanning thirty-four years as a municipal councilor, including nearly twenty years as mayor. The volume can be read as a symbolic text aiming to cement Khreng's political position by the deployment of complementary and mutually reinforcing civic and state hierarchical symbols. It catalogues Khreng's civic achievements in building Hat Yai to the status of the premier city of southern Thailand, which had became by the late 1970s the center of a thriving tourist trade from Malaysia and Singapore. Numerous testimonies from senior bureaucrats praised his achievements. The public honors and positions that Khreng had been awarded were enumerated, including his honorary law degree from Thammasat University, his long presidency of the Municipal Association of Thailand, and his appointment as senior advisor to the Prince of Songkhla University in Hat Yai. Khreng's virtually unopposed election in the 1990 municipal polls—where only one of three districts had been contested—was praised as one of the greatest proofs of his public popularity.[12]

Khreng's long hold on the administration of Hat Yai earned him the unofficial title of "permanent mayor" (*nayok talotkan*). Some journalists have likened Khreng to a *chaopho* ("godfather"), or a *phu mi itthiphon* ("influential person"), suggesting that he was the southern equivalent to the infamous *chaopho* figure, Kamnan Po, of Chonburi Province, Central Thailand. But this is a poor comparison because, although Khreng could certainly be identified as one of the most well-known and connected public figures in Songkhla Province, there were no demonstrated links between him and crime networks, which is a key criteria in the label "*chaopho*." Nor had he ever expressed interest in national party politics, or acted as a canvasser for national politicians—a core characteristic of the stereotypical provincial *chaopho* business figures that became prominent in public and academic discourses on Thai politics in the 1990s. In any case, unlike the northern and northeastern regions of the country, the phenomenon of the rural *chaopho* in southern Thailand is rare.[13] Instead, there are "influential figures," often popularly labeled "*nakleng*," who tend to command more localized bases. There is no doubting, however, that Khreng functioned as an urban boss, as widely feared as he was loved, and he used his considerable connections to maintain simultaneously his political support and to manage the city. Not surprisingly, Khreng denied that he exercised any "influence" for his own benefit, and responded to journalists that he would accept the title of "influential person" only on condition that he be seen as an influence for the public good (*itthiphon thang khwam di*). Khreng insisted that he had never used his public office to aggrandize his own interests at the expense of others, or to harm the community to whose development and welfare he was fully committed. Interestingly, this rhetoric was the same as that used by Democrat leaders such as Chuan Leekpai, who always claimed that they had never done ill to the people or ruled for their own benefit (*mai khoei thamlai prachachon*). Khreng remarked in an interview with *Matichon* journalists in 1993 that it was natural that some of his envious local detractors would attribute his long rule to "influence."[14]

Khreng's local pride was matched by an acute and defensive territoriality. He was assiduous in protecting his reputation against suggestions of corruption or maladministration, and through such means affirmed that his own honor and that of the city's bureaucracy and its residents were inseparably intertwined. His hypersensitivity on such matters is illustrated by the case of a research project produced by a local academic. In 1985, a sociologist of Hat Yai's Prince of Songkhla University, Suraphong Sothanasathian, compiled a research report on the administration of the municipality, based on focus groups, interviews with municipal and central government officials, and townspeople. Attached to his report was a transcript of an interview conducted with a Thai Customs Department official, who claimed that smuggled electronic goods (from Malaysia) valued at 10 million baht were being sold in the markets of Hat Yai. After submitting his report to the university, Suraphong was surprised to be contacted by Khreng's lawyer, who threatened him with a defamation action in the courts unless he withdrew the interview transcript from his report and publicly apologized in the national press. Suraphong acceded to this demand, even though Khreng was not directly named in his interview transcript.[15]

Despite Khreng's officially supported civic image as the wise public-spirited ruler, he attracted criticism for his exercise of favoritism and his preference for personal and direct rule over established procedure. One former deputy-*palat* (deputy-chief clerk) of the municipality remarked that very little could be done in the administration without the personal approval of the mayor, "Whether it was the matter of a toothpick or a pickup truck, all matters had to be approved by Nai Khreng."[16] This meant that senior-ranking career officials of the municipality were often bypassed and, not surprisingly, this was disconcerting for senior *kharatchakan* schooled in highly bureaucratized processes. Architects and businesspeople with matters to discuss went direct to Khreng without passing intermediary officials. In looking at this from Khreng's point of view, we should note that he has long resented the Thai state's centralized and cumbersome bureaucratic control over local government.[17] In this context, Khreng's cultivation of direct personal relationships among senior officials (at levels of provincial governors and politicians controlling the Ministry of the Interior), while conforming to quintessential "Thai-style" personalism, was very practical because it facilitated smooth and timely management in the rigid, centralized, and vertically organized administrative culture that surrounded him. Interestingly, though Suraphong's Hat Yai study of the mid-1980s criticized Khreng's machine politics, it also pointed out that the municipality was overly controlled by bureaucrats and cumbersome procedures, with little scope for meaningful local government initiatives or popular participation, a point made in other municipal studies.[18] The strong hold of the Ministry of the Interior over all aspects of local and provincial government only began to be loosened following decentralization initiatives in the 1990s, culminating in formal constitutional mandates for reform in 1997. Yet decentralization of financial control has been slow, and the provincial governors and municipal chief clerks maintain considerable influence in budget formulation and approval. Ironically, nearly a year after winning the election against Khreng's son, Mayor Phrai Phattano was to complain that the elephantine pace of the bureaucracy was the major cause of his failure to implement his own promised election policies.[19]

Over his long period in office, Khreng's personalism was also essential to the bolstering of his ongoing political legitimacy among key groups in the city. The process of building moral legitimacy was expressed by local commentators in the city as "accumulating *barami*" (*sasom barami*), that is, performing continuous good deeds that reflect moral goodness and power, and that incur debts of obligation upon the recipients of the good deeds.[20] Personalism and the networks that flowed from this leadership style also had a political downside for Khreng. Notably, some leading figures opposing Khreng's continuing rule during the 1990s were former councilors who were unhappy with what they viewed as his control of the council through an exclusive phuak of loyal supporters, to the exclusion of more competent, educated, and qualified citizens. Suchat Intradit, a respected school headmaster who had served as council chairman, summarized the mayor's style as essentially, "*rabop phakphuak, khrueayat*" (using a system of cronies and family members). Chan Lilaphon, another casualty of Khreng's style, recalled that when he was councilor his expertise in economics and business were never called upon by Khreng because, "he viewed me as being of another phuak," that is, outside his inner circle of confidantes.[21]

In the south's largest city with an extensive professional and educated middle class, Khreng maintained effective control and legitimacy by means of a traditional leadership style. It was based on accumulated merit through good works (*barami*) from which he expected recognition and return of his *bunkhun* (kindly deeds), respect for his family name (*trakun*), and acknowledgment of his patronage (*uppatham*). His achievements (*phon ngan*) were visible and tangible. In electoral terms, his votes were assured by the predominantly ethnic Thai working class who repeatedly returned him and his *Thim Kao* to power, while most middle-class voters did not bother turning out for the municipal polls. During the 1980s, voter turnout never exceeded 33 percent of the qualified electorate. Gerrymandering of voting districts seems to have enhanced this electoral grip—it was suggested that the division of the municipality into three constituencies in 1985 had increased *Thim Kao*'s ability to control voting through well-cultivated vote-canvassing networks. The constituency-based results for 1985 showed that voting support was highest for *Thim Kao* in Khreng's home constituency (70 percent), but somewhat lower in the other two.[22] Fifteen years later in the election of 2000, voter turnout had increased, but it still did not exceed 45 percent. In that year, *Thim Kao* won all twenty-four councilor seats in a comprehensive win over its main challenger *Thim Kiattiphum*, led by the Sino-Thai businessman Prayun Wongprichakon. Local journalists judged that this victory had been assured by a combination of "firmly established votes" (*khanaen chattang*), together with the important symbolic role of widely shared reverence (*sattha*) for Khreng.[23]

Khreng cultivated his key political assets (established votes and respectful reverence for his person) by exercising patronage in various forms. As in Bangkok, since the 1970s, neighborhoods in Hat Yai had been organized into "communities" (*chumchon*) that functioned as means to deliver urban services. It was through the chairmen and chairwomen of these *chumchon* (thirty in number) and associated community-based groups (especially housewives' groups, *klum maeban*) that Khreng cultivated loyalties by dispensing various favors. This is a common method in urban machine politics elsewhere in Thailand. A particularly popular treat for neighborhood women is excursions to other provinces. Among many of the lower-level employees of the municipality—seven hundred employees were maintained on a monthly basis with no permanency—Khreng was revered as a kind and benevolent employer. Many of them owed their employment to the personal recommendations of Khreng's dense network of family members and friends, and they thus felt a deep sense of obligation to express gratitude during elections. And, among the permanent municipal staff, Khreng had built strong personal loyalties (some sources suggest up to a third of the total staff), which would then be activated in various forms of direct and indirect canvassing assistance during elections.[24]

Notwithstanding the public benevolence and self-sacrifice that marked Khreng's public persona, a less attractive underside to his rule was exposed when he and his team were challenged. Aside from utilizing carefully nurtured loyalties based on kin and patronage, Khreng's team was said to employ a variety of extra-legal tactics during elections. During the 2000 election, Khreng's team was accused of vote buying among the city's poor by Prayun Wongprichakon. It was widely rumored that his *Thim Kao* padded electoral rolls by arranging for transfers of names of recent immigrants or non-permanent residents onto house certificates prior to elections to ensure voting support. One source suggested that as many as 10,000 names were added to the rolls in this way prior to the 2000 election.[25] Others report that threats were used in order to discourage individuals to stand as candidates against *Thim Kao*. For example, Sombun Phonloetnaphakon, a prominent Hat Yai hotelier, related his experience in 1995 when he was considering running as a candidate in Prayun's *Thim Kiattiphum*. Khreng sent an intermediary to ask Sombun why he hadn't joined *Thim Kao* to participate in developing the city, instead of competing against him. This friendly appeal was followed with a menacing telephone call to Sombun's father, warning that if Sombun campaigned against Khreng, he would, "no longer be considered his friend." Perceiving the menacing threat of retribution in this phrase, Sombun's father persuaded his son not to join Prayun's campaign against *Thim Kao*.[26]

Reinforcing Khreng's patrimonial benevolence was the formidable reputation of his larger family network of allied *trakun*, incorporating the Suwannawongs, the core Thawirat group, and its allied lines. Collectively known as the "*Sakun Sam Thuat*" (the clan of the three great-grandparents), this extensive network traced its origins to the period when Hat Yai had first been established as an *amphoe* in 1917. Following a pattern common in the south, these early family founders had been prominent local leaders appointed by the central Thai state as *phuyaiban* and *kamnan* on the basis of local repute and the size of their *phakphuak*.[27] From this early period, the descendents of the Thawirats inherited positions of local prestige, proving to be able village leaders and generous patrons of schools and temples in the sub-districts of Amphoe Hat Yai. Khreng inherited the mantle of his famous uncle, Kamnan Won, and became the most prominent of a network whose public service, prestige, and identity were intimately tied to the development of the city and its districts' progress. The aspirations of the members of the *Sakun Sam Thuat* to public office reflects a quintessential Thai orientation that associates status mobility with public service and corresponding rank. This was displayed conspicuously in the memorial volume that accompanied the clan's reunion celebration early in 2003.[28]

Prasong Suwannawong (the current Hat Yai mayor and former chief clerk of Songkhla's Mueang District and Hat Yai District) and his cousins Thawisak Thawirat (former province councilor and TRT parliamentary candidate) and Wirachai Suwannawong (lawyer, and former TRT candidate) featured prominently in the memorial publication as the younger generation of the clan that bore the important status markers of government service and university education. Other members of the family were prominent in various positions as councilors of Hat Yai Municipality (e.g., Khreng's brother Khran), or permanent officials of the municipality, as teachers, as *phuyaiban*, and *kamnan* as well as members and chairs of the *tambon* municipalities surrounding Hat Yai. At the city's neighborhood level, the clan's members and their extensive phuak were highly visible. Not all were non-Democrats like the Thawirats and Suwannawongs, but many served as a ready-made network of vote canvassers for Khreng and his *Thim Kao*, and for other family members with political aspirations in Hat Yai's surrounds.

When Prasong became mayor in March 2002, there was general confidence among his supporters that his father's reputation and accumulated achievements would serve as an effective foundation assuring a continuing electoral ascendancy. However, the young mayor faced a changing political environment. Although Khreng's *Thim Kao* had won the January 2000 elections convincingly, there were clear signs that opposition to the group's continued hold on power was growing. In that year, Prayun's *Thim Kiattiphum* had run for all of the seats, with three other teams also competing. Another team leader, "Charlie" Nophawong Na Ayutthaya, campaigned on a platform of upgrading education in municipal schools and addressing Hat Yai's problems. Charlie critiqued Khreng's rule by raising the issue of vested interests (*phonprayot*). Personal assistant to the well-known Songkhla Democrat MP and Deputy Prime Minister Trairong Suwankhiri, Charlie enlisted the senior politician's endorsement in his campaign, although Trairong was careful to emphasize that he was doing this on a personal basis only. In 2000, voter turnout increased by some 15 percent. A "Hat Yai Assembly" promoted by local university academics had conducted workshops encouraging greater voter participation in the cause of democratization. There was a greater emphasis on the importance of a parliamentary-style opposition in council affairs, and even Khreng began wielding the term "*prongsai*" to counter insinuations of dark dealings in the council. Khreng's team won all twenty-four council seats in 2000, but his *Thim Kao* needed to campaign energetically. This was the first municipal contest where campaign rallies and speeches became prominent.[29] Khreng's team countered the demands for an opposition group in council by stressing that *Thim Kao* was so honorable, inclusive, and representative of the community that no opposition faction or scrutiny would ever be necessary. As in the past, Khreng relied on his accumulated *phon ngan* and practical policies for the well-being of the people. These were highlighted in his team's folksy and self-congratulatory motto, "The water flows, the lights are bright, and the roads are convenient."[30] It was a motto clearly based on the famous lines from the thirteenth-century inscription of King Ramkhamhaeng, taught to all Thai schoolchildren, "In the time of King Ramkhamhaeng, this land of Sukhothai is thriving. There are fish in the water and there is rice in the fields." Here was a classic portrait of patrimonial rule, defining popular happiness and its origins in benevolent Thai-style rulership. And, of course, there was a clear message of pragmatic legitimacy here—if it isn't broken, don't fix it.

A more serious challenge to the public image of Khreng's administration—and a harbinger of political opposition to come—was the impact of the destructive flood that struck the city in November 2000, causing some thirty deaths and economic losses exceeding US $220 million. Although Khreng's administration had undertaken preventive action in earlier years, this catastrophic flood took the administration by surprise, severely disrupting trade, tourism, and everyday life. Rumors of Khreng's absence on the day of the flooding were combined with more thoroughgoing criticism of his administration's piecemeal and unsystematic approach to urban development. There was direct political fallout for Khreng's team several months after the flood, when Tharadon Phromsut defeated Khreng's own cousin Wanchai Thawirat in a council by-election by campaigning on a platform of greater scrutiny of council affairs. Tharadon was the owner of a small transport company and the son of a former local *nakleng* with a long-standing grudge against the Suwannawong-Thawirat clan going back to the time of Kamnan Won. He became a one-man opposition to *Thim Kao*, leaking information to the press about council members' minimal discussion of Hat Yai's multi-billion baht budgets and commenting on community radio about the need for an effective opposition. His efforts attracted anonymous death threats by telephone, though Khreng made no public response to Tharadon's criticisms.[31] In the months just prior to Prasong's appointment to replace his father, *Thim Kao*'s political opponents became more vocal in their criticisms. In Prasong's first year of administration, extensive public works were implemented in coordination with central government agencies to alleviate flooding, but in December 2003 further severe inundation indicated that this was not enough.[32] The traumatic memory of the 2000 flood was to be used to powerful effect by Phrai Phatthano in his campaign to unseat the Suwannawong dynasty.

PHRAI PHATTHANO'S COALITION: BUILDING A *KRASAE* OF "CHANGE"

Phrai Phatthano had first signaled an interest in running for mayor in Hat Yai soon after the rumors of Khreng's retirement began to circulate through the city in December 2001. The appointment of Khreng's son as mayor in early 2002 and the discontent that this generated provided a major stimulus for his involvement. But it is doubtful that Phrai would have run had not legislation been pending to introduce a new system of direct mayoral elections. Throughout Thailand, allied legislation for direct elections of executives to PAOs had stimulated a trend for national politicians to become interested in running for provincial office, and there were suspicions that Democrat politicians were "jumping ship" because the national party had no prospects of gaining government. Phrai denied this as a motivation, claiming that he was running because of his commitment to solving Hat Yai's problems, emphasizing that he would never desert the Democrat Party.[33]

From early 2003, Phrai began forming a team of candidates and opened a website to gain feedback from city residents. In May 2003 (after participating in the parliamentary no-confidence debates against

TRT ministers), he announced to the party his intention to leave his parliamentary position to run in the upcoming Hat Yai mayoral election. He first consulted the party's new leader Banyat Banthatthan about resigning as MP. The decision as to when he was to vacate his Constituency 3 seat was in the hands of the party, and there was a clear need to coordinate Phrai's campaign with the party's preparation for the necessary by-election. Phrai's resignation was not to take place until the end of 2003, neatly placing the by-election just before the Hat Yai contest. Already, prominent individuals in the Democrat national leadership had indicated a readiness to endorse Phrai in his mayoral campaign, but without officially declaring it as a party-sponsored contest. In mid-2003, Phrai indicated that his campaign would be grounded on the familiar lines of Democrat moral politics, declaring that Hat Yai had been in the grip of the Suwannawong family for too long, and this hold on power (*phukkhat amnat*) was a version of "dictatorship" (*phadetkan*)—the traditional moral bogey of the Democrats.[34]

In a ceremony on August 3, Phrai openly declared to the Hat Yai public his commitment to run against Prasong as head of the team, "Transparent Hat Yai."[35] On the same day, the chairman of the Democrat branch of Constituency 2 (covering the Hat Yai municipal area) convened a meeting with branch members, who unanimously agreed to assist Phrai in his campaign. The branch members did not seek permission from the sitting Democrat MP Lapsak Laparotakit. They simply took it for granted that they would assist Phrai because he was "*Prachathipat*." Many members had close links with Phrai and his father, having helped campaign with them in the same multi-member constituency prior to the electoral boundary rearrangements of 2000, which had split Hat Yai from its surrounding districts to form a single member constituency.[36] Later the next month, at a rally following the popular Democrat-sponsored "Prachathipat Cup" sports festival held in Songkhla City, Phrai affirmed to the party faithful that in resigning his seat he was not deserting the party, explaining that he had to step down because of his concern for Hat Yai, the place of his birth ("*pen huang bankoet*").[37] His emotionally delivered phrase echoed Chuan Leekpai's habitual mantra to his southern audiences, "I'm worried about the country" (*pen huang banmueang*). Phrai's decision was then enthusiastically endorsed by senior Democrat politicians who took the platform, and in their speeches depicted Phrai's cause as consistent with the Democrat Party's noble tradition of fighting authoritarianism and the current national challenge of fighting Thaksin's "parliamentary dictatorship."

Phrai's entrance into the mayoral contest changed the alignments of the groups opposing Suwannawong rule in Hat Yai. He, in fact, had been encouraged to run by a number of former members of Prayun's *Kiattiphum* team, who were acutely aware that Phrai was the only possible local leadership figure with enough political clout to undertake the formidable task of dislodging the entrenched *Thim Kao*. Phrai highlighted this point to me in saying, "These people can't fight against this [Khreng's] influence. I have to help them to compete against a giant. If I don't come forward, that group will control this city for *another* thirty years." In reinforcing his importance to the contest, Phrai stressed that there was a great deal of fear that Khreng's group would intimidate an opposition team in various ways, but because he was related by blood to the Suwannawongs, he need not fear for his life if he led them.[38] Prayun, who was widely viewed as an eccentric, had come forward to run in the elections once again, despite publicly vowing to retire from local politics after his previous defeat in 2000. Prayun was prepared to ally himself with Phrai, but this became untenable when Phrai decided to run with a newly formed team with a distinctive name. With his dignity dented, Prayun determined to run his own team, but his former leading lieutenants did not follow him. Instead, they joined with Phrai. In fact, Prayun was something of a joke in Hat Yai. For example, pest eradication policy was always prominent in his political platforms, and he seemed oblivious to the fact that everyone knew he was the owner of the largest pest extermination company in the city! He was an irascible personality, and had repeatedly run in elections against Khreng despite his slim chances of success. [39] In American parlance, Prayun was the classic "kamikaze candidate." Phrai Phatthano, by contrast, was anything but a loser.

Phrai brought to the contest his experience as a national politician and a twice-elected MP with skills in oratory and campaign planning, and he commanded attention and respect because of his considerable family prestige, a factor that his father Sawai counted as a critical ingredient in attracting votes.[40] He also deployed cultural capital and strategic skills in the form of a Thammasat University law degree and an MBA from an American university, together with a background as a lecturer in marketing at Hat Yai's principal university (before his entry into politics), as well as experience in operating his own on-line communications business in the city. Phrai's core supporters recognized that in a candidate-to-candidate comparison, Phrai considerably outweighed Prasong. Not only was he locally born and the scion of a prominent political *trakun* with the local status to match Prasong, but his overseas travel, education, and English-language familiarity gave him the symbolic stamp of modernity and internationality (*radap inter*) that overshadowed Prasong's background as a district-level government official with Thai university degrees. Localism and globality needed to be finely balanced in marketing the mayoral candidate before the diverse urban electorate, and Phrai knew that he had to draw the educated middle class out to rallies and polling booths as much as the wage earners and small vendors.

Although much of his public prestige stemmed from his identity as a Democrat politician, Phrai came forward as leader of a broadly based coalition that was committed to ending the Suwannawong regime. Leading figures in his *Hat Yai Prongsai* team (comprising twenty-four councilor and three deputy mayor candidates) did contain Democrat Party members, but Phrai also attracted public figures known for their support for TRT. Among these was the prominent Sino-Thai businessman Chan Lilaphon, a leading member of the Songkhla Chamber of Commerce, and a former Hat Yai municipal councilor. Chan had made it clear to Phrai that he did not want him to use the name of the Democrat Party in the *Thim Hat Yai Prongsai* campaign: "I don't want the national level to come and play politics here," he emphasized to me. Chan saw his role as helping motivate the Sino-Thai traders of the city, who were scared of Khreng's influence, to come out and exercise their voting rights in favor of change.[41] Others were not directly connected to parties, such as two of Phrai's *thesamontri* candidates, the Sino-Thai hotelier Sombun Phonloetnaphakon (non-aligned) and the construction engineer Bunchuai Changsiriwatthanathamrong (also

Sino-Thai), a brother-in-law of Democrat MP Lapsak Laparotakit, who voted Democrat but was not a member. Democrat Party members in Phrai's team included Samrit Bunarat, owner of the *Samila Times* newspaper and a *thesamontri* candidate; Adunsak Mukhem (Muslim), a long-time active Democrat member, community radio broadcaster, and civil society activist; and Phuwit Saichannaphan, a lawyer active in a number of local associations, staunch Democrat member, and parliamentary secretary to Phrai. Among Phrai's team were three former Hat Yai councilors and four former contestants.

Phrai's team of twenty-four councilor candidates spanned a range of occupational groups comprising small business proprietors, teachers, lawyers, and other professionals, representing a cross-section of key groups in the community. Members of Phrai's team were well placed to garner support from a variety of sources, including Democrat Party loyalists as well as members of the important Sino-Thai business community and the professional groups of the city. The presence of the Democrat-aligned newspaper owner Samrit Bunarat was also strategically advantageous, as later events would show. While Phrai's team was broadly non-sectarian in political appearance, the Democrat stalwarts on the team with political experience admitted that the only way to overcome decisively the voting base of the Suwannawongs and *Thim Kao* was to stimulate the stronger countervailing force of popular Democrat loyalties among Hat Yai's people.[42] This was obvious to Phrai, who knew well that his future electoral success, and that of his team, had ultimately to be based on his Democrat affiliation.[43]

Although a number of other opposition teams were being formed in Hat Yai, Phrai's group was recognized as the main contender against Prasong in the approaching election. With professional experience in marketing, Phrai was well placed to help frame policy and build a political image for the team. After consulting widely in the community through Phrai's website, the team devised the name "*Hat Yai Prongsai*" (Transparent Hat Yai), featuring a green logo with a map of the city to highlight the team's concern for the environment. Its key slogan was "Reform Hat Yai." Phrai's challenge was to build a current (*krasae*) for regime change strong enough to undermine the link between the Suwannawong family and the identity of the city. The team's twin emphasis on the environment and transparency was calculated to frame the election narrative in terms of policy and governance, one that could be polemically presented in clear binary opposites. On the theme of environment, much would be made of the impact of the 2000 flood, and what this exposed about the *Thim Kao*'s apparent lack of forward planning, incompetence, and disregard for the populace. On the matter of governance, the evocation of transparency in the usage of the term *prongsai*—a standard trope of good governance discourse in Thailand since the early 1990s—could be contrasted with images of dark and shadowy influence (*itthiphon muet*).

Phrai's campaign approach was not a new formula. His team's approach to the contest borrowed from a previous election for Ban Phlu Municipality, one in which Phrai and his Democrat canvassers had played a leading role. Ban Phlu is a municipality directly to the south of Hat Yai, located in Constituency 3. Here, the long incumbent team of Seri Nuanpheng faced a new challenge by a team led by a medical doctor and former hospital administrator, Dr. Worawat Siwaisarakun. Like Phrai, this contender was the son of a locally esteemed Democrat-aligned politician (a friend and supporter of Phrai's father) and former chairman of the Ban Phlu municipal council. As Phrai was to do in Hat Yai, Dr. Worawat Siwaisarakun drew on his father's local *barami* together with Democrat Party canvassing resources from members of the Constituency 3 Democrat branch. He built a *krasae* by attacking his opponent's mismanagement and allegedly suspect dealings. With management credentials derived from a former position as a hospital administrator in Phuket, and drawing on the social status of his medical background, "Mo" Worawat advanced a platform of "transparency" against his opponents and succeeded in winning the election with his team. Seri failed to gain enough support, despite his emphasis on accumulated *phon ngan* and his status as the president of Thailand's Municipal Association. Seri attributed his defeat as the result of unfair interference by the area's Democrat phuak and to the Democrat art of scandal mongering.[44]

BATTLING FOR LEGITIMACY: RALLIES, PRESS SPECULATION, AND SCANDAL

The eligibility claims that both the contenders projected in their campaigns were grounded in the traditional cultural criteria of family and person-based *barami*, which were essential to cementing locality-based legitimacy. Just as important in their rhetorical performances were policy issues and claims to eligibility that utilized the global clichés of "good government" and participatory management, which had become incorporated into Thai political language over the past decade, i.e., "transparency" (*prongsai*), "good government" (*thamaphiban*), "participation" (*suanruam*), "policy" (*nayobai*), and "vision" (*wisaithat*). These are obligatory tropes of modernity, which, as elsewhere in Thailand, have become integral to the rhetoric of public political competition. So too in the Hat Yai contest, these representations were subsumed into the contestants' proclamations about governance and leadership capacity. Above all, the contest was dominated by contrasting moral narratives about power and trust.

Although Hat Yai's election was due in February 2004, after the expiry of the council's four-year term in January, the campaigning of the two main contesting teams began in mid-September 2003, continuing through to December with door-knocks and several large rallies. The intensity increased considerably in January, when the Provincial Election Commission announced the official election date of February 29 and issued candidates' numbers. During 2003, when Phrai was staging rallies and canvassing in the four city constituencies, Mayor Prasong and his *Thim Kao* were operating on a lower key, relying on community gatherings and meetings that formed part of his established mayoral routine. At this stage, Prasong did not need to rush like his opponent, because he was widely visible as the mayoral incumbent.

Prasong's claims to leadership legitimacy flowed from his mutually reinforcing identities as chief city executive, government official (*kharatchakan*), child of a much loved and respected (and feared) city elder, and inheritor of a prestigious *trakun*. This was symbolized in his popular title, "Palat Oi," which, in typical Thai fashion, served to confer status through former official rank (*palat*), while simultaneously conveying intimacy through his nickname "Oi." From the time he entered office as mayor, large billboards had been erected showing Prasong proudly smiling above scenes of civic life, religious ceremonies, and public works. He instituted a monthly "meet the people" tour as part of his mayoral routines, and from September these were used for canvassing purposes. His status had also been strengthened by receiving a Ministry of the Interior award for "good governance" (*Rangwan Thamaphiban*) in 2002, an award that featured prominently in campaign brochures as a symbol of his administration's modernity and efficiency. Local journalists suspected that this award had been engineered by Khreng through his connections with the Interior Ministry in order to add weight to his son's leadership claims.[45] In election leaflets distributed throughout the city's neighborhoods, Prasong's claims to eligibility evoked the concrete achievements of *Thim Kao* with modern themes of efficiency and community participation. Hat Yai's growth and development were a result of the joint efforts of elected representatives and the people who had continuously elected *Thim Kao*. Together, they would continue to advance the position of Hat Yai as the urban center of the southern region. But overlaying the imagery of urban progress and administration were moral and emotional themes of local intimacy and self-sacrifice, a clear hearkening to the Suwannawong's dynastic legitimacy. These were reinforced in the key slogan of *Thim Kao*, "All our lives fully committed to Hat Yai" (*Thang chiwit thumthae phuea Hat Yai*). While *Thim Kao* enjoyed considerable electoral advantages, it was evidently clear to them that this election would be different from all earlier contests, and in an effort to match the anticipated strength of Phrai's campaign, Prasong committed 3 million baht to hiring a publicity consultant for forthcoming rallies and publicity.[46]

Projecting loyalty to the city and its communities was also the bedrock of Phrai's campaign. Phrai and his team proclaimed themselves as reformers, committed to change and the true progress of the city. They claimed that Hat Yai was managed by an unprofessional and self-interested group that had done little to systematically advance Hat Yai in terms of infrastructure and services, especially education. *Thim Hat Yai Prongsai* aimed to elevate the city to its rightful place as an advanced urban center. A key icon of this advancement was a plan to construct a monorail for tourism and public transport. At the forefront of the team's policies was a cluster of measures that strongly reflected the Thai Rak Thai Party's populist, direct marketing approach to election campaigning, although team members vehemently denied this when I suggested it. These included a scheme to grant all of the thirty-three communities of the city a fund of 1 million baht for development purposes, the abolition of rubbish collection fees, and the abolition of the fees for wastewater treatment, which they argued had been inequitably levied by the previous administration. Linked to this swathe of attractive policies was the projection of Phrai Phatthano as both a modern cosmopolitan leader and a locally born man committed to sacrificing his career in national politics for the good of the city.

Like Prasong, Phrai followed Thai conventions in fusing his identity with his rank in the social hierarchy. In door-knocks for the mayoral campaign, Phrai introduced himself to local people as "*so so*" (*samachik sapha phuthaen ratsadon*, member of parliament); and in rallies he was introduced in the same way. His *trakun* identity was also a critical part of the projection of his leadership legitimacy. Phrai's *trakun* identity and his inherited family *barami* were explicitly displayed at several key early rallies in September by the presence of Sawai Phatthano, who Phrai presented to audiences in his wheelchair. But an equally important dimension of *Thim Prongsai*'s campaign was the attack on Khreng's long hold on power. This was where the campaign rhetoric coincided with long-established Democrat Party discourses against authoritarianism and corruption. Most of the attacks avoided any detailed reference to Prasong's performance as mayor over the past two years or his administrative qualifications. He was presented as simply a pliant puppet of dark influence and his father's grip on power (*phukkhat amnat*). On the few occasions when Prasong *was* depicted in rallies, he was dismissed by speakers—as he was in much street gossip—as a daddy's boy who still referred all key decisions to his father. The major rhetorical objective was to uncouple the Suwannawong family identity from the identity of Hat Yai itself, and this could only be achieved by undermining the established moral and administrative claims of *Thim Kao* and their evocations of Khreng's benevolent legacy. These themes were dramatically highlighted at Phrai's rallies in late 2003.

The large rally held by Phrai's *Thim Hat Yai Prongsai* on October 24 exemplified the articulation of the twin themes of legitimate leadership, administrative efficiency, and their opposites. Before the speeches commenced, a large video screen showed the gruesome scene of floating corpses during the severe Hat Yai flooding of November 2000. Speakers began by using the flood as a leitmotif to critique Khreng, who they accused of having no foresight and no real wisdom (*mai mi panya*). Individual candidates presented themselves and gave the reasons for their candidature, most emphasizing that they were tired of the tight hold on power exercised by Khreng's exclusive group of *Thim Kao* cronies. Khreng's passing of the mayoralty to Prasong was an arrogant exercise in perpetuating authoritarianism (*suepthot phadetkan*), and this system did not allow talented people to join the city's administration. As a result, development in the city was shortsighted, uncoordinated, and many projects were useless and wasteful. A major example of this was the construction of an agricultural market that had never been used, and in fact this market had been built over a natural drainage channel and had caused the flooding of that area in 2000. Compounding this, further speakers claimed, was the favoritism exercised in the awarding of road building contracts, which regularly went to only two or three contractors who were "*phakphuak diaokan*" with Khreng's group. After these speeches, Phrai mounted the stage to enthusiastic applause, following the triumphant announcement that "Phrai Phatthano has woken up the people of Hat Yai."

Criticisms of Khreng's strong hold on Hat Yai and his passing of mayoral power to his son that featured in Phrai's rallies found an echo in street talk, as well as e-mail chat rooms in the city. In November, I witnessed an exchange between neighboring Sino-Thai shopkeepers in the central trading area on Niphat Uthit 2 Road. The owner of a traditional Chinese medicine shop confided to the woman next to him, "They have perpetuated their power but they haven't done anything for the people at all." His neighbor concurred. "This group has held on to power for too long," adding that *Thim Kao* had never really had any system for improving Hat Yai, they simply developed individual projects and then pulled them down to begin again. But what she was most angry about was their assumption that they had the right to govern the city through bestowing the mayoralty on Khreng's son, which was an insult to locals. "We are not dogs, we are people," she exclaimed. Others were pleased that at least there was now some competition for the mayoralty, viewing this as a sign that the city's local politics were maturing.[47]

Although the campaigns enlivened discussion about local politics in Hat Yai, in late 2003 the prospects for Phrai's team were still uncertain. Some people were skeptical and somewhat nervous about Phrai's grandiose policy proposals, such as the overhead monorail, and felt it safer to rely on the familiar governing group. Listening to discussions among some of my die-hard Democrat voting friends at a teashop in Hat Yai Nai (inner Hat Yai), I found it interesting that while unanimous in supporting the Democrats in the upcoming by-election for Constituency 3, some were reluctant to vote for Phrai against *Thim Kao* in the municipality contest. "Why change?," asked Sanit, "If we change, what will happen?" Sanit's friend Chuea clarified his own decision to vote for Phrai by emphasizing, "If Khreng was standing I'd vote for him for sure, but I don't think his son is up to much." Local journalists reported that loyalty to *Thim Kao* was still strong among the chairmen and women of Hat Yai's communities. Prasong's team held an advantage in parading the accumulated achievements of their administration and maintaining networks of canvassers in the neighborhoods. Nonetheless, Phrai's rallies had succeeded in generating interest among the city's middle class, and this, the press reported, was a new thing.[48]

In mid-December, reports of land purchasing irregularities involving the municipality threatened to undermine Prasong's image as inheritor of a responsible and self-sacrificing city administration. News broke in Hat Yai that the Office of the Auditor General had determined that the municipality had purchased land for its wastewater pond at inflated prices, amounting to wastage of 360 million baht. Foul play and collusion among municipal councilors and land brokers (*nai na*) were suspected. Khreng Suwannawong found himself in the humiliating position of being besieged by journalists asking questions about past land transactions. His son, Mayor Prasong, held a press conference where he declared his regret that the good name of the municipality had been impugned by the news reports and affirmed that he would not interfere with official investigations. Following his father, Prasong was using moral outrage and the invocation of the city's honor to deflect suspicions of malpractice. In press interviews, Khreng vehemently denied any involvement in expenditure irregularities and claimed that this was part of a "political game" being played against him and his son. In response, Phrai Phatthano expressed bemusement at Khreng's claim, because the reports had come from central state officials, not politicians. Phrai was correct. He had nothing to do with prompting the investigation. It had, in fact, been initiated by Prayun and other concerned businesspeople of the city several years earlier when they complained to the Auditor General's Office that the price of the land was exorbitant.[49] Nevertheless, the timing of this scandal was fortuitous for Phrai, since he could now point to a concrete case of corruption as an example of the abuses he was aiming to stamp out with a new municipal administration

The *Samila Times* continued to report into January on the land sales controversy, and also ran a story about the municipality's disused agricultural market, constructed at a cost of 30 million baht. These reports had the effect of embarrassing municipal officials and confirming Phrai's denunciations of *Thim Kao*'s administration. Soon after this, the *Samila Times*' senior editor reported that the municipality's publicity department had been instructed by a "senior administrator" not to send news releases to the newspaper because it was opposed to *Thim Kao*. He fervently denied that the *Samila Times* was partisan, and in retaliation accused municipal officials of inappropriately acting in collusion with Prasong's *Thim Kao*. He provocatively entitled his column, "Municipal Public Relations is Not the Business of a Family."[50] Local press coverage in Hat Yai from December served to reinforce publicly Phrai's denunciation of the Suwannawong administration. Added to the lurid images of the November 2000 flood being used by Phrai in his rallies, the land buying scandal provided some concrete justification for *Thim Hat Yai Prongsai*'s demands for political change and administrative transparency in the city. Khreng reacted by lodging charges of slander against the Auditor General's Office, claiming publicly that the office had besmirched his family's honorable name. He argued that there was no clear proof of any conspiracy in the land deal and it was highly suspicious that officials should make such charges public during the lead-up to an election. He concluded that these charges were entirely political in their intent.[51]

Despite this apparent furor, a large number of chairmen and women of Hat Yai's communities—key vote canvassers for the old regime—still professed loyalty to Khreng and his son on the basis of *phon ngan* (results) and *barami*. Many, in fact, admitted that they did not even read the local newspapers that featured reports of the land scandal.[52] In the following months, Phrai's strategy to undermine Khreng's traditional voting base relied on maximizing the formerly dormant middle-class vote and undermining the influence of *Thim Kao*'s canvassers by drawing on residents' Democrat Party attachment.

THE DECISIVE STROKE: DEMOCRAT *KRASAE* AND CHUAN'S BLESSINGS

Beginning in January, the most decisive contributor to the intensification of the political excitement in Hat Yai was the approaching by-election contest between the Democrats and TRT in nearby Constituency 3, set for February 22. Candidate registration for Hat Yai's election took place on January 26, just three weeks before the by-election, and the political atmosphere was strongly influenced by excitement and scandals surrounding this national-level contest. The local press anticipated correctly that Phrai and his team would automatically attract votes owing to his Democrat Party identity, given Hat Yai's history of solid support for the party. Moreover, a Democrat win in the by-election would tend to attract even more votes to Phrai.[53] By virtue of close family and personal connections between Prasong and the TRT candidate Thawisak, and Khreng's known connection with the TRT personality Sano Thianthong, *Thim Kao* could be easily identified as a local political vehicle of TRT interests. The by-election heightened an awareness of party-political identities in the Hat Yai contest, and both of the contesting groups fomented rumors as a resource to undermine their opponent. Prasong's supporters spread the word that Phrai had deserted the Democrats by stepping down to run in the municipal election and was therefore undeserving of election, while Phrai's supporters encouraged rumors that Khreng and Prasong were in league with TRT.

The municipal contest took on a bitter character from the day of candidate registration (January 26), when Khreng and Prasong openly refused to return the respectful *wai* greeting to Phrai and his team. This social snub signified that the contest was now an open family feud.[54] Prasong's family and supporters strongly resented Phrai's use of his Democrat Party credentials in campaigning for the election. The use of nationally prominent politicians to assist Phrai's campaign was seen as an unfair invasion of local politics, and Prasong was now faced with an uneven struggle against local voters' Democrat loyalties. Prasong's sister Patthama (a Hat Yai municipal officer) was particularly upset that rumors were spreading claiming that Prasong was a TRT supporter, clearly aiming to benefit Phrai's campaign. And above all, Prasong's family regarded Phrai's denunciations of the Suwannawong's dynastic pretensions as hypocritical, because Phrai himself had succeeded to his father's political position and he was relying on his family name to gain electoral support.[55] These points were all made by speakers in *Thim Kao*'s rallies in January and February. In the final week of the campaigns following the smashing Democrat by-election victory, any association with TRT was clearly an electoral liability. In order to disassociate itself from rumored connections with the TRT Party, *Thim Kao* erected large placards near the speaker's stand with the words, "*Thim Kao* is not under any political party." During February, Prasong's increasing sense of the changing balance of the contest was signified by the production of a newspaper (*Kanmueang Raisapda*, "Politics Weekly") that attempted to discredit Phrai Phatthano in the eyes of local Democrat voters. This was an unregistered newspaper distributed widely to newsstands throughout the city. Two issues were released before the publisher was arrested for distributing an illegal newspaper. The key articles aimed to spread the rumor that Phrai had deserted the Democrat Party by standing down to run in the Hat Yai mayoralty, and, even more damning, that he had done this against the will of the revered former party leader Chuan Leekpai.[56]

Chuan Leekpai played a decisive role in assuring the Democrat by-election victory on February 22, and he played an equally decisive role in assuring Phrai's win over Prasong a week later. The Democrat by-election victory in Constituency 3 was greeted with jubilation in Hat Yai, although not, of course, among *Thim Kao*'s close supporters. The positive effects of the by-election victory on voters' opinions towards Phrai appear to have been confirmed by an opinion poll released after his win. They showed that the percentage of sampled voters in favor of Phrai increased from 43.5 percent in the first week of February to 52.4 percent in the days immediately following the Democrat win of February 22.[57] Many city residents had attended the final Democrat rally staged on the evening of February 20, opposite the "Big C" department store on the northern edge of the municipality boundary. It was here that Chuan Leekpai, in addition to promoting Wirat Kalayasiri as the new Democrat candidate, openly affirmed his support for Phrai Phatthano's mayoral candidature. Chuan exonerated Phrai from any inconvenience he had caused the party by resigning his Constituency 3 seat, and emphasized that Phrai had expressed concern that his decision would necessitate the use of public money in holding the by-election. Nevertheless, Chuan affirmed, Phrai was motivated by the worthy intention of serving the people of Hat Yai and making it a better city. This was a good thing for the people of Hat Yai. In the final week of the Hat Yai contest, Chuan Leekpai's highly popular protégé Abhisit Vejjajiva assisted Phrai's campaign by visiting the shopping districts of the city. He received an overwhelmingly enthusiastic welcome, particularly among women.

Finally, after extensive advertising, Phrai's team staged two large rallies, featuring Chuan, Abhisit, and Banyat as the main speakers, with ten well-known Democrat MPS from Songkhla, Phatthalung, and Satun also attending. While the three key members of the party leadership wore smart casual clothes, the MPS arrived wearing the conspicuous dark blue Democrat Party jackets, a clear symbolic assertion that this was a Democrat occasion. The mix of Hat Yai Prongsai's green apparel with the Democrat blue was echoed in the audience. Phrai's handbill advertisement highlighted the rallies' key themes, including answers to the questions, "Why must there be change?" and "Have I really discarded the party?" The latter question was clearly a response to Prasong's charges in his scandal sheet. The rally held on February 26 attracted an estimated 5,000–7,000 people, who crammed into a vacant plot of land on Prachathipat Road to listen to Chuan Leekpai and his colleagues, together with Phrai and his assembled team. Speaking in his characteristically soft and sincere tones, Chuan began by thanking the people for delivering a decisive victory in the by-election. He told the audience that he had not wanted Phrai to leave national politics because he was a politician of high quality, but he understood Phrai's motivation to help his hometown. After stressing that the direct election of city mayors was a result of Democrat Party commitment to decentralization and democratization of local government, Chuan added, "I have told Phrai already that the party will not leave him; even though he has not campaigned in the name of the Democrats, he is still with the Democrats." Each speech that followed was greeted with enthusiastic applause as Phrai's case was linked to the principled politics of the Democrat Party—its commitment to democratic and transparent politics, to truthfulness, and honesty.

4.2 The blessings of Chuan. Chuan Leekpai (center) receives garlands with Phrai Phatthano (right) from an adoring crowd at Phrai's final rally. (Source: Samila Times*)*

In contrast to *Thim Hat Yai Prongsai*'s rallies, *Thim Kao* rallies in the critical final week were poorly attended, a clear indication of a shift in the political climate. The handbills advertising *Thim Kao*'s rallies were headed with the exhortation, "Don't vote for anyone if you can't see their results"—evoking a key pragmatic criterion of electability in Thai local politics. *Thim Kao*'s rally, held in the car park next to the Diana department store on February 23, highlights the symbols, styles, and metaphors employed by Prasong's team in their effort to withstand Phrai's Democrat-aided onslaught. The team's rally featured the same musical and visual paraphernalia as their opponents, although its key tune that repeated its motto—"All our lives are fully committed to Hat Yai"—was redolent of military marching songs, possibly geared to a conservative audience. A more striking contrast with Phrai's rallies was the use of a professional announcer, a smartly dressed woman in her mid-30s who addressed the audience using crisp Central Thai diction, somehow out of place among the plain-talking southerners in the audience and the candidates seated on the stage. She was part of the publicity package invested in by Prasong. The forthcoming election, she intoned in an obviously prepared commentary, was about choosing "*good* people, people with *knowledge*, people with *experience*, people with *quality* that, as we *Thim Kao* people know, are under the leadership of an administrator with great *virtue*—Nai Prasong Suwannawong!" The core vocabulary of the announcer's introduction stressed the moral themes of the team's determination to remain committed and loyal to the people, to show respect to seniority, and to never commit wrongs or do evil to ancestors. The emphasis on ancestors (*banphaburut*) and elders (*phu awuso*) was evidently intended to evoke and personalize the themes of continuity and respectful inheritance that Prasong's candidacy represented, clearly intended to be read as the moral opposite of Phrai's insulting attacks on Khreng's patrimony of civic service. It was reinforced by the distinctive vocabulary of a quintessential emotionally based localism, emphasized by a pledge of commitment to Hat Yai's continued development (*phatthana mueang Hat Yai to-nueang*) by "the team which has done and will do service continually for all generations, from the time of your parents through to your children and grandchildren." The councilors who mounted the stage following this thematic introduction devoted their time to enumerating the achievements of their administration while simultaneously rebutting Phrai's accusations that they had "abandoned" (*thotthing*) the people (as symbolized by Phrai in his graphic use of the 2000 flood as a key indictment). Stress was placed on the municipality's achievement of the Ministry of Interior's "good governance" (*thamaphiban*) award, which highlighted their commitment to encouraging community involvement in various projects (such as sports) and the municipality's equal engagement with all ethno-religious groups in promoting festivals and culture. Key good governance terms like "participation" (*suanruam*) and "community-strengthening" (*sang khwam khemkhaeng nai chumchon*) punctuated these pronouncements.

Conspicuous in *Thim Kao*'s enumeration of achievements was the absence of Prasong as a distinct leadership figure. He was implicit rather than clearly profiled in the municipality's achievements. There were at least two reasons that help to explain this absence in the campaign narrative. First, the image of *Thim Kao*, cultivated since its emergence under Khreng, was its collective service and indivisibility from the community; but second, and more pragmatically, was that it was difficult to identify any distinctive measure initiated by Prasong in the short time of his mayoralty. The stress placed on the "good governance" award to Hat Yai in 2002 was foregrounded precisely because it had been gained during Prasong's term, and thus he could claim credit for this urban status marker. Before his own election speech, Prasong was introduced to the audience as a person who had "sacrificed himself working for society continuously," a history illustrated principally by his previous government service as *palat amphoe* in three districts and, most recently, in gaining Hat Yai's good governance award (despite the fact that it had been awarded to the municipality as a corporate body). Prasong's address, diction, and body language betrayed his strong reliance on a *kharatchakan* training and persona. He stood erect, reading from a prepared speech, and delivered his words slowly in regular meter. He was clearly inexperienced in the ways of political histrionics, and more comfortable with the idiom of the benevolent administrator. Curiously, Prasong modulated his sentences in the tones of a Buddhist monk delivering a chant. Instead of employing local southern Thai dialect, as

Phrai was doing, Prasong enunciated in Central Thai, explaining to his audience that he was doing this as an answer to his opponent's claim to cosmopolitanism. This was an obscure rationale, which no one seemed to comprehend, and the older people shouted to him to speak in the local dialect, but he doggedly persisted with his priestly Central Thai cadences.

The essence of Prasong's message was the continuity of *Thim Kao*'s loyal service and pride in the community's collective achievements in building a city, a message imbued with a moral theme of loyalty to locality. He made explicit a core element of his father's model of governance by equating the community with a family united in happiness. He then introduced the theme of "change" to draw contrasts with his team's opponents. He contested criticisms of the "Old Team" as outmoded and unchanging, highlighting that its personnel had always been modified through the years. This was positive and productive change. By contrast, the "change" demanded by his critics was motivated by shallow political opportunism, he claimed. Playing on Democrat rhetoric, he accused an opponent (obviously Phrai) of a lack of true "*udomkan*," which was signified concretely by his team's long commitment to the people. *Thim Kao* was always changing its approaches to improving the city. Milking the word "change" further, Prasong proclaimed that the key change really needed was the removal of people who wanted to use "our territory" (*phaendin khong rao*) for their own interests (again a reference to Phrai). This was a clear delineation of insiders and aliens, friends and enemies of the city, which *Thim Kao* and Prasong embodied. For him to step down would be a desertion of the city, "Do you want me to stop and sit down to watch a person who has not shown any results—a person who has no generosity and no virtue?" He then answered this question with a *coup de grâce* that forged family pride with civic service, "I can't do this. If I allowed this it would be like destroying my birthplace where I have inherited the family name of Suwannawong from my father who has been accepted by the people of Hat Yai for forty years, known to people through the country as 'Brother Khreng,' 'Uncle Khreng,' this, a man who is a model in my heart." This exclamation of filial piety drew enthusiastic applause from a small but loyal crowd. Prasong returned to his address, highlighting that the task of nurturing the city, achieved by *Thim Kao* with the trustful endorsement of Hat Yai's people, was under grave threat by opportunists and vested interests.

4.3 Defending community and family honor against the invading Democrats. Prasong Suwannawong receives audience applause at his first rally.

In his first main rally, Prasong raised the specter of a happy family about to be despoiled by unscrupulous outsiders. This was a direct adoption of his father's model of Hat Yai society and its organic political order. Unfortunately, for him and his team, this imagery was not enough to stem the wave of support for Phrai. Moreover, Khreng deliberately avoided being present at his son's rallies, probably because this would attract Phrai's condemnation and undermine his son's electioneering. In the last days of campaigning, Prasong and his team failed to draw crowds of sufficient size because people were flocking to see Phrai and his popular Democrat sponsors. The last *Thim Kao* rally, on February 27, was scheduled to be held in the large car park in front of Robinson's department store, but the venue was shifted at short notice to an open field opposite Khreng's own home in an apparent effort to attract listeners from Khreng's former voting heartland. On this last evening, the rally attracted only about 500 listeners. Phrai's rally on the same evening, by contrast, drew a crowd of some 7,000 people. At this packed event, prominent Democrat politicians spoke in favor of Phrai as a self-sacrificing representative who had come forward not for himself, but for the people (*phuea pratchachon*) to save Hat Yai from authoritarianism. Thanin Chaisamut, Democrat MP for Satun and a well-known and skilled orator, presented a thinly veiled comparison of Thaksin as a dictatorial leader with Khreng Suwannawong. The precincts of the rally were festooned with small posters bearing the slogan, "People with Courage to Change" (*khon kla plian*).

In the polling of February 29, Phrai emerged victorious over Prasong, gaining 35,755 against 20,625 votes. His team of councilor candidates won twenty-three out of the twenty-four seats. The voter turnout was a record high in the history of Hat Yai municipal politics, amounting to 66.36 percent of the qualified voters (63,402 of 95,536).[58] The leaders of *Thim Hat Yai Prongsai* had known from the beginning that the only way to topple the Suwannawong's *Thim Kao* was to boost the number of active voters beyond the previously small percentage, which had guaranteed Khreng's electoral dominance. Phrai's victory clearly stemmed from a mix of interacting causes and conditions. One local academic suggested that these included five main factors: (1) a widespread desire among the population to change the administration; (2) the appeal of his team's policies; (3) widespread approval of Phrai's qualifications as a leadership figure; (4) the monitoring of the election commission, which minimized voting fraud; and (5) the enthusiasm and confidence generated by the Democrat by-election victory. Another Hat Yai academic credited Phrai's victory to the singular importance of Chuan Leekpai.[59] There is little doubt that it was the Democrat by-election victory and the mobilization that accompanied it, together with the charismatic role of Chuan Leekpai that provided the decisive conditions to mobilize Hat Yai's voters to opt for "change" in their city administration. Had the Democrats lost the by-election, Phrai would surely have failed in his bid, although the by-election victory was almost certain from the beginning. With Phrai identified as a Democrat Party personality, and the by-elections generating a demonstration of popular party loyalty and a stand against entrenched authority consistent with Phrai's message, a pattern of group allegiance was mobilized in such strength that *Thim Kao*'s canvassing networks could not counter it with customary evocations of Khreng's local *barami*, or the more dubious methods of intimidation and selective vote buying that some inhabitants observed during the campaign.

Prior to the December–January period, journalists had tended to assume that Khreng and Prasong's popularity among Hat Yai's community chairmen and women guaranteed that ordinary voters would follow these *hua khanaen*'s customary persuasions. This was not the case, for in all these communities there were Democrat Party members of the Constituency 2 branch, who were assisted by friends from further afield. Although Phrai was not their own constituency MP, these members were emboldened to come out in force to act as his canvassers, and they added considerable impetus to his campaign at the neighborhood level. Women in particular played an important role in advocating votes for Phrai at the neighborhood level. With the exception of Chan Lilaphon (who was a TRT supporter), the non-Democrat members of Phrai's team did not appear to object to the use of the Democrat *krasae* as a mechanism to unseat the Suwannawong regime; after all Phrai's moral denunciation of the Suwannawong's dynastic pretensions was consistent with their own view. From the local perspective of municipal politics Phrai's triumph can be interpreted as a product of local power struggles and the specific history of a dynasty and its opponents; but in the final analysis, it was an electoral outcome stemming from the unprecedented entry of party-based identification into local political life.

SYMBOLIC COMMUNITY AND THE LIMITS OF LOCALISM

A few days before Hat Yai's election, Khreng confided to me that if the election issue was based on criteria of tangible achievements (*phon ngan*), then his son and *Thim Kao* would surely win. But, he stressed, the Democrats were making sure that the election was not about the accumulated sacrifices of devoted local leaders, or about tangible results. Rather, Phrai and the Democrats were building a *krasae* to pursue a utilitarian agenda to capture political territory (*yuet phuenthi*). Khreng's concept of local government as a system of mutual helpfulness and concern, built on idealized southern Thai virtues of, "*rak luk, rak phong*" (Love your children, love your group) did not allow him to comprehend the causes of Phrai's challenge beyond selfish interest. Khreng could not fathom the meaning of his son's appointment to Hat Yai's citizenry outside his own idiom of family service and loyalty to locality, and so local resentment at his nepotism was incomprehensible to him. Therefore, according to this ideology, those who opposed his son were simply creating division and disharmony and not joining a collective effort. With the advent of Phrai's challenge, a new politics had emerged in Hat Yai. For the first time, Khreng's group had been unable to control the main narrative of an election contest. Of course, beyond Khreng's ideology of the happy family were concrete mechanisms of power maintenance. His political power, which in 2002 had allowed him to install his son so confidently in office, was based on his group's capacity to maintain the political field of Hat Yai as a restricted sphere, where contests were based on a delimited range of personalities and issues, and where a small voting base was sustained by patronage. This was no longer feasible in the new environment brought about by the direct election system, the issues of legitimacy and governance that emerged in the city from 2002–04, and the national political struggles that impinged on the Hat Yai contest.

Phrai Phatthano's decision in 2003 to stand in the Hat Yai contest at the head of an anti-Suwannawong coalition was spurred by a combination of local issues aided by the new political conditions represented by decentralization measures that provided for direct elections of executives and gave greater status and power to them. His stunning victory over Khreng Suwannawong's son Prasong in late February 2004 was the result of a calculated gamble that was ultimately successful. It was successful partly because it was based on the strategic use of his father's *barami* and its transferal to the local political arena. It was successful also because of Phrai's ability to mobilize an urban electorate and increase voter turnout by fusing a Democrat-style rhetorical performance of moral outrage (against authoritarianism and cronyism) with a modernistic discourse of urban administrative renovation. But the decisive electoral edge was achieved by the popular impact of the preceding Democrat Party victory in Constituency 3—an event made necessary by Phrai's own resignation and perfectly timed to maximize his and his party's political resources. Phrai's Democrat identity and, more critically, the blessings of the party's icon Chuan Leekpai, were crucial in providing the impetus necessary for victory over Khreng's son and the well-entrenched *Thim Kao*. In Hat Yai's election, local issues and local political history became enmeshed in a national-level political discourse and the Democrat Party leadership's agenda. While the contest demanded attention to matters of policy, vision, and professional capacity among the mayoral contestants, it was shaped, above all, by a powerful moral narrative against which *Thim Kao* could not compete, because Phrai's local cause was symbolically subsumed into a wider political mission embodied by Chuan Leekpai and his opposition to demonic despotism, as well as the broader communalism marked by Democrat Party allegiance.

CHAPTER 5
The Provincial Election: Policy, Phuak, *and Party Allegiance*

IN THAILAND, the field of local politics (*kanmueang thongthin*) is conventionally defined by its practitioners as distinctive from national-level politics (*kanmueang radap chat*) in terms of a number of key differences, including the prosaic issues around candidates' campaigns for election (garbage collection, water supply, etc.), the diversity of competing groups or "teams," which often comprise people with different allegiances at a national political level, and the primarily person and locality-centered election criteria that are accepted by both the contestants and voters alike. Viewed from province, district, and sub-district levels, *kanmueang thongthin* is a sphere of competition and electioneering that many practitioners claim is distinct from party and national politics. This is, however, a convenient fiction. National press commentators often claimed that the year 2004 marked the dramatic entry of party politics into local affairs. It was, however, a further development of trends that were accelerated by the establishment of *tambon* and province administrative organizations in the mid 1990s, and the increased resources available to these organizations. The advent of these local electoral-based organizations expanded considerably the pool of local political aspirants. There has long been an intimate relationship between "local politics" and national-level politics, because of the complementary needs of local political actors and national-level politicians to secure key political resources. For local politicians (whether provincial or *tambon* councilors), the critical resources sought from these connections are endorsements and financial assistance, and for national politicians, the key resources required from local politicians are their local networks that are critical for vote canvassing support.

The elections for the presidency and council of Songkhla's PAO were held on March 14, simultaneously with provincial contests throughout the country, and they followed hard on the heels of Songkhla's dramatic by-election and Hat Yai's mayoral contest. The account that follows shows how the Democrat-endorsed candidate for the presidency (*nayok*) gained decisive symbolic advantage from Democrat affiliation in his effort to defeat the incumbent president, a result that served both his own interests and that of Songkhla's Democrats. Beyond this conspicuous feature of the 2004 competition, however, the contests reveal the critically important linkages between the fields of local and national politics and the centrality (and fragility) of phuak alliances as a structural element underpinning relationships and support among key actors.

As elsewhere in the country in 2004, the provincial election in Songkhla was unprecedented; this was the first contest when province presidents were to be directly elected by popular vote, with parallel polls held for their associated teams of provincial councilors (*so cho*). The intensity of these elections was also conditioned by the national-level rivalry between the major political parties. These parties were keenly observing and selectively sponsoring the provincial contests to assess and nurture support networks in preparation for the 2005 national polls. As much as an incursion of national political parties into provincial politics from above, however, the process can equally be viewed as revealing the opportunistic appropriation of party labels by local political aspirants. In the provincial election campaigns throughout the country, many contesting teams and aspiring *nayok* tried to harness the political capital of the ruling TRT Party and so gain the electoral edge over rival teams. This led to considerable confusion in some provinces where several rival candidates claimed TRT endorsement.[1] Though in most of the country where the political capital of TRT was seen as an advantage for contestants, in Songkhla and the majority of the south's provinces direct links between contesting teams and TRT proved to be an electoral liability, and those who showed the clearest alignment to the regionally dominant Democrat Party generally held the advantage. In Songkhla, the unprecedented labeling of the *nayok* candidates in terms of national party alignments was also a direct consequence of the elections held there in the previous month.

Songkhla's PAO elections brought into strong relief and increasing tension a variety of allegiances and alliances connecting the local and national fields of Songkhla's multi-layered political system. These tensions were revealed in the rivalry between the prominent Democrat MPs Thawon Senniam (and his brother Winai) and Niphon Bunyamani, with the former supporting the incumbent *nayok* Worawit Khaothong, and the latter supporting his younger brother Nawaphon, with the endorsement of prominent national Democrat figures. At the district level, a number of localized conflicts were played out between rival *so cho* candidates. While distinct from the larger battle played out by the PAO presidency candidates, these local contests were critical to the overall results, and had important implications for later alignments among vote-canvassing networks in the national election of 2005. At the top of the pecking order of local politicians, the *so cho* require continued cultivation by PAO faction leaders and national politicians alike. A consideration of one of these district contests highlights the intersection between local and national political imperatives in Songkhla's political world and its significance for the reproduction of the Democrat ascendancy.

ALLIES AND RIVALS: THE PROVINCIAL PRESIDENCY AND *PHUAK* POLITICS

The key contestants in Songkhla's 2004 PAO presidency election, Nawaphon Bunyamani and Worawit Khaothong, had been uneasy allies since Worawit's assumption to the presidency in 1999. In Songkhla, the political alliances between provincial politicians have been shaped by phuak solidarities—tightly knit, informal groups bonded by common interests, personal affinities, and reciprocal obligations. The links binding some of these phuak have been reinforced by affiliation to key Democrat national politicians or prominent local political figures. Worawit Khaothong's rule as president of the Songkhla PAO from 1999 was based on an alliance of various district and phuak-based groups who agreed to back him as a voting bloc in return for gaining positions in key administrative posts, including deputy president (three positions), chairman, and deputy chair positions. One of Worawit's key support groups in the PAO assembly was a Democrat Party–focused phuak headed by Nawaphon Bunyamani, who enjoyed considerable electoral support in the region surrounding the *mueang* district of Songkhla, largely because this was the electoral heartland of his elder brother, the veteran Democrat MP Niphon Bunyamani. Nawaphon was first elected as a *so cho* in 1994, after having worked for five years as assistant to Niphon, who had begun his career as a *so cho* before becoming MP in 1992. Nawaphon's base of support among *so cho* in the PAO assembly was essentially founded on his elder brother Niphon's Constituency 5 Democrat phuak networks, which included *so cho* from the Singhanakhon, Bang Klam, and Khuaniang Districts. Some of

5.1 Nawaphon Bunyamani (center) sharing a laugh with members of the Democrat phuak. The mayor of Songkhla is on the left.

them were prominent Democrat Party branch officials, and all were Democrat supporters and canvassers. In addition, there were prominent Democrat phuak members who ruled the Songkhla Municipality, including the mayor Uthit Chuchuai and his key lieutenants, friends of Niphon since their schooldays (see plate 5.1).

Worawit, who was first elected as *so cho* for his home district of Rattaphum in 1996, came to prominence in provincial politics when he ousted the reigning PAO president in 1999, shortly after positions of PAO presidents (then elected by councilors) were created under new national government legislation, replacing in prominence the former council chairmen (*prathan*). Significantly, he gained power by deposing the new president, the well-known Democrat-connected personality Sithon Sikka (a Muslim), who was secretary to the prominent Songkhla Democrat MP Trairong Suwankhiri. The Democrat phuak surrounding Nawaphon was a key group that guaranteed Worawit's bid for executive power in the PAO assembly by switching support from Sithon Sikka.[2] Nawaphon gained his position of deputy president as a reward for joining Worawit's coalition and undermining the former president. Though Nawaphon's group was clearly identified as, "the Democrat phuak" in Songkhla's PAO, Worawit was also identified as a Democrat supporter, in particular, because he enjoyed a close personal relationship with the two Democrat MP brothers, Thawon and Winai Senniam. Worawit had also acted a key *hua khanaen* supporting Niphon Bunyanani's earlier election campaigns in Constituency 5, where he had many relatives who formed a reliable voting and canvassing pool for the Democrats. Worawit's voting bloc in the PAO also included *so cho* who were connected to other national political parties.

Prior to the PAO elections of 2000, Nawaphon signaled his ambition to become PAO president. At that time, however, the Democrat Party had indicated that it was not prepared to publicly endorse candidates for PAO elections, and this may explain why Nawaphon did not mount a concerted challenge to Worawit.[3] Nawaphon formed an alliance with Worawit, which was reportedly brokered by his brother Niphon who ensured that his younger brother was again given a position as deputy president as a condition of his phuak's voting support. This comprised the Bunyamanis' immediate Democrat phuak of seven *so cho* as well as six others, who were closely connected to leading Democrat Party figures in the province. The latter group included three *so cho* from Amphoe Hat Yai (the largest *amphoe* of the province, which returned a total of nine *so cho*) and three *so cho* who were members of a phuak focused on Surasak Mani, one of Trairong Suwankhiri's long-serving personal assistants. Keen to enter national politics, Surasak later split from the Democrats when his ambition to run as a candidate was thwarted, and his phuak followed him out of the Democrat Party (for further discussion, see chapter 6). In the PAO, however, Surasak's phuak continued to support Worawit, who was careful to maintain a stance of nominal independence from political parties.

Councilors unanimously elected Worawit as PAO president in January 2000.[4] Through a process of clever and pragmatic bargaining with constituent groups of *so cho*, he was able to regain the presidency and ensure a supportive voting bloc in the assembly. With Nawaphon as a deputy, however, he knew that he had an ambitious enemy lurking at his back. Worawit occupied the presidency at a time when PAOs in Thailand were enjoying the advantage of increased funding and autonomy in expenditure, and throughout his period in office, 1999–2003, he built a strong reputation as a skilled administrator bringing much needed and tangible development benefits to the province. A university graduate with an engineering degree and studying for a postgraduate qualification in public administration, Worawit conformed to the image of the new generation of educated local politicians. His local renown was considerably reinforced by his reputation as a *nakleng* with wide connections and commitment to the needs of the province's *chaoban*. Like province administrators throughout the country, Worawit built up a mutually beneficial relationship with a network of building and construction contractors (*phu rapmao*), who regularly provided him with kickbacks, and, in turn, acted as vote canvassers to ensure his continued favors.[5]

There was, however, a seamier side to Worawit's connections and activities. He was widely known to be a gambler and rumored to consort with individuals involved in the drug trade and with gunmen. This did not particularly bother the ordinary people of the province, but Worawit's reputed criminal connections were publicly highlighted when he was identified by provincial officials early in 2003 as a possible candidate for the government's black list of *phu mi itthiphon* ("influential figures") that was mandated under Prime Minister Thaksin's highly publicized, "War on Crime and Influence" campaign. Worawit denied his branding as a "*phu mi itthiphon*," and pointed out to the scoop-hungry local press that he did not meet the official criteria for this identification. He did not own illegal gambling dens, nor was he a drug-seller or engaged in harboring gunmen. The most conspicuous basis for this suspicion, he argued, was that he had many phuak, but this was nothing unusual for any local politician. In fact, he stressed that, "You have to have many phuak if you are a politician, especially the PAO president. If Nayok Thaksin didn't have many phuak, then he wouldn't be the prime minister." In this, Worawit echoed Khreng Suwannawong's affirmation that if he was indeed a person of "influence," it was only influence for the good of the people, and not for his own benefit.[6] Later in 2003, his name was quietly removed from the province's black list, some say because of his close connections with prominent TRT politicians, such as Deputy Minister of the Interior Pracha Malinon.

In terms of national political orientations, Worawit maintained connections both with the Democrat Party cause and among politicians of other parties. He had a close personal friendship with the Songkhla MPs Thawon and Winai Senniam. His own home was located in Amphoe Rattaphum, which was within Thawon's Constituency 6, and he had canvassed on Thawon's behalf during the 2001 elections. His extensive kin network extended into the neighboring *amphoe* of Khuaniang, which came within Niphon's constituency, and he canvassed for Niphon as well. Worawit also enjoyed close connections with prominent politicians from other parties, including Chongchai Thiangtham of the Chat Thai Party, and Pracha Malinon of TRT. Chongchai, a wealthy businessman and deputy secretary-general of Chat Thai, provided substantial financial assistance to aid Worawit's provincial election campaigns. Both of these men gained important cabinet positions when TRT won office in 2001 and formed a coalition with Chat Thai and other parties. Worawit continued to maintain these connections, which brought him under suspicion from Democrat quarters that he was in league with their political opponents.

PREPARING FOR THE ELECTION

From mid-2003, when it was clear that long-awaited legislation was to be introduced to institute direct elections of province presidents, it was clear in Songkhla that the main contestants for PAO president would be Worawit and his ambitious deputy, Nawaphon. Active preparation among the contenders began in August, and by November the leaders declared their team names, members, and campaign messages. Worawit's chances of success for the 2004 PAO election were particularly strong, if considered on the basis of his administrative performance and personal popularity as a committed representative who combined all the modern and traditional qualities associated with a good leader. He prepared to campaign on the achievements of his past administration and on policies that would emphasize his support for schools, the environment, and the promotion of trade. Under his past administration, the income available to the PAO had increased by 100 million baht. Worawit formed his group under the name of *Thim Rak Songkhla* ("The Team that Loves Songkhla").[7] A more pragmatic advantage stemming from Worawit's successful incumbency was that he could draw on the financial backing and canvassing support of the numerous contractors of the province who had benefited from his patronage and wished it to continue.

In contrast to Worawit, Nawaphon was less widely known throughout the province. His main strength was the strong mentorship provided by his elder brother Niphon, who used his influence to mobilize a Democrat-focused phuak that he had cultivated for over a decade as an MP. From September 2003, it became clear that Nawaphon's campaign for PAO president and that of his team of candidate *so cho* would be based strongly on the electoral appeal of the Democrats. In the following months, Nawaphon attended Niphon's large party branch seminars and other rallies in Constituency 5, where he was introduced to audiences as a candidate for the PAO presidency. Nawaphon's planning meetings for developing his campaign and policies all took place at Niphon's home, which was a regular gathering place of his widespread Democrat phuak, and Niphon also helped provide funding for his campaign.

Nawaphon's reliance on Democrat symbolism was clear from the design of his team's logo, which was released in November accompanied by a set of policy diagrams. The logo was designed as a mauve and pale blue circle with the team's name—*Thim Songkhla Phatthana* (Team to Develop Songkhla)—printed within a white ring. Both the color and shape of the logo closely resembled the official Democrat Party insignia. Just as critical to Nawaphon's electoral strategy as his brother's support was an agreement (made at some point during this period, and brokered by Niphon) for senior national-level Democrat politicians to come forward in rallies and news advertisements with their personal endorsements for Nawaphon and his team. These prominent figures included the party-leader Banyat Bantatthan and other leading Democrat personalities such as Senan Kachonprasat and Surin Pitsawan. By late 2003, it was known that the impending by-election, Hat Yai's election, and the provincial election would cluster together, and this would generate a beneficial Democrat *krasae* to aid Nawaphon.

Nawaphon admitted that his close Democrat phuak (centering largely on Songkhla's Amphoe Mueang) were an important core group in his team as well as others who were known party supporters, but not all of his thirty-six *so cho* candidates were Democrats. He emphasized that an important principle in his selection of candidates to run in the districts was their competence and reputations in their localities. He also emphasized that his success would be based on the appeal of his team's policies. That being said, he acknowledged the role of family and phuak connections in assuring voting results for his own individual team members. He assessed the relative importance of policy as against traditional factors of patronage and family alliances in drawing votes in terms of percentages. Sixty percent of overall votes would be drawn by policy and 40 percent would come from voting based on the factors of, "*khwam pen yat phi nong, khwam pen sangkhom uppatham lae kan phuengpha kan—khue khwam pen sangkhom Thai*" (Family identification and being a society of patronage and mutual reliance, that is, being Thai society).[8] In October, by which time he had almost finalized his team's candidate line-up, Nawaphon was not willing to reveal the extent to which his own presidency campaign was going to be reliant on the Democrat Party *krasae*. He admitted that the forthcoming by-election contest would play "some role" in his team's fortunes. It is possible that, at this stage, he did not anticipate the wave of Democrat support that would be unleashed by the combined effects of the Constituency 3 and Hat Yai Municipality contests, but more likely the qualified admission was typical dissimulation by a wily politician. Nonetheless, in viewing the electoral geography of Songkhla Province, he did confess to me that Hat Yai was a particular type of electorate. Hat Yai was different from the rural areas surrounding it where traditional "*itthiphon*" prevailed in influencing voters. "I believe that Hat Yai is a *mueang krasae*—there are many middle-class people and those involved in business. Here, you have to have candidates with high education," he said.[9] Nawaphon's identification of Hat Yai as a "*mueang krasae*" was prescient, because Democrat votes in Hat Yai delivered Nawaphon his victory. Moreover, as events showed, the particular *krasae* that triumphed in Hat Yai and gave him victory was not based on his policies or much on his candidates—as he gravely intoned to me that October—but on the popular enthusiasm generated by the two preceding Democrat electoral triumphs.

CANDIDATES AND THE QUESTION OF PARTY AFFILIATION

The opening rallies of the contesting teams began in November. The actual policies of the major competing teams of Worawit and Nawaphon were similar, with both advancing programs that addressed a range of acknowledged development needs in their province. The competition for voters' support turned not on policies and issues of "*kan phatthana*," but rather on key eligibility criteria concerning the candidates' personal qualities and their affiliation with political parties. Nawaphon was able to more successfully appropriate the important symbolic capital of Democrat Party support, and in doing so, he managed to compensate for Worawit's advantage of greater personal appeal among people in the province.

The issues of national political party involvement in local politics, and local politicians' party affiliations, were kept in the forefront by Songkhla's local press during 2003. Journalists of *Focus Phak Tai* and *Samila Times* followed national journalistic commentary in viewing the national significance of local contests in the light of TRT's declared objectives of capturing up to twenty seats from the Democrats in the south in the next national elections. Given that these papers were read mainly in the province's urban centers of Hat Yai, Songkhla, and the larger market towns, the impact of this reportage was probably minimal among ordinary voters in the rural districts, though press speculation did reflect much of the anti-TRT rumor that circulated among communities, much of it spread by Democrat vote canvassers. From November 2003, when three contesting teams in Songkhla presented themselves to the public in opening rallies, the local press began to speculate about TRT party affiliations.[10] Nawaphon's reliance on his prominent Democrat elder brother Niphon in his campaign was already clear. In addition, Nawaphon gained celebrity endorsement in attracting the support of the popular southern *luk thung* singer Ekkachai Siriwichai, who was a staunch Democrat Party loyalist. Ekkachai performed at Nawaphon's *Thim Songkhla Phatthana* opening rally on November 12, and was prominent in Nawaphon's newspaper election advertisements from this time onwards.[11] Worawit Khaothong had well-known connections with leading TRT figures, but he also enjoyed the personal support of the prominent Songkhla Democrat MPs Thawon and Winai Senniam. In his first rally (also held on November 12), Worawit declared that he was not running under any political party banner or benefiting from unofficial party support. Those politicians helping promote his candidature, he stated, were doing so only in a private capacity.[12]

In contrast to Worawit, the political interests of the third contestant, General Suchat Chanthonchotikun, were more openly tied to TRT. Suchat had briefly served as a New Aspiration Party MP for Songkhla. First elected in March 1992, he had been defeated in September of the same year, a victim of the surge of Democrat support following the overthrow of the Suchinda Khraprayun government. Suchat was now a member of the TRT Party's coordinating committee for the province. He openly declared that he had been encouraged to come forward by the prominent southern TRT figure Wira Musikaphong, a former colleague in the New Aspiration Party (which merged with TRT in 2002). Suchat revealed that the current Interior Minister Wan Muhamad Nor Matha (also formerly NAP) had helped him gain official permission from the TRT leadership to use the name and logo of TRT in his campaign. Suchat's team bore a name that clearly resonated with its patron national party—*Thim Thai Rak Songkhla*—and his major policy emphasis was the coordination of development projects with the new government-appointed "CEO" governor of the province.[13] Suchat's effort was clearly part of a strategy devised by Wira and Wan Noor to try to catalyze non-Democrat groups in the province and widen the TRT voting base as a preliminary to the Songkhla by-election and the 2005 national elections. Ultimately, however, Suchat was unable to assemble enough *so cho* candidates and was forced to restrict his campaign to the presidency only, with associated executives.

With Suchat's success in gaining permission to use the TRT logo for his campaign, suspicions of Worawit's TRT connections should perhaps have abated, but this was not the case. By January 2004, the popular enthusiasm for the Democrats began to render any identification with TRT an electoral liability. In late January, as the by-election campaigns for Constituency 3 gained momentum, the election contests for the Hat Yai Municipality and the Songkhla PAO became progressively subsumed within the struggle between the Democrats and TRT, with calls on wider loyalties overshadowing the local dimensions of those contests. At the final rallies in support of Wirat Kalayasiri, the Democrat Party leader Banyat Banthatthan and senior advisor Chuan Leekpai simultaneously called on voters to support Phrai Phatthano and Nawaphon Bunyamani in their campaigns, and in the process they blurred the distinction between official party support and personal endorsement for candidates.

Democrat Party victory in the by-election and de facto support in the Hat Yai rallies of late February added decisive strength to Nawaphon's campaign—Nawaphon had made sure that he was visible to voters in the Hat Yai rallies and in the canvassing processions. In particular, this helped to divert public attention away from an emerging scandal involving Nawaphon and his alleged pledging of an official provincial vehicle to secure repayment of gambling debts. Some suspected this was a set-up by his rival. Until late January, Worawit had gained the upper hand at the hustings by calling Nawaphon's integrity into question over this issue of the pledged Mercedes Benz.[14]

While monitored by the local press, Nawaphon's suspected impropriety was overshadowed by the Democrat campaign momentum which was buttressed by more lurid scandals about vote buying and the misuse of state power by TRT government ministers in the lead-up to the by-election. With the stunning Democrat victory over TRT on February 22, Nawaphon's personal flaws became less important. The PAO presidency election came to be represented in symbolic terms as part of a wider Democrat moral crusade against the dictatorial designs of the TRT giant. Worawit's professed party-political neutrality was already under suspicion by the press, who reported that he had planned for Thaksin's sister and prominent TRT Party figure Yaowapha Wongsawat to attend a rally in Hat Yai the previous November.[15] A week before the Constituency 3 by-election, TRT Party heavyweight Pracha Malinon visited the province, ostensibly in his capacity as deputy minister of the interior to inspect various development programs, but also in his position as TRT Party official to monitor the TRT campaign. He also met with Worawit, whose campaign by this time was now being described by the press as "under the name of TRT."[16]

By early March, the PAO campaigns had developed a new complexion. With the Democrat landslide victory in Constituency 3, and Phrai Phatthano's Democrat-endorsed victory in Hat Yai close on its heels in late February, Worawit's suspected affiliation with TRT was a major electoral liability for him and a clear asset for Nawaphon. Nawaphon's final rallies were attended by Democrat Party leader Banyat Banthatthan and accompanied by video screenings showing the endorsements of Sanan Kachonprasat, Surin Pitsuwan, and Trairong Suwankiri. At these rallies, Worawit's *Thim Rak Songkhla* was identified as a TRT team and thus an archenemy of true Democrats. This image was reinforced by rumors spread by Nawaphon's vote canvassers among ordinary voters at the district and village level.[17] Nawaphon's newspaper and rally advertisements included the proclamation, "The Democrats add the strength of fellowship to help Nawaphon become president of the PAO."[18]

In the critical final week of the campaigns, Worawit tried to publicly discount the widespread rumors of his identification with TRT and opposition to the Democrats. He could not afford to alienate his many ordinary supporters who were also traditional Democrat voters. At his rallies, he made the point that his family had always supported the Democrats and that he himself had been a key vote canvasser for Niphon Bunyamani in Constituency 5.[19] To aid his cause in denying the allegations, Worawit enlisted the help of his Democrat MP friends, the Senniam brothers. In their capacity as Democrat MPs, the Senniams proclaimed that the Democrat Party had not officially declared that it would support specific teams in Songkhla's PAO elections. A full-page declaration on this point was made by Winai Senniam and printed in the local newspapers.[20] To further help distance Worawit from TRT and to separate Nawaphon's campaign from association with the Democrats, a flier was circulated throughout the province in blue and white Democrat colors, signed by the Senniam brothers and featuring their portraits. It announced solemnly that, "The Democrat Party has declared not to officially send candidates to stand for the provincial election." The Senniam-endorsed flier emphasized that Worawit had welcomed Pracha Malinon in January only in his official position as PAO president, and not in any political capacity, and to reinforce this, the reverse side featured pictures of the Democrat-affiliated mayor of Songkhla welcoming TRT ministers.[21] Notably the flier did not address the fact that Pracha Malinon had mounted the stage in Worawit's support during one of his November rallies in Ranot District. Having miscalculated by trying to capitalize on his TRT connections early in his campaign, Worawit was now trying to contain the debates in the *nayok* contest to an autonomous sphere of provincial-level politics to benefit from his strongest ground of eligibility—his personal performance as incumbent *nayok* and his local image as a generous and trustworthy *nakleng*-type leader. The final election results showed that although he was unsuccessful in this, it was only by a slim margin, and he remained popular in the province.

NAWAPHON'S LIMITED VICTORY: THE PERSISTENCE OF LOCALISM

The voting results for Songkhla's PAO poll of March 14 showed the decisive role of Democrat *krasae* in delivering Nawaphon a victory. He won the *nayok* contest by a majority of just over 22,000 votes, or 46 percent of the province vote, compared to Worawit's 43 percent (see table 5.1 below). Furthermore, Nawaphon's victory was entirely owing to the significant majority he gained in the province voting constituency of Amphoe Hat Yai, which holds the largest number of voters in the province, incorporating the electorates of national Constituencies 2 and 3. The upsurge of loyalty to the Democrat Party generated by the by-election and the Hat Yai elections thus impacted on the provincial election in a geographically specific way. In the urban and peri-urban districts of Hat Yai, Nawaphon gained a majority of over 30,000 votes, which compensated for his losses to Worawit in nine of Songkhla's sixteen *amphoe*. Local-level support for Worawit was conspicuous in the overwhelming support that he gained in his rural home *amphoe* of Rattaphum, where his votes were more than twice those of Nawaphon. By contrast, Nawaphon gained only a narrow victory in his own home *amphoe*, the largely urban district of Songkhla. Despite Nawaphon's win, the results showed the persistence of Worawit's popularity among voters and his canvassing networks. They indicate that many voters—despite their Democrat allegiance regularly expressed in national elections—had resisted the pressures to vote on party lines.

From one perspective, Songkhla's PAO contest might be viewed as a surrogate national election. This, at least, was the way the *nayok* elections were represented by Nawaphon's team and the leading Democrat figures who presented him to the province's electorate. Democrat orators in the Constituency 3 by-election had presented the contest to the electorate as an opportunity to affirm Democrat Party strength and declare opposition to the national administration of Thaksin and the TRT Party. This symbolic imperative had infused the rhetoric of the succeeding Hat Yai elections and then the provincial contest. Nawaphon had benefited by preemptively appropriating Democrat symbolism and sponsorship, which served to simultaneously boost his electoral appeal and undermine Worawit's superior person-based eligibility claims. There is no doubt that the TRT national leadership was viewing the PAO president contests in the south as a test of strength and support. The elections had brought out into the open a number of political aspirants, such as Suchat Chanthonchotikun, who aimed to capitalize on explicit TRT sponsorship. If Suchat's performance was viewed as a test of TRT's goals in Songkhla, then that party had

TABLE 5.1

District (*amphoe*) Results for the March 2004 PAO Presidency Election

Amphoe	Worawit Khaothong (Candidate No. 1)	Nawaphon Bunyamani (Candidate No. 2)	Suchat Chanthonchotikun (Candidate No. 3)
Mueang Songkhla	24,237	26,689	3,808
Hat Yai	42,752	73,111	11,627
Sadao	17,363	20,560	2,656
Chana	20,875	19,922	4,232
Thepha	13,397	12,488	2,992
Rattaphum	20,475	9,998	1,599
Ranot	15,584	12,372	1,953
Sabayoi	10,819	9,030	5,025
Singhanakhon	14,057	18,224	2,046
Sathingphra	8,104	11,871	2,104
Khuaniang	8,619	7,087	339
Nathawi	12,947	10,791	5,335
Bang Klam	6,183	5,580	643
Namom	4,083	6,214	1,458
Krasaesin	3,599	3,637	905
Khlong Hoikhong	6,747	4,727	782
Total Votes	**230,041**	**252,298**	**47,504**

Source: Provincial Election Commission, Songkhla

clearly failed to gain ground; however, it was Worawit who emerged as the strongest potential contender against the Democrats, and later in 2004, it was revealed that he had accepted TRT candidacy for the upcoming national election.

Despite Nawaphon's strategic success in drawing on the Democrat Party *krasae* that energized Hat Yai, the PAO elections in Songkhla were not entirely conducted, or perceived by voters, on national political party lines. For example, the composition of the respective leaders' *so cho* teams was not clearly based on party-political allegiance.

Nawaphon's team, for example, included a *so cho* who supported Surasak Mani, a renegade Democrat and an aspirant for selection as TRT candidate for Constituency 8. Worawit's team included a *so cho* of Bang Klam who was a well-known Democrat supporter and close relative of Wirat Kalayasiri, the newly elected Democrat MP for Constituency 3. So too, the voting pattern for *so cho* candidates showed a more complicated pattern than the *nayok* votes, revealing that at the district and sub-district levels, voters continued to evaluate candidates on person-based eligibility criteria and customary affiliations of family loyalties. Of the thirty-six PAO council seats, Nawaphon's team members gained seventeen, Worawit's team won thirteen, while a further six seat winners had campaigned as independents. In Amphoe Hat Yai, where Nawaphon gained a decisive majority of votes for his own *nayok* candidacy, voters returned five members of his nine-member *so cho* team, three under Worawit's banner, and one independent. Voters were clearly splitting their preferences between the *nayok* and the *so cho* ballot papers. Worawit suffered a personal defeat as a *nayok* candidate, but his own team actually gained a respectable thirteen seats in the PAO assembly. Nawaphon's team gained more seats (seventeen), but the decisive group was the six independents, who held the balance of power in the assembly. The factional tussles after the election saw Nawaphon succeed in forming a slim majority of one in the assembly (nineteen of thirty-six councilors). He did this by persuading an independent councilor to move to his side and by cleverly poaching a Worawit team member in Khuaniang District (as related below).[22]

The teams of the two contestants were essentially composed of phuak with varied levels of loyalty to the team leaders. As noted already, the teams comprised each leader's core phuak combined with other individuals whose interests were served by attaching themselves to these teams. Close connections with Democrat Party branches reinforced the phuak solidarities of a number of Nawaphon's *so cho* team members, and furnished vote canvassers for him at the district level. Many of these also acted as vote canvassers for the Democrats in national-level elections. The loyalties and affiliations that connected the individuals composing these team groups and their canvassing support networks at the district level were not entirely convertible to predictable canvassing alignments in national political contests. That being said, Worawit Khaothong clearly based his later bid for national politics as a TRT candidate on his healthy performance and support levels in the province competition. Songkhla's Democrat politicians were also keeping an eye on local district-based contests, and the outcomes were important. The account that follows considers one district-based contest and highlights how *so cho* fortunes were bound up with Democrat Party agendas and phuak alliances.

THE TUSSLE IN KHUANIANG: THE FALL OF *SO CHO* SAWIANG

Within the province-wide battle of the PAO presidency, a number of district-level tussles were taking place among *so cho* contestants. Driven essentially by local issues and accumulated conflicts, they also revealed the significant interconnection between the fields of local and national politics and how Democrat interests are intimately interwoven with the fortunes of local political players. In the election contest in Khuaniang District, a long-serving member of Niphon Bunyamani's constituency-based phuak lost voters' support and legitimacy in a contest fought on local issues, and in the process lost Niphon's critical patronage. Though the loser turned against the party, Niphon and Nawaphon brought the victor into their Democrat phuak through the clever exercise of patronage, converting apparent defeat into a Democrat gain. Democrat MPs of Songkhla, as elsewhere, need to continually cultivate relationships among key local political actors to nurture the networks so vital to securing voting bases (*thansiang*). This involves the maintenance of a vital balance between their own political needs and those of local politicians. The case of *So Cho* Sawiang of Khuaniang highlights the ways that political bonds, however infused by the cultural norms of phuak loyalty, can break under the accumulated strain of diverging interests and local political dynamics.

Sawiang Chaisiri, a lawyer by training, was first elected to the Provincial Assembly as a representative for Khuaniang in 1991, and thereafter succeeded in maintaining this office through another four elections until his final downfall in 2004.[23] Sawiang had first impressed the voters of Khuaniang by energetically lobbying for budget resources for local projects. As a newly elected *so cho*, Sawiang was active in attending funerals and marriage ceremonies, and was liberal in donating ice and drinks for these occasions. He ingratiated himself with key groups, in particular schoolteachers, whose support proved important in elections because of their high esteem among villagers. With the vital support of his wife, Sawiang established housewives groups (*klum maeban*) around the district, and these groups provided further canvassing strength in periodic elections, together with his and his wife's kin networks. In his second term, Sawiang won local acclaim in a project providing computers to local schools. From 1992, Sawiang acted as a vote canvasser for the Democrats and was noticed by Niphon Bunyamani, who first won election that year. Sawiang joined the Democrat Party and thereafter became a key vote canvasser for the party in Khuaniang District. Niphon's financial support reinforced Sawiang's patronage resources as a *so cho*. He was particularly active in distributing T-shirts (with his name clearly emblazoned on them) to school and police sports teams, housewives groups, and aerobics clubs throughout the district. In the PAO assembly, Sawiang was a member of Nawaphon Bunyamani's emerging Democrat phuak. At the same time, he cultivated his own district-based phuak who canvassed for him and were mobilized during national elections for the Democrats.

Despite his early successes, however, Sawiang's popularity was wearing thin in the district by the later 1990s. He focused more and more on his own business schemes and was seldom seen in the district. Furthermore, he embarked on a land development scheme that collapsed under the impact of the 1997 financial crisis, and he failed to repay local people who had paid deposits for their lost building allotments. Just as serious, he was increasingly suspected of taking substantial commissions on the sales of computers to local schools, and the opposition of local schoolteachers to his shady practices signaled increasing erosion in his voting support. In addition, he made promises to local people about road-building projects that he did not keep, earning him the local sobriquet of "the bullshitting *so cho*." In the PAO elections of 2000, Sawiang defeated his less well-known local opponent, but his overall votes had declined and his margin of victory was not impressive. Local critics argued that the key reason for his victory was the financial support of Niphon Bunyamani, which had enabled him to buy votes to top up his declining pool of support.

On the eve of the PAO elections in late 2003, Sawiang was firmly ensconced in the Democrat Party's Constituency 5 branch structure, where he was chairman. He was re-elected to that post in September. Niphon Bunyamani knew about the rumblings of dissatisfaction from the voters of Khuaniang, but he was reluctant to abandon his long-time key vote canvasser and phuak member though he knew he was now a poor electoral bet. As a long-time member of Nawaphon's Democrat-based phuak in the PAO, Sawiang was included in his *Songkhla Phatthana* team of *so cho* candidates for the 2004 contest. In Khuaniang, local resentment of Sawiang had brought forward a new candidate, the local teacher Mit Kaeopradit ("Khru Mit"), who from 2002 began laying the groundwork of his campaign to topple Sawiang. Mit adopted the same technique as Sawiang in getting himself known and liked by voters, but he did it more systematically. He laid out a plan to visit every village in the district and spend at least fifteen minutes talking to each householder. He also had T-shirts printed and distributed to housewives groups, sports teams, and aerobics groups. His message was that Khuaniang had not been adequately developed, and that Sawiang was corrupt and self-serving. As the election approached, Mit secured the support of a number of Sawiang's former vote canvassers who had become disillusioned with him. He was even able to undermine Sawiang in his own voting stronghold of Tambon Bang Liang by gaining the support of one of his wife's relatives, a prominent village headman who had long disliked Sawiang. Together with a dense kin network in Tambon Huai Luek, Mit also gained the vital support of schoolteachers, among whom he was well known through his position as a committee member of the district's teachers association. Mit joined Worawit's team of *so cho* candidates, though he has emphasized since that he was really running as an independent, and did not want to be controlled by any group.[24]

Khru Mit's campaign against the Democrat-aligned Sawiang in the district PAO contest was successful, with Mit gaining 8,438 votes against his opponent's 7,150. He had campaigned on purely local issues of development and a negative campaign against his opponent's suspect character and slovenly record. Sawiang did not give up easily, however, and managed to have the victor disqualified by Songkhla's Provincial Election Commission on the grounds that Mit had donated money (200 baht) to a temple during the campaign period. In the by-election for the district that followed in May 2004, Sawiang again failed, this time at the hands of Khru Mit's younger brother, who campaigned in his stead. Sawiang's defeat was not such a liability for the Democrat phuak as it first appeared, because Nawaphon, with his brother's aid, successfully drew Mit across to support their team in the new PAO assembly. This process of cajoling, known as "*dueng*" (pulling), was successfully applied to another independent *so cho*, giving Nawaphon a majority of one in the PAO assembly—a critical necessity for the passing of the PAO budget. Mit was the last to be "pulled across." Before his disqualification by the PEC and the calling of the by-election, Mit attended the first assembly of the PAO, where he voted in support of Nawaphon's nominee for PAO assembly chairman. This was an explicit slap-in-the-face to Worawit, and served to confirm Nawaphon's supremacy over the assembly and Mit's alliance with the new PAO president.

The background to Mit's new alignment with the Democrat phuak was Nawaphon's support of 700,000 baht (supplied apparently through Niphon) to aid Mit's brother's campaign against Sawiang, which was successful. Obliged to the Democrat phuak for his assistance, Mit came forward to act as canvasser for the party in the 2005 national election, supporting the new Democrat candidate for Constituency 5. For his part, Sawiang was outraged when he heard that the Bunyamanis had supported his rival behind his back, and he left the Democrat Party. As for Mit, his victory (despite subsequent disqualification) spurred his own political ambitions in local politics. His brother was a fairly lackluster representative, but Mit worked as the de facto *so cho* of the district, aiming to gain election in the future. Experience taught him to be pragmatic and realize that the Democrat phuak of Nawaphon and his elder brother was an indispensable support for his new career. As he explained to me in the presence of a friend of his who resented the ubiquitous influence of the Democrats in local politics, "You have to realize that you can't get anything done unless you are with this Democrat phuak."[25]

The character of the contest in Amphoe Khuaniang in 2004 shows how specifically local issues engaged voters' attention in the election for councilors, despite its portrayal as a party conflict by the Democrats and by the press at the level of the presidency battle. Just as significant, it reveals how local political actors need to draw on wider resources of support, and how obligations and affiliations through phuak are the principal vehicle for this resource building. Among political actors with concrete ambitions, however, these phuak bonds are durable only so far as all interests are served. In the case of Sawiang, his departure from the Democrat phuak and party was spurred by a clear divergence of interests and benefits. To him, the phuak had not given him enough support, while to the key phuak members (especially Niphon) he had shown that he could not command the trust and affections of the electorate and would thus be unable to secure votes for the party.

DEMOCRAT *KRASAE*, LOCALISM, AND THE BALANCING ACT

Although the provincial *nayok* election results revealed the power of the Democrat Party's symbolic resources and popular loyalties, the contest also exposed the resilience of localism in the strong performance of Worawit Khaothong. The provincial election contests revealed more complex processes than a simple trend of "local politics" converging with national party agendas. In Songkhla, the campaigns and voting results showed the persistence of more traditional locality-centered forms of evaluation in group alignments and electoral preferences, focusing on family, phuak affiliation, and personality. Nawaphon Bunyamani's Democrat-endorsed campaign for the province presidency proved to be successful at the expense of his main rival, the popular and experienced former PAO president Worawit Khaothong. In this sense, his victory was a Democrat Party victory; but his winning margin over his rival was not spectacular, and it relied exclusively on his voting majority in the populous and urbanized districts of Hat Yai that were energized by the pro-Democrat enthusiasm of the by-election and municipal contests. Just as striking was that the voting results for the *nayok* candidates showed how popular Worawit still was among voters in the province. Measured by the voters' responses in the district-based *so cho* contests, many of them resisted viewing the provincial election as party-based.

Nevertheless, the PAO elections were used by the Democrats and political aspirants to marshal resources for the forthcoming national-level contest. The presidency election served as a testing ground for opponents of the Democrat ascendancy in the province, and the contest actually produced the Democrats' most formidable enemy in Worawit Khaothong, not the official TRT candidate Suchat Chanthonchotikun. Worawit's impressive performance in the face of the Democrat *krasae* had shown the strength of more locally and person-based evaluations of political eligibility in Songkhla. His message could quite comfortably be accommodated under TRT's banner—he was a committed local leader dedicated to developing the province and serving the people. After his defeat, Worawit openly revealed his ties to the TRT Party and gained TRT endorsement to stand for Constituency 5, which included two districts where he had gained clear majorities in the PAO elections and where networks of strong canvassers were available.[26] Worawit's turn to TRT reportedly dismayed the Senniam brothers, who had genuinely believed his professions of independence from TRT during his campaign.

As brought into relief during the provincial elections, the political system in the south reflects patterns of political group formation that are well established throughout Thailand, where "local" political actors are intimately connected with national politicians in a quest for complementary political resources. Phuak solidarities, as Michael Nelson has emphasized in his studies of Chachoensao Province and elsewhere, play a critical role as a fundamental structural pattern in group formation and identification.[27] In most parts of Thailand, provincial and local-level bases for a party structure are weak or completely absent, leaving phuak-based alliance as the dominant pattern of identification among local political actors, in contrast to the Democrat-dominated south, where there is a well-established and active party branch system with office-bearers and committees. Here, durable party branch structures and commitment to membership do have an effect on shaping political alignments and commitments. Nevertheless, phuak-based relations, as elsewhere, are the primary "glue" that keeps key political players together. Sustaining the Democrat Party political ascendancy in Songkhla relies on the maintenance of a delicate balance between the ambitions of local politicians and the needs of their patrons and allies, the national politicians. Phuak durability and longevity relies on the performance of these mutual needs.

In the months approaching the 2005 national elections in Songkhla, a number of the strongest non-Democrat contenders in the PAO contest, including Worawit, were encouraged to come forward as TRT candidates. In their efforts to undermine the long-standing Democrat Party ascendancy, these contenders attempted to maximize their political resources by marshalling TRT Party national *krasae*, bolstered by solidarities and loyalties that drew on family, phuak, and person-centered eligibility claims. The following chapters explore the dynamics of these contests.

Part IV

The 2005 Election: Democrat *Udomkan* and Other Persuasions

CHAPTER 6

Southern Democrats at Bay: The 2005 National Election

IN THAILAND'S national election of February 2005, the southern Democrats confronted the greatest challenge to their long regional electoral ascendancy. To be sure, the Songkhla by-election victory of 2004 proved that the great majority of the southern electorate still faithfully responded to the party's tried-and-trusted calls to unity against the immoral political "other." Yet the resources commanded by the nationally dominant TRT were considerable, and the Democrats at the national level were in tatters, with a party leadership unable to compete with Thaksin's public image and populist policies. The south remained the only coherent base of the party and a TRT victory there would spell the death knell of the national party and any possible parliamentary opposition to Thaksin's political juggernaut. As it turned out, in 2005, the southern Democrats scored an overwhelming regional victory against TRT. Though the final voting figures suggest that the Democrat triumph in the south was an easy one, at the level of certain constituencies it was a tough struggle against some strong challengers.

In this and the two chapters that follow, I examine the campaigns of the parties and candidates in those Songkhla constituencies that witnessed the fiercest competition between the Democrats and their TRT Party challengers. At the national level, the Democrat Party faced a grave predicament, and fierce challenges were also anticipated in its southern heartland. In Songkhla itself, three Democrat constituencies were particularly vulnerable to TRT attack because the party's own candidates were either novices, or completely new. By contrast, those TRT candidates who came forward to challenge the novice Democrats marshaled impressive cultural and material resources, and they employed these to the full in their efforts to organize supporters and persuade voters. Significantly, all three of these challengers to the local Democrat ascendancy had formerly been closely connected to their opponents, whether by phuak, or by formal party affiliation.

THE GATHERING STORM: DEMOCRAT TROUBLES AND THE TRT ADVANCE

Just a year after mounting their spectacular defense of core party territory against TRT in the showcase by-election for Constituency 3, Songkhla's Democrats faced a more concerted TRT onslaught in the February 2005 national polls. After the by-election victory, Democrat fortunes at a national level during 2004 were decidedly mixed. In August, an impressive Democrat win in the Bangkok gubernatorial election was hailed by the party's leaders and other commentators as a significant urban middle-class protest vote against Thaksin's autocratic governing methods. In a field of fifteen contenders, Democrat Party candidate Aphirak Kosayodhin won the Bangkok governorship with 40.6 percent of the total votes cast, far ahead of TRT-sponsored Pavena Hongsakul with 26.6 percent.[1] But the Bangkok victory was the only good news in an otherwise bleak year for the party, and it was no guide to the national political preferences of the urban electorate, as was to be shown in TRT's success in the metropolis in 2005. In July, leading Democrat figures Sanan Khachonprasat and Anek Laothamatas left the party to form the new Mahachon Party. The parting was amicable, but it thinned the leadership, and Mahachon's focus on the northeast (with support from some leading NGO activists) weakened the Democrats' already tenuous electoral resources in that region. This was not the worst of the news, however, for early in August, four of the five Democrat MPs in the southern border provinces of Narathiwat, Pattani, and Yala defected to join TRT. Soon after, more party-switching cases were publicized, with the most embarrassing defection being that of Thawi Suraban, Democrat MP for Constituency 1 in Trang, the home province of the party's venerated icon, Chuan Leekpai. These renegade Democrats were all long-serving parliamentarians with strong voter bases, and journalists suggested there were good prospects for TRT winning a substantial number of southern seats in the upcoming national elections. The Democrats claimed that their southern MPs were being bought off, and other sources indicated that the defections had been prompted by cash payments from TRT of up to 25 million baht. Lapsak Lapharotkit, the standing Democrat member for Hat Yai, revealed to colleagues and party members that he had been approached by a TRT intermediary to resign from parliament in exchange for a substantial cash payment, but he had refused.[2]

The TRT government's full four-year term of office was due to expire in January 2005, but national-level campaigning by both parties began in October 2004, well before a definitive date was set for the dissolution of parliament and the national polls. In the constituencies, party candidates were already making preparations in October, and in November TRT formally publicized the party's candidates for the south.[3] In December, after some speculation of an early election, the date for the national polls was finally announced as February 6.[4] Throughout October–December, Prime Minister Thaksin capitalized to the full on his advantages of incumbency; numerous major infrastructure projects were announced aimed towards building and reinforcing electoral support in key regions, including Bangkok. Through trendy "mobile cabinet meetings" and "workshops" held in provincial centers, development projects were publicized as rewards for future electoral support.

Despite the confident electioneering of the government party, a major problem for TRT emerged in the first month of campaigning, when at Tak Bai in the southern Muslim-majority border province of Narathiwat, some eighty-five Muslim villagers were killed by the military in circumstances that pointed to official incompetence and unwarranted brutality. The Democrats, especially in the south, took full advantage of this controversial event to again question Thaksin's claims to sound and effective government. The prime minister's nationwide popularity suffered from widespread consternation and anger over the Tak Bai incident, but from late December, Thaksin gained a major boost following his highly publicized efforts to manage recovery operations in the wake of the tsunami tidal wave devastation on the Andaman coast provinces of southern Thailand.[5] Most commentators agreed that Thaksin's aim to win four hundred parliamentary seats nationally was entirely possible, and that the Democrats had no answer to his government's record of policy implementation. In particular, the Democrats were seen to be handicapped by the colorless party leader Banyat Banthatthan, who was unable to project a leadership image capable of competing with Thaksin's powerful public persona.[6]

TRT's campaign message stressed the government's proven record as a policy/performance-based organization responsive to the people's needs and headed by a decisive leader of international renown. Arguing that over the past four years TRT had "repaired" the damage of the 1997 crisis by restoring economic growth and attacking poverty and social problems, the party presented its next term as a period of "strengthening." The party announced fourteen draft policy measures, including deferred repayment loans for university students, establishment of village banks, and tax relief for householders caring for elderly parents. In response, the Democrats highlighted as their main issue the defense of constitutional democracy based on checks and balances against Thaksin's monopolistic "parliamentary dictatorship." The DP slogan "at least 201" stressed the aim to gain a minimum number of MPs necessary to permit parliamentary censure motions against the prime minister. The slogan was a gesture of defiance, but also an admission that the Democrats were doomed to become a parliamentary minority once more. Arguing for sustainable as opposed to shallow populist solutions to pressing socioeconomic problems, Democrat policies actually resembled TRT's raft of handouts, with promises of "free" elementary education, allowances for the elderly, unemployment relief, and vocational training. The Mahachon Party stressed public participation and decentralization, but its main policies appeared very similar to the Democrats. The Chat Thai Party, TRT's declining coalition partner led by the elderly former Prime Minister Banhan Silpa-acha, focused its campaign around Banhan's earlier prime ministerial record and the commitment of candidates to deliver development benefits to constituents. Chat Thai campaigning featured no criticism of the Thaksin government, since the party held out the hope of retaining its tenuous status as a minor government coalition partner.

Notwithstanding Thaksin's triumphant national *krasae*, the Democrat-dominated south stood out as the distinctive and stubborn bastion of opposition in the nation, with particular challenges for the governing party. In contrast to the extravagant boasts made earlier in 2004, TRT gave no specific targets for the number of seats that the party expected to wrest from the southern Democrats. In fact, Thaksin made it clear that TRT was targeting the northeast and the northern regions, where his party's polls indicated an overwhelming level of popularity. TRT did not need to win in the south to achieve its overall goal of winning a convincing parliamentary majority. Nevertheless, the fact of southern defiance posed an annoying challenge to TRT's legitimacy claims. In November, TRT announced that its polls indicated that it would win 244 House seats out of the four hundred available through direct voting, and at least seventy seats out of the remaining one hundred party-list seats.[7] In typical style, TRT used these polling results as a public marketing tool, claiming that in the south the Democrats had only a "marginal" lead over TRT in overall popularity. Such pompous claims, however, contrasted starkly with the party's internal assessments of its southern candidates' chances. The party ranked its candidates into three categories—A, B, and C—according to whether they were very strong candidates, tough competitors with a fifty-fifty chance, or were likely to be defeated. Although not highly publicized, these categories were linked to the levels of funding that TRT provided to its constituency candidates. Officially, Thaksin and his spokesmen claimed that the party counseled all candidates to keep within the legal campaign spending limits (set by the Election Commission of Thailand at 1 million baht); but this was hardly likely given that actual TRT funding levels for its candidates were much higher than this. It was generally accepted that successful campaigns in 2005 would require candidates to spend an average of 8 million baht.[8] TRT's relatively low estimates of clear victory over the southern Democrats were indicated by the party's ranking of its southern candidates, which contrasted strikingly with the other regions. Thus, while in Thailand's northeast, TRT was fielding 105 A-grade, twenty-seven B-grade and three C-grade candidates, in the southern constituencies it fielded only three A-grade contenders, with the remainder comprising seventeen B-grade and thirty-three C-grade candidates. Particular attention was being given to defeating the Democrats in Chuan Leekpai's home province of Trang, where the TRT leadership hoped that a symbolic victory could be won by former Democrats now running as TRT candidates. TRT spokesmen claimed that Chuan Leekpai would be so occupied bolstering Democrat loyalties in Trang that he would have little time to assist his party's campaign elsewhere in the south. Notably, two of the TRT's grade "B" candidates were contesting seats in Songkhla Province: Worawit Khaothong and Sunthon Pathumthong.[9]

In Songkhla, Phrai Phatthano's outstanding Democrat-sponsored triumph in Hat Yai had demonstrated the force of Democrat loyalty in the urban electorate, and the surge of pro-Democrat support in that city was also crucial in delivering victory to Nawaphon Bunyamani's team at the provincial polls. However, Songkhla's Democrats faced some new challenges in this election contest. Nawaphon's own narrow victory had already shown that non-Democrat networks were strong, and that Worawit Khaothong's impressive performance was a sign that prominent local politicians running for TRT could draw support among ordinary voters. In this 2005 contest, the long-incumbent Democrats faced a situation that was starkly different from 2001, when they had campaigned on a clear and attractive message of returning Chuan Leekpai as prime minister. Now, out of office for four years and with no hope of gaining a parliamentary majority, the party had to validate its electoral claims in terms of its usefulness as an opposition party. Never before had the enemies of the Democrats in Songkhla enjoyed such an opportunity to crystallize their opposition and undermine their enemy's long-standing hegemony. Harnessing TRT's powerful *krasae*, non-Democrats now had a powerful tool to supplement their local claims to eligibility in running against Democrat legitimacy. The Songkhla Democrats recognized that three of their eight constituencies were vulnerable to assault by TRT because in two of them they were fielding new candidates (Constituencies 5 and 8) and the sitting member for the third, Wirat Kalayasiri of Constituency 3, had been an MP for only twelve months. Just as important, these TRT candidates claimed strong qualifications for local support.

DEMOCRAT WORRIES IN SONGKHLA: VULNERABLE SEATS, NEW FACES

Viewed overall, the Songkhla Democrats enjoyed obvious advantages over their TRT enemies because they could draw on long-established networks of support and a strong foundational loyalty among voters. Vulnerability, however, was exposed when the party was presenting new candidates and when strong rivals with powerful local credentials contested succession. In five of Songkhla's eight constituencies, where established MPs were defending their turf, the Democrats were rightly confident of absolute victory. Here, the Democrats' *thansiang* (voter base) was reinforced by the continuing relationship between parliamentarians and their electorates. These relationships are cultivated on an on-going basis through customary practices such as attending funerals, ordination ceremonies, and other public events, patronizing local organizations, and addressing constituents' varied problems on an individual basis. Personal prestige and identification with the party are self-reinforcing in Democrat MPs' efforts to maintain local support, or at least such is the ideal. But a change in representation, such as occurred in three constituencies in Songkhla, threatened to disrupt the relationship between electorate and party, particularly in the face of the unprecedented assault being prepared by the TRT for February 2005. On the eve of the elections, according to leading Songkhla Democrats, all seats could be comfortably defended, except those three constituencies where their candidates were new. In these three constituencies, somewhat different conditions and challenges faced the new Democrat candidates and their party branch activists.

In the important suburban and rural seat of Constituency 3, the Democrat MP Wirat Kalayasiri was a newcomer, although he had worked hard since his by-election victory nearly twelve months earlier to establish a presence in the electorate and in parliament. In early January, Wirat was keen to inform me that he had already given some twenty addresses in parliament. He was acutely aware that his visibility and importance to his constituents had to be reinforced through radio and television exposure.[10] As well as extending his presence in the constituency, Wirat faced the challenge of rebuilding the core group of branch officials after several key members had followed Phrai Phatthano into the Hat Yai City administration. More seriously, several branch officials had resigned from the party to join the new TRT candidate, Sunthon Pathumthong, the popular district head of Amphoe Hat Yai (a relative of Phrai and once a strong Democrat supporter). Although Wirat himself was openly confident, some leading Democrat officials from other branches confided to me that the candidature of Sunthon was going to pose a particular challenge to Wirat.

Constituency 5 is renowned as the solid voting heartland of Niphon Bunyamani, a Democrat MP since 1992. For this election, however, a new candidate was necessary because Niphon was standing as a party-list candidate, in keeping with his seniority in the party (he was a deputy secretary-general). Carved out of a larger multi-member constituency in the electoral redistributions of 2000, Constituency 5 (now merged with other constituencies, since 2007) covered part of the fishing zone of eastern Songkhla extending into the center of the province to incorporate rubber-growing and fishing districts fronting Songkhla Lake. The electorate included a substantial minority of Muslims (approx. 20 percent of the voting population), many of them pursuing livelihoods based on small-scale fishing, with a strong concentration in the Singhanakhon District, the site of the original port of the old *mueang* of Singhora. In September, the party chose Praphon Ekkuru, Niphon's nominee, to run for the seat.[11] Although inexperienced as a candidate for political office, Praphon had long been a Democrat Party member, and is the nephew of the influential and former long-serving mayor of Songkhla township, Prayot Ekkuru, well known as a Democrat phuak member. Praphon is a wealthy owner of fishing trawlers and food-processing factories, and a long-standing friend of Niphon, who he has supported in previous elections. He has particular influence because of his position as president of the Songkhla

Fishermen's Federation, whose membership boasts well-connected business figures in the province. Praphon's phuak members, drawn from the Fisherman's Federation, are an important electoral asset (see plate 6.1). His strongest base of support is in Songkhla township itself (located in Constituency 1), even though he had a large number of relatives in areas of Constituency 5, who, according to custom, were expected to supply assured votes for him. Praphon himself admitted that without a well-established personal vote base in Constituency 5, and due to his lack of experience, he would need to rely heavily on the support of senior Democrat leaders to promote the *krasae* of the national party (*krasae phak*) to carry him through.[12] Just as important, he needed to rely on his friend Niphon's former party branch workers, as well as Niphon and his brother Nawaphon's *hua khanaen* in the districts and villages of the constituency. Praphon's task was a tough one, because he faced a strong opponent in the TRT candidate, the former long-serving PAO president, Worawit Khaothong.

In Constituency 8, the Democrats faced a similar challenge of assuring succession of party representation with a new candidate

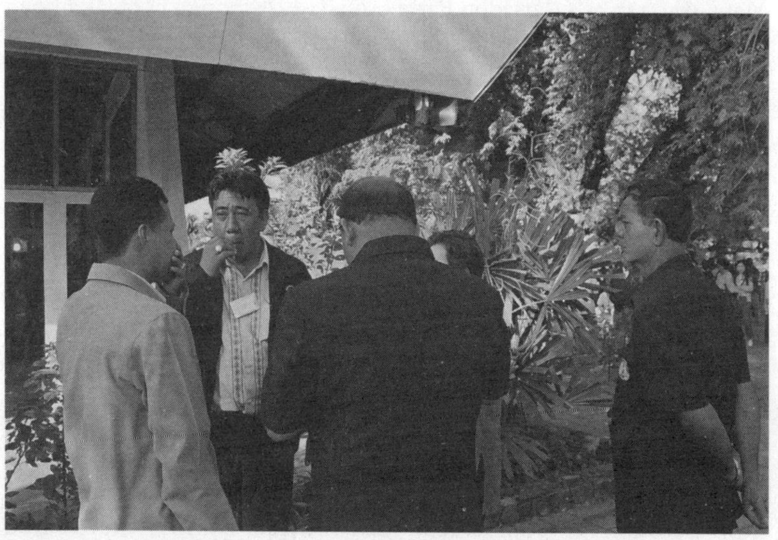

6.1 Praphon Ekkuru (second from left) with phuak *supporters from the Songkhla fishermen's federation on the day of his registration as Democrat Party candidate.*

in the face of a popular local figure running under the TRT banner. Constituency 8 encompassed a majority Muslim area dominated by small-scale rubber growers. Its boundaries extended along the coast southwards from Songkhla's Mueang District to the northern border of Pattani Province. Muslims comprised some 70 percent of the overall population in the communities of Constituency 8, with ethnic Thai Buddhists predominating in its northernmost *amphoe* of Na Mom, and Muslims dominating the remaining two *amphoe* of Chana and Thepha. These districts have provided a solid base for the Democrat Party for decades. The Muslim Democrat MP Wichit Suwit, (formerly a police Lt.-Colonel) had been re-elected for these and surrounding districts since 1992. First recruited to stand as a Democrat candidate by his university classmate Trairong Suwankhiri, Wichit had shared the former multi-member Constituency 3 (then encompassing Thepha and adjoining districts of Nathawi and Sadao) with Trairong until the electoral redistributions of 2000, when new single-member constituencies were created.[13] In 2001, Wichit successfully defended his Constituency 8 seat against the former Democrat activist, Surasak Mani, who ran as a Ratsadon Party candidate. Although popular among both Buddhists and Muslims of the electorate, Wichit gained victory in 2001 with the narrowest margin of all eight of Songkhla's Democrat MPs (14,503 votes), facing strong opponents in Surasak Mani as well as the Muslim New Aspiration Party candidate. The problem facing the Democrats was that Wichit, now aged sixty-four, had suffered from ill health for several years and was unable to undertake his constituency work adequately. This was a weakness that Surasak had been capitalizing on for some time in promoting his own claims as a committed local representative.

For some months, it was unclear just who would be selected as the Democrat candidate to replace Wichit Suwit for Constituency 8. In September, there was speculation that Wichit would be nominated as a party-list candidate and that his eldest son Naracha would run for the constituency. There were, however, some reservations expressed among Democrat branch officials because they feared Naracha was not well-enough known by local voters, and that he could not compete in popularity against Surasak.[14] In October, the province-level Democrat committee rejected Naracha's nomination and enjoined his father to run again, but Wichit declined on grounds of ill health. His son was eventually confirmed as the Democrat Party candidate in December. Naracha, a young man in his mid-thirties, faced a challenge in confronting the experienced and wily Surasak. Nevertheless, he could claim political experience through his work as personal parliamentary assistant to his father as well as membership of a number of parliamentary standing committees. He could also claim advantages over Surasak in terms of his higher education (an MBA gained in London) and his experience overseas.[15] In addition to Surasak's charge that Naracha's candidature was an attempt to perpetuate the prestige and power of the Suwit family (*phukkhat amnat trakun*) in the locality, the Democrats of the constituency also faced the challenge of authenticating Naracha as a qualified and democratically chosen candidate. As with Praphon in Constituency 5, Naracha's campaign required reinforcement with the strong symbolic resources wielded by senior Democrat politicians, particularly Chuan Leekpai. It is no coincidence that during the campaign in January 2005, Chuan Leekpai spent a full morning accompanying Naracha on his campaign cavalcade through Chana township to strengthen the young Muslim Democrat candidate's image.

THE NON-DEMOCRATS: DIFFERENT PARTIES, FAMILIAR FACES

The non-Democrat parties contesting the polls were, in order of support and resources, the TRT, Chat Thai, and the new Mahachon Party. This reflected the changing alignment of parties that occurred at the national level in the years 2002–04. The New Aspiration Party, which had fielded candidates in all of Songkhla's constituencies in 2001, had merged with TRT during 2002, while the Ratsadon Party was transmuted into Mahachon in 2004. Chat Thai, the only government coalition partner that had resisted complete absorption into TRT, had only intermittently run in elections in Songkhla since losing its briefly held seat in the province in 1992. As in the rest of the country, it was very clear that the major contest was to be between the Democrats and

TRT. In Songkhla, in common with the countrywide pattern, many non-Democrats contenders were invariably drawn to TRT as a vehicle to advance their political fortunes, though only a few were chosen. The strongest candidates were actively cultivated by the TRT leadership.

The parties arrayed against the Democrats featured a large number of familiar faces who had contested under different parties in previous elections. This reflected the standard pattern of fluid political affiliation among non-Democrat aspirants in Songkhla and elsewhere in the south. With its overwhelming advantages of popularity and financial resources, TRT enjoyed the luxury of picking the best non-Democrat contenders, while Chat Thai and Mahachon were left with less impressive aspirants. This was not a serious issue for Mahachon, which was focusing its major efforts on the northeast, as well as the three southern Muslim border provinces. In Songkhla, Mahachon ran only four candidates. In Constituency 2, they fielded an old Democrat renegade Naruchat Bunsuwan, a failed Ratsadon Party candidate for Constituency 5 in 2001. In Constituency 5, they ran Police Lt.-Colonel Kamonchai Sirirangsi, a political unknown who had failed to gain selection as a TRT candidate. In Constituency 7, there was the prominent local Muslim figure, Sithon Sikka, the former PAO *nayok*. A former Democrat phuak member, Sithon had run unsuccessfully as a Ratsadon Party candidate in the 2001 elections. Informants within the Democrat Party branches pointed out to me that the small number of Mahachon candidates reflected the fact that Sanan Khachonprasat did not want to antagonize his former faction members among the Democrat MPs of Songkhla and had made an agreement not to mount competitors against them. This is believable, since Mahachon did not run in most constituencies controlled by Sanan's old Democrat faction—Thawon Senniam (Constituency 6), Winai Senniam (Constituency 4), and Chuea Ratchasi (Constituency 1). Thawon Senniam publicly denied that any agreements had been made with Sanan, but Songkhla's Mahachon candidates claimed this to be so.[16]

The Chat Thai Party's candidates comprised a varied assortment of political aspirants, including well-known campaign veterans with a persistent record of electoral failure under other parties, as well as complete newcomers to national politics. They included the ever-persistent ex-Democrat Chamlaeng Mongkhonnitphakun, who had been rejected as a TRT candidate for the Songkhla by-election and had resigned his TRT membership to run in Constituency 2 under the Chat Thai banner. In the Muslim-majority electorate of Constituency 8, Chat Thai fielded the Muslim candidate Santhat Matbasa, a twice-serving deputy *nayok* of Songkhla's PAO. Chat Thai had not commanded a presence in Songkhla since the early 1990s, when Nikon Chamnong had served as a local MP before being defeated in the watershed September 1992 elections. The Songkhla-born Nikon was a senior party-list Chat Thai politician who held one of the few cabinet positions (deputy minister of communications) in Thaksin's coalition, and it was hoped that he could lend his prestige to the Chat Thai campaign in Songkhla. However, the Chat Thai line-up in the province was unimpressive, except in Constituency 3, where the party fielded Niran Kaenyakun, the ambitious former TRT aspirant who had been rejected by that party on the eve of the by-election a year earlier. Impressed with Niran's credentials and local support base, Nikon had personally recruited Niran to the party. A Chat Thai poll in December classified Niran as a level "A" candidate with good prospects.[17] Wirat Kalayasiri, however, dismissed Niran as posing a serious challenge to him, judging that he was capable of winning votes only in his own home *tambon* of Nam Noi, which had been his voting base as a provincial councilor. This assessment turned out to be correct, and Niran was to gain little over four thousand votes.

TRT CHALLENGERS: REPUTE, SUPPORT, AND RESOURCES

To the Democrat MPs and their key party supporters, none of the Chat Thai and Mahachon candidates posed any danger to their three most vulnerable seats in Constituencies 3, 5, and 8. Everybody knew that it was the TRT candidates and their combined resources of local and party support that represented the real threat. Here, the new and unblooded Democrat contenders faced a challenge to assert their personal credentials as parliamentary representatives. Since mid-2003, senior TRT officials had been scanning the Songkhla constituencies for eligible candidates for the 2005 national election, and numerous political aspirants had attempted to attract the party's attention. In keeping with its established formula for electoral success elsewhere in the country, TRT aimed to win seats by recruiting candidates with strong local reputations and support that were founded on the well-established electoral criteria of kin connections and the vote-canvassing influence of their local phuak constellations. To these traditional local factors of support, TRT aimed to inject the considerable force of its triumphant nationwide *krasae*—its media-driven message of policy successes fused with the image of Thaksin as national leader. For Songkhla, the TRT easily identified Constituencies 3, 5, and 8 as the Democrats' weakest points. By September 2004, the preferred candidates had been cultivated and selections were confirmed on the basis of secret popularity polling in the constituencies. These candidates and their supporters had a number of reasons to be optimistic that they commanded sufficient political resources to contest the Democrat ascendancy in their districts.

Sunthon Pathumthong: The Good *nai amphoe*

Sunthon Pathumthong enjoyed exceptional qualifications and high eligibility as a political candidate in Constituency 3, which the Democrats recognized when they first sought him out as a successor to replace his relative Phrai Phatthano. Unfortunately for the Democrats, Sunthon fell short on the one key criterion of party loyalty, because in late 2003, it was found that he had been successfully courted by TRT. It was only by pure accident that Sunthon had not stood against Wirat Kalayasiri for TRT in the February 2004 by-election as a result of neglecting to resign his membership in the Democrat Party within the required time span stipulated by electoral law. Although Sunthon was a career civil servant with no prior political experience (except for lending his influence for many years in favor of the Democrats), he was well placed to garner electoral support as a TRT candidate. In fact, he was confirmed as a TRT candidate as early as April 2004 when he was transferred back to Hat Yai from exile in Phangnga Province to resume his former post of *nai amphoe* and thus use his position to build foundations for voter support (*wang thansiang*). As a TRT member and candidate, Sunthon enjoyed the full benefits of TRT government patronage. Moreover, he had everything to gain and nothing to lose by running for office under the TRT banner. Classified by the party as a category "B" candidate, he was in receipt of at least 6 million baht from the TRT coffers for running his campaign. Furthermore, if he lost the election, he was able to return to his government job with a promotion to higher rank.[18]

As outlined by one of his optimistic campaign assistants, Sunthon's political eligibility had a number of advantages, including his high general public visibility as *nai amphoe* involved in numerous local development activities in many parts of Constituency 3 (which overlapped with the territory of Amphoe Hat Yai). For this, he had won the prestigious "*Khon Di Si Songkhla*" award for public service in the province in 2002. By virtue of his position and long service in the *amphoe* of Hat Yai, Sunthon commanded a detailed knowledge of the district and its problems, and—important for the task of building canvassing networks—he could draw on his links with *tambon* and village leaders as well as key community associations, such as housewives groups (*klum maeban*). Not the least, his voter support was seen to be enhanced by the fact of his local origins (he was born in Ban Phlu), and he and his wife's considerable family networks (*yat phi nong*) in the district. Key supporters of Sunthon estimated that the *khrueayat* factor (family networks) in the constituency doubly favored him, because of his kin affiliation to the locally prestigious Sawai Phatthano and his son Phrai. By exploiting this *thansiang* of the Phatthano family through drawing on common kinship connections and the substantial Phatthano family *barami*, it was hoped that Sunthon could split voters' loyalties away from the Democrats. In this calculation, Phatthano family *barami* could be separated from the strength of the family's Democrat Party association.[19]

Sunthon commenced laying the foundations for electoral support well before the official campaigning period began. He used the considerable advantages of his position as *nai amphoe* to garner popularity with the public as well as seek concrete campaigning support. An example of the former was his offer to residents of the *amphoe* that they could obtain gun licenses free from the usual onerous bureaucratic checks and procedures. This was not tied to any specific request for votes, but it was a tactic that was recognized by residents as an effort by Sunthon to gain general goodwill. More specifically, Sunthon personally approached local people with promises of rewards should they support his forthcoming campaign. One informant, a Democrat loyalist connected to Sunthon by distant marriage ties, recalled that he visited her home twice asking for her support as a vote canvasser. In return for this service, Sunthon promised that he would use his influence to obtain the transfer of her husband, an army sergeant, from his distant posting in Singanakhon District to Hat Yai, where they lived. She declined Sunthon's offer. Other informal methods used by Sunthon during this period were reported to include the distribution of coupons that allowed potential vote canvassers to treat friends to free meals at hotels.

On an organizational level, Sunthon needed to marshal the concrete support of networks for vote-canvassing purposes. It is not possible to assemble a comprehensive listing of all of the *hua khanaen* supporting Sunthon in Constituency 3, but through observation and interviews with a variety of informants, we can identify some key groups who provided support and their reasons for doing so. One key supporter was Seri Nuanpheng, a prominent TRT member and director of the party's campaign in the Ban Phlu area in the previous by-election. As already noted, Seri was the former mayor of Ban Phlu Municipality. His support was critical because Sunthon was using Ban Phlu, his own birthplace, as his key base to demonstrate support in the constituency. As a former Democrat phuak member, Sunthon and his wife (a widely connected teacher) had earlier lent their influence in backing Seri's opponent Worawat in his victorious campaign for the Ban Phlu mayoralty. This had created some resentment on Seri's part, but ultimately not enough to prevent him from cooperating in the cause of aiding TRT. Although Seri did not openly admit it, a victory by Sunthon would clearly further his prospects for future re-election as Ban Phlu's mayor.

Seri presided over a team of local supporters, both current and former municipal councilors, called "*Thim Santitham*." This was a unique local organization that assumed the character of a small political party, focusing on issues around local government and development. Originally formed as an organization to contest the Ban Phlu municipal elections, it continued in operation after Seri's election defeat in 2003. It comprised some twenty core members who met regularly and conducted discussions. Although presided over by Seri and holding its gatherings at a meeting room attached to Seri's home, the group debated issues and took decisions by vote. Members included both TRT and some Democrat supporters. *Thim Santitham* placed a priority on local issues, and the matter of offering support to Sunthon's campaign was debated in terms of the benefits the municipality would gain from Sunthon as a local member. The group voted formally to support Sunthon's candidature. Connected to *Thim Santitham* was a wider network represented by over a hundred local people belonging to an affiliated group called "*Yat Santitham*," comprising close relatives of Seri's team. It was this extensive family network that provided the core canvassing support and practical assistance for Sunthon in Ban Phlu.[20] Beyond his heartland base of Ban Phlu itself, Sunthon was aiming for assistance from the *kamnan* and *phuyaiban* throughout the constituency who had thrown their weight behind Thawisak in the by-election—notably those in the *tambon* of Khuan Lang and Khu Tao—but additionally further *tambon* councilors known to Sunthon in his capacity as *nai amphoe*.

By late December, a few weeks before he was due to officially resign and take up his TRT candidature, Sunthon's campaign assistants were confident that his strong family and phuak connections with the Phatthano family were effectively fragmenting the local Democrat organization. A former close assistant of Phrai and party branch secretary had become head of the TRT election coordination center, and several other leading Democrat branch officials also defected to join Sunthon's campaign. It was known that Sunthon and his canvassers were spreading the word in the electorate that he had the blessings of Sawai Phatthano. Sunthon was clearly hoping that Sawai's substantial personal *barami* could be split from its Democrat Party associations in boosting his local legitimacy. Commenting on how this reflected on the particular foundations of popular Democrat political support in Constituency 3, one Democrat branch official in Hat Yai pointed out, "*Udomkan* is part of it, but *yat* [kin] are also part of it."[21] Some journalists and Democrat officials were certain that strong family obligations were impelling

6.2 Sunthon Pathumthong (center) on a neighborhood door-knock, January 2005.

Sawai and his son Phrai to offer clandestine support to Sunthon's TRT campaign. There was certainly substance to these suspicions, for it became clear after official candidate campaigning began in January that Police Sergeant Chum, a prominent bodyguard of Sawai and Phrai—and long identified as a solid Democrat—was giving the support of his small phuak to Sunthon in both canvassing and the arrangement of rallies. Although openly present at Sunthon's rallies, these phuak members were careful not to wear TRT jackets. I first encountered this group as Democrat canvassers in the 2004 by-election and canvassers for Phrai in his mayoral campaign. Responding to my direct enquiry about the meaning of his support for a non-Democrat, one of Chum's young followers, Mohammad, remarked with a smile of embarrassment, "We are helping Nai Sunthon because he is a good person." Chum later confided to me that he had lent support as a vote canvasser in Sunthon's TRT campaign because of personal esteem and loyalty, not through any pressure from Sawai or Phrai.[22]

In preparing his campaign for Constituency 3, Sunthon directed his attention to undermining both the Democrats' constituency network base and their claims to voters' foundational loyalty and trust.

He did this by taking advantage of the range of concrete patronage resources available to him in his position as a government official. Just as important in his electoral strategy were kinship solidarities and the symbolic resources represented by his reputation as a "good person" and a locally born citizen.

Worawit Khaothong: The *Nakleng Nayok*

During the contest for the Songkhla PAO presidency in 2004, Worawit Khaothong had been careful to downplay his party's political alignments. His narrow electoral defeat at the hands of Nawaphon Bunyamani showed that he enjoyed a high popularity throughout the province, but particularly in his home district of Ratthaphum and the nearby *amphoe* of Khuaniang and Bang Klam, which fell within Constituency 5. Worawit had been publicly ambivalent about his connection with national political parties, attempting to restrict the election to local issues. Local journalists had tried to link him with the TRT Party, but he had denied that he was benefiting from any direct affiliation. He had been helped in his rallies by the two local Democrat Party personalities Thawon and Winai Senniam, who had stressed the non-party basis of their public support for their friend. At the same time, however, Worawit received funding support from close associates in the national political world, notably Chongchai Thiangtham, a prominent Chat Thai Party politician of Suphanburi (secretary-general of the party and former deputy minister for Labor) and the influential TRT Deputy Minister of the Interior Pracha Malinon. After the PAO election defeat, Worawit publicly aligned himself with TRT. His appointment as the party's official candidate for Constituency 5 was publicized in September.[23]

Worawit's many supporters in the constituency were confident that he had a strong chance against the new Democrat candidate because he could draw on a high local reputation as a former PAO president with *phakphuak* and family networks that were even more extensive than those of Niphon Bunyamani, who had dominated Constituency 5 as Democrat MP through an extensive collection of phuak. In the past, Worawit had acted as a key *hua khanaen* for Niphon, and his dense network of canvassers had helped to ensure Niphon's electoral success. Now, however, Worawit aimed to use his networks to help defeat the Democrats. In contrast to Sunthon in Constituency 3, whose eligibility was based on local origins and professional expertise as *nai amphoe*, Worawit could claim a record of political success as a long-serving local representative whose position had been gained through elections and vindicated in tangible form in public works and other services to the locality. Worawit could draw on a high local reputation as a *nakleng*-style leader, with *phakphuak* and family networks that were even more extensive than Niphon's. Widespread local knowledge of his close connections with illegal gambling dens and suspicions of his involvement with crime and *mue puen* (gunmen) did nothing to diminish Worawit's popularity. As one of his main vote canvassers in Khuaniang emphasized:

> He lost the [PAO] election because of the strong *krasae* of the Democrat Party, but if the competition with Nawaphon had been based on ability and personal qualities, he would have swept the polls. In this forthcoming national election, on a person-for-person basis, many people here see that he has a much better chance of success than Praphon. This is because he has many *hua khanaen* and a strong vote base in every area and because he is a *nakleng*. He is widely known and generous, and has many *phakphuak* and close friends.[24]

Informants close to Worawit estimated that he had spent 40 million baht in the PAO election campaign of 2004, which included his own funds as well as money from national-level political connections and business contractors in the province. His personal funds had been exhausted in the PAO campaign, and he could not expect further support from the business contractors. Yet for the national election, he was able to draw on considerable funding from the TRT party's central organization, supplemented by support from some close friends. This amounted to an estimated 14 million baht.[25]

Surasak Mani: The Local Hero

TRT's candidate for Constituency 8 was Surasak Mani, a man whose background and situation is somewhat different from that of Sunthon and Worawit. To be sure, they all shared a former allegiance to the Democrats, but Surasak was the only one who had run in national politics before. He had also been a senior Democrat Party figure in the province, not just a phuak member who lent assistance in elections, like Sunthon and Worawit. On the other hand, he had never held office in local government or administration like these two men. Surasak was born in the Chana District of humble origins. His parents were small-scale rubber growers and his early education was gained when he served as a novice monk in a Songkhla temple. Surasak later gained a bachelor's degree in business administration and later another degree in political science. In his mid-50s, he could boast of practical political experience spanning over twenty years, gained mainly in his capacity as a Democrat Party branch official and as the long-serving assistant of the prominent Songkhla Democrat MP Trairong Suwankhiri. According to Surasak, he left the Democrats in 2000 because he was denied a promised opportunity to stand as a candidate for the newly established Constituency 8. In describing the circumstances surrounding Surasak's departure, Democrats in the constituency pointed out that at that time Trairong had counseled him to be patient and stay with the party to wait for a future opportunity, but Surasak felt betrayed and hurt (*noichai*), and left the party harboring deep resentment.[26]

Over the years of his work for the Democrat Party, Surasak built a strong phuak in the districts of Chana, Na Mom, and Thepha, which comprised a group of senior party branch members, chief among whom were local *tambon* politicians and PAO councilors. These men shared Surasak's sense of betrayal and defected with him *en masse* from the Democrat Party. One of his phuak members, Thip Phromphet, a provincial councilor, explained the general feeling in the phuak that the party's refusal to grant candidature to Surasak for the 2001 elections had demonstrated that "the Democrats are not democratic" (*Prachathipat mai pen prachathipatai*).[27] With the support of this phuak, Surasak campaigned in the 2001 elections under the Ratsadon Party banner, choosing this party for no other reason than that it was the only party needing a candidate in the constituency.[28] Among his phuak and the people of the constituency generally, Surasak enjoyed strong support from Buddhists and Muslims alike. This was shown in the 2001 election when Surasak's high personal reputation and the effectiveness of his phuak support garnered him an impressive 20,418 votes. He came in second to the incumbent Democrat MP Wichit Suwit (34,503 votes) and attracted more votes than the New Aspiration Party (17,403), which courted support among the constituency's majority Muslim population with a Muslim candidate. By contrast, the TRT candidate for Constituency 8 had attracted only 1,003 votes, ranking a poor fifth among the contenders.

Although defeated in 2001, Surasak continued to nurture his political ambitions. Committed to "doing whatever is useful for society," he promoted a variety of activities among communities, which ensured his public visibility. Without the benefit of support from a political party, he funded these various community-related activities himself, with income derived from his five mobile telephone shops in Hat Yai and profits from fish farms. In conducting these community development activities, Surasak simultaneously sought to expand both his reputation and voting base. As one phuak member expressed it with a knowing smile, by promoting community projects, Surasak was "*ha siang tai din talot*" (always canvassing for votes underground). One of the highly visible projects in 2003 was an arrangement to ensure that young villagers obtained motorcycle licenses and training in traffic safety. In October, with the cooperation of Chana's technical school and the provincial traffic police, Surasak staged a large meeting to publicize this effort. It was a measure calculated to gain popularity and future votes, because Surasak was addressing an issue of great concern to families in the area. Surasak ensured wide publicity for such efforts by acting as a regular speaker on Hat Yai's community radio stations. Well before his formal announcement as a candidate, Surasak made it publicly known that he was hoping to run in the next elections under the TRT banner. When I first met Surasak in October 2003, he was confident that he would gain selection by TRT as their candidate for Constituency 8 because of his high public profile. In September 2004, he was officially declared TRT's candidate, and in November he was given a category "C" by the party, which signified a fairly slim measure of confidence in his victory. By late December, however, a poll conducted by the newspaper *Krungthep Thurakit* suggested that Surasak would actually win against the young Democrat newcomer Naracha Suwit.[29] According to one of his close associates, TRT funded Surasak to the tune of approximately 7 million baht.[30]

Democrat spokespeople in the Constituency 8 branch were reluctant to admit that Surasak posed any danger to their campaign; however, some senior party members elsewhere in the province were worried. Thamanun Selimin, a well-known Muslim Democrat loyalist and province-level party branch chairman (*Prathan Changwat*), confessed that Surasak was "dangerous" because he possessed the popular

6.3 Surasak Mani extolling his local commitment and the benefits of Thaksin's politics at a Thepha District rally.

qualities of a *nakleng—chaithueng, khon thi kwangkhwang* (close to the people, generous), together with considerable financial resources supplied by TRT. Thamanun emphasized that in 2001 Wichit Suwit had won the seat by only some fourteen thousand votes, and since that time, he had been ill and unable to visit people in his constituency. Prior to the election, Wichit himself expressed concern and admitted to me that his lack of public appearances in the constituency over the past year was a weak point for the Democrats.[31] In Thepha District, a local village headman and Democrat *hua khanaen* pointed out that although local people were still strongly supportive of the Democrat Party, when the personal qualities (*tua bukkhon*) of Surasak and Naracha were compared, Surasak was clearly the stronger. Moreover, he added, Surasak's phuak of close supporters, comprising *tambon* and province-level councilors, was active and ever-present in the district.[32] This was true, particularly in the rubber-growing district of Amphoe Thepha, where two of the district's three provincial councilors were active members of Surasak's phuak. These men tried to capitalize on their own political capital and channel it into voter support for Surasak. Thip Phromphet, one of these councilors, had a range of *phon ngan* (tangible achievements) to his credit among local communities, represented in particular by income-generating projects and local computer centers. His projects spanned at least a hundred activity-based community groups in Thepha, and he hoped to garner support for Surasak through them.[33]

A further factor working in Surasak's favor was the absorption of the New Aspiration Party into TRT—this meant that the Muslim supporters who had formerly voted for that party, largely because of their admiration for Wan Noor and his Muslim *Wadah* faction, would transfer support to the TRT candidate. It was ironic perhaps, as one of Surasak's Muslim assistants remarked, that the Buddhist Surasak appeared to be more popular among Muslim voters than Thai-Buddhists. Most of the constituency's Buddhists—35 percent of the constituency's voting population—were concentrated in its northern district of Na Mom, and here Democrat support was strong. However, the party support in the electorate was not aligned on ethno-religious lines because the Democrats had always enjoyed strong Muslim support and, for many years, the Democrats had been careful to present at least one Muslim candidate in Songkhla's Muslim majority districts. When campaigning began in earnest in January, Surasak's tacticians believed that of the three *amphoe* of the constituency, Thepha would vote predominantly TRT, Na Mom would vote Democrat, and the main battleground for votes would be Chana, the most populous and developed *amphoe*.[34]

WEIGHING THE ODDS: STRENGTHS AND WEAKNESSESS

TRT had endorsed its candidates in Songkhla according to the same criteria it applied elsewhere, criteria that prioritized local repute as the key factor in electability. In all three of the Democrats' vulnerable constituencies, the TRT candidates expressed confidence that if personal factors (*patchai tua bukkhon*) on a candidate-to-candidate basis counted, then they stood a fighting chance against their Democrat rivals. In addition, Sunthon and Worawit counted their extended families in these constituencies as providing a core voting and canvassing base. They also commanded extensive financial resources derived from their sponsoring party, and, in the case of Worawit, sponsorship from rich patrons. Worawit commanded about 14 million baht in funds, Sunthon somewhat less (though probably more than the 6 million baht that his brother admitted to me), and Surasak was given at least 7 million baht (though he complained to me that his funding was less than he had received as a Ratsadon Party candidate in 2001). Sunthon and Surasaks' Democrat opponents (Wirat and Naracha) were relying largely on party funds, but Worawit's opponent Praphon could supplement party funds with his own considerable business-derived wealth. The TRT challengers pronounced strong messages of local development and aimed to maximize their appeal with the predictable claim that electing members to the government party would deliver rapid and preferential constituency benefits.

Yet two factors weighed in the Democrats' favor and against the TRT contenders in these three constituencies. The first was the specter of the formidable Democrat Party *krasae* that could be generated by the party's orators. If strong enough, this "tide" of popularity could outweigh any deficiency in candidates' personal attributes and local repute. As one of Hat Yai's local newspaper editors confided to me a month prior to the election, it was the existence or not of a strong Democrat Party "tide" that would determine Democrat success or failure against TRT in the province. He predicted (correctly, as it turned out) that Chuan Leekpai's role as the symbol of the party would be absolutely crucial to bolstering the fortunes of the weaker Democrat candidates. Reinforcing this Democrat advantage was the second factor—the unpopularity of Thaksin in the region, a resentment that had grown considerably over the past year in the wake of the increasing border violence. This widespread resentment against Thaksin prevented Songkhla's TRT challengers from calling on Thaksin's leadership image as an electioneering asset, one that was readily available to their compatriots in Bangkok, the north, and the northeast.

CHAPTER 7

The Campaigns: Symbols and Rhetorical Performances

IN THE campaigns for the February 2005 national election in Songkhla, the TRT challengers and Democrat defenders both employed the full repertoire of well-established tactics commonly used to seek votes in the south and the country generally. These techniques of persuasion extend from legally prescribed formal and public activities to informal and illegal methods. This chapter examines the symbolic dimensions of the public efforts made by the competing parties and candidates to persuade voters, encompassing the performative arenas of election rallies, ritualized face-to-face encounters, and the use of value-laden language to project electoral eligibility and denounce opponents. Strategically deployed rumor and public scandal, always important in Democrat campaigns, also played an important role in demonizing their TRT opponents.

For TRT candidates, a symbolic foundation was needed to counter the calls on voters' foundational loyalties by Democrat canvassers and that party's formidable orators. While the TRT contenders in the Democrats' three vulnerable constituencies of Songkhla Province enjoyed advantages in the key resources of local repute as well as finances, they were hamstrung by both organizational and symbolic disadvantages. Popular hostility toward Thaksin in the south had increased over 2004 as the border violence escalated. The ongoing "fire in the south" which the Democrats claimed had been created by

Thaksin's wrong-headed policies was a major trump card wielded by the party, and was skillfully used to erode Thaksin's legitimacy among many in the electorate. Against this, the local TRT candidates had no answer, and they were unable to use Thaksin fully as a party leadership symbol in their campaigns. They were also restricted in their own rhetorical ambit because any criticism of the publicly revered Chuan Leekpai would draw disapproval from ordinary voters. While Chuan and the Democrat leadership roamed the region freely to aid candidates' campaigns, Thaksin did not come to the south to help his candidates, leaving this job to a number of his TRT lieutenants. A major vote-buying scandal surrounding government minister Newin Chitchop was skillfully fueled by Songkhla's Democrat MPs in mid-January, and seems to have caused the cancellation of a planned visit by the prime minister. At the organizational level, there was little cooperation among the TRT contestants, who had more contact with the Bangkok party center than with each other. The TRT constituency campaigns were thus largely isolated from each other, unlike those of the Democrats, whose party members circulated through each other's electoral districts as did key party leaders.

THE TRT ASSAULT: LOCALISM, *PHON NGAN*, AND DEVELOPMENT

Through their advertising and direct communication with people on door-knocking tours and at public rallies, the TRT candidates Sunthon, Surasak, and Worawit (together with their supporters) attempted to craft a basis for their eligibility and trustworthiness that drew on two contrasting yet complementary sources: traditional and conservative local loyalties embodied in their personal qualities and histories, together with *phuak* loyalties and webs of person-community obligations; and the progressive imagery attached to TRT as a modern, performance and policy-based organization with a proven record of success and a decisive national leader. TRT's astounding electoral success in the rest of the country was based on this fusion (see plate 7.2).[1] In regions such as northeastern Thailand, the apparent contradiction between locally entrenched *barami*-focused voter bases and modernistic national-level policy delivery was resolved (or perhaps obscured) by the compatibility between local peoples' long-standing pragmatic criteria of "*phon ngan*" (results, achievements) and the wider discourse of "*phatthana*" (development). As Callahan and McCargo highlight, moral evaluations of candidates are also important in the northeast, and elections are viewed as a means of selecting trusted candidates to deliver tangible benefits to the electorate.[2] By contrast, in Songkhla—as elsewhere in the Democrat-dominated south—TRT candidates, however prominent they were, faced the supreme challenge of contending with popular understandings of national politics as moral contests, not simply choices about constituency-focused development or local repute. At the same time, the tough competition mounted against the Democrats in some constituencies would show that the eligibility criteria of personality-repute and achievement (*phon ngan)* could seriously threaten party-based voter loyalty.

Songkhla's TRT candidates shared a common approach in emphasizing their own personal qualities and the pragmatic advantages afforded to people by electing members of a party guaranteed to gain government. It reflected the efficiency-centered and materialist discourse pronounced triumphantly by Thaksin in his national election proclamations, evoking the idea of political representation as a matter of service delivery and meeting concrete needs. Sunthon Pathumthong's appeal to voters' trust in Constituency 3 was articulated in familiar idioms that centered on his local origins, local family ties, love for and knowledge of the locality, and *phon ngan*—criteria of eligibility that were well recognized in Songkhla's local-level politics, as we have seen. The critical task was to harness these personal credentials to the identity and achievements of the national level TRT party and define the stakes of the national election primarily in terms of development opportunities and material progress for the constituency, thus contesting the Democrat portrait of the electoral battle as an issue of morality and power. The emphasis was embodied in Sunthon's core campaign slogan, "Choose the person that we love—choose the party that has shown results."

Like Sunthon, Surasak's public claims to electoral worth in Constituency 8 were made on the basis of his closeness to the area and his proven record of activities that had borne very tangible and practical results. As he emphasized to local journalists in November 2004, he had achieved results even though he had "worked outside parliament." As far as he was concerned, the violence prevailing in the southern border provinces should not be at the forefront of election talk, rather the emphasis should be on *kan phatthana* (development) and *thongthin* (local matters). He announced a group of policies to uplift the district, including a plan to establish Amphoe Chana as a central marketing point for singing birds in the effort to bring income to local people, a proposal to promote an increase in the selling price of rubber tree timber, and a project to construct sports stadiums in every *amphoe*.[3] Surasak's slogan on billboards and brochures emphasized his local development message, "Please give me the opportunity for four years to provide development to Constituency 8 that you will see front and back." This idea was reinforced by large roadside billboards that portrayed Thaksin and Surasak as soccer players, together with inset photographs of development themes in the electorate. The billboard design was somewhat comical (probably unintentionally), with Thaksin and Surasak's heads appearing transposed onto pictures of different bodies. Nevertheless, the soccer player image was clearly aiming to impress parents and the youth of the electorate, and project the idea of teamwork (see plate 7.1).

7.1 Floating heads: One of Surasak Mani's TRT election billboards with Thaksin and himself portrayed as soccer players.

Worawit's billboard posters in Constituency 5 reflected the same objective of melding his local repute to the development opportunities offered by the prospect of electing a member into the government party. Naturally, Worawit's billboards highlighted his local origins and his former status as president of the PAO (together with his familiar nickname, "Nayok Chai"):

> *When the time comes . . .*
> *together we will develop Songkhla Province*
> *Worawit Khaothong* ("Nayok Chai")
> *A local person*

7.2 One of Worawit Khaothong's TRT election billboards. The slogans read: "It is time to develop Songkhla Province together" (middle), and "A local person" (bottom).

Another style of poster for Worawit featured a quotation from Thaksin Shinawatra, "Choose a person of the government party who can arrange for funds to come to the area." This slogan underlined the clear advantages to be gained by constituents if they returned members for the incumbent government, highlighting the way that Thaksin's administration aimed to de-legitimize parliamentary opposition.

Meeting the People

In common with electioneering practice, TRT candidates' chief means of directly contacting voters was through walks and tours through constituencies and by delivering speeches at rallies. Both methods served the dual purposes of communicating to voters and giving them some evidence of support through local people's responses and attendance. These activities began soon after the announcement of the election date in December, well before the candidacy registration date of January 10, the day when party numbers were issued.[4] The standard pattern for door-knocks (*kho pratu*) is to arrange for local supporters to accompany the candidates' entourages through their neighborhoods in the mornings and afternoons. In Hat Yai's suburban areas incorporated by Constituency 3, Sunthon had been able to garner support from *tambon* councilors who met him in their localities and assisted in handing out brochures to residents. He was followed by attractive female university students who had been hired to help, as well as assistants clad in party jackets who attached stickers and larger posters to doors and walls. Sunthon's prominent status as *nai amphoe* drew a greater amount of public attention than many of the non-Democrat candidates in other constituencies.

Sunthon's early morning visit to Tambon Khlong Hae on January 27 is a good example of his brisk and confident style that reflected his assurance and status as an experienced public official reintroducing himself to the public in a somewhat different guise. Accompanied by a group of seven assistants, he greeted residents face to face, stopping occasionally in front of individual homes to impart the key message of his own campaign. Ironically, his first encounter on entering the streets of Khong Hae was with a local Democrat supporter, a woman shopkeeper (and a Democrat Party member known to me). Her small shop was emblazoned with Democrat stickers, some of them dating from the 2001 election and featuring Chuan Leekpai in his prime ministerial robes of office. Sunthon managed this potentially embarrassing encounter breezily. He expressed mock surprise at the swathe of Democrat posters in the shop—"Oh! Prachathipat!"—and though the woman scowled in annoyance and refused to offer the customary *wai* (prayer gesture) of respect, he offered a smile and recited his rehearsed appeal to elect a "local" person (*khon phuenthi*) of the government party (*fai ratthaban*) who would benefit the locality. "You don't have to elect a member of the opposition," he declared, before walking away under the glare of the diehard Democrat loyalist. Just as Phrai Phatthano had invoked his established public rank as "*so so*" (member of parliament) in his door-knocks during the Hat Yai mayoral campaign, so too Sunthon referred to himself as "Nai Amphoe Sunthon" when announcing his arrival in neighborhood doorways. Some local people greeted him with a deferential *wai* to signal their respect. Short requests accompanied these encounters, "Please take this opportunity to elect a member of government that will help Hat Yai," or "This is a chance to change your party and change your representative," or, more explicitly against the Democrats, "You don't have to vote for the opposition, you've voted for them for a long time already—please use this opportunity to support a candidate who will work in the government."

Following Sunthon's door-knock, I spoke with his personal secretary who told me that it had been a success; however, direct evidence for this claim, based on people's polite smiles and ritualized public deference, was ambiguous. Out of more than three hundred households canvassed in the neighborhood that morning, I noticed that only one resident greeted Sunthon with open acclamation. A number of the district's *tambon* councilors that followed the entourage remarked to me that they were supporting TRT because the government party offered an opportunity for furthering "local development." Their public accompaniment of Sunthon was a symbolic indication of this support to the Khlong Hae residents. But to read from the sponsorship of local councilors a wider support for Sunthon was a mistake. After his departure from Khlong Hae, for example, many residents ripped the TRT stickers from their walls and tore up the TRT brochures.

Sunthon could be more confident of support on his own home turf of Ban Phlu Municipality, where Seri's "Santitham" group reinforced person-based loyalties to Sunthon's extended family with constant neighborhood-level visits and daily injunctions at local teahouses. Elsewhere, particularly in the solidly Democrat areas of the Hat Yai suburbs, informal persuasion was needed. Sunthon's method here was to try to persuade people to change their habitual voting practices at the constituency level, while still respecting their sense of obligation to the Democrats. This was the job given to Police Sergeant Chum's phuak. Enjoying extensive familiarity with constituency families through their service with Phrai Phatthano and the Democrats, Chum's young phuak members approached local people during and after Sunthon's door-knocks and advised people to vote for TRT on the candidate ballot paper, while continuing to affirm old loyalties by voting Democrat on the party-list ballot papers.[5] In addition, Sunthon tried to capitalize on his close relations with the Phatthano family. He also had the rumor spread throughout neighborhoods that the highly respected former Democrat MP Sawai Phatthano had given his personal blessing to his campaign. Sunthon's effort to appropriate the force of Sawai's considerable repute to his electoral advantage was to engender a struggle with the sitting DP member Wirat Kalayasiri over Sawai's personal *barami*. The struggle between the two candidates to claim Sawai's authorized support and *barami* was prominent in gossip among both Sunthon and Wirat's key supporters throughout late December and early January. The issue was also picked up in the local press, by which time Wirat had publicly proclaimed Sawai's support.[6]

In rural districts, methods of meeting voters face-to-face in the campaigns were necessarily different from those employed in suburban and city residential areas. In the rural areas of Constituencies 5 and 3, and in the predominantly rubber-producing electorate of Constituency 8, settlements were widely dispersed. Here, candidates focused on touring market areas where people gathered in late afternoons or early mornings. Surasak based his canvassing on meeting people directly by visiting all villages in the constituency and conducting small rallies. From the day the election was announced, he embarked on an ambitious program that involved holding small rallies at five villages a day. As with

Sunthon, Surasak faced the challenge of requesting the votes of people who had long voted Democrat. He emphasized in a private discussion with me that his only hope was to campaign on the basis of his own personal qualities (*tua bukkhon*) and not rely so heavily on images of the TRT party. He stressed that, "If I campaign on the basis of 'party' too much I will fail for sure because many people do not like Thaksin." In admitting to local hostility to Thaksin, Surasak was acknowledging the effects of the Tak Bai incident (October 25, 2004) on popular sentiment in his Muslim-dominated constituency. Since Tak Bai, Democrat members had been actively distributing copies of DVD portrayals of the grisly event among the Muslim communities. Moreover, in the Buddhist areas of the constituency he had to be particularly careful, because people held Chuan Leekpai in high regard. In many villages he was only permitted by the headmen to hold his rallies if he promised not to criticize Chuan Leekpai. "In this rural constituency, many of the villagers have little education," he noted, "and, in fact, sometimes the *chaoban* don't even know that Chuan is no longer the prime minister!" In his talk with villagers, Surasak tried to separate the popular veneration for Chuan from identification with the current Democrat Party by emphasizing that the contest was now not between Thaksin and Chuan, but between Thaksin and Banyat, the new Democrat Party leader.[7] In his speeches to villagers, he drew on peoples' pity for Chuan, now in poor health, and criticized the Democrats for forcing this venerable ex-leader to travel extensively to attend Democrat election rallies. Surasak was well aware that he was far better known by local people than his young Democrat opponent Naracha. His public electioneering strategy aimed to maximize this personal eligibility by conveying the message that voting for the government party was the means to bring development benefits to the locality through the vehicle of a committed and experienced public figure, namely himself.

Surasak contrasted his campaign with his fellow TRT candidate Sunthon Pathumthong in Constituency 3. He noted that Sunthon's constituency was a highly urban one, where people tended to vote for parties, but here in the countryside (*chonnabot*), people focused on the personal characteristics (*tua bukkhon*) of candidates. As a politician, he needed to make the most of these dominant cultural sensibilities.

He needed to rely, he explained, on culture (*watthanatham*) for his repute and image making. His continuous work in the constituency in promoting development activities was something that earned him *sattha* (reverence). But he also knew from villagers' own talk that they felt sympathy for him (*songsan*), because he had worked so hard in the district without any support from political parties. Announcements by Surasak's assistants that he was traveling to each of the 224 villages in the constituency were deliberately calculated to impress people with Surasak's conscientious commitment and sacrifices to serve the people. He hoped that both of these traditional sentiments of *sattha* and *songsan* could be harnessed towards advancing his electoral objective. In these village visits, Surasak presented himself as an ordinary *chaoban*. Instead of donning a TRT party jacket, he wore an ordinary checkered shirt with old jeans and wrapped a *pha khaoma* cloth around his waist. His speeches commonly began with accounts of his own humble birth and his early life working on his parents' small rubber plantation. Local commitment was the foundation of his message, and TRT was promoted as the proven vehicle to deliver development benefits to the area. Surasak's village visits commonly lasted for an hour and a half and attracted fairly small audiences—ranging from twenty to fifty people, but he was confident that many more residents listened to his amplified platform addresses from their homes.

Compromised Performances

Most TRT candidates in Songkhla aimed to mount a number of medium- and large-scale rallies (*wethi klang*, *wethi yai*). The medium-sized rallies were a means to address groups of people at an *amphoe* level, while the larger rallies were timed to be held close to election day and aimed to draw greater numbers of listeners because of the attractions of prominent TRT politicians. Ultimately, however, the medium-sized TRT rallies were somewhat limited as spectacles because they could not project a wider party presence. Since the TRT candidates were concentrating on their individual constituency battles, they did not gather at each other's rallies, in contrast to the Democrat events, where even medium-sized rallies presented a spectacle of party solidarity and the wider Democrat community with the attendance of party MPs and branch members from neighboring constituencies. In fact, Songkhla's TRT candidates rarely consulted each other at all throughout the election period. They relied above all on communication with the party center in Bangkok and through their own patrons in the party hierarchy. The TRT candidates were counting on a boost to their campaigns by the appearance of the party's *kongthap yai* (large army). Plans were being made for Prime Minister Thaksin himself to attend a large rally on January 23 in the Sadao District (on the border of Constituencies 7 and 8), but on January 16 a major scandal broke out surrounding Newin Chitchop (TRT deputy minister for agriculture), who had visited Hat Yai and was alleged to have held meetings to plan large-scale vote buying. As a result of this widely reported scandal, Thaksin's planned visit to the Songkhla constituencies was cancelled.[8] Although TRT spokesmen denied that Thaksin's cancelled visit had anything to do with the Newin scandal, it was clear that the reports had damaged the image of the party locally. It is probable, as local journalists suggested, that the TRT leadership feared that further visits by prominent TRT figures would be used by Songkhla's Democrat propaganda machine (headed by the wily Thawon Senniam) to further undermine local TRT campaigns in the province. During the critical campaign period from the middle of January onwards, Songkhla's TRT candidates were largely left to fend for themselves without the presence of their party's heavyweights, except for a rally appearance by Wan Noor and Wira in the Chana District in aid of Surasak's campaign on January 24. Thaksin himself concentrated on campaigning in the much more receptive northeastern region.[9]

TRT Rallies: Trustworthy Local Representatives for Development

In their final rallies, the TRT candidates and core supporters did their best to fuse the strength of localism, the personal repute of candidates, and the practical values of *phon ngan* to the national TRT party message of efficiency, successful achievement, and practical policy-based government. Sunthon's rally highlights the central features of these attempts to construct a framework of eligibility to counteract Democrat claims to popular loyalty. Like his opening rally held on January 10, Sunthon's final rally was staged in the heart of his home territory on a large sports field fronting Ban Phlu's largest temple, Wat Thep Chumnum. This time the large speaker's platform, flanked with VDO screens and speakers, was erected at the narrow end of the field to accommodate the larger numbers of listeners, who included villagers from distant *tambon* in the constituency transported to the venue by *kamnan*, *phuyaiban*, and *tambon* councilors. Plastic chairs had been set up to accommodate the listeners, although they were not all occupied. Later arrivals, including sunburned villagers bussed in by canvassers from outlying areas, sat in groups with friends and family on the grass. Sunthon estimated that there were five thousand people in the audience, but those present at the height of the rally (at 9:00 p.m.) probably numbered only half that figure. The deliberate location of the final rally in Sunthon's core home territory reflected a pattern commonly found in Thailand, where family-based and personal networks are concentrated close to candidates' homes.[10] Niran Kaenyakun, the Chat Thai candidate, also held his final rally in his immediate home *tambon* of Nam Noi. Sunthon needed to present a spectacle of support that would have an impact in the electorate, and in this, he shared with the Democrats the knowledge that attendance at rallies was a subject of common gossip in village and neighborhood teahouses, and that it played some role in impressing undecided or wavering voters.

Like Democrat rallies, this event can also be read as political theater and spectacle. In this case, Sunthon and his main supporters were attempting to construct a symbolic apparatus of solidarity founded on a sense of communal identification in support of a dedicated local personality, one that aimed to shift loyalties from the Democrats to the TRT Party. In the final week of the campaign, the key theme of Sunthon's final rally was reflected in new posters mounted throughout the constituency that featured the single word "*plian*" (change). The family and communal basis of Suthon's eligibility as candidate had been unashamedly advertised in literature distributed with his candidate brochures announcing that he was confident in relying on the strength of "*rabop khrueayat*" (the family system) as his main support. As the visitors started entering the venue at 6:30 p.m., the loudspeakers played the TRT Party song ("*Rak Thai Rak Thai*," Love TRT) interspersed with excerpts from Thaksin's speeches proclaiming past achievements and future goals of the TRT government.

By 7:00 p.m., the announcer Phayom Phromphet, a well-known *so cho* and technical school principal, took over the proceedings. So Cho Phayom, a popular local figure and experienced speaker, adopted a tone of jovial familiarity to introduce a number of local *tambon* politicians who mounted the podium and spoke of Sunthon's virtues and commitments to local development. Following the standard political rally format, a pre-recorded video program was then projected onto the large screens flanking the dais. The program portrayed the various environments of Hat Yai, stressing the city's importance as a commercial and population center, then focusing on scenes of Sunthon as *nai amphoe* involved in a range of development activities throughout the communities, featuring in particular close-up scenes of him shaking hands or otherwise greeting ordinary people. After this panorama of scenes demonstrating Sunthon's dedication to the locality, there followed testimonials in the form of television interviews, where local people praised Sunthon's efforts in assisting them during the disastrous floods of 2000 and for bringing various TRT programs to the locality (such as the *uea-athon* housing program). The dramatic verbal narrative accompanying the VDO program and the language of the speakers set the main themes dominating the rally event. Key terms were repeated to drive home local identification and Sunthon's personal qualities of eligibility—this was "Our Nai Amphoe Sunthon," with *khwam samat* (ability) and *khwam tangchai* (determination)—all of these qualities mirrored the qualities of Thaksin Shinawatra's government, which was founded, so they affirmed, on *nayobai* (policy) and a commitment to *kanphatthana* (development). Phayom followed with a rousing introduction to Sunthon, proclaiming, "Now, the time has come for Hat Yai to have change. This is a time for change! Change our representative from one party to the representative of a party who can bring funding from the government to this locality of ours (*phuenthi khong rao*)!"

Sunthon's own speech was dominated by the same key vocabulary. His address aimed to reinforce the meaning of the election as a simple matter of voters making a choice to ensure the development of the area and tangible improvement to their lives and their children's opportunities. This mirrored TRT's discourses at a national level, which defined politics as a matter of efficient administration (*kan borihan*) and reflected long-standing associations of proper government with stability and security.[11] The theme of administration was an idiom that suited Sunthon's own background as a government official. He deliberately assumed a southern Thai accent for his audience, but it was controlled by the measured speaking rhythm of the typical senior *kharatchakan*—clear, confident, efficient, and tinged with a touch of benevolence. He did not offer polemics, and he avoided any reference to southern Democrat charges of the government's use of state power in these elections, or to the serious violence pervading the neighboring border provinces—issues that were central in the Democrat Party rallies. The issues of the election were narrowed and funneled into the uncontroversial and practical questions of local development and the promised benefits to the families of the electorate. Sunthon proclaimed that TRT offered *phonprayot* (benefits) to the people of the locality, and his job was to act as the people's representative to assure that funds would be delivered. He confided that he turned to support TRT because it was an effective policy-based government. He had decided to stand as candidate because becoming a member of the government party was the only way he could translate his commitment to the locality into useful results. Supporting the opposition party was no use, he affirmed, because the opposition Democrats could not access funding for development. In claiming this, he was echoing Thaksin's mantra that supporting the government party would assure development benefits to localities, whereas supporting a party consigned to parliamentary opposition was of no practical significance to the people. Like the TRT leader, Sunthon was oversimplifying and misrepresenting the parliamentary system and the rights of all parliamentarians to lobby for their localities. It highlighted the ways that the Thaksin administration was aiming to shape the meaning of parliamentary representation in Thailand towards a Singaporean one-party state model—a system of rewards and punishments to constituencies.

Not surprisingly, in his account of his decision to join TRT, Sunthon did not elaborate on his former identity as a loyal member of Hat

Yai's Democrat phuak that centered on Sawai and Phrai Phattano. His change was expressed as a reflection of his deeper loyalty to the locality of his birth and his commitment to be of practical service to the people. His reference to the Democrats was, in fact, deliberately guarded. Instead of naming the Democrat Party, he referred to "another party" that people had elected in the constituency for many years, a party for whose constant support they had "received nothing" in return. Sunthon spoke of the numerous achievements of the TRT government, echoing the TRT slogan of four years of "repair" and a further four years of "building" strength in society. He related these to the audience in personal terms, emphasizing that these were "good things" for people and their children. He concluded with an exhortation to his listeners that it was critically important to bring about change in the party representation of this constituency, and made a personal appeal to members of the audience to canvass for extra votes in his support:

> If you vote for TRT—and TRT will be returned to government for sure this time—the policies of TRT will definitely be delivered to Amphoe Hat Yai and Constituency 3. Mother and fathers, brothers and sisters, why must you vote for me, Nai Amphoe Sunthon? Vote for Nai Amphoe Sunthon and there will be useful benefits [*phonbrayot*]. There will be benefits following government policies that will be shown in this area of Constituency 3 of ours for sure.
>
> I'm asking you—and I've never asked you for anything before—I'm asking you truly, please give me your votes for building opportunities, building the future for mothers and fathers, and your children. I'm confident that mothers and fathers, and brothers and sisters here have decided already. We have ten thousand votes assured here already, but this is not enough. You must go back home and urge your relatives as well—if each person here asks another ten people each, then through your determination you will surely get Nai Amphoe Sunthon Pathumthong for your representative. The approaching election day, February 6, will show if Hat Yai can change or not. I think that Hat Yai people are brave enough [*kla*] to change—change in order to build things that are good for themselves and their children.

Sunthon's appeal was followed by an address from a senior member of the TRT government, Wissanu Khrueangam, one of Thaksin's deputy prime ministers. Wissanu arrived late to Sunthon's Ban Phlu rally, after speaking at Worawit Khaothong's final TRT rally in Constituency 5, held in Amphoe Singhanakhon. Most local political observers judged that after the Newin Chitchop scandal of mid-January, TRT was wary of sending senior cabinet figures to assist local TRT candidates. In any case, Wissanu was probably the only suitable choice because he was both a native of Songkhla and also uncontroversial. His presence reinforced the conservative, paternalistic, and state-centered representation of government as "administration." Before joining the TRT government, Wissanu had been an exemplary bureaucrat, serving many of Thailand's governments as cabinet secretary. He was presented to the audience as an experienced public official qualified to judge the quality of Thaksin's government. Wissanu's major theme was the importance of stability for national development, and in this, he reinforced Sunthon's portrayal of the function of government as one of furthering development and progress (*khwam charoen*). Prime Minister Thaksin's administration, he stressed, was the only elected government that had ever served its full term in Thailand's history. Speaking from his own long experience as a cabinet secretary to seven of Thailand's governments, he pointed out that previous governments had been unable to implement policy because they were composed of unstable coalitions.

Wissanu elaborated on the theme of stability by emphasizing how in the last four years the TRT government had successfully devised and implemented policies that were long-needed for the country. To do this in the future, the government needed a firm majority. Prime Minister Thaksin's government represented a new era in Thai politics—an era where much-needed social and economic policy could be effectively implemented. This election in Constituency 3 was about sending a well-qualified local representative to parliament who would act to inform government ministers about the needs of the locality. In turn, relevant development would flow to the people of the locality. As a TRT MP, Sunthon would thus be a crucial link between the people and the TRT government, and his intimate knowledge of the needs of the area would be critical in order to guide projects. To help people comprehend the nature of this link, Wissanu drew on the example of the famous Tinsulanonda Bridge linking Ko Yo Island to Songkhla township and Singkhanakhon. Without the construction of the Tinsulanonda Bridge, the people of Ko Yo would have remained isolated and bereft of development. In portraying Sunthon metaphorically as this vital connecting bridge, he simultaneously evoked the image of the highly revered Songkhla-born Prem Tinsulanonda, former benevolent military ruler of the county. Wissanu reinforced the eligibility criteria that had been stressed throughout the evening, reiterating the key terms *khwam samat* (ability), *khwam tangchai* (determination), and, above all *nayobai* (policy) and *phatthana* (development). In electing Sunthon, the people would be assuring themselves of government attention. It was that simple.

DEMOCRAT RIPOSTE: DEMONIZING THAKSIN AND INVOKING THE POTENCY OF *UDOMKAN*

The Democrats of Songkhla countered the person-focused, localist, and development-based campaigns of their TRT rivals with a counter-representation of politics and eligibility that was founded on a critique of Thaksin's governing practices as "parliamentary dictatorship," and an emotive call to party loyalty based on a perennial *udomkan* that linked virtuous representatives with loyal voters in a common cause. The national party had attempted to devise competitive policies to TRT's swathe of populist initiatives. These were advanced under the rubric of, "Building People, Building the Future," which incorporated key policies concerning education and welfare. The aim was to free people of debt and build self-dependence by encouraging education and reducing centralized government. These various policy statements seemed to be thin copies of TRT programs. Moreover, their effectiveness was unproven, unlike the TRT initiatives, which, despite considerable criticism, had been embraced with enthusiasm in much of the country. Despite the Democrats' policy-based efforts, it was clear that TRT would win the election nationally by a large margin.

By January 2005, the national party changed tack to emphasize that the key Democrat election objective was to win a critical minimum number of seats (201 seats) in order to form a parliamentary opposition that was strong enough to mount no-confidence motions. The main campaign message thus became one of affirming the importance of maintaining a viable political opposition to Thaksin's TRT government. Unlike the 2001 Democrat campaigns in the south, when the tangible prospect of being returned to government with Chuan Leekpai as prime minister could be dangled before voters, in 2005 the task was to affirm the moral and political worth of returning a principled opposition party. Not surprisingly therefore, the dominant slogan on Democrat Party candidate's billboards and posters stressed the identity and continuity of the party with the assertive statement: "*Udomkan mai khoei plian*"—"[Our] *udomkan* Has Never Changed." The overarching theme and symbolism of the Democrat campaigning was the identity of the party itself as an enduring moral entity. The party and its *udomkan* were presented as a timeless essence that distilled the best of democratic ideals. The perfection of this embodiment was all the more clear when it was contrasted with its moral opposite, the TRT government and its amoral leader.

Democrat Resources: Symbols, Scandals, and Demons

The Democrats in Songkhla were unable to draw on the considerable national party resources that had been available to them in the by-election. Nevertheless, they enjoyed a number of advantages, even in the vulnerable constituencies. The by-election exit polls had highlighted considerable resentment among voters against the TRT government, in particular a widespread view that Thaksin was responsible for generating the disturbances in the border provinces. These animosities had increased during 2004 as the violence in these provinces worsened and spread into the southern parts of Songkhla itself. The Democrats had taken full advantage of this situation to condemn the government, and they targeted the Muslim communities of the electorates by distributing DVD coverage of the Tak Bai incident. Another highly tangible impact of the border disturbances was the dramatic slump in tourism, particularly to Hat Yai City, which seriously affected incomes of many people, from hotel owners to vendors and tuk-tuk drivers. These issues, of major concern to ordinary people of the province, were highlighted in the Democrat rallies in the 2005 campaign.

On an organizational level, and in stark contrast to the largely individual campaigns of the TRT candidates, the Democrats benefited from a high degree of cooperation and coordination between their parliamentarians, candidates, and party branch members. In rallies and in canvassing, candidates could count on the presence of other Democrat party members and speakers from around the province. They could thus present a strong spectacle of unity even at the level of middle-sized and small party rallies.[12] Medium and large rallies were organized at the junction of two or three constituency boundaries so that maximum effect could be achieved by concentration. The symbolic resources of the party—although they were strained by campaign demands throughout other parts of the country—were strategically deployed where they were most needed; hence the party's most powerful speakers and revered leaders, especially Chuan Leekpai, were used to buttress candidates' campaigns in the most vulnerable constituencies.

Integral to the Democrats' campaigning arsenal was its skill in sniffing out election malpractice among opponents and its ability to foment public scandal in the media. Democrat accusations of widespread vote buying and arbitrary uses of state power by TRT leaders played a key role in setting the crisis atmosphere that pervaded the Songkhla by-election, winning the moral high ground for the Democrats in that contest. So too, in mid-January 2005, with a remarkable ring of déjà vu, a major scandal was identified and publicized by the Democrats in Hat Yai. It concerned an alleged vote-buying exercise by Deputy Minister for Agriculture Newin Chitchop, who held a "conference" on January 16 at Hat Yai's Rubber Research Institute with numerous officials and TRT vote canvassers from Satun and Phatthalung Provinces. The exposure of the incident revealed just how pervasive was the Democrat spy network. The gathering was first identified as suspicious by a Provincial Election Commission official, retired Police-Colonel Mongkon Bunchum, a highly experienced PEC committee member. Mongkon had approached various canvassers gathered outside the meeting venue on January 16. Pretending to be a vote canvasser from the same province (he was familiar with the distinctive Phatthalung accent), he was told after making general inquiries that the men were gathering to "receive money." The news of this meeting also spread to a number of local journalists, one of whom was able to enter the conference room and tape the proceedings. He recorded a voice (allegedly Newin's) giving instructions to canvassers to buy votes, and promising rewards of 100,000 baht each to major canvassers if TRT was successful in the polls. Rewards were to be dispensed by provincial governors. This journalist informed Thawon Senniam, who also attempted to enter the meeting and confront Newin. The event attracted national press coverage and featured as a leading scoop in Songkhla's local newspapers. Though the central ECT in Bangkok claimed that it could not confirm the authenticity of the tape recording or identify the voice, the suspicious circumstances pointed to a deliberate attempt by TRT to buy votes. Mongkon openly revealed his identity to the press, and following this, both he and the local journalist (from the *Samila Times*) received threatening phone calls.[13] Thaksin distanced himself from Newin over the matter, and TRT itself was protected under law because charges could only be laid against individuals, not the party. Moreover, as a minister, Newin could not be classified as a candidate, and was technically not chargeable. Newin was finally cleared of the charges by the central ECT on February 17, on grounds that evidence was insufficient, but by this time the damage was already done. Coming at a critical time two weeks before the polling date, the Newin scandal was used at Songkhla's Democrat rallies to substantiate their claims of TRT perfidy. Thawon Senniam was the Democrat hero of the day, and he solemnly recounted the dastardly event before the party's rally audiences. The Newin scandal gave an important boost to Democrat efforts to undermine the legitimacy claims of the TRT candidates, and just as importantly, it prompted Thaksin to cancel a planned campaign trip to the south.[14]

The Democrat Campaigns: *Barami, Udomkan,* and Amoral Enemies

The Democrat candidates, assisted by their core leadership (*kaennam*) groups in the branches, employed the standard methods of door-knocking and personal appearances—combined with a mixture of small and medium rallies—to reach the maximum number of people in their constituencies. This was particularly important to new candidates, such as Naracha Suwit in Constituency 8, who needed to familiarize voters with his presence. In this, he was assisted by his father Wichit (former Democrat MP for the constituency) and his brother Atswin (deputy president of the Songkhla PAO) as well as his mother, who was widely respected. As in other constituencies, Democrat parliamentarians' wives played an important part in projecting their husbands' presence in the electorates and bolstering their popularity. In Naracha's case, the visible support of his parents highlighted the transfer of their *barami* to the son. Naracha's campaign was also assisted by the presence of Chatchai Sirirat, personal assistant and nephew of the prominent Songkhla Democrat Trairong Suwankhiri, who had represented the districts around Chana for many years as an MP. Chatchai, a skilled speaker and a staunch advocate of the party's *udomkan*, was sent to buttress Naracha's electioneering efforts and represent the authoritative voice of his uncle Trairong.[15] In the Democrat rallies, Chatchai acted to remind the electorate of Trairong's *barami* in the constituency.

TABLE 7.1

Canvassing Itinerary for Naracha Suwit (DP), June 26, 2005

Time	Activity
6:00–10:00 a.m.	- Walk in Sunday market, Maikan Bridge - Door-knock in Maikan Bridge District
11:00 a.m	- Visit villages - Attend ceremony at Hua Din to pay respects to Muslim religious teachers ("*thambun to-khru*") - Meet housewives group (*klum maeban*)
12:00 noon	- Visit factory ("S2K") and talk to workers
1:00 p.m	- Walk and door-knock in Noen Phichit Village
3:00–4:00 p.m	- Meet people at Noen Phichit village's Sunday market
4:00–6:30 p.m.	- Rally (without screen) at Noen Phichit Temple
7:00–10:00 p.m.	- Rally (with screen) at Phrompradit Temple School

Naracha's TRT opponent Surasak charged that Wichit had been neglecting the electorate, and in response to this charge, Naracha needed to make extra efforts to compensate for his father's absences owing to ill health over the past two years. To this end, he underwent a grueling daily regime of visits and speechmaking that committed him to campaigning at least sixteen hours a day. The example shown in table 7.1, taken from handwritten plans drawn up by his father for each day, highlights the range of Naracha's daily activities during the campaign. On the occasions when I attended Naracha's evening rallies held at the village and *tambon* level, he was frequently so tired that he could hardly string his sentences together coherently.

For more experienced Democrat campaigners like Wirat Kalayasiri, the demands of electioneering were not quite as taxing, partly because he was already known in the constituency, and also because he could rely on key branch members and other Democrat supporters to substitute for him in door-knocks when necessary. Nevertheless, Wirat was particularly busy in the evenings, usually rushing between speaking engagements at up to three rallies and also speaking at Democrat rallies to show support for colleagues in neighboring constituencies.

At the Democrat rallies, the speakers addressed common themes. Suffusing the rhetoric and content of the Democrat speeches—and common to the themes of all the Democrat speakers—was the stress on the moral gulf separating honorable Democrat politics from the unscrupulous, nepotistic, and authoritarian practices of Thaksin and his TRT government, a party that aimed to benefit the rich. TRT's materialistic, venal, and corrupt politics exemplified by rampant vote buying and use of state power—illustrated in particular by the example of the Newin Chitchop "money-for-votes" scandal—were contrasted with the pure motives of the Democrat opposition and its moral politics that upheld the sanctity of legal democratic processes. Commitment to this moral politics bound the Democrat Party to the southern people in a bond of trust. This image of a Democrat moral political community, united by a long history of mutual trust and loyalty, was skillfully invoked by Chatchai Sirirat at one of Naracha's rallies in the Na Mom District staged on the grounds of the Ban Phring monastery in late

January. In this forceful address to local villagers, Chatchai invoked his uncle Trairong's name to drive home his message:

> Dr. Trairong is very worried about Songkhla Province. He told me, "Now Songkhla Province has eight people [Democrat candidates]—but even if one of them loses in one of these constituencies, I will lose face." It's likely that you have made your decision already. I have met with brothers and sisters in many villagers, particularly in Amphoe Na Mom. They tell me, "*Phak Prachathipat*, doesn't have to come and give speeches here at all—even if you didn't come, we have chosen the [Democrat] party already." Some people have been party members since the time of Khlai La-ongmani. They have been party members for a very long time. Everywhere in Songkhla Province, there is a long-standing attachment to the Democrat Party already.

Devotion to this moral politics demanded that in this election loyal supporters returned the Democrats as a strong parliamentary opposition with a mission to scrutinize the government's conduct.

Democrat speakers made strong efforts to counter the persistent claims of TRT candidates—claims constantly reinforced by Thaksin's public pronouncements—that the key issue of this election was simply a matter of returning members to the government party in order to deliver efficiently development funding to localities. Democrat speakers therefore emphasized that returning members of parliament was an important matter of national importance. The role of the parliamentarian, in addition to representing the particular needs of localities, was to deliberate and debate on the making of national laws. Therefore, voters needed to trust the party in its choice of highly qualified and dedicated candidates to fight in a common cause against a government that was ruining the democratic process and misgoverning the country. There was no greater example of misgovernment than the problems of the Muslim-majority border provinces, which were highlighted in all the rallies.

In their arguments, Democrat Party orators interspersed concrete critiques of TRT policy weaknesses (often contrasting them with earlier Democrat government policies) with moral arguments, crafted to encourage the audience's feelings of political solidarity by appealing to their sense of trust, collective party loyalty, and honor. TRT's attempts to gain an unassailable majority in parliament in this election were represented by speakers not only as a prelude to further "parliamentary dictatorship," but also an insult to southern Thai honor. This was exemplified by Thaksin's focus on gaining a powerful symbolic victory in the Democrat heartland by targeting Chuan Leekpai's home province of Trang. The following extract from a speech by the Democrats' Constituency 4 branch chairman at one of Naracha Suwit's rallies is a typical example of this type of emotional appeal:

> Two days ago, I watched Thaksin interviewed on television. A journalist asked him what constituency he wanted to win most in Thailand. Thaksin answered that the seat he most wanted TRT to win was Constituency 1 in Trang Province! This is the birthplace of Chuan Leekpai! It shows he wants *mansai* (to inflict humiliation). This shows the character of the leadership of Thaksin Shinawatra. We are southern people. . . . I am confident that the Democrat party is a political institution that the people of Songkhla, the southern people, must depend on (*phuengphing*).

Other arguments marshaled against Thaksin tapped folk beliefs. During a speech in Thepha District, Niphon Bunyamani pronounced that never in Thailand's history had a national leader brought so much bad luck to the country as Thaksin. Echoing national press reports of a prominent soothsayer pronouncing Thaksin as a harbinger of bad luck, and drawing on a common topic of village talk, Niphon argued that the recent tsunami disaster was just one in a string of misfortunes that had befallen the country since Thaksin's accession to power. According to Niphon, these events—which included the bird flu epidemic and the southern violence—were proof that Thaksin's rule was deeply inauspicious.[16]

Wirat Demonstrates His Achievements and Claims Sawai Phatthano's *Barami*

Aside from these common themes focusing on undermining the legitimacy of TRT and upholding Democrat Party political integrity, the

Democrat candidates also needed to address specific issues relevant to the particular challenges facing them in their own constituencies. For Wirat, competing against Sunthon's campaign message that stressed *phon ngan* and local development interests meant using the rallies as a forum where he could demonstrate his performance in parliament and his practical achievements since gaining election a year earlier. Accordingly, the video program that was screened before Wirat's speeches featured scenes of him walking through the constituency and speaking in parliament during no-confidence debates against the government.

Wirat's rallies also provided the opportunity for him to deny effectively the stories spread by TRT canvassers that the revered former local Democrat MP Sawai Phatthano was secretly in favor of his opponent Sunthon Pathumthong. During the first week of January, Wirat had personally approached Sawai to gain his permission to produce billboards featuring Sawai's portrait alongside his own (see plate 7.3). For Wirat, this was the most potent means of symbolically disempowering Sunthon and scotching the rumors of Sawai's clandestine support.[17] The billboards were erected throughout the constituency and were mounted behind the speaking rostrum during rallies, together with others featuring Banyat and Chuan. In all his rallies held from January onwards, Wirat emphasized to his audiences that Sawai had granted him permission to display these posters. In this way, he publicly reclaimed the force of Sawai's local *barami* as an electioneering resource.

Naracha's Modernity and Southern *Udomkan* vs. Surasak's Political Promiscuity

Naracha's rallies were similarly used as an opportunity to counter the claims of Surasak and undermine his eligibility in Constituency 8. In addition to promoting his own candidacy by publicizing his self-sacrifice and commitment to practical local development, Surasak attacked his Democrat opponent's credentials by claiming that Naracha's candidacy was not gained by merit, but was rather an attempt by his family to perpetuate a political dynasty. In an effort to rebut this accusation convincingly, Naracha stressed to his audiences that he was well qualified for political life through his experience as his father's personal assistant

7.3 Wirat Kalayasiri claims veteran Democrat MP *Sawai Phatthano's* barami. *Billboard erected in Constituency 3.*

and his work in parliamentary standing committees. Most importantly, he emphasized that he had been chosen to stand for the seat according to the established procedures of Democrat Party pre-selection, through a voting process by a committee comprising MPs at the province level, which was later confirmed at the national party level. Not surprisingly, he omitted any reference to the party's vacillation about his candidature during 2004.

Naracha also played up his educational qualifications, which included bachelor's and master's degrees, both gained overseas. Through this, he presented himself as well qualified to serve at the level of national politics. Moreover his anecdotes of his experiences and observations during his study overseas (in India and the UK), together with his ability to speak English, highlighted his modernity and cosmopolitanism.

Naracha did not explicitly attack Surasak—he left that role to others—but by virtue of a clear contrast with his own sophisticated background, Naracha's TRT opponent was made to appear an ignorant country bumpkin and hardly fit to take on the responsibilities of a national-level legislator. Naracha admitted to his comparative youth as a parliamentary candidate aged just thirty-five, but he argued that this was an advantage, not a drawback, because he would be well placed to relate to the young people of the constituency and promote useful projects to enrich their lives, including educational seminars on public affairs and local issues.

Naracha left it to the other speakers to explicitly criticize his TRT opponent, and Surasak had given his detractors plenty of ammunition. His most critical weak point was his earlier Democrat affiliation and his subsequent defection. On his brochures and name cards, Surasak had listed as one of his political credentials his long service to the Democrat MP Trairong Suwankhiri. Local Democrats regarded this as completely unacceptable, given the fact that Surasak was competing against his old party. His political desertion laid him wide open to attack for committing the most heinous sin for the Democrats—abandoning the party, and thus revealing his lack of sacred *udomkan*. Surasak was lambasted as the embodiment of naked opportunism, without ideals and without loyalty, a representative of the selfish motivations exemplified by the politicians in all the non-Democrat parties of the country. Against the pathetic figure of Surasak, Naracha was projected as a "child of the party," committed to an *udomkan* that could not be purchased by rich political parties. One skilled Democrat orator, a *so cho* from Singhanakhon, demolished Surasak's claims to eligibility and simultaneously elevated Naracha as an embodiment of the party's *udomkan* in these terms:

> Who is Surasak and where does he come from? Surasak was the secretary of Dr. Trairong. He was not satisfied with *Prachathipat*. Where did he go the last time? I forget!—Oh yes, he went to the Ratsadon [Party]. We see that today Thaksin wanted him to go with Thai Rak Thai [Party]. People of this type, they don't have *udomkan*. They are people without dedication, without any commitment. The people of our home (*khon*

> *ban rao*) don't want them! The people of our home don't like them! Yesterday they were with one party. Today they go with the Chat Thai Party! The people of our home don't like this! Today Naracha Suwit is presented in the name of the Democrat Party. You have to believe that this boy has substance—he has bachelor's and master's degrees. We present this boy to you with assurance! Whoever we offer, we offer with assurance. We inform our brothers and sisters that this is the type of representative for a Democrat constituency. Brothers and sisters don't retreat from this! This party and its commitment is what we all depend on. I remind you brothers and sisters, go into the polling booth on the 6th [February]. There are two ballot papers. . . Brothers and sisters don't be confused. Don't think about Surasak, forget him, don't think about Chat Thai, forget it! Write the number 4, on both ballots and that day brothers and sisters will gain the Democrat Party for this district and the country. If we become the opposition party, then let it be a strong opposition, and if it becomes the government, then let it be the face of the southern Thai people and then a southerner [Banyat] will be prime minister for three terms!

Rolled into the space of less than two minutes, this Democrat speaker rhetorically compressed a cluster of potent binary opposites that located the qualities of the individual candidates Naracha and Surasak within a wider moral struggle. This struggle was framed by key cultural norms: fidelity against faithlessness, the safe intimacy of home against alien outsiders, the transcendent wisdom of a permanent party against unprincipled and disloyal opportunists, and the collective political wisdom and honor of proud southerners against amoral and promiscuous political opponents.

EMBODYING THE DEMOCRAT SOUTH: THE PRESENCE OF CHUAN

The most potent electoral advantage wielded by the Democrats in the south was Chuan Leekpai, whose appearance in the electorates, whether in person or as a visual image on billboards, condensed the meaning of Democrat virtues expressed in the evocative slogan, "The *udomkan* that never changes." In the Democrats' vulnerable constituencies of Songkhla, the TRT candidates knew that they could not directly compete with the symbolic force of Chuan in rallying loyalty among ordinary people, whether Buddhists or Muslims. In early January, Surasak Mani confided to me with a sense of frustration and resentment, "They [the Democrat Party] will use Chuan. This is my weak point. People are still devoted [to Chuan]. Even if Chuan doesn't come here, they'll have his picture stuck all over the place—and they'll get votes that way.[18] As a veteran former Democrat, Surasak knew how the party deployed its symbols, and his predictions were correct. As the election campaigns increased in intensity in mid-January, there was a palpable change in the character of the Democrat Party billboards. In the first half of the campaign period, posters featured candidates' portraits together with smaller pictures of party-leader Banyat and Chuan. Two weeks before the election date, these were being supplemented, and sometimes replaced entirely, by large posters featuring only the face of Chuan together with his handwritten personal appeal to the voting public.

Although Chuan was unwell (at least this was the news spread among the electorate) and had limited time because of the high demand for his presence in many other constituencies—particularly in the south—the geography of his visits in Songkhla show that he was skillfully deployed to bolster popular support in the most hotly contested constituencies. Accompanied by Niphon Bunyamani (Democrat campaign director for the Muslim border provinces), Chuan was brought through Songkhla on his way to and from visits to the provinces of Yala, Pattani, and Narathiwat, where the Democrats aimed to win seats from TRT (the Muslim *Wadah* group of the former National Aspiration Party). On these tours, Chuan spent much of his time assisting Naracha's campaign in Constituency 8, visiting Chana and Thepha on two occasions in the space of four weeks.

On the afternoon of January 27, the Constituency 8 Democrat Party branch arranged a rally in front of Thepha railway station adjoining the town's market as a prelude to Chuan's visit. The event began at 3:30 p.m., and as party officials delivered their addresses, Naracha, his parents and other party members circulated the town canvassing and publicizing Chuan's arrival. Chuan did not arrive until the sun had already set, by which time hundreds of townspeople in this predominantly Muslim township had gathered in anticipation. About a hundred plastic chairs were set up to accommodate listeners, but by dusk the waiting crowd was so large that it filled the adjacent market area and eager onlookers spilled out into the nearby streets. Provincial buses were unable to pass through the market area, and had to be diverted by the police.

Chuan's arrival (at around 8:00 p.m.) generated a flurry of excitement, and it was only with difficulty that he was able to reach the speaking platform mounted on the back of a pickup truck. With children playing in front of the truck and Naracha standing respectfully at his side, Chuan commenced his address in his characteristically intimate and humble manner. Apologizing for the brevity of his appearance, he began by reminding listeners that Songkhla people had voted overwhelmingly for the party in the 2001 elections, gaining victory in all eight seats. With the exception of the border provinces, where the party had been unable to win six seats, the whole of the south had returned Democrat representatives, and this, he stressed, had made the party very proud. He pronounced with gravity that this showed how much the party owed the people, "I tell all parliamentarians that they should never forget the moral debt that we owe to the people" (*ya luem bunkhun khong prachachon*). Chuan tailored his talk to this predominantly Muslim audience in a district that was feeling the destabilizing effects of the violence in nearby Pattani Province. He had recently been assisting the campaigns in the Muslim border provinces, and reported to the audience that people there were welcoming the Democrat Party. This showed that people realized that the TRT government in the past four years was the direct cause of the problems of insecurity and violence. Never in a hundred years had so many deaths occurred as in this period presided over by Thaksin's government (loud cheers and clapping followed). TRT was using the democratic electoral system as a tool (*khrueang meu*) to expand its dictatorial power and control over all arms of government and the media. Never in all his long years in politics had he witnessed this. At the same time, Thaksin and his government were making themselves rich, "They're getting richer, but not us!" (loud cheers)

Chuan closed his address at Thepha with an exhortation to the audience to return Naracha to parliament, reminding them that, "I love *phi nong* and I thank *phi nong*." As Chuan was driven away, Niphon Bunyamani stayed on to address the crowd. He did so in his usual aggressive and colloquial manner:

> You've just heard Nai Chuan speak. He has not much time because there are many places to visit—he is tired and we didn't even have time to eat on our way. You've heard Nai Chuan, who has been prime minister of this country twice. He has governed with honesty and without corruption, unlike the present government. This is Nai Chuan, the child of an ordinary villager (*luk chaoban*). *This* is what our party is all about! (loud cheers and claps)

Niphon continued with a particular emphasis on stories of TRT vote buying in the district, and responded with pugnacious defiance, "We know they are offering you 1,000 baht for votes, so take as much of their money as you can, but vote *Prachathipat*."

Chuan's final tour through Songkhla took place four days before polling day. Traveling from Pattani in the morning, Chuan first stopped at Chana township where he accompanied Naracha on a canvassing cavalcade. In the early afternoon, he was then driven to Wirat's constituency on the outskirts of Hat Yai, where he spoke briefly to eager crowds that had been waiting for several hours. He then proceeded to Khuaniang and Singhanakhon, populous districts in the hotly contested Constituency 5, and thence to Phatthalung. Chuan's visit to Singhanakhon was timed to coincide with the largest of the Democrat rallies, strategically positioned so as to bolster support for Praphon's campaign against his popular TRT rival, Worawit. The excitement prevailing among the crowds that assembled to catch a glimpse of Chuan during his brief visits in Songkhla Province showed the continuing drawing power of this Democrat Party icon. In his brief addresses, Chuan condensed two fundamental themes—he represented the election as a heroic and uneven struggle to uphold democratic processes against the TRT government's use of money and state power in these elections, and to oppose Thaksin's disastrous policies towards the border provinces. In their support for this great task, he praised ordinary Democrat voters for their steadfast loyalty to the party.

Chuan's visit to a district of Wirat's Constituency 3, on the edge of Hat Yai, generated great excitement and anticipation, and is worth describing here (see plate 7.4). Under a hot noonday sun on February 2, several hundred people gathered under awnings to await Chuan's arrival at the sports field fronting the Wat Thep Chumnum School in Ban Phlu. The waiting crowd was dominated by middle-aged women, but among them were also a number of civil servants taking advantage of their lunch hour to attend. Most of the women held bunches of flowers to present to Chuan. They were addressed by Democrat members of party branches from Constituencies 2 and 3. The speakers included a branch official who was also a public servant. He emphasized that he was speaking in his capacity as a Democrat member and pointed out that he was on his lunch break, so his political activity was legitimate. The crowd waited for nearly two hours for Chuan's arrival. During the long wait, branch officials clad in party jackets took turns to fill the time by speaking about Democrat policies and the evils of Thaksin's government. Nathawut, the Constituency 3 branch chairman, took the opportunity to refer to Sunthon's new campaign posters as a way to reinforce the theme of Democrat loyalty: "Nai Amphoe Sunthon's posters say 'Change,' 'Change,' 'Change'—but don't take any notice! We are dedicated to *udomkan*, and our *udomkan hasn't changed.*" Sensing the occasion, and aware of listeners' growing impatience, speakers began focusing on the theme of Chuan's moral leadership. They drew comparisons between the present government and previous Democrat governments. As prime minister, Chuan demonstrated his clean-handedness (*mue sa-at*) and had never pressured officials to promote the Democrat Party or his own power.

A few minutes before Chuan's van entered the sports ground, Wirat arrived to prepare the listeners. He stressed that the visit would be short because Chuan was busy helping other constituencies and was very tired. The theme was a common one used to highlight the former leader's sacrifices for his party. Excited by Chuan's imminent arrival, women rushed to the front gateway and, with some difficulty, were formed into two lines by officials to flank Chuan's entrance. Wirat, still speaking from the podium on the other side of the field, was ignored in all the excitement. Chuan never reached the podium from the gate because he was crowded by scores of delighted female well-wishers as he stepped out of his van. Somehow, a party official managed to bring Chuan a portable microphone, and in the short space of less than two minutes before leaving, he could do no more than apologize for his brief visit and promote Wirat's campaign for Constituency 3, emphasizing that voters needed to choose the party's number for both ballot papers and ensure that all family members turned out to vote for the Democrats on polling day. After this lightening visit, Chuan went on to a similar gathering in Khlong Hae District, near a busy shopping area close to the Prince of Songkhla University. Here he was joined by Democrat MPs Wirat, Lapsak, and also Phrai Phatthano, whose crippled father Sawai was also brought to greet Chuan. Chuan's visits to Hat Yai were directed towards reinforcing Wirat's campaign in Constituency 3, but they were also seen as benefiting Lapsak's campaign in the heart of Hat Yai City. Whether or not Phrai was offering clandestine encouragement

7.4 The southern Democrat icon arrives: Chuan Leekpai crowded by proud admirers on his visit to Ban Phlu (Constituency 3), February 2, 2005.

to Sunthon, as had been rumored earlier, his presence beside Chuan at the Khlong Hae rally favored Wirat's cause by visibly associating his family with Chuan and the Democrats in general. Among many ordinary people of the Hat Yai electorates, Chuan's visits, however brief, bestowed honor (*kiat*) upon them and made them feel proud that they were objects of Chuan's personal concern.

The significance of Chuan's presence, both in person and as an image on billboards, in the election landscape of Songkhla was openly acknowledged by TRT protagonists such as Surasak. That the personal appearances of Chuan during January–February had made a tangible difference to the contests in the vulnerable Democrat constituencies was attested to by a number of vote canvassers and candidates on both sides. Somdet, a Democrat *hua khanaen* known to me in Thepha, had been worried about Surasak's growing popularity in that area during late January. He confided to me that Naracha could just not compete with Surasak on the basis of *tua bukkhon* (personal characteristics). When I contacted Somdet after Chuan's visit to Thepha, however, he was reassured. Since Chuan's visit to Thepha, he told me that, "The people feel great sympathy [*songsan*] for Nai Chuan," and "Everything has now returned to normal." In short, Democrat loyalty had been restored and renewed, and he was now confident that Naracha would defeat his TRT opponent.[19] Several hours after Chuan's visit to Ban Phlu on February 2, I asked Seri Nuanpheng (Sunthon's campaign organizer in Ban Phlu) about TRT campaign progress. He confided that, "Things are not going very well and I'm not at all confident."[20] As for Worawit in Constituency 5, up to the middle of the last week of the campaigns, TRT polls and even newspapers (such as *Matichon*) had identified him as a clear winner for TRT against Praphon. After Chuan's visit to Singhanakhon and the large rally on February 2, however, Democrat politicians were confident they would now have no problems.[21]

The appearances of Chuan provided a tangible boost to the morale and fortunes of the Democrats in the Songkhla constituencies. Where individual candidates such as Naracha and Praphon were weak in local repute, or where fortunes were threatened by strong local competitors, Chuan served to cloak them in his transcendent *barami* and elicit *khwam songsan* (sympathy) for his own sacrifices. He strengthened candidates' shaky individual credentials with an invocation to voters of a wider moral presence—the party's history of moral politics and its everlasting *udomkan*.

SYMBOLS AND SOLIDARITIES

The rhetorical performances of the Democrats were crafted to draw on powerful idioms of trust and communality—idioms that were rooted in long-established cultural paradigms connected to values of group solidarity and personal morality. The irony is that the Democrats' opponents also grounded their eligibility claims on the culturally normative grounds of personal integrity, faithfulness to locality, and trustworthiness. As with the province and municipality contests, however, these non-Democrat claims confronted another very powerful symbolic idea in the immanent presence of the Democrat Party as a political community with a sacred collective essence of *udomkan*. To most ordinary voters, Democrat *udomkan* was not something with formal analytical properties, and Democrat orators knew this. When I mentioned to one of them that few ordinary Democrat voters could ever delineate Democrat *udomkan* to me, he explained that, "Thai people don't like thinking on too many levels—you have to make the message simple." To MPs and party activists alike, the most effective way to explain the *udomkan* of the Democrats is to personify it and evoke an enemy who had no *udomkan*. It is here where the presence of Chuan Leekpai and other iconic Democrat leaders of the past (such as Seni Pramoj) played a critical role in symbolizing party identity and *udomkan* in the 2005 election campaigns. Conversely, the demonization of Thaksin and the denigration of the TRT Party in Songkhla acted to evoke amoral political "others" who could never be entrusted with the peoples' votes.

Exemplified in the speeches of Democrat orators in 2005, southern Democrat rhetoric evoked a highly simplified (and demanding) construct of southern morality, an objectification of virtues which in their daily lives and relationships people rarely can, or do, follow.

Yet this should not discount the importance of *udomkan* as a cluster of ideals proclaiming perfect loyalty, fidelity, and trust. Nor is this representation of Democrat loyalty entirely parochial. Rather, it reflects the idea that exemplary southern Democrat leaders represent the best qualities of ordinary southerners in the task of taking care of the nation. But not all southern voters are enamored of the Democrats, and nor are they necessarily interested in elections. Symbolic politics, as the following chapter examines, needs a strong foundation in pragmatic organization and the deployment of money. The Democrat victories in their vulnerable constituencies needed strong foundations in support groups and instrumental counter-strategies to combat their opponents' resources and repute.

CHAPTER 8

Alliances and Persuasions: Vote Canvassers and the Uses of Money

THE PROCESS of seeking votes (*ha siang*) in Songkhla, as elsewhere in Thailand, involves the use of all possible means of persuasion, whether legal or illegal. These multiple methods draw on resources ranging from personal repute, friendship and influence, to hard cash. In the public arenas of rallies and in street and village-level encounters, the contesting parties and candidates during the campaigns of 2005 in Songkhla asserted a mixture of policy, party identity, and personality as the key foundations for candidate eligibility and voter decision-making. In the TRT-Democrat struggle, the competing symbolic narratives of the parties centered respectively on policy performance and political morality. Critically important as these symbolic strategies were in competing for votes, especially for the Democrats, they had to be accompanied by equally important direct and instrumental methods that relied on networks of vote canvassers (*hua khanaen*) and the distribution of money. Forming and sustaining *hua khanaen* groups was a critical task for candidates in the 2005 election; so too was the strategic use of money by both the Democrats and the TRT candidates, as is shown in this chapter in the case of Songkhla's Constituency "X."

WHO ARE THE *HUA KHANAEN*?—ROLES AND RELATIONSHIPS

The "*hua khanaen*" (literally meaning "head of the vote") are central actors in Thai electioneering practice, particularly in rural areas, and the south is no exception to this pattern. *Hua khanaen* have been variously defined in terms of their functional roles and relationship to candidates. In his now-classic study on Thai electoral practice in the early 1990s, Sombat Chanthawong argues, ". . . it is accepted that the *hua khanaen* is nearly the most important (if not *the* most important) person in determining the candidates' electoral success."[1] The translation of the Thai term *hua khanaen* to mean "vote canvasser" is generally more appropriate as a characterization of these groups than an alternative translation as "vote broker," since the latter idea implies that a narrow financial and profit-based motivation underlies the relationships between *hua khanaen* and political candidates.[2] While this depiction is certainly applicable to many who undertake vote canvassing, a variety of motivations and relationships underlie the practices and networks of *hua khanaen*. Those who act as *hua khanaen* include friends and relatives who expect no reward for assisting candidates or their key followers, but also those known as "*hua khanaen rapchang*," who undertake canvassing for hire. In between these extremes is a grey area where political advocacy and desire for remuneration are intermingled.[3]

In Songkhla, the term "*hua khanaen*" is often interpreted as shorthand for "*hua khanaen rapchang*." Vote canvassers and key supporters of candidates are often reluctant to accept the designation of *hua khanaen*, because it carries this negative moral connotation of a canvasser-for-hire. One of the most effective rhetorical strategies of Democrat politicians is to brand vote-buying canvassers and vote-selling electors as prostitutes. This is made doubly powerful by juxtaposing ideal southern female virtue with the stereotyped venality displayed by vote-selling northeasterners, whose political promiscuity is explicitly paralleled with the sexual promiscuity and mercenary habits attributed to northeastern prostitutes. Khran Thawirat, the main organizer of the TRT campaign for Constituency 3 in 2001 and a major canvasser for his nephew in the 2004 by-election, refused to accept the title of *hua khanaen* when I proposed this term for his political role. He emphasized to me that he was definitely not a *hua khanaen*, but rather a "supporter of the TRT party."[4] Hat Yai journalists and a number of local politicians were certain that Khran had indeed been remunerated for his efforts by TRT, both in 2001 and in 2004 (in cash and in kind, with a Toyota van). Khran would no doubt regard this as compensation for his work rather than a hire fee, since he was a TRT Party member. Similarly, Charan, a councilor for Tambon Khu Tao (also in Constituency 3) refused this designation. Though described by one of his closest friends and fellow phuak members as a "*hua khanaen*" for the Democrats, Charan refused to associate this label with himself when I spoke to him about his political activities in national-level elections. Rather, he described his efforts as "helping look for votes" (*chuai ha siang*), explaining that he was not a *hua khanaen*, if by this term it was implied that he was a "*hua khanaen rapchang*." Charan recounted that he had willingly canvassed for the Democrat MPs of his district, and that he was a strong believer in Democrat *udomkan*. His long record of canvassing support stretched back to the days of Sawai Phatthano, who he respected as a politician of high integrity. The most he had ever expected from his vote-seeking assistance for the Democrats, he insisted, was payment for his petrol expenses.[5]

As already outlined (chapter 5), it has long been the practice among national-level politicians (whether Democrat or non-Democrat) to cultivate support networks among province/*tambon* level political figures and *tambon* and village leaders (*kamnan/phuyaiban*).[6] The establishment of *tambon* administrative organizations in the decentralization reforms of the early to mid-1990s heightened the importance of local-level electoral politics and reduced the former centrality of the village heads and *kamnan* as vote canvassers, generating an expanded group of *tambon*-level politicians whose political resources commanded attention from national politicians and parties. As seen in the PAO elections of March 2004, supporting and recognizing the needs of local politicians is a necessity for constituency MPs in the important task of building and sustaining voting support among ordinary people. In Songkhla, the Democrat MPs invest considerable time and effort in maintaining the bonds of mutual support between themselves and local politicians, especially when these politicians are doubly connected to them through party membership.[7]

In the activity of cultivating relations among local politicians, the incumbent MPs (and their adversaries) fulfill patronage and support roles, which are commonly articulated by local politicians as key attributes of the generous and loyal *nakleng*. As expressed by a long-term Democrat Party member and branch committee member in a typical self-ascribed cultural formulation, "You can't be a politician here in the south unless you are a *nakleng*—you have to have many *phakphuak* and be generous."[8] The mutually reinforcing relationship between personal fame and generosity are summarized in the commonly used euphemism for the *nakleng*-type person—*khon chaikwang* (a person with a wide heart). These qualities are not restricted to the hyper-masculine version of the *nakleng* as a "tough guy," but also apply to outwardly gentle people, such as Chuan Leekpai and prominent women. This point was further reinforced to me by a number of Democrat Party branch officials of one constituency, who were dissatisfied at the low level of financial help received from their own Democrat MP in meeting expenses incurred in working for the party and sacrificing their time. They compared him unfavorably to Niphon Bunyamani, who they portrayed as a true *nakleng* in his generosity to his fellow Democrat phuak members, saying, "You can't be a good MP if you're *khiniao*" (stingy). As already seen in the case of Sawiang Chaisiri, Niphon's long-serving *hua khanaen* of Khuaniang (to whom we will return in this chapter), local politicians, even those who are long-serving party branch officials, nurture their own political ambitions and expend resources in sustaining their own phuak for political support in their localities. If support to them is withdrawn or insufficient, they may feel justified in withdrawing their allegiance and canvassing support. Among the Democrats of the south, phuak and party connections are closely interwoven, and though phuak norms sometimes outweigh party obligations, party loyalty can also counteract the tensions that often arise from divergent expectations among phuak members. The general portrayal of Thailand's *hua khanaen* as independent of party structures derives from a model based on systems prevailing in the central and northeastern regions.[9] This needs to be modified in the case of the Democrat-dominated south, where party membership and allegiance do have meaning for many of those who emerge during elections to act as canvassers.

The effectiveness of the *hua khanaen* system is predicated on the multi-layered character of Thai social relationships and the cultural meanings and normative imperatives that define them (despite the volatility of such relationships). In calling for votes, *hua khanaen* of all levels draw on the obligations and loyalties derived from patron-client relations, family connections, strong friendships (*phakphuak* solidarities), and mutual self-interest. *Hua khanaen* are commonly organized by political candidates and their key lieutenants into a broad hierarchical system extending from principal *hua khanaen* (*hua khanaen lak*), through to supporting *hua khanaen* (*hua khanaen rong*), and even groups below this (*hua khanaen lek*, or *hua khanaen yoi*).[10] The activities of *hua khanaen* are multiple, extending from assisting in rallies and door-knocks, to face-to-face persuasion of friends, relatives, and neighbors, to "vote buying" (i.e., the exchange of goods or cash for votes). It should be said, though, that the now-standard models of *hua khanaen* and their system derive from studies conducted during the early to mid-1990s, a period that can be described as the peak period of vote buying in election campaigns (although it is still widespread). These accounts focused in detail on the poverty-stricken northeast or the central regions, areas where popular commitment to political parties is generally judged as weak or non-existent, and where voters are focused on a cluster of priorities that include local development and the personalities and tangible achievements (*phon ngan*) of their local parliamentary representatives. In this context, the payment of money to electors for votes via canvassers played an important role in candidates' electoral performance, though it was not necessarily decisive.[11]

It would be fair to judge that in rural areas vote buying has become the established *necessary* condition—although not the *sufficient* condition—for political candidates' electoral success. In this context, the *hua khanaen* function as vote-getting contractors, employing their own prestige and circles of influence and contacts in localities to accumulate voting banks for political candidates who offer the best payment for their services. The party affiliation of candidates has often been judged as generally unimportant as a factor in the vote-seeking process.[12] In southern provinces such as Songkhla, however, where Democrat Party branches are strong and the party enjoys a strong foundational loyalty among ordinary people, the phenomenon of party identification adds another dimension to relations between *hua khanaen* and voters. The account that follows shows how the formation of *hua khanaen* groups in Constituency 5 was influenced by different types of allegiance that were sometimes in tension, extending from phuak solidarities and local sentiment to patron-client obligations and party-political commitment.

FORMING *HUA KHANAEN* GROUPS IN CONSTITUENCY 5

The Canvassers for Thai Rak Thai

In his campaign for election in Constituency 5 under the TRT banner, Worawit (popularly known as "Nayok Chai") could call on a large group of supporters. His particular links with these groups were varied, ranging from close family ties and friendship and phuak bonds, to patronage links forged during his years as PAO president through the assistance he extended to groups and individuals (for example, his donations to mosques). It was these actions that earned Worawit a reputation as a widely connected man of power (*khon kwangkhwang*), and a generous and trustworthy *nakleng*. The high level of popular support that Worawit enjoyed in Constituency 5 was demonstrated in the votes cast for him in the PAO elections of the previous year. Constituency 5 comprised three *amphoe* (Bang Klam, Khuaniang, and Singhanakhon) with the addition of two *tambon* from the adjacent *amphoe* of Rattaphum, which is Worawit's own home territory. Despite the substantial weight of Democrat Party support that had been thrown behind his rival Nawaphon during the provincial elections, Worawit gained narrow victories in Bang Klam and Khuaniang. He lost in Singhanakhon by some four thousand votes, but was overwhelmingly victorious in his home *amphoe* of Rattaphum. Notwithstanding the strong basic loyalties of ordinary people to the Democrats in these areas, Worawit aimed to maximize his chances of election by capitalizing on his personal repute.

Not surprisingly, a key group of Worawit's *hua khanaen* were those who canvassed for him in the 2004 PAO elections. Another group were *tambon* councilors, village and district headmen. A third component was a renegade group of former Democrat *hua khanaen* that were supporters of Sawiang Chaisiri, who had until very recently been the right-hand man of Democrat MP Niphon Bunyamani in Khuaniang. The following profiles of some of Worawit's *hua khanaen* highlight the salient relationships, interests, and motivations that underlay these support groups in the constituency.[13]

Among Worawit's principal canvassers (*hua khanaen lak*) were those who had assisted him in the PAO presidency contest of the previous year. They included Mrs. Uthai, his aunt (aged sixty-four). A retired teacher, Mrs. Uthai is widely respected among the schoolteachers of the district as a "generous" and helpful person (*khon kwangkhwang*). She has numerous friends in the teaching fraternity and many former students (*luksit*) who hold her in high esteem. During the PAO elections, she donated funds to support Worawit's campaign. In the national election campaign, Mrs. Uthai was unable to provide financial support to her nephew, but she extended support by canvassing for votes among her wide circle of friends and associates in the teaching fraternity and among her former students. There was also Mr. Somwong (aged sixty-two), a relative of Worawit. Somwong is a construction contractor, and during his years as PAO president Worawit favored Somwong with lucrative construction contracts. During former PAO elections, he provided Worawit with funding support, but by this time his own funds were exhausted. While Somwong could not offer money, he did offer his help to canvass for votes. In this group of key former canvassers, there was Sawat (aged forty). Sawat is known as a *nakleng*, and a "generous person" (*chaikwang*) in Amphoe Rattaphum, with a wide circle of friends and acquaintances by virtue of his ownership and operation of illegal gambling dens in numerous localities. A close friend and former school classmate of Worawit's (*run diao kan*), Sawat acted as Worawit's *hua khanaen* in all prior elections. This time, as previously, he acted as *hua khanaen* in seeking votes for Worawit among the numerous members of the district's gambling fraternity. Another key canvasser was Mr. Prapha (aged fifty-six). Prapha is a self-employed businessman with a wide reputation in Khuaniang District as a "generous person." He was suspected by police of drug dealing, and listed in Songkhla

Province's "black book" by officials as an "influential person" (*phu mi itthiphon*) during Thaksin's "War on Drugs" campaign. Worawit used his influence as PAO president to have his name removed from the black book. Prapha acted as a *hua khanaen* for Worawit in every provincial election, and in the national-level campaign he came forward once more to assist.

For his principal canvassers at village and *tambon* levels, Worawit drew from the ranks of local politicians, *kamnan*, and *phuyaiban*. This followed a well-established pattern adopted by candidates in national electoral contests throughout Thailand.[14] In the constituency's *amphoe* of Khuaniang and Bang Klam, Worawit could count on strong support, and even in the largest district, Amphoe Singhanakhon (where he had lost to the Democrats in the provincial election), he claimed some prominent local figures as canvassers. He knew many of these local figures personally through his work as PAO president, had assisted some personally in their own election campaigns, and was generally held in high esteem. As one local politician and supporter observed admiringly of Worawit, he conformed to a popular model of the *nakleng* leader with its cluster of complementary moral and material qualities—he was generous and open to all people, regardless of their social standing. He was attractive, had good character, and was not a snob ("*mi nata di, mai thue tua, lae mi nisai di, pen khon kwangkhwang*").[15]

Though a large proportion of these local politicians, *kamnan*, and *phuyaiban* had already acted as Worawit's *hua khanaen* in the PAO elections, others had supported Nawaphon's Democrat-backed team and now switched their support to Worawit. Amphoe Khuaniang is a good example. Here, of the nine *tambon* councilors of Tambon Bang Riang acting as TRT *hua khanaen*, five had earlier been *hua khanaen* of Nawaphon. In Tambon Rattaphum, the number of former Nawaphon canvassers in Worawit's canvassing group was four of ten local politicians. In Tambon Khuan So, it was two of seven, and in Tambon Huai Luek, two out of five. All professed that their main motive for throwing their support behind Worawit was that he was a person of the locality (*khon phuenthi*), against whom the new Democrat candidate (Praphon) could not compete in terms of proven personal qualities and local links. Informing this locally focused and person-based preference for Worawit was a view that it was time for a change in representation. This was particularly strong in Khuaniang, where many felt that the area had been Niphon Bunyamani's fiefdom for too long. Sawiang's self-serving period as PAO councilor had reinforced resentment of the Democrat phuak. Niphon's departure as local MP and the appearance of his relatively unknown protégé Praphon as Democrat candidate presented an opportunity to engineer a change, focusing on the popular local figure of "Nayok Chai."

Aside from the admiration for Worawit that was cited as a key motivation by the local politicians who came forward as his *hua khanaen*, there were clear links of patronage and personal obligation that bound some of these local politicians to the TRT candidate. For example, Worawit had formerly provided financial assistance to the *tambon* councilors Mr. Asai of Khuaniang and Mr. Sombun of Bang Klam in their own election campaigns. They made it clear that they felt morally bound to reciprocate this assistance. Multiple ties of mutual interest linked Worawit with prominent local figures. Kamnan Samli of a Muslim-majority sub-district in Amphoe Bang Klam had a close association with Worawit through a joint construction business that gained contracts during his PAO presidency. Worawit had helped fund Samli's successful campaign for election as his *tambon*'s *kamnan*, and Samli in turn helped Worawit by acting as his principal *hua khanaen* in Tambon Ban Han during provincial elections. In these national elections, Samli acted as Worawit's *hua khanaen lak*, in charge of TRT canvassing at the *tambon* level. Highly respected in the local Muslim community, Samli was able to appeal to other community leaders to transfer their canvassing support from the Democrats to Worawit. Among those who responded to his appeals was a highly respected local imam who made his preference clear by hanging a large TRT banner in front of his house, which was located in front of the village mosque. In late 2004, Worawit visited this imam—and others in the constituency—and donated funds to the mosque in an effort to cement loyalty. Community leaders and local politicians in other districts of the constituency also indicated that they were acting as *hua khanaen* for Worawit because they had been asked to do so by respected senior figures (*phuyai*) in their areas.

In Amphoe Khuaniang, Worawit gained further vote-canvassing assistance from a rather unexpected quarter, in the form of a phuak headed by Sawiang Chaisiri. Until mid-2004, Sawiang had been a key Democrat *hua khanaen* for Niphon Bunyamani. The circumstances surrounding Sawiang's defection from the Democrats illustrate how allegiance to the party among middle-ranking supporters is often highly contingent on the maintenance of very pragmatic political interests, despite Democrat rhetoric about the strength of *udomkan* as the binding essence of the party. At the same time, these relations are interpreted in terms of the ideals of phuak loyalty. As we have seen, Sawiang failed to gain re-election as PAO councilor when he campaigned as a member of Nawaphon's team. He did manage to have the victor, Khru Mit, disqualified by the Provincial Election Commission, yet he was defeated in the following by-election at the expense of Mit's brother, who was clandestinely funded by the key members of the constituency-wide Democrat phuak (Nawaphon and his elder brother Niphon). Sawiang attributed his own electoral failure not to the disapproval of the voters or his own deficiencies as a representative, but to an act of betrayal by his phuak. Sawiang's close friends emphasized that his subsequent action to support Worawit's TRT candidature was motivated by a spirit of revenge (*kaekhaen*) against Niphon and Nawaphon Bunyamani. Sawiang formally resigned from the Democrat Party and his position as party branch chairman for Constituency 5. He then contacted Worawit through a mutual friend and offered his services as a vote canvasser for TRT.[16]

Sawiang was not fully trusted by Worawit, partly because of his history of long service with the Democrats and his record of shady business dealings, but also because Sawiang and his wife were known to be in debt. He was thus judged as likely to pocket funds given to him for campaign expenses and vote buying. According to a friend of Worawit, during an initial first face-to-face meeting of the two men, Sawiang was compelled to make a sacred pledge (*saban*) that he would not betray or cheat Worawit during the campaign—if Sawiang did so, Worawit assured him that he would arrange for him to be shot dead. But despite the question marks about Sawiang's trustworthiness, Worawit accepted his offer of assistance, because he could assemble a group of around ten key supporters to assist him. These supporters were members of Sawiang's phuak as well as relatives who had served as his own *hua khanaen* in PAO elections and had performed roles as regular canvassers for the Democrats in national election campaigns. As in the case of Surasak Mani's defection from the Democrats in Constituency 8 some years earlier, loyalty to Sawiang among his phuak members was stronger than loyalty to the Democrat Party.

The Democrat *Hua Khanaen*

Though well known in Songkhla township, Praphon Ekkuru was a new candidate for the Democrats with few connections in Constituency 5. For his *hua khanaen* and campaigning workers, Praphon, therefore, had to rely on Democrat branch members and regular supporters who had been regular campaigners for Niphon Bunyamani. Niphon's brother Nawaphon, now the PAO president, also added his appeals to strengthen the level of Democrat support. The number of Democrat *hua khanaen* in Constituency 5 was much smaller than the number who came forward to assist their TRT rival. In Amphoe Khuaniang, the ranks of the regular Democrat *hua khanaen* had been thinned by Sawiang and his phuak's breakaway. The Democrat *hua khanaen* were distinguished largely by their characteristics as diehard party members and others, who, though not party members, were staunch loyalists for whom support for the Democrats was more important than any regard for the candidate. Personal connections did play a role, however, and some of these *hua khanaen* had received personal appeals from—or otherwise felt bound by—loyalty to relatives, friends, and patrons in the Democrat fraternity. This was a key factor in the support given by Khru Mit, elder brother of the newly elected PAO representative for Khuaniang. Just as Worawit's *hua khanaen* group included some who had formerly supported Nawaphon in the PAO elections, so too among the Democrat *hua khanaen* there were a number (three out of nine in Khuaniang, for example) who had canvassed for Worawit in the province-level contest of the previous year. This shift in support highlights the fact that some staunch Democrats who had earlier exercised personal preference for Worawit in the provincial election saw provincial politics as a qualitatively different type of contest to national political battles.

For them, national politics demanded a concerted demonstration of party allegiance, beyond considerations of *phon ngan*, localism, and personality that they had employed in the provincial contest. Others felt obliged to shift their support away from Worawit to the Democrats in response to personal appeals made by respected superiors (*phuyai*), through family pressure and a sense of obligation, or a combination of these. The outline below illustrates the character of Praphon's main *hua khanaen* support-base in Constituency 5.

In Amphoe Khuaniang and its municipality, Sawiang's departure from the Democrats' canvassing ranks was compensated for in part by the successful recruitment of his local political rival, Mit Kaeopradit, who had gained a strong following by opposing Sawiang in the PAO election contest. Mit had supported Nawaphon in the PAO assembly, and above all was obliged to the Democrat phuak for funding his brother's election to the PAO, which served as a proxy endorsement for himself. Another important principal canvasser for the Democrats was Chalat, president of the Khuaniang Municipality. Chalat was also deputy chairman of the Constituency 5 Democrat Party branch and a long-serving party member. Through loyalty to the Democrat phuak, Chalat canvassed for Sawiang in the PAO elections. A hard-line Democrat loyalist, Chalat's commitment to the party was not affected by Sawiang's defection, and in the February national elections he acted as the head of all Democrat canvassing for Praphon in the municipal area. For this purpose, Praphon gave him funds to hold feasts (*liang*) for the youth and residents of the municipality in order to garner support before the official beginning of the campaign period (after which time such activities are officially illegal). Another principal canvasser in Khuaniang Municipality was Mrs. Urathai. Urathai (aged thirty-five) is a self-employed businesswoman and a municipal councilor who was elected to the position in 2004, as a member of Chalat's winning team whose core group were all members of the Democrat-connected phuak. A long-standing Democrat Party member and a highly trusted lieutenant of Chalat, Urathai was placed in charge of Democrat campaign cavalcades and door-knocks in the Khuaniang municipal area.

The principal *hua khanaen* for the Democrats in Constituency 5 were tied by both party loyalties and personal links with key Democrat figures, with most of them having no former connection with Praphon, the new candidate. They included Mr. Udom. Udom is president of the Rattaphum TAO and a close friend of Nawaphon Bunyamani since their schooldays together (*run dio kan*). He gained critical funding support from Nawaphon in his election campaign for TAO president. Udom acted as a *hua khanaen* supporting Nawaphon's PAO presidency campaign and for the 2005 national contest he lent his unqualified support as a *hua khanaen lak* for Praphon's campaign. Udom was placed in overall charge of all Democrat campaign activities for Tambon Rattaphum and was entrusted by Praphon with funds for the pre-election feasting of the villagers. Mr. Komen, the *nayok* of the Khuan So TAO, had acted as a *hua khanaen* for Worawit's PAO team, but for the 2005 election, he lent support to the Democrat candidacy of Praphon because of a special request made by his relative, the *so cho* Mr. Phan. Phan is a long-serving and popular *so cho* of Amphoe Bang Klam. He came forward as one of the main *hua khanaen* supporting Praphon's Democrat Party candidacy in that district, even though he had gained re-election to the PAO as a member of Worawit's team. A regular supporter of the Democrats but an admirer of Worawit, Phan felt especially obliged to offer canvassing assistance to Praphon because of his close kin connection with the new Constituency 3 Democrat MP Wirat Kalayasiri (himself a native of Bang Klam). In fact, most of Phan's canvassers for his PAO campaign swung behind the Democrats as a result of his urging.

THE *HUA KHANAEN* FACTOR: ASSESSING THE FORCES

Based on the relative numbers of *hua khanaen* supporting the TRT and Democrat contenders in Constituency 5, Worawit as TRT candidate was clearly the stronger player. He was able to gain the support of the greater number of prominent community figures and the majority of the local politicians at the *tambon* level. The figures below (table 8.1) represent estimates by the *amphoe*-level campaign directors of the two contending candidates' numbers of *hua khanaen*. These estimates show clearly that the TRT candidate's *hua khanaen* outnumbered those of the Democrat Party by a ratio of two-to-one in Constituency 5. But this simple arithmetic did not add up to a winning formula for Worawit. Though *hua khanaen* are universally regarded as a critical factor in determining outcomes in Thailand's electoral politics, a number of countervailing realities were also at play in this constituency and Songkhla generally, and they proved to be decisive, no matter how strong the personal credentials of the individual TRT candidates and the local reputations of their *hua khanaen*. One reality, shared throughout the country, is that the number of *hua khanaen* alone cannot guarantee candidates' success if they do not undertake their principal duties as planned, particularly the task of dispensing money allocated by parties and candidates for vote buying.[17]

TABLE 8.1

Estimates of *Hua Khanaen* Numbers for DP and TRT Candidates, Constituency 5

Amphoe	Praphon's (DP) *Hua Khanaen*	Worawit's (TRT) *Hua Khanaen*
Bang Klam	120	300
Khuaninang	150	500
Singhanakhon	400	700

Source: Estimates provided by *amphoe*-level campaign directors of Democrat and TRT parties

Just as important in the regional context is the fact that the southern constituencies are not level playing fields. No matter how many *hua khanaen* acted as advocates for the TRT contenders, they had to face long-standing popular loyalties to the Democrat Party among ordinary voters. A product of this loyalty is a profusion of small-scale canvassers. Democrat canvassing is undertaken not only by prominent party members occupying key positions in branches, but also by ordinary members and Democrat loyalists who are widely dispersed throughout communities. Among the Democrat Party membership everyone is, by definition, an advocate for the party, even the humblest vendor or tuk-tuk driver. Women in particular are conspicuous among these ordinary advocates, both in rural and urban areas of the province. In early 2005, this meant that the numbers of *hua khanaen* identified for

Constituency 5, as above, underestimates the cumulative force of the numerous ordinary Democrat supporters who lent their assistance in informal settings and on a continuing basis. As one key informant—a local politician with long experience—emphasized, "Worawit has many more *hua khanaen lak* than the Democrats, but the Democrats have many more *hua khanaen rong*, and they seek votes automatically on a personal level" (*ha siang kan-eng doi atanomat*). The capacity for spontaneous mobilization among ordinary Democrat sympathizers had been demonstrated in Phrai Phatthano's campaign for the Hat Yai mayoralty the year before. It was vividly demonstrated again in 2005, in Constituency 3, where a small group of women from Hat Yai (technically outside the constituency boundary) operated as a mobile flying squad to distribute candidate cards and show the Democrat banner in areas missed by the Democrats' candidate, Wirat. The same type of spontaneity was displayed in Constituency 5.

The composition of the *hua khanaen* groups as political formations reflect a range of relationships that are embedded in Thai patterns of sociality. They might be expressed perhaps in terms of a continuum of relations extending from deep emotional connections to mercenary interests. As expressed in the terms given by the various *hua khanaen* themselves, they spanned relations of benevolence-respect (*napthue khaorop*), patron-clientage (*luk phi luk nong*), intra-generational loyalties (*run diao kan*), love and loyalty among friends (*pen phuan rak*), and the mutual dependence deriving from complementary political and material interests (*phuengpha asai sueng kan lae kan*). To this, however, we must add a further relationship of loyalty that is distinctive among many of the Democrat *hua khanaen* and it even applies to many of the Democrat loyalists who are not party members. This is a deep attachment to the idea of the party—an attachment and commitment that is very resilient and independent of personal calculation or interest. Against this level of hard-line commitment, Worawit could not compete for loyalty. Hence, despite the apparent weakness of Praphon's credentials as a candidate, he could still gain unswerving support, even if it was from a smaller group. And beyond this relatively small group of *hua khanaen lak*, there were hundreds more ordinary Democrat Party loyalists who practiced their advocacy for the party in the intimate settings of teahouses, market places, and village neighborhoods.

Those TRT candidates in Songkhla, like Worawit, who could command key political resources such as large numbers of *hua khanaen*, high personal prestige, and considerable electioneering funds, still found that they were unable to either control or predict the voting behavior of the *chaoban* (villagers, ordinary people). The section following investigates the activities of *hua khanaen* in connection with the distribution of money among *chaoban*, many of whom demonstrated that while they were happy to accept cash, would not change their Democrat vote. Others accepted money from both parties and voted for the highest bidder.

"SOUTHERNERS CANNOT BE BOUGHT!" ("BUT, WE'LL TAKE THE MONEY ANYWAY"): VOTE BUYING IN CONSTITUENCY "X"

There is a widely expressed view in Songkhla that vote buying in the province, and in the south generally (at least until very recently) is minimal, and far less prevalent than in other regions of Thailand. Other evidence suggests otherwise, however, and reports of election monitoring agencies during the 1990s (such as Pollwatch) indicate that the exchange of cash for votes during national elections in the south, while not reaching the levels prevalent in the northeast, has been practiced widely in the region for at least a decade.[18] Local politicians in Songkhla with experience both as canvassers and contenders point out that direct vote buying (i.e., votes-for-cash) has been prevalent during elections at all levels (local, provincial, and national) for two decades.[19] The claim that vote buying is foreign to the south is strongly affirmed by southern Democrat politicians, and is used to fuse the image of a pure and honorable party with an image of pure and honorable southern voters. In Democrat rhetoric and imagery it is the eternally evil others, i.e., opposing parties, that use money as their main method of seeking votes. These parties are temporary (*phak chaphokit*) and devoid of enduring political principles (*mai mi udomkan*); they are the antithesis of the Democrats and represent a corruption of pure political values. After the Democrat victory in the Songkhla by-election of 2004, Thawon Senniam made the triumphant claim that, "The southern people can't be bought." Repeated as a headline in the national press, it was a calculated statement designed to taunt and label TRT as an unprincipled party that relied on money for its electoral success, and it also functioned, predictably, as a rallying cry to express and mobilize southern regional pride.

Notwithstanding the persistent Democrat Party rhetoric that distances the party from the morally sordid business of distributing money for votes, the practice of vote buying has been documented among southern Democrats. In Songkhla, former Democrat activists privately admit to have engaged in vote buying, although party loyalists vehemently deny this. When I pressed some prominent local journalists on the evidence of Democrat vote buying, they admitted that it did take place but also stressed that the incidence of Democrat vote buying has been very low in comparison with other parties. Some Democrat members reinforce their denials of vote buying by pointing out that the party is "too poor" to buy votes. This common response highlights one of the popular images of the Democrats as a party of ordinary people, but it denies the reality that candidates can use their own funds to support the practice. Probably more significant in explaining the low level of Democrat vote buying in the south, however, is the very practical fact that for over a decade the party's electoral popularity has been so strong that vote buying has been unnecessary to the task of securing voting majorities. Thus, in referring to what appears to be an absence of vote buying in the past, southern Democrat Party orators can portray the result of a hegemonic electoral advantage as a product of popular political ethics.

The use of money and other legally proscribed methods of persuasion were widespread in Songkhla's 2005 elections. Openly reported by election commission officials at all levels, these illegal and clandestine practices ran the gamut from pressure by state officials (mainly police), bias among Provincial Election Commission workers, feasting, the offering of bribes in the form of gifts, and attempts to buy votes with hard cash.[20] The widely reported case of Newin Chitchop's vote-buying conference in Hat Yai on January 16 was only the most spectacular of the accusations brought against TRT by the Democrats in Songkhla. In Constituencies 3 and 8, the Democrat candidates and branch officials claimed that the TRT candidates were compiling lists of names of voters for the purposes of vote buying and that they were using their considerable funds from TRT to hire many *hua khanaen* for this purpose. Not surprisingly, the TRT candidates and key supporters denied this. One of Sunthon's personal assistants admitted that money had to be used for feasting and for the expenses of *hua khanaen*, stressing that, "everyone does this, including the Democrats," but she denied that in Constituency 3 the party directly paid people for their votes.[21]

The Democrats found that lists of names on standard printed forms (with provisions for names, addresses, and telephone numbers) were being used by TRT *hua khanaen*, and claimed that this was clear evidence of TRT methods of preparation for vote buying. TRT organizers denied that the forms were being used for these purposes, but their alternative explanations were not entirely consistent. One explanation was that these forms were used to help compile targeted voting figures for the TRT candidate. Another explanation was that the forms were used to gather names of people for enrollment as TRT Party members.[22] Surasak Mani argued that Democrat allegations of TRT's rampant vote buying were an example of the well-established ploy of the Democrats to de-legitimize their opponents through spreading rumors at all levels. Moreover, he argued, the Democrats were even more culpable of the illegal practices of which they were accusing him:

> Regarding the Democrat claims of our use of state power [*amnat rat*], I can tell you that when the Democrats were in government they used state power in elections and bought votes far more than we [Surasak and his supporters] did—because they sent soldiers and police to control us—we couldn't go anywhere. In the 2001 elections, when I was running as Ratsadon Party candidate against them in this constituency, they [the Democrats] said I was buying votes and told the Provincial Election Commission I was doing this—I spent half a day at the PEC office in Songkhla explaining myself to the officials. Last week, they said [at the Democrat rally in Chana], 'Surasak is paying people 1,000 baht

> each for votes!' If I go and sit with my *phuak* in a teahouse [*ran namcha*] for a chat, the Democrats will spread a rumor that I was paying them 5,000 baht each as *hua khanaen*! In this method of rumor, the Democrats are experts. Games like this make the people confused.[23]

Notwithstanding Surasak's fervent denials, vote buying by TRT candidates did take place in many constituencies in Songkhla, and it was not simply a rumor concocted by the Democrats, though these were also effective in undermining their opponents. Muslim residents in the Thepha District confirm that Surasak's *hua khanaen* were active in distributing money among their communities.[24] At the same time, the practice of vote buying was not restricted to TRT candidates, even though that party deployed the most money. Rumors, accusations, and denials are a central feature of political contests in Thailand, and the proliferation of rumors surrounding vote buying, combined with the skills exercised in concealing it, make it difficult to identify in concrete terms. But the numerous accounts given by ordinary voters at village and neighborhood levels as well as the confidential statements of PEC officials, who were in touch with their own local informants, confirm its prevalence during the 2005 election.

The following account of the deployment of money in Songkhla's Constituency "X" shows how the contending candidates, through their *hua khanaen* groups, attempted to use vote buying to determine the outcome of voting in one of the province's most hotly contested constituencies. Due to the controversial nature of this information and the danger to informants, I have deliberately disguised the identity of this Songkhla constituency, the candidates, and their canvassers. Based on information from key informants close to organizers of both parties, this account shows how *hua khanaen* were employed to identify voters, and how the vote-buying method was not, in the final analysis, effective enough to determine the outcome. Partly, at least, this was because the TRT effort to purchase votes was sabotaged by the venal behavior of the candidate's own TRT *hua khanaen*, in combination with a skillful Democrat strategy involving rumor and carefully targeted counter vote buying. But in addition, and most critically, the election result in Constituency "X" was determined by the choices of the inscrutable voters themselves, who for varying reasons supplied the Democrat candidate with his critical winning vote, even though many were willing to accept monetary payments from TRT.

MONEY AND THE STRUGGLE FOR VOTES IN CONSTITUENCY "X"

The election contest in Constituency "X" was probably the hardest-fought contest in the whole province. The TRT candidate, "Tim" was a highly popular local politician and the Democrat candidate "Nut" was new. The contest presented a dilemma to many people in this constituency who had regularly voted for the Democrat Party in national elections, because here the TRT Party had cleverly selected a candidate universally known, with numerous practical achievements (*phon ngan*) to his credit. At the same time, voters were asked to support the Democrat Party and demonstrate their historical loyalty, despite the fact that they had little knowledge of the individual candidate. It was clear to local observers that in formulating a choice, the voters of Constituency "X" were compelled to juggle between two key principles of candidate eligibility represented by each of the contestants: the popularity of the person (*niyom tua bukkhon*) and the strength of party identification (*niyom phak*). As with all the other constituencies where TRT had strong contestants, Tim needed to harness his popularity to the TRT *krasae* and emphasize the importance of local development issues as key points of persuasion in his public campaign. In this process, his major challenge was to overcome the inertia of habitual Democrat support. Conversely, Nut needed to emphasize the enduring qualities of the Democrat Party, appeal to voters' loyalty, and harness all the rhetorical and symbolic force of senior Democrat orators to counter the strength of Tim's calls to voters' sense of localism and the attractions of a development-centered idea of political representation.

One of Tim's key *hua khanaen*, Khun Soem, an active local-level politician and former TAO president, portrayed the spread of voters' dispositions in Constituency "X" in the approximate proportions noted below (table 8.2). He emphasized the significance of conflicting loyalties to "person" and "party" in the same body of voters. Based on these types of estimates and classifications of voters, the contending candidates in Constituency "X" deployed money through *hua khanaen* to assure themselves a decisive margin of victory.

TABLE 8.2

Voters' Dispositions Towards the Election in Constituency "X"

Level of Party-Based Attachment	*Level of Person-Based Attachment*
Democrat Party 70%	"Nut" (DP)20%
TRT and others 30%	"Tim" (TRT) 50%
	Undecided 10%
	No interest in politics, but happy to take money for votes 20%

Source: Khun Soem, leading TRT *hua khanaen*

Tim's Use of Money—Identifying Target Votes and Employing *Hua Khanaen*

Tim began organizing his *hua khanaen* network in earnest in November, following formal notification of his selection as a TRT candidate. In each of the constituency's three *amphoe*, he gathered his *hua khanaen lak* together for a meeting and treated them to a feast, where he also explained the themes of his public campaign. Shortly after this, around the time of the formal declaration of the polling date, he chose election directors (*phu amnuaikan lueaktang*) from among his *hua khanaen lak* to take charge of electoral centers in each *amphoe*. These close supporters were entrusted with recruiting further *hua khanaen* in their districts of responsibility. The phases of Tim's organizing of *hua khanaen* and his use of funds coincided with the reception of financial support from the TRT party center. The first tranche of funds arrived in December, amounting to 1 million baht, which he used for payments to *hua khanaen* who were to use these funds to feast people in their localities. His second tranche was sent in January, the month of candidate registration, to fund production of large billboards and cover further *hua khanaen* expenses. His final installment came in the last week of electioneering, with the sum calculated on the basis of voters lists sent to the party. For this, Tim received at least 14 million baht, supplemented with funds from a number of highly placed supporters.

Targeting the voters was a three-stage process overseen by Tim's *amphoe*-based election directors:

> FIRST STAGE: *Hua khanaen* were instructed to identify up to fifty people each and to submit their names for party membership. This was done by collecting and photocopying people's identity cards and submitting them to the *amphoe* election center. For this work, each *hua khanaen* was paid between 1,000 to 1,500 baht.
>
> SECOND STAGE: Each *hua khanaen* was instructed to collect the names of as many close family and friends (*yat phi nong*) as they could identify and write details on pre-printed forms.
>
> THIRD STAGE: This was similar to the second stage process, but involved a wider group of voters, and the election directors crosschecked the canvassers' lists, in order to eliminate duplicate names. Once the *amphoe* directors had finalized the voters' lists and confirmed that they had reached the vote target set by Tim, they called in the *hua khanaen* and paid them each 1,000 baht. This payment was to cover petrol expenses, but it was also a fee for *hua khanaen* to maintain contact with the voters they had identified on the lists and to ensure that Democrat *hua khanaen* did not attempt to poach their votes.

The objective in compiling these lists was twofold. First, the aim was to identify a target number of voters sufficient to secure a clear winning margin of votes for each *amphoe*, based on estimates of enrolled voters and anticipating the level of potential support for the Democrats based on voting figures in the 2001 election. Second, these targeted votes were to be doubly secured by payments delivered by the *hua khanaen* to the groups of family, friends, and neighbors that they had approached and identified by name on the lists. The payment for votes per person listed was calculated at a rate of 200 baht per head. In all *amphoe*, the number of names submitted by *hua khanaen* exceeded the calculated target number of votes set by the directors, but these were accepted anyway, presumably in the expectation that they would assure an ample victory (see table 8.3). Tim's vote target was 44,000, which corresponded roughly with the number of votes gained by the winning Democrat candidate in the 2001 elections for Constituency "X." Although 44,000 votes represented just 39 percent of all qualified voters, it could be expected that roughly the same proportion of voters would exercise their rights as the previous election of 2001, which was around 74 percent. On the assumption that the same proportion of the electorate would exercise their voting rights in 2005, a vote of 44,000 represented 53 percent of the total expected constituency ballots (82,972), which would assure a victory for Tim. Tim would need to allow for the factor of spoilt ballots, which had equaled 3.25 percent of all ballots cast in Constituency "X" in 2001, but this factor would also affect other candidates.[25]

TABLE 8.3

Tim's (TRT) Vote Targets and Payments Made to *Hua Khanaen* for Vote Buying

Districts in Constituency	No. of Registered Voters	Voters Targeted for Payments	Actual No. of Names On List	Vote Buying Expenditures	Expected Non-Effective Payments	Vote Target
Amphoe A	24,016	15,000	17,000	3.4 M baht	3,000 voters	12,000
Amphoe B	55,987	25,000	30,000	6 M baht	7,000 voters	18,000
Amphoe C	18,437	13,000	16,000	3.2 M baht	5,000 voters	8,000
2 Tambon	13,685	8,000	10,000	2 M baht	2,000 voters	6,000

Source: Confidential informants serving as TRT *amphoe*-based campaign directors

Early in the final week of the election period (around February 1), Tim's TRT election directors in each *amphoe* called in the *hua khanaen* to present copies of their voters' lists. Each *hua khanaen* was paid between 1,000–2,000 baht in advance as a fee to cover the distribution of money to voters, those with a large number of names receiving higher payment. This was a personal payment, made to ensure that the vote-buying money was actually delivered to voters, since the practice of *hua khanaen* keeping vote-buying money for themselves is a common problem faced by candidates and their campaign supporters throughout the country, and Constituency "X" was no exception.[26] The *hua khanaen* were then given the vote-buying money calculated at 200 baht per listed name. In some cases, *hua khanaen* submitted lists and collected vote-buying money on behalf of other *hua khanaen* in their local phuak.

To ensure that the money actually reached the listed voters, the *amphoe* directors attempted to monitor the delivery of money in this last week of the campaign by organizing a group of trusted followers to check households that were targeted. However, not all the *hua khanaen* could be checked in this way, given the large territory to be covered. Moverover, some *hua khanaen* objected to being followed. As one *amphoe* director explained, "If we follow them personally, they say 'why are you doing this, don't you trust me?'" To try and confirm that listed voters had actually received promised payments from *hua khanaen*, organizers devised a system whereby printed stickers were affixed to the walls of houses after payments were made. These colored stickers featured a picture of Tim with the statement, "This house votes for Nai Tim—a person of our locality—Thai Rak Thai."

Tim's campaign directors tried to ensure the efficient delivery of vote-buying money in the week before polling day, but thousands of baht did not reach the listed voters as promised. Some *hua khanaen* did not distribute the money at all, some gave the payments only to close family members and kept the balance of the money, while others paid only 100 baht to each listed voter and pocketed the remaining 100 baht for themselves. As in other constituencies, these *hua khanaen* had been recruited by the candidate's close supporters, his *hua khanaen lak*, and most of them had offered their services willingly and professed support for Tim as the best candidate on the basis of his local ties and reputation. Despite these professions of loyalty, pecuniary interests clearly held sway among certain groups of them. As expressed by Tim's "Amphoe A" election director, "As soon as the money came through, their character changed."

There were limits to *hua khanaen* commitment in Tim's campaign, and it was, notably, the *chaoban* themselves who alerted Tim's *amphoe*-level directors to this problem. In "Amphoe A," a major case of *hua khanaen* deception was detected the day before polling day when a group of *chaoban* arrived at the director's office to complain that they had not received their promised money from the *hua khanaen*, Mr. Chop. Chop was given money on the basis of his name lists of six hundred voters (totaling 120,000 baht). Tim's *amphoe* election director went straight to Chop's home to make enquiries, and found that Chop had distributed money to only half (three hundred) of the people on his lists, retaining for himself the unexpended balance of 60,000 baht. Chop gave the lame excuse that he was intending to distribute the money that same evening. The director demanded the money from Chop and arranged for other *hua khanaen* to pass it on to the *chaoban*. But in many other cases, the unpaid money was never recovered. The uneven distribution of payments by some groups among Tim's *hua khanaen* alienated many people in Constituency "X," causing considerable resentment against the *hua khanaen*, which then impacted negatively on Tim. Disappointed voters who did not receive the promised money, or who found that they received less than their neighbors, responded to this state of affairs by withholding their votes from Tim and voting for the Democrats in an act of spiteful revenge (*prachot*). Tim's betrayal at the hands of his *hua khanaen* in the last week of the campaign passed a considerable advantage to the local Democrats, who were past masters at sowing discord and confusion among their opponents.

Nut's Use of Money—Outbidding TRT and Planting Rumors

As a Democrat candidate, Nut held one major advantage over Tim. He could draw on a heritage of strong Democrat support among voters and rely on many ordinary Democrat members canvassing in informal ways at the local level. Nevertheless, because of the very strong current of person-based popularity enjoyed by Tim in this election, and because he was a new and untried candidate, Nut could not take this support entirely for granted in this obviously close contest. In the task of targeting eligible voters for payment, Nut enjoyed an advantage over his rival, because the selected *hua khanaen* he assigned to the task were mainly Democrat Party members who, aside from needing payment for their petrol expenses, were not undertaking the work with the expectation of personal profit. Nut's approach to vote buying was characterized by a more careful targeting of voters than Tim and his campaign directors. His *hua khanaen* employed two key methods, both of which were designed to "outbid" his opponent, a process that required careful intelligence gathering and timing.[27]

The primary technique employed by the Democrats in Constituency "X" was to delegate village-level *hua khanaen* to approach those households identified as having voters who were politically uncommitted or undecided about the candidates. Lists of these households were compiled after agreements with household members were made at least a week in advance of the polling date. Then, during the three days up to and including election eve ("*khuen ma hon*," the night of the howling dog), payments of between 1,500–2,000 baht were made. This method is well known as "*sue baep yok khrua*" (buying the household). The second approach was calibrated to follow the TRT vote-buying efforts, and took place shortly before polling day. In this second method, the Democrat *hua khanaen* identified those voters who had already received payments from Tim's *hua khanaen* and found out the actual sums received by these voters. They then paid individuals a higher amount than they had received from TRT, amounting to between 300–500 baht. In delivering the money following either of these methods, Nut's *hua khanaen* had to devise a technique to avoid being detected by ubiquitous police patrols, which were deliberately favoring the TRT candidate by holding up the Democrat *hua khanaen* in their pickup trucks in the evenings. To overcome this obstacle, the Democrat *hua khanaen* made arrangements with groups of local youth, who were able to visit and pay the targeted households without arousing police suspicion.

Informants close to Nut's major Democrat Party *hua khanaen* estimate that he devoted a total amount of some 10 million baht in vote buying. The money was not drawn from official party funds (unlike most of Tim's TRT money), but was drawn from Nut's own substantial reserves built up from the profits gained from his own private business. Although Nut employed less money than Tim (10 million compared to over 14 million baht), he spent more money per individual and household than his TRT opponent, who had adopted a blanket approach to his vote buying. Nut's targeted strategy was ultimately far more effective in persuading the uncommitted and undecided middle-ground of voters who comprised an estimated 30 percent of the Constituency "X" voting population. But in addition, Nut gained from the widespread dissatisfaction generated by the stories of Tim's self-interested *hua khanaen*, who had withheld money from people who had agreed to vote for him. Nut's *hua khanaen* took full advantage of this betrayal and spread rumors in communities that considerably inflated the dimensions of TRT *hua khanaen* misdeeds.

VOTER RESILIENCE AND THE AMBIGUOUS ROLE OF MONEY

Just how decisively the vote-buying activity of either candidate affected the final result of the elections in Constituency "X" cannot be fully determined. Nut emerged the victor for the Democrats by a margin of some 15,000 votes, while Tim, the defeated TRT candidate, fell short of his voting target (44,000) by at least 10,000 votes. Informants close to the TRT *amphoe*-level election directors confided to me their own view that a key factor in Tim's electoral failure was the betrayal by the *hua khanaen* and the consequent resentment directed against Tim by the *chaoban* who had not received their promised money. A friend of Tim's told me a few days after the election that Tim had decided to have one of the main culprits (Mr. Chop) shot for not following instructions, but then had decided that it wasn't worth the trouble to kill him.

Several points, however, seem clear in relation to the question of money and votes in Constituency "X," and they are applicable to other constituencies in Songkhla. First is the reality of the practice of vote buying among the Democrats, despite the high moral claims of party leaders and orators that the party is clean-handed, honorable, and relies on the strength of its *udomkan*, not the power of money, to secure allegiance and votes. That being said, it has to be accepted that because of the strength of Democrat Party popular support in the south, vote buying is only necessary for the party's candidates in the toughest-fought contests, and even here, the Democrats engage in highly targeted vote buying and the judicious deployment of funds among voters who are identified as uncommitted. This highly selective pattern of targeted vote buying can be more easily obscured and is far less visible than methods of other parties, giving ordinary Democrat loyalists the impression that it is entirely absent from party practice in the region.

A second point to be drawn from this account of Constituency "X" is that ordinary voters, especially in rural areas of the province, take it for granted that they will be offered money by *hua khanaen*. In the case of Tim's vote-buying program, money seems to have been treated by many recipients more as a token gift offering than a direct bribe, since he was already a highly popular figure among many locals. On the other hand, cash-in-the-hand is of considerable value for poorer rural residents, and per-head payments of 200 baht on a household basis may accumulate to 600–1,000 baht, which does represent a useful amount of money. It is also clear that the commitments made by *hua khanaen* to pay money in Constituency "X" were taken seriously by many voters, and they were disappointed when it was not forthcoming. But, perhaps the most important point is that even though there is a widespread acceptance of money payments offered by *hua khanaen*, the money itself is not compelling enough to persuade many voters to shift their habitual preference for the Democrat Party. There are also practical reasons that allow for this voter resilience. Changes to vote-counting methods were introduced by new electoral legislation from 1997, so that ballot counting (formerly counted at local polling stations) was undertaken at constituency-level centers, making it well nigh impossible for *hua khanaen* to check whether recipients of money had actually cast votes according to instructions.[28]

A week after polling day, I visited a village known to me in Constituency "X" and sat talking with a number of the residents on the porch of Uncle Bun's house. I had come to the village with Aet, an army sergeant who worked at a military recruiting station in another district of the constituency. Aet had already told me of the widespread stories of Tim's *hua khanaen* keeping the vote-buying money. Aet suggested that I ask Uncle Bun (his father) whether the stories of vote buying were true. Uncle Bun confirmed this, saying that Tim's *hua khanaen* had come to his home and given him 200 baht. A neighbor sitting with us mentioned that some large families in the village had received between 800–1,000 baht from the TRT *hua khanaen*. "But," Uncle Bun said, smiling to his neighbor, "we voted Democrat anyway." He added, "I didn't do anything wrong, or commit a sin, because *they* gave me the money—*I* didn't ask for it." The neighbor giggled and admitted that, "Everyone knows that Tim's *hua khanaen* kept a lot of money and didn't give it to the *chaoban*." To villagers like Uncle Bun and his neighbor, getting the money was a nice thing, but they reserved the right to vote as they wanted, and they both voted Democrat. Uncle Bun was adamantly opposed to the TRT party, because it was a party of the rich dedicated to "eating the country" (*kin mueang*). He and all his neighbors were voting Democrat, because it was "the party of the southern people" (*Prachathipat pen phak khong khon tai*) and they believed Thaksin was colluding with his *phakphuak* of businessmen cronies to destroy the country. Uncle Bun and his neighbor's revelations highlight a high level of voter resilience and agency in the face of money offered for their votes. Uncle Bun's neighbor gave a portrayal of *chaoban* and the *hua khanaen* by means of a natural metaphor that highlighted how, in the final analysis, it was the *chaoban* that maintained control over their own choices:

> We are like a turtle with only its head above the water—you can't see how big the rest of its body is—so, just like the turtle, the *hua khanaen* who pay money can't tell how many people will vote for their party after the *chaoban* accept their money.

CHAPTER 9

Interpreting the Democrats' Southern Triumph

IN SONGKHLA, as elsewhere in the south, the Democrat Party candidates emerged as clear victors after polling day on February 6, 2005, notwithstanding some tough individual contests mounted by their TRT opponents. This regional success in the context of national failure revealed the Democrat-dominated south to be once more the great anomaly in Thailand's political landscape. At the national level, TRT's sweeping election win had been predicted months earlier, but many commentators were still surprised at the extent of TRT's wholesale rout of the Democrats and other rivals. Thaksin's party gained 61 percent of the vote and won 377 of 500 parliamentary seats (comprising 400 constituency and 100 party-list seats). Aided by the provisions of the 1997 constitution, and guaranteed comprehensive constituency-based success through its absorption of older rival parties, TRT made history by becoming the first political party to win enough seats to form a single-party government. On a national scale, the results were interpreted as a popular endorsement of TRT's delivery of populist policy promises and its performance-orientated approach to governance, as well as a vote of confidence in Prime Minister Thaksin Shinawatra's leadership style. Thaksin's highly publicized efforts during the tsunami disaster on the eve of the election were seen to have played a particularly important role in boosting public support, especially among voters in Bangkok.[1]

The election results highlighted the inability of the Democrat Party to compete with TRT in terms of policies and leadership image. The Democrats won just ninety-nine seats overall, down from 130 in the 2001 national election. Acknowledging this poor national performance, Banyat Banthatthan stood down as party head and the national party leadership began exploring better ways to reach the electorate and construct a clearer public image.[2] But within TRT's national triumph was a conspicuous and irritating regional failure, because TRT had been unable to make inroads into the Democrats' southern stronghold. TRT had in fact lost seats in the south (the seats held by the former *Wadah* politicians in the three border provinces), while the Democrat Party had not only withstood the assault, but had also increased its constituency seats from forty-eight (gained in 2001) to fifty-two of the south's fifty-four seats. Without the comprehensive southern support that delivered over half of its parliamentarians, the Democrats would have been all but wiped off the political map as a contender in national politics. Southern voters' rejection of TRT stood out as a clear rebuttal to the prime minister, who attempted to downplay this rejection as southerners' "misunderstanding" of his government's policies, particularly his measures adopted towards the border province disturbances.[3]

As Pasuk Phongpaichit and Chris Baker observed, the 2005 election results confirmed that there was a clear line dividing the south from the rest of the country in Thailand's national political geography, reaffirming in even starker terms than 2001 the strength of southern support for the Democrats.[4] The Democrat victories in all but two of the south's fifty-four constituencies stood out in sharp relief against the TRT electoral triumph in most other regions (see table 9.1). TRT's campaign formulas had been proven supremely successful everywhere but in the south. How was this conspicuous regional failure to be explained? The reasons given by scholars, press commentators, and politicians after the election were both specific and general—they identified specific reasons applying to the TRT loss in the three border provinces of Narathiwat, Pattani, and Yala, and familiar general factors for the rest of the south. The vote against TRT in the border provinces was viewed as a direct protest vote against the government's heavy-handed and violent handling of the border problems, exemplified particularly by the Tak Bai tragedy. Notably, in these provinces none of the former Democrat MPs who defected to TRT gained election, whereas the new Democrat candidates sent to run for seats were successful in all but one constituency. This Democrat win in the three Muslim-majority provinces was less a conversion to Democrat *udomkan* than a strong negative vote against Thaksin.[5] Nonetheless, the loyalty of the rest of the southern electorate to the Democrat Party was clear.

TABLE 9.1

2005 National Election Results: Distribution of Seats by Party and Region

Party	Bangkok	Center	North	South	N'east	Const'y	Party List	Total
TRT	32	80	71	1	126	310	67	377
Democrat	4	7	5	52	2	70	26	96
Chat Thai	1	10	-	1	6	18	7	25
Mahachon	-	-	-	-	2	2	-	2
Total	**37**	**97**	**76**	**54**	**136**	**400**	**100**	**500**

Source: Election Commission of Thailand

The overwhelming level of support given to the Democrats and the low popularity of TRT in the south were explained by scholars in post-election press reports in terms of a range of factors. The high reputation of Chuan Leekpai was cited as an important factor influencing southerners' votes, but notably the commentators were also drawn to distinguishing "southerners" in terms of their distinctive political attitudes. One scholar from the National Institute of Development Administration argued that TRT "could not outplay the Democrats in the south because the people there were opposed to the excessive use of state power." Moreover, opposition to Thaksin's government could be further explained by the fact that, "Southerners also do not like capitalists."[6] Anek Laothamatas, a prominent political science academic and former Democrat deputy party leader, gave his view that most voters in the country, including Bangkokians, looked for short-term gain "at the expense of long-term security of democracy." Southerners, by contrast, were distinctive in their political attitudes because they "did not vote for policies but for ideology." This news interview was reported in English, but one assumes that Anek used the Thai term "*udomkan*" in his press interview. He added that, "They [southerners] wanted Thai Rak Thai to know this country belongs to them as well. They wanted a balance of power. They did not care what Thai Rak Thai offered them."[7] Nikon Chamnong, who supervised Chat Thai Party campaigns in the south, offered the view that the Democrats were too strong to be beaten there because of their stable voting base, adding that, "Southerners and Democrats had a strong bonding and people were motivated to protect their party, after seeing it attacked in other regions."[8]

THE SONGKHLA RESULTS

The voting results in Songkhla revealed the continuing strength of Democrat support in that province and the success of the party's campaigns in each of its eight constituencies (see table 9.2). The Democrats emerged as victors in their three most vulnerable constituencies, showing how misplaced had been the confidence of the TRT contenders Sunthon, Surasak, and Worawit. In Constituency 3, Sunthon had attracted 22,291 votes as the TRT candidate, fewer than Thawisak Thawirat had in the February 2004 by-election (26,636 votes). This represented only 23.6 percent of the total vote (compared to Thawisak's 32.8 percent). Against TRT, Wirat for the Democrats had gained an impressive 67,631 votes of the total of 94,351 valid votes cast, which was somewhat less that Phrai had gained in 2001 in percentage terms (71.6 to 78.6 percent), but nevertheless impressive, particularly given Sunthon's claims to popularity in the electorate. A comparison between constituency and party-list voting also shows that a proportion of Sunthon's supporters had split their votes and continued to show support for the Democrat Party through their party-list votes. The same pattern of ballot-splitting was conspicuous in Constituencies 5 and 8, suggesting that it was the person-based popularity of Worawit and Surasak that drew votes more than identification with the TRT

Party, and that popular loyalty to the Democrats still remained strong even among those who voted for individual TRT candidates.

TABLE 9.2

Songkhla Province:
Constituency and Party-List Votes, February 2005 General Election

Constituency	Ballot	TRT	DEM	CTP	MCP	FFP*
1	Const.	22,750	**56,997**	2,624	–	–
	PL	18,431	**58,910**	4,036	525	206
2	Const.	14,459	**54,407**	2,111	1,180	–
	PL	14,516	**54,512**	1,761	792	108
3	Const.	22,291	**67,631**	4,429	–	–
	PL	18,099	**71,896**	3,038	599	250
4	Const.	17,360	**49,604**	2,835	–	–
	PL	12,423	**52,663**	2,762	499	347
5	Const.	33,039	**47,680**	2,535	570	–
	PL	20,537	**58,319**	2,202	957	537
6	Const.	15,909	**59,571**	1,528	–	–
	PL	14,884	**59,394**	1,914	1,060	201
7	Const.	25,159	**43,848**	2,152	12,736	240
	PL	20,797	**51,564**	2,282	7,971	527
8	Const.	27,551	**45,065**	11,428	2,638	–
	PL	18,105	**60,654**	5,770	1,674	398
Total	Const.	**178,518**	**424,803**	**29,642**	**17,124**	**240**
	%	27.45	65.32	4.56	2.63	0.04
	PL	137,792	467,912	23,768	14,077	1,023
	%	20.54	69.74	3.54	2.10	0.71

Source: Compiled from the constituency office returns of the Songkhla Provincial Election Commission

* FFP = Farmers' Force Party

In Constituency 8, Surasak received 27,551 votes, representing 31.7 percent of the popular vote in a field of four candidates—this was 7,000 more votes than he had gained in 2001 when he ran under the

Ratsadon Party banner (and gained 20,418, or 26.8 percent of the vote in a field of six candidates). Despite Naracha Suwit's weaker personal credentials, he defeated Surasak convincingly in Constituency 8, polling an impressive 45,065 votes for the Democrats—over 10,000 votes more than his father had achieved in the previous elections—and increasing the Democrat constituency vote from 45.2 percent (in 2001) to 51.9 percent. In 2001, the New Aspiration Party candidate had attracted a considerable number of votes from Muslims among the electorate (over 17,000), but in 2005 it was clear that many of these votes had not been transferred to TRT to benefit Surasak. Instead, the Chat Thai candidate (a popular provincial councilor and former *phuak* ally of Surasak's) who gained over 10,000 votes seems to have attracted some of this former NAP support. Significantly, a third of the electors voting for Surasak (some 9,000) did not support TRT in the party-list ballot, but cast their votes for the Democrats. The Democrats gained over 60,000 votes, an impressive 70 percent of the total votes in the Constituency 8 party-list ballot.

As we have seen, the toughest TRT-Democrat battle occurred in Constituency 5 between the popular Worawit Khaothong and the new Democrat candidate Praphon. But here the Democrats had also scored victory, with Praphon gaining 47,680 votes over Worawit with 33,039. Worawit's vote score was impressive, for he won the highest number of votes of all TRT candidates in the province. In this tussle, the Democrats emerged with a lower total proportion of constituency votes than in 2001 (56.8 percent in 2005 compared to nearly 69 percent in 2001). Worawit had clearly attracted a strong level of person-based support, but as with the other strong TRT candidates, this did not reflect support for the TRT Party as such. Worawit attracted 39.4 percent of the constituency vote, but only 23.8 percent of voters opted for TRT in their party-list ballot choice. Conversely, while Praphon gained 56 percent of constituency votes, his party attracted over 10,000 more votes for the party list, representing 69 percent, or exactly the level of support given the Democrats in the constituency ballot of 2001.

Clearly, high levels of person-based popularity and local identification among the strongest TRT candidates had not been enough to undermine the strength of foundational loyalties to the Democrat Party in Songkhla.

Just as significant in these candidates' defeat was the widespread popular animosity towards the TRT government and Thaksin Shinawatra, in particular. The Democrat Party exit polls taken after the by-election of 2004 had already indicated the strength of voters' opinions, including their considerable resentment towards the Thaksin government for stirring up troubles in the border provinces. The Democrat campaigns for the 2005 elections in Songkhla were based largely on demonizing Thaksin as the Democrat Party's moral antithesis, and this was effective. The TRT candidates and their key supporters were clear about the prominence of this factor in their electoral defeat. After the election, Surasak Mani gave his view that the electorate of Constituency 8 had not voted against him personally—they had, he claimed, voted against the Thaksin government, who his Democrat opponents had demonized by distributing DVD disks with lurid portrayals of the mistreatment of Muslims at Tak Bai.[9] Surasak's point was vividly illustrated to me in a teahouse after the election in Thepha District, when a villager pointed to one of Surasak's supporters wearing his TRT Party jacket emblazoned with Surasak's name, and explained, "*khon di, tae phak phit*" (a good person, but wrong party). In Constituency 5, where Muslim voters comprised between 20–25 percent of the electorate in each of the constituency's three *amphoe*, Democrat branch members and supporters had also distributed DVD disks of the Tak Bai demonstration to encourage hostility to Thaksin.[10]

In Constituency 3, Somsri Wongsakun, personal assistant to Sunthon Pathumthong, was confused and frustrated by TRT's poor showing in the vote figures, because during the campaign the people had appeared to welcome Sunthon warmly on his "door-knock" visits to neighborhoods, but this publicly expressed goodwill had not been translated into votes. Personally, Sunthon was well liked but his candidature for TRT was a handicap, and dislike of Thaksin and TRT and the emotional commitment to the Democrats were too strong to be displaced by Sunthon's personal repute alone. As Somsri emphasized, "The people here are Democrat. They like Nai Sunthon, but they don't want Thai Rak Thai. Their view is that this party [TRT] is not the party of southern Thai people. But if Sunthon had stood for the Democrats he would have won for sure."[11]

Southern Culture and Stubborn Belief: Verdicts from the Democrats' Opponents

In assessing their failure to break the Democrats' electoral hold on the constituencies, TRT supporters in Songkhla viewed the specific campaign tactics of the Democrats as important. Fomenting scandal and rumor to undermine enemies was the Democrats' stock-in-trade and was used to great effect in 2005 in Songkhla. But to veteran opponents of the Democrats this reflected the importance of a deeper phenomenon involved, which was the high level of popular trust for the party and its leaders among ordinary voters. In identifying the key reasons for their failure to dislodge the Democrats, frustrated TRT campaign leaders pointed, above all, to factors of southern "political culture" (*watthanatham thang kanmueang*) and what appeared to them as the irrational bond (*khwam phukphan*) between voters and the Democrat Party.

The day after the election, I sat in the café of a Hat Yai hotel with two disconsolate TRT supporters, Seri Nuanpheng, a key organizer for TRT in Constituency 3 and his friend and assistant Achan Chit, a retired technical college teacher and former member of Songkhla's PAO. I had come to know these men over the past two years as strong admirers of Thaksin Shinawatra and his TRT party, who they saw as representing a new policy and performance-based politics. As we talked, I asked them to offer an explanation for TRT's failure to shift the loyalties of the electorate in Songkhla and the south, despite their party's considerable electoral advantages of government incumbency and ample campaign funds. Their explanation of the key factors behind their own candidates' defeat and TRT's overall failure in the region are an interesting commentary on constructs of regional cultural identity and the iconic status of the Democrats in the province. With a pained expression, Seri pronounced his verdict:

> Right now, whoever stands as a TRT candidate here [in Songkhla Province] will lose. I'm not judging this through Nai Sunthon's ability to conduct a campaign, or his qualifications. He was a good candidate, but he lost anyway! In elections for parliamentarians in the south, they [southerners] don't evaluate politics through understanding

> [*khwam khaochai*], but through belief [*khwam chuea*]. If they were to use understanding and reason, they would evaluate policies. Prime Minister Thaksin has advanced policies to establish the 30-baht hospital insurance scheme, to abolish corruption, suppress the drug trade, and many other policies, *but it's no use*! When people *believe* in what the Democrat Party tells them, policies aren't considered, however good these are. Their judgment is based on *belief*!

Achan Chit expanded on his friend's assessment:

> It's difficult to analyze southern Thai politics according to any principles of political science [*rathasat*], because the Democrat Party is a political party that expresses the regionalism [*phak niyom*] of the south. The party has the ability to generate feelings among southerners—that it is a symbol of southern identity, and that it *belongs* to southerners, and above all, the [Democrat] party is highly trusted.

Achan Chit's reference to "political science" underlined his frustration that formulating a political campaign on policy, however relevant to peoples' material needs and local development issues, was not an effective calculus for winning against the force of myth and the power of trust engendered by the Democrats. For both of these men, the political significance of this popular trust was that voters believed implicitly in the truth of the rumors spread by southern Democrat politicians that TRT candidates and supporters were engaged in comprehensive vote buying and using state officials in their electioneering. In short, the Democrats had won by romancing southern voters into once again affirming emotional loyalties against their own TRT Party and candidates that—unjustly, according to Seri and Chit—had been damned by Democrat orators as evil enemies of democracy and the noble "political culture" of southerners, one that eschewed vote buying and resisted intimidation by officials. Their favored party had literally been out-performed.

Manop Patumthong, the brother and principal campaign advisor of Sunthon in Constituency 3, put forward a similar analysis of fundamental emotional bonds linking the Democrat Party and local voters:

> This [election result] is about political culture. . . . rooted deeply in southern Thai culture is a strong dislike of authoritarianism and a deep hostility to state power. . . . and also an attachment to *phuak phong*. Nai Sunthon has strong connections with the locality among village and sub-district headmen in his position as *nai amphoe*, and he has many family members in the area, but this was just not enough [to succeed]. If we analyze this result deeply, we see that the people here were afraid that the Democrat Party would lose, so they made a special effort to vote for them. . . . It's clear that, deep down, southern Thai people can understand and evaluate policies well, but in the final analysis, policies aren't important for them to consider because they are "*khon tai*" [southerners]. . . . and, it doesn't matter to them if the TRT candidate is also a southerner. The fact is that they identify the Democrats as the party of the southern people, so they will choose them.

There was a strong degree of similarity in the judgments of local civil society advocates and these TRT supporters in their pronouncements about the cultural foundations of the southern Thai bond with the Democrats. Seri Pathumwan, a local politician and a vote canvasser for Worawit in Constituency 5, is also a strong supporter of local NGOs and the civil society movement. He supported Worawit as the TRT candidate because he believed that the government party offered the possibility of bringing tangible development benefits to the ordinary people of the province and introducing a "policy-based" politics to the south. The popular support given to the Democrats signaled to him that the people of his constituency were not prepared to accept a new way of assessing the political eligibility of candidates or parties. In his frustration at the continuing ascendancy of the Democrats in his constituency, Seri exclaimed, "The *chaoban* are stubborn (*due*) and keep to their trust in the Democrats, even if they get no real benefits from them. If I were Thaksin now, I would drop the price of rubber to 10 baht and then see what they think! No matter what this government has done for them, they don't care! They stick to this crazy belief in the Democrats."[12]

Seri's argument echoes the views of the pro-civil society southern folklore scholars who identify the basis of loyalty to the Democrats as rooted in traditional phuak loyalties and reverence for leaders who embody *nakleng* qualities of skillfulness, courage, and fidelity. The similarities in judgment between the TRT supporters and civil society advocates lie in claims to the cultural foundations of this loyalty and political outlook, expressed as a politics founded on "belief" (*khwam chuea*), not analysis (*kan wikhro*). The difference in interpretation between these groups is their contrasting emphasis on the power balance in the people-party relationship. The TRT supporters (including Seri Pathumwan) see the *chaoban* as complicit in the reproduction of the myth of the Democrats as the embodiment of southern sensibility and morality, while the folklore scholars see the *chaoban* essentially as victims of the Democrat Party's calculated manipulation of their traditional cultural symbols, norms, and relationships.

It is understandable that in their immediate post-election despondency, these TRT campaign leaders in Songkhla should naturalize the relationship between the Democrats and their southern voters as an irreducible bond and in the process paradoxically mirror the southern Democrats' own discourse that the party represents the highest political virtues of the people of the region as honest, forthright, trustworthy, loyal, and congenitally sensitive to signs of corruption and authoritarianism. Yet the campaigns in some constituencies had been a close-run thing for the Democrats in Songkhla and the south, calling on all their renowned resources of scandal mongering and rhetoric to capture the moral high ground in a desperate contest for political legitimacy. And as Seri Nuanpheng and his friend Chit knew all too well, for them it had been as much a struggle against a highly organized local and regional Democrat political machine as it had been a symbolic contest for the hearts and minds of voters. Their distinction between rationality and emotion in their political models, contrasting modern "rational" TRT politics and "emotional" (thus irrational) Democrat loyalties, was hardly convincing, and it simplified both their own and the Democrats' techniques of mobilization, which had relied strongly on basic solidarities of kinship and phuak affiliation. In 2005, the TRT Party made a determined effort and employed a variety of methods to undermine the multi-faceted Democrat political ascendancy. In this, they failed, despite overwhelming success elsewhere in Thailand and considerable superiority in financial resources. On both symbolic and pragmatic levels, and despite strong efforts in some constituencies, they were unable to undermine effectively the Democrats' dense phuak-based support networks, combat their strategic use of scandal, and shift the broadly based emotional loyalties and myths connecting ordinary people to the party.

Part V

Anatomy of the Democrat Political Ascendancy

CHAPTER 10

Symbols and Solidarities: Anatomy of the Democrat Ascendancy

IN THAILAND'S south in 2005, the Democrat Party's anomalous regional victory in the context of its national failure was achieved by tried-and-trusted campaigning methods—a judicious mix of rhetorical romance, ritual displays of communal solidarity, a touch of scandal, denunciation of their opponents' use of money, and a thoroughgoing demonization of Thaksin as government leader. To be sure, voters elsewhere in the country were highly critical of Thaksin's governing style, his nepotism, rampant money-saturated populism, restrictions on press freedom, and a conspicuous failure to deal with the southern crisis. Yet this disapproval was not strong enough to translate into many Democrat wins in constituencies, except in the south. As already outlined, commentators offered various explanations of the Democrats' regional triumph in 2005. Some centered on specific issues to explain the TRT defeat, such as the effects of the escalating southern border insurgency in provoking hostility to Thaksin. Others had advanced "culture"-based explanations resting on southern Thai "personality," or the standard truism about the habitual "regionalism" (*phumiphak niyom*) of the majority of southern voters who embraced the Democrats as "the party of the south."

How do we account for the continuing electoral dominance of the Democrat Party in southern Thailand and its stubborn persistence in the heyday of Thaksin's rule, an era which many commentators pronounced as heralding the transformation of both governance and electoral politics? Earlier chapters presented accounts of four election campaigns at close quarters and explored the dynamics of political group formation and allegiance as I encountered them directly in Songkhla Province during the eventful years of 2004–05. This chapter brings together some key themes that have emerged in these accounts concerning the character of symbols and solidarities in the political world of the south. These accounts have brought into relief the contours of what I call the multi-level "Democrat ascendancy." It is an ascendancy that is forged from the dynamic interaction between political resources that I describe here as "poetics," "symbolism," "social-familial" bonds and "organization," all of which inform and shape loyalty and solidarity among different groups within the constellation of actors that engage with the party at various levels. These dimensions of meaning, practice, and structuring interact. They reinforce each other, but also exist in tension. I am not proposing that politics is played out on a static bedrock of cultural norms. Rather, political action and choice in the south, as elsewhere in Thailand, involve the active manipulation of key symbols—by political actors at all levels, from candidates, to canvassers, to voters—to rationalize and legitimize behavior, to forge relationships, to categorize group identity, and to comprehend political eligibility.

The Democrat ascendancy in Songkhla is always under threat, from both inside and outside the party and its constituent groups. As elsewhere in the country among the connected political networks centering on patrons and phuak, political players at various levels are periodically activated to function as "bases" of support for elections. These "voting bases," evoked as solid entities and factors by journalists, scholars, and politicians alike as the primary foundation for predicting electoral performance, are in reality never inert or passive, whether in the south or any other region. These solidarities and linkages need constant cultivation at many levels; otherwise, they will dissipate and be claimed by others. The Democrat ascendancy requires constant nurturing and reproduction. This is done by balancing the interests of key players with party interests and phuak loyalties among the crucial middle and upper ranks of followers who have their own political ambitions in local and provincial spheres. The constituency politicians, as everywhere else in the country, need to keep in constant touch with constituents by attending funerals and numerous functions to bestow *kiat* (honor) on people and display their own closeness with the localities (*samphat phuenthi*). Visibility is everything—the *chaoban* want to be acknowledged and the politicians need to be seen. In addition, "the party" needs to be presented and constantly authenticated in the presence of ordinary voters and party members. In election campaigns, the party and its orators serve to translate the meaning of political issues to the electorate by presenting convincing performances of political paradigms, which play the critical role of defining the purpose and place of the party and its community of supporters in Thailand's broader political world. Pragmatic alliances—that is, instrumental and interest-driven affiliations—and symbolic idioms both play a critical role in generating and reproducing the south's pro-Democrat political solidarities. These processes shape a political ascendancy and voting heartland, which—despite the spats, disputes, and double-crosses constantly being played out among middle-level political aspirants within the party and associated phuak—can be imagined vividly by ordinary voters as the home of a trustful and honorable political fellowship within the nation.

By "poetics," I refer to the active performative delivery of rhetoric and the powerful evocation of social-cultural metaphors that are central to political identification and the symbolic construction of political community. In his finely nuanced ethnographic study of the performance of identity among Cretan men, Michael Herzfeld writes, "The successful performance of selfhood depends upon an ability to identify the self with larger categories of identity."[1] This clearly applies to the way that the Democrat Party is literally "performed" at its political rallies. Democrat political performances, as we have seen, are undertaken through oratory, usually in the powerful collective ritual context of rallies. The effectiveness of these performances derives from their capacity to articulate received truisms about the noble Democrat "political self," a shared identity binding politicians, party activists, and ordinary people alike in an intimate political community. Rally performances are indeed the essence of the Democrat Party's ideal public self—bold, assertive, and defiant.

By "symbolism," I refer to the idealized representations of political action and virtue that serve to define the boundaries of a "symbolic community" against those who might compromise its existence. As William Connolly notes, "Identity requires difference in order to be, and it converts difference into otherness in order to secure its own self-certainty."[2] My point here is that the force and effectiveness of Democrat Party evocations of "southern Thai political culture" stem from the persuasiveness of an idealized representation of the southern Thai person as citizen and voter. The party projects a moral paradigm of the good citizen (trustworthiness, loyalty, truthfulness) onto the electorate and names this paradigm "the political culture of southerners" (*watthanatham khong khon tai*). Yet, this is not a one-way process of objectification. In this construction of an idealized southern Thai political person, ordinary citizens participate actively. The Democrat seduction of the southern electorate is not based on narrow parochialism, but on a moral politics that resonates with shared cultural norms of trust and loyalty tied to ideals of leadership eligibility. "Southern Thai political culture" is a symbolic construction where two imagined primordialisms unite—the pure and timeless party, and the noble and incorruptible southern citizen. But at the same time, this is not an exclusive construction, since southern Democrat supporters see themselves as part of a broader national Democrat Party community. My point here differs markedly from the arguments advanced by the Thai political commentator Chai-anan Samudavanija and southern Thai folklore scholars, who have proposed that regional pride is ruthlessly used by the Democrat Party as an electoral tool, implying by this that southern voters are the innocent pawns of a scheming party agenda that exploits simple parochial loyalties.[3] The process of party-people identification, I suggest, is more nuanced and mutual than this simple depiction of symbolic exploitation.

Two other culturally informed dimensions of solidarity and integration, which I label collectively here as "social-familial bonds," interact with the poetic and symbolic dynamics that inform people-party identification. They are kinship links and repute (*barami*), and phuak affiliation. Notably these dimensions of identification and solidarity serve to reinforce as well as undermine and compete with party-linked identification. Phuak solidarities serve to consolidate the collective commitments among the middle and upper groups of the province's Democrat Party membership. Phuak linkages among friends and work associates among these political actors may be based on earlier connections forged over time during childhood, schooldays, and work experience. These generalized "social phuak" loyalties are drawn upon when members enter political life, and thus to some extent might be then described as "political phuak," because they find affirmation by mutual assistance rendered in common political activity. It is quite common for an individual to belong to numerous other phuak (which I describe here as "social phuak") that have nothing to do with their political activity, and often such phuak may be affiliated to non-Democrat political parties. Other phuak bonds develop through the experience of common activity within the party and these phuak might be portrayed as tightly knit sub-groups within the party structure, such as the leading phuak figure described by Thongchai later in this chapter, who financially assists him so that he can maintain his political activity as a committed party activist.

As we have already seen, phuak membership and identity has both structural and symbolic importance. Widely evoked as representing an ideal of loyalty and commitment, the phuak is, however, capable of fracturing when individuals find that their ambitions are not served. Significantly, when an individual splits away from a phuak, such an action is justified in moral and normative terms. *Trakun* identity and the accumulated repute generated by forms of public service are an important resource used in calling on electoral support, and kin affiliations are fundamental, even among Democrat politicians whose party commitment is publicly affirmed through *udomkan*. Primordial loyalties of blood are widely accepted as a principle of political support among national and local-level politicians. However, political divisions within family networks are not uncommon, and Democrat Party identity has been a more powerful and countervailing force than *trakun* loyalty in electoral politics in Songkhla, at least up to the present.

The organizational structure of the Democrat Party allows wide participation in party activities and in so doing serves to create a relatively permanent group of supporters. It is a pattern that no other party in the province has succeeded in reproducing. The wide distribution of party members throughout neighborhoods and villages—often occupying positions of prominence—gives the party a pervasive presence in Songkhla, contributing strongly to popular identification with the Democrats. In the following sections of this chapter, I elaborate on these mutually reinforcing poetic-symbolic and structural-organizational themes.

METAPHORS OF LOYALTY AND INTIMACY

Ordinary southern Democrat voters and members express their connection with the party in terms of personal intimacy and visceral loyalties, evoking values and ideals commonly applied in the south to interpersonal relationships, collective bonds to groups, and ancestral attachments to place. As expressed freely by women supporters, loyalty to the party is not a matter for cerebral reflection; it is about irreducible matters of the heart—*Prachathipat yu nai chai* (The Democrats are in my heart) or *chai Prachathipat* (a Democrat heart). Even among men, this attachment is often evoked in the strong terms of an idealized fidelity between lovers—*rak diao, chai diao* (I love only one, my heart is with one). It is hardly surprising therefore, that in late 2003 when the prominent Democrat MP Niphon Bunyamani organized entertainment for a meeting of Democrat Party branch officials at his home, he invited the popular southern *luk thung* entertainer Ekkachai Siriwichai to sing the well-known song *Khon Tai Rak Ching* (Southerners Love Truly). Bodily or natural metaphors are also commonly used to express these bonds—*fang luek* (rooted deeply), or *Prachathipat yu nai sai-lueat* (The Democrats are in my veins).

Visceral expressions reinforce other commonplace signifiers of the party's centrality to ordinary people, such as the common reference to the age of the party and the duration of its presence in the region ("The party is old," "The party has been here a long time"). For many ordinary supporters these compressed matter-of-fact phrases are enough to highlight the historical nexus binding the party-people relationship, but often this historical dimension is reinforced by the introduction of an evocative depiction of grandparents and parents on their deathbeds urging their children to always vote Democrat. In this way, the party is authorized not simply by its age as a national political institution, but by a narrative that invokes the wishes of wise and respected family elders. Another metaphor connects the party to a familiar old house (*ban kao*), where families return for comfort and solace. The shared dimension of Democrat Party identification is powerfully reinforced by the parallels commonly drawn between fidelity among friends and fidelity to the party. Hence, the powerful alliterative declaration: "*Mai thing phak, Mai thing phuak*" (Don't abandon the party and don't abandon the group). Phuak loyalty is both a social reality and a popular cultural ideal underpinning social relations and loyalties in the south. Connecting party loyalty to phuak loyalty is therefore a powerful association, even if it is contradicted in practice.

In discussions about voting alternatives and the advantages of the TRT Party over the Democrats in terms of policies, many people stressed to me that in the final analysis if they didn't vote Democrat they would not sleep at night and they couldn't face their friends for the shame (*phop phuak mai dai—ai phuean*). In short, they felt that there was something unnatural about voting for a party other than the Democrats. Voting Democrat has become a socialized convention reinforced by peer and family pressure.[4] Deeply internalized through socialization, this voting loyalty acts as a counterweight to the temptation to vote for alternative parties; this is admitted not only by rural folk with limited education, but also by quite highly educated individuals. Sombun, for example, is a prosperous electrical contractor of Hat Yai, a Sino-Thai with a university degree in electrical engineering. He acted as a vote canvasser for Worawit Khaothong in the PAO election of March 2004, but in February 2005, he could not bring himself to vote for TRT in the national election. He confided to me, "I can't really explain it, but during a number of national elections in the past and in this one too, I left home determined not to vote Democrat anymore, but once I entered the polling booth something happened and I found myself changing my mind and voting for the Democrats once again."[5]

PERCEIVING THE PARTY

Popular metaphors and expressions evoking the people-Democrat Party nexus often suggest an absence of considered reflection about political issues among ordinary southern voters, a point often made by opponents of the Democrats in Songkhla. This oversimplifies the reality that many Democrat supporters do indeed see the weaknesses of their party. Since the advent of Thaksin Shinawatra's TRT government and its emphasis on decisive policy-oriented action, many committed Democrat branch officials in Songkhla pointed out to me that Thaksin's leadership contrasted with the generally slow and hesitant performance of the Democrats when in government during the 1990s. Although the virtue and integrity of the much-revered Chuan Leekpai, former party leader and prime minister, are never doubted, Democrat supporters admit that there were faults with his less-than-decisive governing style. But this is not enough to dislodge commitment to the party, because what underlies the fundamental allegiance of Democrat supporters in Songkhla—among both rural and urban dwellers of a wide range of occupational backgrounds—is an evaluation of eligibility that centers on the issue of trust. To its supporters in Songkhla Province, and elsewhere in the south, what makes the Democrat Party trustworthy is its credentials as a distinctive representative organization in a national political world dominated by power-seekers, money, the absence of principles, and corruption. Thaksin's first period in office from 2001–05 did nothing but confirm a deep distrust that power holders were bent on "eating the country" (*kin mueang*) and practicing rampant cronyism (*len phak, len phuak*). A number of themes stand out in people's accounts of the identity of the party. These portraits vary in sophistication depending on people's education, interest in politics, and monitoring of the news media; but nevertheless, many of these accounts extend well beyond the simple knee jerk regional loyalties attributed to southern Democrat supporters.

The Authentic Institution

Prominent among the popular criteria that accord eligibility to the Democrat Party is its distinctive characteristic as a collective institution with no single owner or founder (*mai mi chaokhong*). In contrast to almost all existing political parties in Thailand, it has not been created, and nor is it controlled, by one powerful person. The collective nature of the party's origins, linked to its foundation on a set of principles, reinforces another key characteristic of the party as an authentic and enduring political institution (*sathaban kanmueang*). Contrasts are continually made between the Democrat Party as an authentic political institution and other parties as only special purpose parties (*phak chaphokit*) that make their appearance only during elections.

A Democratic Institution for Ordinary People

Supporters at all levels argue that the party is distinctive because of its governing structure, which promotes ability and accessibility. The governance of the party is deemed to embody the democratic ideal by virtue of the fact that its leadership and office-bearers at all levels are elected. This leads to a further critical dimension frequently emphasized by ordinary supporters—that the party is accessible to committed people, who can rise through the ranks according to their efforts and merit. Throughout the years following the TRT victory in 2001, this quality was emphasized in contrast to the nepotistic and paternalistic practices of Prime Minister Thaksin in appointing government ministers and key military office-holders. The TRT Party itself was seen as a creature of Thaksin, totally dependent on his money and personality, unlike the struggling but worthy Democrats. These themes of the party's qualities as a firmly established, accessible institution allowing able and worthy people to rise, and encouraging ordinary people to participate, are not abstract ideas. They can be easily illustrated, whether by reference to the stories about exemplary local MPs, the supreme example of Chuan Leekpai's rise from temple boy to law graduate and prime minister, or by branch office-bearers and ordinary members in accounts of their own involvement in the party.

A Clean and Morally Upright Party

Democrat Party politicians and supporters are adamant in their claim that voters, at least Democrat voters in the south, cannot be "bought." In Songkhla, there is a widely held view that vote buying in the south is low compared to the high levels of its incidence in Thailand's poverty-stricken northeast. But vote buying certainly exists in the south and its emergence coincides with its rise as a countrywide phenomenon since the late 1980s, with the advent of civilian governments, business-backed parties, and provincial political machines. During the March 1992 elections, more instances of vote buying were reported in the south than any other region of the country, while in 1995 monitoring agencies reported substantial levels of vote buying in the south, including among the Democrats.[6]

In Songkhla, during the by-election in February 2004 and later in the 2005 general election, evidence points to widespread distribution of cash-for-votes on behalf of the TRT candidates, even though this party was heavily defeated. In Songkhla, we have seen that the Democrats also engaged in vote buying, but this took place on a smaller scale and was highly selective. First-hand knowledge of the practice is therefore less visible among ordinary Democrat voters, and it is thus easier for the party to sustain its image as a clean party. Indeed, the fact that the Democrats generally do not *need* to buy votes—even if this perennially cash-strapped party had the financial capacity to do so—is testament to the strong foundation loyalty that the party inspires.

The legitimacy claims of the Democrat Party are based heavily on its image and declared principles of honesty, trustworthiness, and "clean-handedness" (*suesat*, *sucharit*), and this is echoed by ordinary supporters in Songkhla who claim that abhorrence of vote buying is the party's major distinguishing virtue. The powerful moral denigration invoked against vote buying in the south needs to be understood in terms of strong culturally normative elements that are tapped by Democrat leaders and perpetuated in local folklore about the party. The right to vote (*sit lueaktang*) is proclaimed a sacred possession (*sing saksit*) and to be "bought" signifies amorality as well as loss of personal dignity (*sia saksi*). Democrat speakers are adept at evoking both individual dignity as well as the collective self-worth of southerners (*saksi khong khon tai*, the dignity of southerners) in presenting the party as the moral exemplar of southern virtues in the political realm. To be "bought" connotes loss of dignity and reduction to the despised historical status of a *phrai* (a bonded commoner in the pre-modern Thai social structure). More powerful than this negative image of a purchased *phrai* is the equation of a bought voter with a prostitute. Money offered by other parties does not have to be refused, however, as the Songkhla Democrat MP Niphon Bunyamani intoned at a political rally, "Take the money offered by Thai Rak Thai but vote for *Prachathipat*."

In Songkhla, Democrat voters give both moral and practical reasons for the party's clean record. In a type of circular logic, it is argued that the party is committed to clean politics but also a key reason not to buy votes is that the party is poor. Being poor makes the party more worthy of support and reinforces its popular image as a struggling and heroic band of underdogs defending democratic institutions against parties of the rich and powerful that gain power through illegitimate means. The Democrat Party's record of particular success in the south, despite lack of resources, helps to ennoble ordinary voters because it underlines the consistent strength of willing commitment and loyalty.

A Strong and Enduring *Udomkan*

Though they are quick to affirm that the Democrat Party and its supporters are distinguished from other parties by *udomkan*, ordinary supporters in Songkhla have difficulty explaining just what this *udomkan* is. Among rural villagers, the party's *udomkan* may be described simply as "the party has existed for a long time." Even among urban-dwellers, the notion has a very vague meaning. For example, two female assistants in a gold shop in Hat Yai informed me cheerfully that the Democrat *udomkan* was "to vote Democrat" (*udomkan khong Prachathipat khue: lueak Prachathipat*). At its most definite, expressed by more well-read and seasoned party branch office-holders, or urban businesspeople, the *udomkan* is explained variously as opposition to authoritarianism, moral uprightness (opposition to vote buying), and the opportunity for all to gain elective office-holding in the party on the basis of merit, not of wealth.

For most people, in fact, it is easier to define *udomkan* by its absence in political opponents. A lack of *udomkan* is exemplified by political parties that emerge momentarily, base their support on money and vote buying, are dependent on wealthy leaders, and, in particular, it is shown by politicians who change their party. Ultimately, those who lack *udomkan* are seen as lacking commitment and long-term loyalty. The positive quality of the Democrat Party and its supporters, evoked as a community united by *udomkan*, emerges most clearly in the context of electoral contests and other occasions where the party's enemies are invariably defined as the antithesis of its *udomkan*. To emphasize the importance of *udomkan*, Democrat supporters in Songkhla frequently refer to examples of the electoral failure of politicians who have left the Democrat Party. A prime example is Wira Musikaphong, a prominent former Democrat who had helped engineer the damaging "January 10" party split of 1987. After his defection, Wira failed in all attempts to contest southern seats against Democrat candidates under other party banners. Democrat politicians often encapsulate *udomkan* in vivid images tailored to the character and lifestyles of their audiences. For example, at a small rally held in a Muslim fishing village in his constituency in late 2003, Nipon Bunyamani likened the party's *udomkan* to the unity of fishermen staying together in their small boat during a storm at sea. This, he proclaimed, was the Democrat Party spirit, unlike other parties, whose self-interested politicians selfishly jump out of the party boat in times of trouble.

To many of the Democrats' southern voters, the party's cherished *udomkan* remains impossible to define in the abstract; it becomes clear only when it visualized and evoked, either in the guise of enemies that can be portrayed as its antithesis or in terms of exemplary leaders who can be admired as embodying the *udomkan* of the party.

The Chuan Factor—Embodying the Party

The popular veneration for former party leader and twice-serving Prime Minister Chuan Leekpai must be counted as a critical—indeed the most critical—factor behind the overwhelming support enjoyed by the Democrat Party in the south. Chuan's role in attracting electoral support for the Democrats in the south has not simply been a result of popular pride generated by the opportunity of having a southerner as a national leader; it stems more from Chuan's iconic significance as an embodiment of ideal political and social virtues. Short in stature, quietly spoken, bespectacled, and with the pale complexion that betrays his Chinese heritage, Chuan might appear to be an improbable figurehead in a region where dark-skinned features and masculine postures prevail as one of the dominant models of the tough Democrat politician. Nonetheless, Chuan's carefully cultivated public persona and gravely intoned pronouncements serve to make tangible for ordinary people the bond between moral and political values that the Democrat Party propounds as its guiding *udomkan*.

Through Chuan, the *udomkan* is identifiable because it articulates with commonly held ideals and paradigms of southern virtue. Loyalty is a recurring theme in Chuan's speeches, where accounts of his own life feature prominently. His loyalty to ordinary people—*chaoban*—is expressed in his gratefulness to the people for their trust expressed in voting for him and by his oft-mentioned accounts of his mother's sacrifices for his education. These articulate with a commitment to serving the nation. His loyalty to and identification with ordinary people expresses the ideal self-sacrificing and down-to-earth (*tit din*) virtues of a member of parliament who recognizes that legitimacy flows from the people (*prachachon*), and that "a politician should never discard the people who have voted with purity," i.e., without the pressure of money for their votes.[7] These dispositions resonate with strongly held social and religious values attached to the practice of returning merit (*topthaen bunkhun*).

To his audiences, Chuan's repeated personal accounts of his political life and devotion to the Democrat Party reinforce the values of loyalty and constancy that are associated in the south with the loyalty to one's friendship group (phuak), and this contrasts with the near-universal practice of non-Democrat politicians changing their party allegiance.[8] Chuan lives an ordinary life and has not enriched himself through political office; in fact, it is well known that he is the poorest man among his Democrat Party colleagues. In addition to embodying these widely accepted virtues, Chuan is revered for his qualities of courage and his skills in parliamentary debate where he has earned the sobriquet, "the honey-coated razor."[9] Ordinary people in Songkhla, as elsewhere in the south, admire Chuan because he shows he has "the heart of a *nakleng*." This popular image combines the valued attributes of courage in speaking out (regardless of the consequences), persistence in the face of adversity, and unqualified self-sacrifice and loyalty, whatever the consequences. Chuan's rhetorical self-deprecation as a servant of the *chaoban* serves to elevate him even further as an icon to his audiences, so that when he solemnly intones his standard opening line, "*phom pen huang banmueang*" (I'm worried about the country), it conveys a communal imperative to join him to protect the community against those enemies who threaten its very existence.

Chuan is referred to in the south as "*Nai Hua Chuan*" (Leader Chuan) and by the older generation he is affectionately called "*luk Chuan*" (Son Chuan). Popular reverence is affirmed by numerous households who proudly mount his framed portraits and posters in places of honor on their walls; sometimes the portraits are positioned even higher than ancestral and spirit shrines (see plate 10.1). His popularity among women, notably *maekha* (women vendors), is particularly strong. Whenever Chuan is the featured speaker at Democrat rallies, women are a conspicuous presence and their enthusiasm in bestowing garlands on Chuan often interrupts his speeches for long periods. In 2003, when Chuan stepped down from party leadership and the pedestrian Banyat Banthatthan was elected in his place, some journalists speculated that this signaled the decline of Democrat Party support in the south.[10] This did not occur and, in fact, Chuan, now senior advisor to the party, remained busier than ever as a key campaigning asset and rallying symbol for the party in the south, despite his oft-reported failing health. This was powerfully revealed during the critical by-election in Songkhla's Constituency 3 early in 2004, when Chuan attracted crowds of supporters to the Democrat rallies. Here the TRT Party, although triumphant in all other by-elections held since its overwhelming national victory in 2001, was convincingly defeated.

A clear recognition of the popular reverence accorded to Chuan in Songkhla was shown during the principal TRT rally before the by-election, when Thaksin was careful to show respect to Chuan's qualities—he even described Chuan as "*narak*" (loveable, cute) and carefully focused his criticism on the Democrat Party in general. In the by-election campaign, Democrat workers traveling in caravans of pickup trucks through outlying districts of the constituency discarded calls to support the individual candidate by name or number and reverted to the abbreviated but powerful catch-cries, "If you love Nai

10.1 Chuan as a household icon. Portraits such as this grace many homes of ordinary southerners.

Hua Chuan, vote Democrat," or "Vote for the party of Nai Chuan." Despite Chuan's apparently poor health, he continued to act as a critical party rallying symbol in the 2005 election. Here, the Democrats in the south skillfully played on the "sympathy" (*songsan*) factor by reminding voters of Chuan's determination and sacrifice for the party and people. In Songkhla, posters featuring Chuan were deployed strategically throughout the campaign. In early January, billboards for candidates began to feature the portraits of both Banyat (the party leader) as well as Chuan, but two weeks before polling day many of these were replaced by billboards that showed only Chuan and the party number.

Reverence for Chuan in the south might actually be interpreted not as regionally distinctive at all, but typical of the importance of morally powerful leadership figures in Thai society generally. Chuan's particular significance to the south, however, is based on a symbolism that articulates with the particular blend of paradigms—individualism, egalitarianism, fierce collective loyalty, and assertiveness—that southerners habitually attribute to their ideal selves. In the person of Chuan are condensed the key attributes of an ideal Democrat and an ideal southerner—a courageous and skilled advocate of parliamentary democracy, a man of humble origins who advanced through education and merit, a man schooled in the law and an able orator, and a national leader with a proven record of commitment to virtue, honesty, sacrifice, loyalty to the people, and to political principles. The Democrat Party slogan printed on candidates' posters, "The ideology has not changed" (*udomkan mai plianplaeng*), was literally embodied in the person of Chuan. The Democrat campaign slogan of unchanging *udomkan* was parodied by TRT speakers and juxtaposed with the TRT message of newness and change, but this rhetorical play on contrasts was a pointless exercise. For in this small phrase was a powerful emotional language of loyalty, integrity, and self-sacrifice for a greater good (the party and the nation) which was condensed in the person of Chuan.

POLITICAL RALLIES: PERFORMING THE PARTY-SOUTH NEXUS

Political rallies are the most powerful means by which the Democrat Party in the south mobilizes and affirms identity and popular allegiance. Democrat rallies are potent rituals where symbols of political community are enacted and enunciated through rhetorical performances. Audiences treat large rallies simultaneously as part entertainment, part festive celebration, and part political lesson. As forums for the display of oratory and humor, political rallies are not unique to the south, however, non-southern Democrats themselves often remark on the distinctiveness of the southern Thai penchant for admiring lengthy displays of political oratory. During the 2004 Songkhla by-election, Democrat members and parliamentarians from

Bangkok expressed genuine awe at the stamina of both rally speakers and their audiences in enduring these marathons. There is some empirical basis for these observations in the form of surveys, which suggest that many southerners view rallies as a source of political information in greater proportions than people of other regions.[11] In early 2003, the Democrat Party apparently conducted a poll which revealed that in the south a high proportion of respondents (65 percent) indicated that their major source of political information was gleaned from political rallies, in contrast to other regions of Thailand where the majority of people gained news from radio, television, and newspapers.[12] During the by-election campaign in February 2004, Thaksin denigrated Democrat rallies as "festivals of abuse" (*thesakan da*). At the same time, however, he warned his audience not to attend the Democrat rallies, knowing that they would have a powerful effect on voters' decision-making. Whether or not it is true that Democrat rhetorical performance in the south owes its popularity to the cultural provenance of the *nang talung* and *li-ke* dramas—which folklorists argue are rooted in the cultural memory of southerners—it is clear that marathon sessions of oratory are widely perceived to be the marks of good politicians and the key distinction of the Democrats.

Democrat rallies act as dramatic public arenas where the collective face of "*Prachathipat*" is presented to the people of the constituencies. Aside from the specific political issues being addressed, all rally oratory is fused by a dominant narrative that affirms a "we/us" group against a demonic or unworthy political "other" who lacks the precious properties of "*Prachathipat*." It is a narrative that retells the struggles of virtuous and truthful men serving the people tirelessly in a common cause. The party is presented vividly on video screens, with solemn commentary, as an ideal tableau of dutiful politicians dedicated to serving the people and upholding constitutional rule through incorruptible behavior and moral rectitude. Democrat politicians present themselves as following in the footsteps of the founding fathers of the party (Khuang Aphaiwong and Seni Pramoj), who exemplified the spirit of political heroism, championing the interests of the people against the trickery and subterfuge of military dictators and upstart business-tycoon politicians alike.

The oratorical skills of individual politicians vary considerably. The great favorites of southern audiences are the comic and mocking Trairong Suwankhiri and the grave and lucid Chuan Leekpai, but others play important roles in rally spectacles, often specializing in speaking about key issues arising from their own constituencies or their parliamentary and party functions. Information, entertainment, and moral disquisitions are combined and calibrated. As rhetorical performances, rallies serve a number of simultaneous functions. They mediate political realities by dramatizing the stakes of political contest; they perform the history and identity of the party, and in the process translate its formal *udomkan* into the comprehensible cultural vocabulary of trust and loyalty.

SOLIDARITIES: *PHAKPHUAK*, PATRONAGE, AND FAMILIES

Phakphuak

One evening early in September 2003, I, was confronted with an expression of group loyalty that flew in the face of all official pronouncements of the Democrat Party and its exalted claims to party identity based on political ideals: "*mai mi udomkan, mi tae phakphuak*!" (There is no *udomkan*, there is only the phuak.) The forceful claim was made by the personal assistant of Niphon Bunyamani, the long-serving Democrat MP for Constituency 5 in Songkhla Province. Speaking as we sat in a van on the way to a small party rally in Singhanakhon District, Khun Don was responding to my invitation to define the Democrat Party's "*udomkan*," but his assertive exclamation wiped out any further reference to matters of Democrat political ideology from our exchange. Another staunch Democrat follower expressed a complementary view with the same wry humor, relegating *udomkan* to a performative role only, and not as the ultimate ground of his party commitment: "Where's my *udomkan*? Well, I leave that on the back of my truck and bring it out when I mount the speaker's platform." Don's assertion that *phakphuak* was the only thing that mattered was a statement about the critical importance of personal relationships and group loyalty in southern Thai social and political organization. Don had been a close friend of

Niphon's since their schooldays together, and was his assistant since the late 1980s when Niphon began his political career as a provincial councilor. Since that time, Don has assisted Niphon in a wide range of capacities, from organizing rallies to acting as Niphon's representative at funeral ceremonies. Don is a full-time civil servant working in a regional office of a central government ministry in the city of Songkhla, but his work for Niphon is not restricted by the demands of his salaried work, because his immediate superior at work is also a Democrat Party supporter, and as a member of Don's *phakphuak*, he naturally allows Don to take time off for Democrat Party work whenever required.

As used by Don, the term *phakphuak* describes a group united by friendship and common commitments, in this case, political work. However, the term resonates beyond this to encompass other dimensions and meanings. On the same evening that Khun Don made his statement about the sovereignty of group loyalty above party-political ideology, I sat with a group of Muslim community elders in a village in Singhanakhon District, while Democrat branch leaders prepared the stage for Niphon's rally. One of them, a village headman, turned to me, smiling, and pointed to Niphon, saying "*mi phakphuak yoe*." The nearest equivalent to a common expression in English is, "He has many connections." But there is a critical difference here, because the expression in Thai is not only about the significance of connections between individuals, but connections with groups (literally: "He has many groups"). Though it was difficult for me to discern whether the statement was made in a spirit of criticism or admiration, it nevertheless described two interacting elements in the function of the phuak. It summarized the practical bases of Niphon's influence as well as the symbolic foundations of his status.

Phuak identity and affiliation represent both instrumental utility (through connections) and proclaim status and power. Some argue that phuak-based loyalties are more pronounced among the southern Thai than elsewhere. Though this is impossible to demonstrate, what is clear is that southerners believe this to be so. In Niphon's case, his many phuak connections contribute to his reputation as a politician with the heart of a *nakleng*, a decisive and strong leader who can get things done. In practical terms, Niphon's ability to get things done in his electorate—whether for himself, his party, or his constituents—depends on his capacity to access and mobilize support and assistance at a range of levels. This is facilitated not only by his formal rights and qualifications as an MP but by the more informal means of phuak connections across a range of spheres. In terms of status, Niphon's reputation is based on public recognition of the size and number of his phuak, and wide public knowledge about the practical efficacy of these connections. Phuak connections enable Niphon to have soccer T-shirts displaying his name and party printed free-of-charge by a friend who owns a factory, so that he can distribute them to school teams throughout his constituency. It is his phuak connections that allow him to help families in his constituency in matters ranging from children's enrollment at schools to assistance in criminal court cases. A phuak identity is not something to be hidden, it is important that it be displayed. It is not surprising, therefore, that when Niphon spoke to Muslim fishermen at a rally in Tambon Sathing-Mo about their problems, he emphasized that he was close friends with the mayor of Songkhla Municipality, Uthit Chuchai, and that they would cooperate together to help. He further demonstrated his phuak connections that evening by inviting his close friend Praphon Ekkuru, president of the powerful Songkhla Fisherman's Association, to speak at the rally. It was no coincidence that during 2004, Niphon succeeded in having Praphon endorsed as the new Democrat candidate for his own Constituency 5, or that Niphon had persuaded his friend to come forward as a candidate even though Praphon had been flirting with the idea of joining TRT.

While the common connotation of phuak membership is egalitarian, political phuak have leaders and core members. This more complex pattern of phuak formation and identification is exemplified in the affiliations of Thongchai, a Democrat committee member. Thongchai has a number of phuak, one of which comprises friends from his own residential community and another, which has developed over time through his intense involvement with Democrat Party activities in the province. Although Thongchai is formally attached to his own constituency branch, his friendships and relationships among Democrat Party activists extend well beyond his own electoral constituency. He is a committed party member and a skilled political speaker (*nak phut*). Not surprisingly, strong friendships and bonds have evolved as a result of shared political commitments. Interestingly, Thongchai, together with his friend and political associate Nun (chairman of his party branch), have not developed a strong connection with the Democrat MP for his own constituency.[13] Thongchai and Nun see themselves as having stronger bonds with Niphon Bunyamani and count themselves as belonging to an extensive Democrat-oriented phuak of which Niphon is a leading figure, even though Niphon's constituency is located quite a distance away. "Niphon knows that we don't have any money but that we are genuine in our commitment, so he helps us. . . . He'll give Nun 3,000 baht and Nun doesn't have to ask. . . . If we go to Bangkok and visit Niphon, he'll take us to meet senior Democrat politicians and ask us to sit down and eat with him at his home," he explained.

Nun describes Niphon as a *phuean fung* (close friend) as well as a true *nakleng*. These two terms are important in defining the nature of valued social relations among phuak members. Even though there may appear to be contradictory elements of equality and hierarchy co-existing in the relationship with Niphon, they are actually resolved by the positive evaluation of Niphon as a *nakleng*. Niphon fulfills the ideal role attributed to a *nakleng* because he is generous (*chaikwang*), and at the same time is not aloof (*mai thue tua*). He treats them as intimate friends and understands their needs without having to be told. As both social and emotional formations, it is hardly surprising that phuak have a dual complexion that combines an egalitarian mode of fellowship with a de facto hierarchy, usually masked by a fictive masculine equality. This is conveyed well in the equation of masculine intimacy with the practice of sitting and sharing food. When Trairong Suwankhiri told a reporter that he was not close to a local politician, he encapsulated this in the brief colloquial phrase, "*mai khoei kin duai kan* (We have never eaten together)."[14] Similarly, when a prominent Songkhla Democrat phuak figure, Prayot Ekkuru, explained to me why he thought Abhisit Vejjajiva had failed to draw enough votes to gain the party leadership in 2003, he pronounced that "he never came and sat to eat with his phuak," meaning that he was too aloof and did not cultivate fellowship.[15]

Within the party, the practice of patronage is widespread, but not expressed as such. As in Thai society generally, it is articulated in terms of "helping" and mutual reciprocity (*chuaikan*).[16] For example, Thongchai is close to Thanom (a good friend of Niphon) who is the chairman of another Democrat Party branch in Songkhla. Thanom finances many party activities from his own pocket and has helped Thongchai with funds to start his own small business. Notably, Thongchai does not describe Thanom as a *phi liang*, or patron, but as a friend in the same phuak. For both Niphon and Thanom, Thongchai gives assistance whenever asked, usually speaking at election rallies of the party or in support of Democrat-affiliated candidates for provincial and *tambon*-level elections. Thongchai's depiction of relationships in his phuak closely resembles a patron-client system, and he readily admits that his notion of phuak is very close to that of *boriwan* (or patron-based entourage). The difference perhaps, Thongchai insists, lies in the fact that he does not expect regular support from either Niphon or Thanom. Rather, the occasional reciprocities between them affirm the loyalties and devotion expected of phuak members whose common link and identity (though now more diffuse) is based on their political commitments as "*Khon Prachathipat*" (Democrat people).

The development of these phuak-type bonds, nested within the Democrat Party structure among its activists at the provincial level, give to the party the structural and emotional qualities of an extended phuak. These qualities act to strengthen the bonds of identification among groups within the party. But though the phuak formations and consciousness that are generated within the Democrat Party in Songkhla tend towards furthering solidarity, they can also provide the conditions for division and defection. This is clear in the political history of Surasak Mani, the Democrat defector who stood for election in Songkhla's Constituency 8 as a TRT candidate in February 2005. Surasak's departure from the Democrats followed the lines of an oft-repeated story in Songkhla. That is, the party promotion structure could not contain his increasing political ambitions. Surasak's loyal phuak of local politicians left the Democrat Party with him. During 2003, Surasak and his *phakphuak* joined the TRT Party, and he was eventually chosen (on the basis of a TRT poll) as a candidate. As it turned out, however, Surasak's personal popularity in the district and the support of his *phakphuak*, reinforced by the policy-oriented messages of the TRT campaign and money resources, were not enough to secure electoral success. His phuak was clearly important in spreading his repute, but the members could not dislodge the multiple strengths that reinforced Democrat allegiance among voters.

We have also seen the same rupturing of phuak bonds exemplified in the case of Sawiang Chaisiri, Niphon Bunyamani's long-serving *hua khanaen* of Khuaniang and Democrat Party branch chairman of Constituency 5. Sawiang split from the Democrats following his defeat in the PAO election re-run in Khuaniang because he believed that he had been betrayed by Niphon and Nawaphon, who had supported the rival candidate. Not only did Sawiang leave the Democrat Party and shift his support as *hua khanaen* for Worawit Khaothong as TRT candidate, but he also took his own phuak of former Democrat supporters with him. The frequent defections from and splitting of phuak never, of course, invalidate the importance of phuak allegiance as a critical normative value for people. As in all societies, where the ideal construct of "friendship"—or in my own case in Australia, "mateship"—is never de-valued by individual experiences of betrayal and disappointment, so too, in Thailand and the south, the normative power of phuak persists. The critical point here is that when someone splits from a phuak, the justification for the defection is always articulated in terms of the very norms that legitimize phuak membership. Hence, Sawiang claimed justification because his fellow phuak members—Niphon Bunyamani and his brother—had breached the rule of unqualified loyalty and support. This released him from any obligations they may have expected in the future.

Phuak groupings and loyalties remain integral to the structuring of alliances among key Democrat political actors as well as their opponents. Maintaining the Democrat ascendancy requires that such phuak obligations are served and respected, though the reality of an individual's ambitions and diverging interests ensure that phuak are volatile, and that larger constellations of these phuak are subject to fragmentation. Yet the coherence of the party as an organization at the province level is not entirely reducible to these phuak reciprocities and loyalties.

Trakun, Barami, and Family Bonds

In an important paper on manipulation and social relations in Thai society, Jeremy Kemp has argued that kinship as a major structural form, "offers considerable opportunities for self-interested manipulation because it is a moral code which indicates what *should* be irrespective of immediate likes or advantage."[17] Family networks (*khrueayat*, *yat phi nong*) play a central role in Thai political life, whether in the guise of providing voting bases for relatives who are candidates, or in the form of political lineages (*trakun*) that form the core of entourages and ramifying clusters of *phakphuak*. Wealth is one critical factor that underlies the influence and prestige of the most well-known political families in the Thai political world, although it is not the only factor, and is somewhat less important with the leading political families in Songkhla Province. In Thailand, the merit-filled repute (*barami*) accruing from accumulated good works is an important bond of obligation that is widely accepted as a tangible political resource among parliamentarians and candidates and voters.[18] The south is no exception to this basic structural and symbolic reality informing Thai political life. In Songkhla, some of the most prominent families are those connected more with local rather than national politics, notably the extended clan of the Suwannawong and Thawirat families. Khreng Suwanawong was mayor of the city of Hat Yai for thirty years, supported by a number of relatives who served as councilors. His public legitimacy was derived from his demonstrated sacrifice and devotion to the public good, a practice that simultaneously reinforced the honor (*saksi*) of his *trakun*.

In the Democrat Party, a number of Songkhla families have played an important role, and their reputation has served to enrich the mythology of the party as an institution of worthy representatives. In so doing, they provide a tangible symbolic resource for the Democrats in sustaining popular identification with the party. Until the late 1990s, the two brothers Amnuai and Trairong Suwankhiri were important constituency parliamentarians. The *trakun* of Suwankhiri carries high status owing to the fact that it originated with one of the early governors of the *mueang* of Songkhla. Amnuai and Trairong's father was a renowned *kamnan* of the Sathingphra District with a reputation as a bold, able, and generous *nakleng*. Both sons served in a variety of ministerial posts when the

Democrats were in office (although Trairong's actual performance as a government minister was not particularly impressive), and Trairong, in particular, enjoys a high reputation as a powerful and charismatic public orator in the traditional southern Thai *nang talung* style.

Trairong Suwankhiri is an example of a Songkhla Democrat politician who has built a reputation greater than his father's. In the case of Phrai Phatthano, we see a rather different situation. Until 2003, when he resigned his seat to successfully run in the Hat Yai mayoral election, Phrai was the Democrat member for Constituency 3. An able politician and talented speaker, Phrai has nevertheless depended much on the local reputation of his father, Sawai, a long-serving Democrat MP who served in numerous government ministries. Sawai Phatthano's enduring *barami* among the communities of Constituency 3 (comprising both suburban and rural areas) is based not so much on his record of ministerial service but his reputation as an approachable, generous, and self-sacrificing representative. Sawai represents a popular ideal of the Democrat MP and, in particular, his qualities of self-sacrifice are claimed by Hat Yai residents to be evident in the fact that he never became conspicuously wealthy, judging by his lifestyle and his very ordinary wooden home. Sawai's humble circumstances are not a myth spread by the Democrats—his difficult financial circumstances were reported in a major national newspaper in the context of discussions about the low levels of government pensions for retired MPs.[19] It is to Sawai Phatthano that Niphon Bunyamani refers constantly when he repeats in his speeches that the Democrat Party is a "poor party" (*pen phak khon chon*) with self-sacrificing representatives close to the people (*klaichit chaoban*). Niphon could hardly refer to himself in this context due to his wealth.

The story of Sawai's career path also conforms to the ideal model of the life of a southern Democrat politician—a person of humble background dedicated to improving himself by education and qualified to undertake a political career through the study of law. Mentored by the locally renowned Songkhla lawyer and Democrat MP Khlai La-ongmani (a founding member of the Democrat Party in 1946), Sawai studied law at Thammasat University and when in Bangkok he lived in the home of his mentor Khlai.[20] He then returned to Hat Yai to work as a lawyer until he was persuaded to stand for election under the Democrat banner in 1975. Local people frequently affirm that Sawai has considerable *barami* and that his son Phrai has benefited from such widespread esteem; however, there is nothing wrong with this because Phrai has demonstrated well his skills in parliament and followed his father's example by keeping close contact with his constituents. In this way, Sawai's *barami* is seen by many people in and around Hat Yai to be honored and recognized by the son.

It is frequently claimed that one of the virtues of the Democrat Party is its uncompromising commitment to democratic processes in the choice of candidates through committee deliberation and voting. It is notable, however, that when the children of Democrat MPs are nominated to succeed their parents as candidates in their own electorates they are invariably endorsed. This was the case with Phrai Phatthano succeeding his father, and more recently in the case of Naracha Suwit succeeding his father Wichit in Constituency 8. Although the qualifications and abilities of the candidates are considered in the procedures of Democrat Party candidate selection, it is equally clear that the party gives priority to the tangible electoral significance of family repute in selecting these candidates. In the case of Constituency 3, this practice appeared to be vindicated by the election results for 2001, which showed Phrai Phatthano's constituency registering the highest votes for the Democrats in the whole province.

Repute generated by prominent political families is a positive factor in sustaining popular allegiance to the Democrat Party because, ideally, it helps to reinforce other symbolic and organizational dimensions of solidarity. However, it can also create complications when family loyalties cut across party allegiance and when sitting members change their political focus and take their followers elsewhere. This situation occurred in Constituency 3 when Phrai Phatthano resigned as MP to run for mayor in Hat Yai. The party appears to have given the Phatthano family the first option in nominating a successor to Phrai, but circumstances worked against family-based political continuity in the electorate because Phrai's younger brother was inexperienced and another relative, Sunthon Pathumthong, prevaricated. As we have seen, Sunthon, related to the Phatthanos through Phrai's mother, served as Hat Yai's *nai amphoe* for some five years. Formerly, as a Democrat supporter, he assisted members of the Democrat phuak in canvassing for local and national government elections. His connection to the Democrats in Hat Yai was well known by the Ministry of the Interior, and after TRT gained office in 2001, Sunthon was deliberately held back from promotions because of his demonstrated Democrat connections. In mid-2003, he was transferred to another province as punishment. Late in 2003, it was found that Sunthon had joined TRT and that he was being groomed to stand as a candidate in Constituency 3 against the Democrats. The Phatthano family's options for assuring family continuity in the constituency were now exhausted, and instead a protégé of the influential Songkhla MP Thawon Senniam (member for Constituency 6) was put forward and finally accepted to run as the Democrat candidate.

At the ground level, these events presented a number of challenges. Most obvious was the fact that a core group of Phrai's supporters in the Democrat Party branch (his *kaennam*) followed him to concentrate on preparing for the Hat Yai election, slated to take place only a week after the Constituency 3 by-election. As a result, the new candidate, Wirat Kalayasiri, had to rely on the assistance of his mentor Thawon Senniam for the provision of key personnel. As it turned out, the by-election of February 2004 delivered a resounding defeat to TRT. Despite this triumph, which also gave critical impetus for Phrai's win in the Hat Yai mayoral election, it became clear later that Phrai's inner group, some of whom had worked with his father for many years, would not be returning to support the work of the party in Constituency 3, but would concentrate on helping Phrai as mayor. As a result, in the twelve months leading up to the national elections, Wirat faced multiple challenges as the new Democrat MP. He needed to build a reputation by demonstrating his skills in parliamentary debate, re-build his branch party network, and foster goodwill in the area despite his lack of strong family ties in the constituency.

In the Constituency 3 contest of 2005, family identity and repute were important to the two main competitors. One issue centered on the role of Sawai Phatthano as political sponsor and symbol. TRT selected Sunthon Pathumthong to run in the constituency for precisely the same reasons that had formerly made him an asset to the Democrat Party—namely, that he had a good local reputation through his work as *amphoe* administrator and that he had a large family network. Through the Ministry of the Interior, the TRT leaders engineered Sunthon's re-appointment to the Hat Yai District as *nai amphoe* (in mid-2004) so that he could begin to build electoral support. In his travels in the constituency, Sunthon spread the news that he had the blessings of his relative, the revered Sawai Phatthano. Some of my sources in Hat Yai suggested that this was in fact the case, and that Phrai Phatthano was also supporting Sunthon as an expression of family allegiance. It is impossible to confirm this one way or the other, but Sunthon was certainly asking for Sawai's endorsement. In the local context, Sawai's support was a critical factor, and Wirat was worried enough about it to meet with Sawai in early December 2004 and gain assurances that the famous man was not offering help to Sunthon, either morally or materially. To reinforce this publicly, Wirat gained permission to display Sawai's portrait paired with his own picture on large billboards posted around the constituency and mounted on the stage during his election rallies. Linking himself symbolically with Sawai's *barami* thus served to help bond Wirat both to the Democrat Party pantheon of worthy men and to the locality.

Though publicly the matter of the Phatthano family's loyalties now seemed resolved in favor of Wirat and the Democrats, the reality appears somewhat more complicated. Most conspicuously, a core group of Phrai's canvassers were assisting Sunthon in vote seeking, headed by Police Sergeant Chum, a former police bodyguard to Phrai who had been a long-serving retainer of Sawai. They affirmed that Sunthon was a "good person" and they were helping him, while Chum later denied that he was acting under instructions from Phrai. Phrai's behavior during this period was ambivalent. He was conspicuously absent from Hat Yai (ostensibly on mayoral business) during the weeks leading up to the election and after he returned he played no part in any Democrat election rallies, activity that might be expected of him given his position as an office-bearer at the national level. As it turned out, however, Sunthon's efforts to gain election under the TRT banner failed, demonstrating that in the south family connections are often not powerful enough to counteract popular loyalties to the Democrat Party. In extending informal support to Sunthon, the Phatthano family fulfilled traditional kinship obligations so central to Thai cultural patterns but did so in such a way so as not to compromise their public identification with the Democrat Party, which is one of the key foundations of their public prestige and political legitimacy. More disappointing for Sunthon, however, was that his own wife's family, despite her entreaties on Sunthon's behalf, refused to support him and voted Democrat. This was highly ironic, given Sunthon's declaration in his campaign leaflets that he was relying on "the family system" (*rabop khrueayat*) for votes. Over a year later, Sunthon was still angry about this and refused to speak to his sisters-in-law.

Kinship bonds might be viewed as non-negotiable ties that override other bases of political alliance and support, and such bonds are certainly evoked as such by political candidates in their assessments of electability, whether in local or national political spheres. Democrat politicians in the south commonly make the distinction between family-based and person-based voting support percentages and "party-based" (or "party-*krasae*") factors.[21] But despite the common enunciation of the kinship bond as a cultural-emotional fact that transcends all other principles of affiliation, political divisions are not so clearly drawn in practice, as we have also seen with the notable transgressions of the phaphuak ideal of intra-group loyalty. There are numerous examples of this transgression in Songkhla. For example, in Hat Yai, the Lapharotkit family is divided between Democrat and TRT allegiance, with Lapsak (MP for Constituency 2) and a number of close relations maintaining loyalty to the Democrat Party, while his elder brother Bunloet and his nephew support TRT. In Constituency 3, despite Sunthon's appeal to his kin groups to support him, close relatives, including his cousin Nathawut, chairman of the Democrat Party branch, staunchly maintained their Democrat Party allegiance. So too, in Constituency 8, close relatives of the TRT aspirant Surasak Mani in the Chana District maintained Democrat allegiance and refused to vote TRT.

MEMORY, PARTY MEMBERSHIP, AND BRANCH ORGANIZATION

Reinforcing the emotional and communal dimensions of Democrat Party identity that are evoked at the party's rallies is the very concrete and persistent "presence" of the party in various guises, in the form of party branches, the engagement of ordinary people in branch activities, an inclusive party membership that spans all ethno-religious groupings, and a history of representation that can be evoked and made immediate through memory and stories. The continuity of the Democrat presence in the province is evoked by the memory of Khlai La-ongmani, who was one of the founding members of the Democrat Party.[22] Khlai, a Sino-Thai lawyer of Songkhla town, was continually elected as a Democrat MP until his retirement in the late 1970s. He was not ambitious for cabinet positions and was never prominent among the Democrats at the national level, but he was highly respected as a dedicated local representative who always worked hard for his constituents. His life is recalled by Songkhla Democrat MPs and older party members alike as the model of a worthy Democrat politician in terms of his commitment to constituents, his education, and his loyalty. The son of a Chinese-born rubber grower, Khlai worked hard at his education, finally attaining a law degree before entering politics. In Democrat rallies, Niphon Bunyamani and other Songkhla Democrats evoke Khlai's dedication to the party as a paradigm of "*Prachathipat*" loyalty. As Niphon intoned at one of his rallies late in 2003, "Khlai La-ongmani never abandoned the party (*mai khoei thing phak*), regardless of the party's fortunes—he said that those politicians who changed parties were like graveyard ghosts, people without a home."

The continuity of the Democrat presence in Songkhla, together with the active involvement in the party's affairs of all ethno-linguistic groups, Sino-Thai, ethnic Thai Buddhists, and Muslims (both Thai and Malay speaking), gives to the Democrats a strong sense of inclusiveness. Although the Muslim-based *Wadah* group (originally Democrat Party renegades) of the New Aspiration Party attracted support among Songkhla Muslims, Democrat allegiance among them has always been high, and the party has for a long time included Muslims among its constituency politicians. Muslims remain very active among party branch officials around the province. In the urban constituency of Hat Yai (Constituency 2), party branch officials represent a cross-section of all these major groups in the community. The chairman is Muslim, the two vice chairmen are Muslim and Sino-Thai respectively, the treasurer is Sino-Thai, and the secretary is Thai-Buddhist. The branch secretaries in Constituencies 5, 7, and 8 are Muslims. So too, the Sino-Thai are prominent in the branches as office-bearers and active members.

Since the early 1970s, the Democrats have been organized—in theory, at least—along the lines of a "mass bureaucratic" party, with an emphasis on membership and branches to facilitate territorial penetration.[23] In this, the Democrats have experienced mixed success and, in the north and northeast, the branches are weak with often only a nominal existence. In Bangkok, one study showed that the branches only functioned during election campaigns, and did not play the ostensibly "educational" role formally declared for them.[24] But in the south, the branch system and emphasis on membership have been highly effective in establishing an ongoing and multi-level resource of party support. While other parties, notably the New Aspiration Party, also emphasized party branches, they have been less successful in establishing enduring organizational structures. In Songkhla, the NAP created no enduring infrastructure that could form a possible base for organization, and the non-Democrat groups in the province have no equivalent structures to ensure cross-district coordination within the province. TRT coordination centers have risen during election periods and then disappeared. Despite attempts of local TRT supporters to promote permanent establishment of branches, they received no support from the TRT Party center.

The Democrat Party branches serve a range of purposes. From one perspective, we might view the branches as providing an organizational framework for the perpetuation of phuak and patron-client groupings among Democrat MPs and local politicians. Key office-bearers in some branches are *tambon* councilors or even *so cho*. Nonetheless, these positions are elective positions, not appointments, and although elections may be engineered by parliamentarians, the branches should not be simply assumed to be the creatures of Democrat parliamentarians in providing voting support for factional power play within the party, as one scholar has proposed.[25] Strong personalized loyalties do play a part in linking branch officials with MPs and this has consequences for the composition of branches. This can be seen in the case of Phrai Phatthano's departure from his Constituency 3 seat to run in the Hat Yai election, when a number of key branch office-holders followed him to concentrate on the mayoral election. Nevertheless, when Wirat Kalasiri became the new MP for Constituency 3, the old chairman remained in his position and the branch was still largely intact, despite the fact that several other office-holders defected from the party to assist Sunthon Pathumthong's TRT campaign.

Formally constituted under the regulations of the national party, the Democrat Party branches and their office-bearers are, technically at least, independent of the parliamentarians, although close working relationships are essential. Branches are capable of acting without the formal authorization of the parliamentarian, as was the case when in August 2003 the Constituency 2 branch spontaneously convened a meeting and unanimously resolved to support Phrai Phatthano's mayoral campaign. In Songkhla, there is a high level of cooperation between branch members in election campaigning, and this is most often a result of the spontaneous initiative of the members themselves, not the result of instructions from sitting Democrat members. Most often, members communicate among their friends, mobilizing extensive horizontal linkages of support. So, when Thongchai (committee member of the Constituency 2 branch) drove sixty kilometers from Hat Yai to Thepha township to address a party rally, he did so at the request of a friend who was a Constituency 8 branch member, not the constituency's Democrat candidate. Though they may be attached to phuak and be assisted by patrons, many key office-bearers remain faithful to the idea of the party despite periodic interpersonal conflicts among phuak. These are the Democrat Party's diehards—they provide the organizational spine and the continuity that structures the Democrat presence at the local level (see plate 10.2). And when Prida, a female member of the Constituency 2 branch, gathered together a group of her friends to canvass in the neighborhoods of Wirat Kalayasiri's Constituency 3, she did so after telephoning a friend in Wirat's branch, not Wirat himself.

10.2 Democrat diehards: Party branch officials. These office-bearers of Hat Yai's Constituency 2 branch assure the continuity and strength of the party's presence at the constituency level.

As with other parties, the Democrat Party receives funding from the Election Commission of Thailand (together with other parties) in order to promote "political party development" and to diffuse basic principles of parliamentary democracy. I observed a number of these events during 2003. The formal components of these sponsored events took the form of presentations given by MPs from other provinces or constituencies. Speakers took pains to present entertaining lectures based on their experiences of travels in other countries and described, in simple terms, the government systems operating in foreign countries. But when representatives of the Provincial Election

Commission departed from the meetings, restraint disappeared and the speakers launched into diatribes against the Thaksin government. MPs, speakers, and other party officials confessed that there were limits to their listeners' patience in assimilating democratic theory. All ideas needed to be concretized in terms of comprehensible values such as *ruamchai*, *samakkhi*, and *suesat*, and speakers needed to extol the virtues and loyalty of revered party leaders of the past. At Niphon Bunyamani's small rallies and meetings during 2003, the occasions commonly ended with karaoke singing in order to maintain an atmosphere of fun and entertainment. Membership of the party is as much about fellowship and fun and enjoying oratory as it is about learning *udomkan*.

Why, then, might we ask, have party branches forged firm foundations in the south while their counterparts in most other parts of the country have a nominal and tenuous existence? Without the benefit of detailed studies for other parts of Thailand, I can only make tentative suggestions here. At a structural level, we might judge that the branches maintain an effective role in the party's support infrastructure because of the intersection between phuak and politicians at various levels, reflected in the overlaps between these networks and branch officials. The branches have retained continuity in Songkhla since the time when the Democrats were only one of a number of political parties represented in the province. With the surge of electoral success experienced in the late 1980s onwards, these branches were able to expand their infrastructure, and beginning in 1992, when the Democrats gained all seats, they extended their presence even further. Democrat Party incumbency in government for most of the 1990s helped to further consolidate support and participation. The cumulative growth of branches was accompanied by an expansion in membership, and although only a minority of members actively participates in the ongoing administrative affairs of branches, this has produced an extensive network of supporters whose help can be called on during election campaigns.

It is above all this pervasive basic presence of the party that contributes to the sense of fellowship and intimate familiarity that dominate sentiments about the party. In fact, "the party" does not stand outside people's lives but exists alongside them. Support networks for the Democrats ramify well beyond the branch officials themselves, involving friends and families who willingly emerge to participate in canvassing cavalcades and politicians' door-knocks. During January and February 2005, Hat Yai's Constitutency 2 Democrat Party branch office was regularly crowded with supporters, including women and their teenage children. As I sat one afternoon at the branch headquarters talking to party supporters, Somphon, the branch secretary, highlighted his own definition of being a Democrat. Casting his gaze fondly around the office where men, women, youth, and children spanning three generations sat happily on the floor folding brochures, he confided proudly, "*This* is *Prachathipat*." By contrast, the TRT candidate had no such automatic infrastructure of support and resorted to hiring pretty university students to carry banners and distribute leaflets for him. To Somphon, the meaning of the party is palpable. It is a long-established family and fellowship of faithful believers.

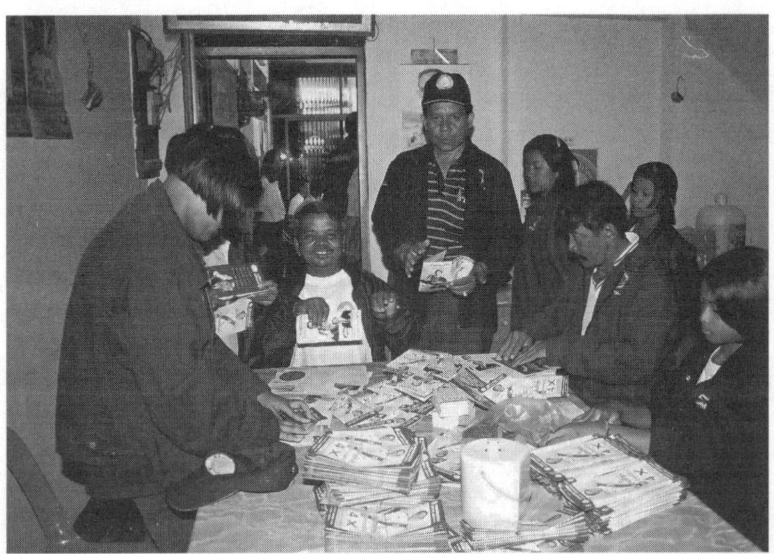

10.3 The Democrat family. Party members and their children fold election fliers in Hat Yai's Democrat Party branch headquarters.

CHAPTER **11**

Conclusion: Performing Political Identity

IN THIS BOOK, I have explored the play of symbols and the organization of groups in election campaigns in a southern Thai province. Though rarely studied in any depth, and even less from the close-grained level of constituencies, election contests in Thailand are important social dramas where cultural categories are articulated and manipulated by political actors as strategic resources. In the process of electoral contestation, these symbols (through language, images, and performance) function to articulate ideals of collective identity, loyalty, leadership, moral worth, and trust that have meaning to the broader political community of ordinary voters. Even though such ideals are widely contradicted in everyday practice—by political actors and voters alike—these constructions of moral ideals and archetypal groups (the ideal party, the ideal southern citizen) serve to establish boundaries, evoke allegiances, and identify enemies. They are, in short, necessary inventions or fictions—essential tools that help people navigate their political world, whether they are leaders or followers.

The cut-and-thrust of political campaigns can be treated as a window into Thai cultural formations just as much as other more sedate or picturesque rituals. But "culture," as Thamora Fishel has demonstrated well in her account of the symbology of power in Phetchaburi politics, is not a static corpus of determined meanings, but rather a vocabulary used actively to position and legitimize actors' claims and actions.

Moral discourses are central to the exercise and legitimizing of power and political eligibility in Thailand. In political contestation, struggles for the moral high ground are as central as the deployment of other resources; they are about the ownership and manipulation of more powerful symbols and meanings than one's competitors.[1]

In such struggles, as we have seen in Songkhla, the *barami* of one player is just as likely to be condemned by rivals as *itthiphon* (influence), its moral opposite. Political symbolism in the south, as everywhere else in the country, deals with the morality of power and the moral legitimacy of leadership, projected in the idioms of reciprocity, hierarchy, communality, and also modernity. The national media centered in Bangkok certainly plays an important role in the building and undermining of political reputations. Yet, idioms of reciprocity and communal identification are important symbolic foundations for enduring political legitimacy, as seen in the very contrasting cases of Banhan Silpa-acha in Suphanburi and Chuan Leekpai in his home province of Trang and the south in general, among both urban and rural voters.[2] Whether this confirms the putative distinction that is habitually made between "Bangkok" and "the provinces" with regard to contrasting "political culture," based on rationality and tradition respectively, remains to be established, since the typical "Bangkok voter" is an academic and media construction.[3] In his deservedly famous essay on the "two democracies" of the urban middle classes and rural voters in Thailand, Anek Laothamatas highlighted distinctions in perceptions of elections in Thailand, yet this portrait itself helps to perpetuate the same broad metropolitan-rural distinctions.[4] Recent research on electioneering and vote canvassing practices in Bangkok localities shows that in lower-middle-class and working-class neighborhoods, personalism and *phuak* relations are just as significant in the mobilization of voters' allegiances as they are in rural areas. Similarly, in an exploration of electoral practices and voters' attitudes in a district of Chiang Mai Province during 2005–06, Andrew Walker shows that there is great variability and complexity in people's voting criteria around a range of principles.[5]

It is reasonable enough to examine electoral contests primarily in mechanical terms as a cluster of campaigning techniques. Equally, political symbolism can be a primary focus. But neither approach, taken alone, is sufficient to illuminate the question of how the Democrat Party maintains its ascendancy in southern Thailand, or how it so tenaciously denied the TRT Party inroads into this threatened heartland during 2004–05. In this book, I have treated Democrat Party campaigning "technique" as critically important in assuring its success in electoral contests in the south, but other perspectives are equally important in illuminating the multi-faceted electoral dominance of the party. Significantly, the accounts and experiences of the Democrat Party's opponents in Songkhla help to confirm the party's multi-level electoral resources and symbolic advantages. The Democrat campaigning technique is certainly a critical factor, as Khreng Suwannawong complained, "These Democrats have so many methods of trickery, it gives me a headache."[6] This expresses the widespread image of Democrat politicians as professional and unscrupulous tricksters. But wily technique is not the only, or even principal, obstacle faced by southern rivals of the Democrats. They are acutely aware of the popular mystique surrounding Democrat Party allegiance and the palpable depth of many ordinary voters' emotional ties—ties which these opponents failed to dislodge in their policy-oriented blandishments and their deployment of person-based political capital.

To appreciate the nature of the Democrat ascendancy in Songkhla and the south, the "party" itself needs to be viewed in a number of guises. First, the Democrat Party is a campaigning machine directed to achieving the electoral support of a parliamentary organization. Second, it is also a dynamic collection of teams and key followers shaped by *phuak* affiliation, without whose support and coherence electoral success would be impossible. Lastly, perhaps most critically, the party is a potent idea and image. We can, then, understand the phenomenon of the Democrat Party ascendancy in the south by viewing its maintenance and reproduction at several levels: (1) canny pragmatic electoral tactics aimed at discrediting opponents through scandal and rumor; (2) management by politicians of phuak alliances to sustain support among key middlemen/women; and (3) for the broader community of ordinary voters, mobilization of powerful idioms of trust and moral potency expressed in the rhetorical performances of rallies and accumulated folklore surrounding exemplary politicians, past struggles and sacrifices.

It is ultimately impossible, and I think pointless, to verify the primordialist claims (enunciated both by southern academics and ordinary voters) that "southerners" embrace cultural (and thus political) values that are markedly distinct from people in other regions. Claims that southerners' attachment to personal honor, to phuak, and to family are stronger than elsewhere in Thailand are difficult to demonstrate, though they are made frequently enough by politicians, scholars, and ordinary people alike (both in and outside the south) in their efforts to explain the continuing bond between the south and the Democrats. There is an apparent contradiction in the common local assertion that the party is "the party of the southern people" (*Prachathipat pen phak khong khon tai*) because quite clearly a significant minority of southerners do not support the Democrats, while others remain indifferent to politics entirely. Does this mean that non-Democrat southerners are somehow "un-southern?" Nobody could say that Surasak Mani or Worawit Khaothong were any less "southern" simply because they supported a different national political party. Indeed, these men embody more clearly the ascribed archetypes of southern *nakleng* than many Democrat politicians. The qualities of Surasak Mani or Worawit Khaothong are fully embraced within the spheres of local and provincial politics, where schemes of eligibility accord importance to local repute, commitment, and to "*phon ngan*," manifested in roads, bridges, and services. By contrast, as many people in Songkhla highlight, the southerner-Democrat Party identity nexus is seen to have particular and special applicability to a national scale of politics, which is often expressed by them as "a special stage" (*wethi phiset*) where the prosaic matters of local *phon ngan* are overshadowed by bigger considerations. There is, of course, always a struggle over these principles of eligibility, as seen in the strong claims of Worawith Khaothong. But so far, Democrat orators have managed to convince audiences that party loyalty is necessary in order to beat back the enemies of true political virtue. In the arena of national political competition, the Democrats have a privileged place. On this broader stage, southern difference "performs" before the nation to complement and enrich the distinctiveness of the party.

My concern has not been to verify or deny the objective reality of southern cultural "difference," but to explore the *assertion of difference*, the forms it takes and why such assertion of difference is important to actors in the context of political competition. Many southern voters believe that their "difference," their noble political values that apparently mark them as southerners, corresponds to and complements the difference of the Democrats as a distinctive party in the nation. Ethnographic research cannot *explain* the putative "difference" of southerners, but what it can reveal and record (as I have tried to do in this book) are the various meanings of party affiliation as they are articulated both by ordinary people through their metaphors and aphorisms and by party leaders in their rhetorical performances. These show us that the southerners who habitually support the Democrat Party believe that the party is distinct as a trustworthy political representative. It does not simply *represent* the south, as suggested in the frequently voiced truncated affirmations that, "The Democrats are the party of the southern people." Embedded in this shorthand phrase is something more—a conviction that the party represents the *very best* of the values to which voters aspire and attribute to ideal leaders.

Widespread popular identification with the party as a "party of the south" is not based on a parochial sense among ordinary voters that the party serves regional interests. Rather, it is an idea that the party is the guardian of a moral political community of the nation at large, expressed by a party that is also national in its span. It is thus "regionalist" in some of its key foundational elements, but not parochial. The simultaneous assertions of southern and Democrat difference condensed in the affirmation, "*Prachathipat pen phak khong khon tai*," are highly nationalistic in intent. They proclaim the idea that, "We are the true representatives of what the Thai nation and its politics could and should be." So, according to this patriotic logic, Chuan Leekpai is both an ornament to the south and an ornament to the nation. The same reverence is accorded to the Songkhla-born Prem Tinsulanonda, though he occupies a place far above electoral politics (as president of the king's Privy Council).

Democrat Party leaders in the south have helped to cultivate a powerful myth that they are the guardians of a noble "political culture of the southern people." It is a myth founded upon the production of evocative images of loyalty, integrity, and truthfulness. The Democrat Party is presented to the southern electorate and accepted by large numbers of people as embodying an ideal political institution with noble leaders, and these features are evoked and reproduced in both specific political and general social settings through rhetoric and performance that resonate with widely shared cultural models of public virtue. Here, we can well apply Edmund Leach's important observation that, "Ritual action and belief are alike to be understood as forms of symbolic statement about the social order."[7] The party presents itself in symbols that are coherent and recognizable, and the community of supporters recognizes and reinvents itself in these symbols as an ideal political community. It is a mutual appropriation based on assertions of difference. It may be trickery but it works both ways, and is meaningful and effective in fostering solidarity.

Democrat voters articulate their allegiance to the party at varying levels of sophistication, but the bond with the Democrats is widely shared across occupational groups and lifestyles. In Songkhla, it is clear that Hat Yai's urban middle-class voters are just as strongly attached to the idea of the party as are humble fishing folk or rubber cultivators in the rural and coastal districts. At the core of this allegiance is a deep trust in the principled integrity of the party and its reciprocal loyalty to the people. This trust persists despite the clear deviation of the Democrat Party's politicians from these ideals in practice (evidenced in the 1995 land acquisition scandal), and the party's patent inability when in government to address decisively key problems facing the nation. The burden of evoking popular trust rests on the efforts of exemplary leaders, most prominently Chuan Leekpai. So far, other parties and their leaders have not been able to demonstrate convincingly to the majority of the southern electorate that they deserve an equivalent level of trust. In Songkhla, those civil society advocates and folklore scholars who despise the Democrats for stealing the noble political culture of the people for selfish political ends are conscious that they have to be very careful in what they say or publish about the Democrats or their icon, Chuan.

Represented by its politicians and embraced by many people as a trusted political guardian, the Democrat Party mediates and translates political reality. In one of his rallies in Songkhla during 2003, Niphon Bunyamani appealed to his listeners by saying, "We must build a wall here in the south against the TRT Party." As we have seen, throughout 2004–05, the Democrats succeeded in constructing this wall, built on a symbolic foundation of trust that distinguished the intimate community of the party from an unprincipled and predatory political "other," embodied by Thaksin but including local followers of TRT. Despite strenuous efforts, Thaksin Shinawatra and the TRT Party were unable to breach this wall and demonstrate convincingly to an ever-suspicious southern electorate that they were not self-serving and predatory opportunists, notwithstanding their demonstrable *phon ngan*. Local TRT candidates were often acknowledged as "good people," but they were doomed because they followed the "wrong party". During the 2005 national elections held in Songkhla and elsewhere in the south, Democrat orators were able to convincingly represent Thaksin as the moral antithesis both to Democrat principles and to basic "southern" political norms. The TRT *krasae* of efficiency was unable to compete with the Democrat *krasae* of morality and the image of the southern electorate as an ideal, politically righteous phuak, bonded by trust, loyalty, and integrity.

THE IMAGE OF THE DEMOCRATS

The well-recognized political downside to the Democrat Party's comprehensive ascendancy in the south has been the erosion of the party's identity and legitimacy as a truly national organization. Since Chuan's first accession to the prime ministership in 1992, and increasingly since the 1995 election, a major campaign trump card for opposing parties (in the north and northeast especially) has been the accusation that the Democrats are a southern party. There is no evidence that Chuan's administration favored the south unduly in development programs and policies, nonetheless, the image stuck.[8] Academics and political commentators remark that the blessing of reliable support in the Buddhist-majority south has become a curse for the Democrats, who are now shackled with the status of a "regional party."[9] Southern Democrat Party activists are acutely aware of this conundrum, though they are bemused by the view that their political motivations are narrow, because their own political vision is national in scope.

In February 2005, though Democrat Party branch leaders in Songkhla were jubilant when the party's impressive defense of the southern constituencies became known, they were also depressed to learn of their party's humiliating losses in all other regions, especially Bangkok. Despite the southern Democrats' heroic defense against TRT, Thaksin and his party still ruled the nation. In December 2005, I attended a conference of the southern Democrat Party branches, held in Nakhon Si Thammarat. Here the branch members were congratulated and thanked by party elder Chuan Leekpai and by the new young party leader, Chuan's protégé Abhisit Vejjajiva, a Bangkokian, but well respected in the south (not least because of his cultivation of a Chuan-like persona). There were strong affirmations of southern Democrat solidarity made at this gathering, but the main questions being posed in speeches and the associated branch-based workshops were: "How do we expand the Democrat Party into Thailand's other regions, particularly the northeast, where Thaksin and TRT are overwhelmingly popular?," and "How can we get northeastern voters to see the importance of the Democrat Party's critiques of the Thaksin government, as we do?" No answers were forthcoming to address the challenge of expanding the Democrats' base of true believers beyond the solid south and the party's beleaguered outposts in Bangkok and a few scattered provinces.

In addition to this "regional party" identification problem was an even bigger one facing the Democrats—the party's clear failure to fashion competitive policies and a saleable national electoral image to compete with the policy-focused marketing of Thaksin's new TRT.[10] This failure was exposed dramatically by Thaksin's smashing national victory of 2005, which gained him a single-party majority government for the first time in the nation's history. Banyat as Democrat leader had been simply "unmarketable."[11] Updating the party to compete with modern electoral politics had become imperative, even though the old *udomkan*-based theme still worked its magic in the south. The challenge, it appeared, was to "re-brand" the Democrats under their new leader

Abhisit and to adopt media-savvy techniques and attractive policies to win back Bangkok, the north, and the northeast.[12] To this end, from April 2006, Abhisit began unveiling a set of issue-based policies to form the basis of a new Democrat platform, while affirming the importance of moral integrity as the defining quality for an alternative national leader (namely, himself).[13]

For the south, (that is, the Thai Buddhist majority south), the Thaksin era has crystallized loyalty to the Democrats even further. At the regional level, the future of the Democrat Party ascendancy in the south will depend on a balance of pragmatics and poetics: the extent to which intersecting and multi-level phuak networks can maintain coherence in the face of individual members' political ambitions, and whether the dominant myths of the party maintain their emotional hold on ordinary people and help them make sense of unfolding political events and crises in the country.

EPILOGUE

The Democrats: Surviving Thaksin and Beyond

FOLLOWING THAKSIN'S crushing electoral victory of February 2005, few could have foreseen that nineteen months later a "democratic coup" would topple the Thaksin government and give the Democrat Party a chance to revive its ambitions to gain government. In the early months of 2006 the party played a role in fuelling the atmosphere of crisis and confrontation that set the stage for the army's subsequent coup in September, particularly by launching a boycott against the snap April elections and also by pursuing a successful court case against the election commissioners for negligence in the conduct of those elections. As in the past, however, it was others who demonstrated in Bangkok's streets and parks while the Democrat leadership stood in the wings and pronounced their commitment to change through parliamentary process and the law. The controversial April elections were declared invalid by the courts in May, but this only fuelled increasing polarization between pro- and anti-Thaksin groups. In the south, opposition to Thaksin was given even greater legitimacy by the statements of the region's revered hero, elder statesman Prem Tinsulanonda, who ominously pronounced that the military would remain loyal to the king and nation. On September 19, 2006, the military seized power, ejected Thaksin from office, and promised to restore democratic government under a revised constitution. The Democrat leadership made no explicit criticism of the military's seizure of power. The coup makers achieved what the

Democrat Party in opposition could never have done: they removed the Thaksin government, proceeded to dismember his support networks in and outside the bureaucracy, and began framing a new constitution that would assure a weak multi-party system of government in the future. At the end of May 2007 the courts found Thaksin's Thai Rak Thai Party guilty of electoral fraud and in the same hearing exonerated the Democrats from similar charges laid during the April elections. These circumstances gave the Democrats a clear chance to form a coalition government in future, and, not surprisingly, the party leadership supported the new constitution and advocated a quick election to restore parliament. In the referendum on the government-sponsored draft constitution in August 2007, southern voters overwhelmingly voted in favor of the new constitution, registering the highest proportion of "yes" votes of any region in the country.

This epilogue summarizes the fortunes of the Democrats and the resonance of recent national political dramas in its southern heartland. At the time of writing (October 2007), the party is girding itself for an election that has been scheduled for December. As I highlight below, the recent survival and revival of the party under its new leader Abhisit Vejjajiva have been achieved under circumstances essentially shaped by other key political groups and forces. This is typical of the history of the Democrats, who have been beneficiaries more than initiators of key events in Thailand's fraught political history. Whether Thailand's voters will give the Democrats another chance in national government depends much on the party's capacity to attract votes in the metropolis and in the north and northeast. In short, it depends on the party's ability to expand its repertoire of key political symbols beyond those that regularly harness the electoral loyalty of its southern constituency.

A BOYCOTT, HEROES, AND A COUP

After the election of early 2005 the Democrats continued to lambaste Thaksin's regime in parliament, critiquing his failure to manage the southern border turbulence and exposing instances of "policy corruption." But the party was not the major force behind the upsurge of widespread extra-parliamentary protest against Thaksin's rule which ultimately forced him to dissolve parliament. This began with the efforts of the disgruntled media magnate Sonthi Limthongkun, who from late 2005 mobilized public rallies opposing Thaksin after his TV show was axed under government pressure. Sonthi's rallies became the focus of a much wider anti-Thaksin opposition from January 2006 after the controversial sale of the Thaksin family's Shincorp telecom shares to Singapore's state investment company, Temasek Holdings. Widespread outrage was sparked over the Shinawatra family's gains from what was discovered to be a tax-free transaction, and added to this was patriotic indignation roused by the sale of these telecom resources to a foreign company.

With the new party leader Abhisit stressing the party's specifically parliamentary role, the Democrats stood aloof from Sonthi Limthongkun's rallies, though some key cases of alleged cronyism and corruption highlighted by Sonthi—such as irregularities surrounding the purchase of "CTX" bomb scanners for the new national airport—had already been the subject of Democrat politicians' investigations (notably Sirichok Sopha, of Songkhla). Public protests against the government and street confrontations between anti- and pro-Thaksin demonstrators escalated to the point where in February Thaksin was pressured (by the Privy Council President, Prem Tinsulanonda) to dissolve parliament and call an election to resolve the crisis. Given TRT's massive and continuing electoral support in the north and northeast, it was clear that this new election would deliver him another crushing victory. Immediately following the announcement for the April national polls, the Democrat, Chat Thai, and Mahachon parties declared an election boycott, asserting that what was needed was political reform, and that another election would simply consolidate a corrupt and crony-ridden regime.[1] In Songkhla, Democrat politicians and their faithful voters once more expressed united opposition to Thaksin and TRT. On election day, April 2, the majority of southern voters cast "no-votes" on their ballots as a protest against Thaksin's continued rule. In thirty-eight of the south's fifty-four constituencies, including all eight in Songkhla, the TRT candidates ran unopposed and failed to gain the constitutionally mandated 20 percent of total votes cast to win seats. The south once again stood out as a political bloc, matching the opposition that had emerged to Thaksin in the metropolis.[2]

The Election Commission declared a second round of "by-elections" on April 23 to fill the vacant seats, but this failed to deliver a full parliament due to the continuing boycott and the effects of the "no-vote" ballots. In Songkhla, as elsewhere in the country, smaller parties were urged to come forward by TRT to allow the government party to contest with token opponents so as to avoid the 20 percent rule, but these alternative candidates were actively discouraged by Democrat supporters. In the city of Songkhla dozens of protestors besieged the election center to block the candidates of minor political parties from registering to run in seven vacant constituencies.[3] Some TRT supporters protested against these activities, and electoral fraud charges were later filed against the Democrats for allegedly organizing them.[4] On election day the protest was symbolically reinforced by the act of destroying ballot papers. Outside Bangkok it was Songkhla Province where public ballot-tearing was the most prevalent, with seven voters destroying their papers before cameramen and crowds at polling stations, and being arrested by police as a consequence. Although it was the People's Alliance for Democracy (PAD) that had appealed to the public to destroy their ballots, the people who did so in Songkhla were mainly female Democrat Party members (five of the seven). This second round of elections also failed to return members to constituencies due to the inability of one-horse TRT candidates to gain required minimum votes. Again the south was conspicuous, with ten constituencies in seven southern provinces returning no MPS.[5] In Songkhla, only one TRT candidate gained election in the face of the Democrat boycott. This was in Constituency 8, where Surasak Mani gained just over 20 percent of the votes required for his election. Though the April polling results were declared invalid in early May, the irrepressible Surasak now proudly displays the title "former MP" on his name cards.

The March-April election period was plagued by controversy. Before the second round of elections, the press reported allegations that TRT was paying minor parties to contest against its candidates so as to escape the 20 percent requirement. These charges were made by one of the southern Democrats' great scandal mongers, Suthep Thueaksuban, of

Surat Thani, who claimed that he had clear evidence.[6] The pressure of publicity forced the Election Commission of Thailand to establish an investigating panel, which found that the Phatthana Chat Thai Party had bribed an ECT official to manipulate data so that candidates appeared qualified to contest. Though two small parties were dissolved, the ECT stopped short of charging TRT as the paymaster in this fraud, despite some compelling evidence.[7] The Democrats also complained of the decisions and procedures surrounding the second round of elections, arguing that it was illegal for failed candidates in the first round to contest different constituencies in the by-election. Again Songkhla was at the center of this controversy, where election directors in three constituencies resigned on the eve of new candidacy registrations (April 19–20). They claimed that the registration period was too short and they feared violating the constitution because they would not have enough time to check candidates' qualifications.[8] At the same time the Songkhla Democrats' parliamentary firebrand Thawon Senniam filed charges of negligence against the three ECT commissioners on behalf of the party. He alleged that they arranged the second round of elections without a royal decree and that they had allowed candidates who had failed to gain 20 percent of votes in the first round to switch to other constituencies for the April 23 polls.

Since the total number of MPs elected in April fell short of the number legally required for the convening of parliament, a major constitutional problem now emerged. After the second round of polls failed to deliver enough members, the king summoned judges of the country's constitutional and administrative courts to an audience where he expressed grave disapproval of an election that had delivered a single party to an incomplete parliament. Shunning the appeal of the PAD to exercise his constitutional prerogative and appoint a new prime minister to resolve the crisis, the king hinted that it was appropriate to nullify the elections, and instructed court judges to act decisively to find a solution to the "mess." Steeled by the king's counsel, on May 8 the Constitutional Court annulled the April election. This, however, was not the end of political crisis and confrontation. The annulment of the April elections was accompanied by the judges' recommendation for the ECT commissioners to resign so that public confidence could be restored, but they refused. Thawon Senniam's case against the commissioners proceeded through the criminal court and in mid-July a guilty verdict was reached and all three commissioners were jailed. Among the Democrat fraternity in Songkhla, both Thawon and his polical protégé Wirat Kalayasiri (who had helped him prepare the legal case) were treated as heroes in the perpetual battle against authoritarianism. Thawon published a book on the case early the next year with a dramatic subtitle in English: "The Man Who Beat Goliath."[9]

Following the appointment of new election commissioners, a fresh election was announced for October. Meanwhile, Thaksin, having returned from a "leave-of-absence" prior to the April polls, and having previously declared he would not resume the prime ministership, made it clear that he would lead TRT in the October election. At the same time, the future of both TRT and the Democrats was unclear, since both faced court proceedings on charges of electoral fraud and bribing the minor political parties: against TRT for paying them to contest, and against the Democrats for paying the leaders of these parties to implicate TRT in the deal as well as preventing political candidates of smaller parties from registering. Between July and August a tense atmosphere prevailed throughout the country, featuring more demonstrations demanding the ousting of the Thaksin government, rumors and denials of impending military coups, and a suspected bomb plot against Thaksin's life. Songkhla's Democrats prepared for the impending election contest with confidence. Their new national leader Abhisit challenged Thaksin to a televised debate and announced his party's reworked policies under the heading of "The People's Agenda," featuring a new slogan "The People Come First." The policy included measures for reducing petrol prices, raising the minimum wage, and introducing a "sufficiency economy fund" to aid villagers, but it drew criticism from specialists as being too vague and no match for TRT's established populist agenda.[10]

The anticipated election contest of October never came. Instead, and unexpectedly for most, a military group led by Thailand's army commander-in-chief General Sonthi Bunyaratkalin staged a "Democratic" putch on the evening of September 19.[11] Calling themselves the "Council of Democratic Reform under Constitutional

Monarchy" (CDR), the military coup makers claimed that their seizure of power was necessary because of the historically unprecedented disunity that had been fostered by Thaksin's administration, together with corruption, political interference in the state's independent agencies, and "actions verging on lèse-majesté against the king."[12] In the capital during the following days, the tanks and soldiers were welcomed by many with jubilation. The junta immediately banned political activities and placed key TRT ministers under house arrest. On October 1 former army commander and Privy Councilor Surayut Chulanont was appointed prime minister under an interim constitution and the CDR was renamed the Council for National Security. The public was promised that elections would be held as soon as possible following the drafting of a new constitution, which would then be presented to the people for approval by referendum.

THE SAVING VERDICT

Though the military coup d'état clearly contradicted the Democrat Party's cherished opposition to dictatorship, General Sonthi's putch was accepted among the party's politicians and the membership as the only way to end the political crisis and break Thaksin's hold on power.[13] The coup makers quickly set out to neutralize Thaksin's extensive political support networks and investigate irregularities in the financial transactions of Thaksin and his family through an "Assets Scrutiny Committee." All of this was welcome to the Democrats, but the most critical issue to be faced over the next year was whether the party could survive charges of electoral fraud brought against both the Democrats and TRT by the Office of the Attorney-General. This raised the real prospect of dissolution for both parties. Soon after taking power the junta had issued a pronouncement (No. 7) that the executives of disbanded political parties would be disqualified from contesting elections for five years, an ominous signal for senior politicians of TRT and the Democrats.

From January to April 2007 the Democrats' legal team submitted its defence testimony against the fraud charges to the Constitution

Tribunal (appointed to replace the Constitution Court), with a closing statement in early May. In April, a month prior to the court's scheduled final verdict on May 30, the testimonies of Abhisit Vejjajiva and Suthep Thueaksuban were published and distributed to party branches and sold in shops, embellished with photographs of party rallies, Democrat heroes and TRT villains.[14] Despite the solemn claims on the covers of these books that the party was defending itself against untruths spread by TRT, Democrat politicians and party members privately remained unsure about their prospects for survival, especially after officials suggested that both the TRT and Democrat parties were likely to be dissolved because of their weak defense testimony.[15] As the date of the court's verdict drew closer, the general view, reported in the press, was that it would be a political impossibility for the court to dissolve only one of the two main parties, because chaos would break out. A week before the verdict was to be delivered, the king spoke to the court judges, counseling them to be firm and not bow to mounting public pressure.[16] On May 30, the court spent fives hours reporting on the case against the Democrats (and two other small parties). The party was cleared of all four charges of electoral fraud brought against it, including hiring members of a small party (Prachathipatai Kaona) to discredit TRT and the obstruction of candidate registration in Songkhla Province. The case against dissolution was dismissed and Democrat supporters were jubilant. By contrast, the judgment and evidence deployed against TRT was damning. In another five-hour disquisition the court ruled that two senior key party members (Thamarak Itsarangkun na Ayutthaya and Pongsak Ruktaphongphaisan) had illegally paid smaller parties to contest the second round of elections in April 2006 so as to circumvent the minimum voter turnout rules of 20 percent. Further, the TRT party executive was implicated in this fraud by virtue of complicit knowledge, which justified the court's verdict to dissolve TRT and ban its 111 executives from participating in politics for five years.[17]

PARTY REVIVAL AND A REFERENDUM

With a new lease on life after escaping dissolution, Abhisit and his party made strong efforts to present themselves to the public as a viable governing party with an able and far-seeing leader. With the insurgency in the four southern border provinces in its fourth year and showing little sign of abatement, a major task for the Democrats was to suggest convincing policies for a region of which they claimed special knowledge. They were, however, hardly in a position to criticize the efforts of Prime Minister Surayut, who had since the previous November introduced a range of initiatives, beginning with an official apology to borderland Muslims for the heavy-handed approach to the deep south (symbolized by the violent events of Krue Se and Tak Bai in 2004) and including the resuscitation of the Southern Border Provinces Administrative Center. In mid-July the party released its policy on the south at a study seminar in Hat Yai. Attended by three hundred ordinary party members and other invited participants from the border provinces, the occasion was used to present Abhisit as a committed leader dedicated to solving problems. The message of the seminar was summed up by the key slogan on the seminar video screen, "Abhisit is worried about the southern people," which echoed his mentor Chuan Leekpai's common avuncular expression to audiences: "I'm worried about the country." It was also the title of the party's monthly newsletter for July, which publicized Abhisit's policy themes for addressing the border problems.[18] He presented the party's direction to problem-solving under six headings, including: "Stop the cycle of violence"; "Build an atmosphere of harmony"; Develop the economy of villagers", "Make a full effort in developing education"; "Enhance participation among all relevant groups"; and "Use diplomacy to enhance the understanding of neighboring countries." As he and other party leaders had argued on earlier occasions, Abhisit stressed that the crisis in the south was a national problem, and every political party needed to assign the highest importance to solving it.

The meeting in Hat Yai concluded on July 15 with a press release from Deputy Party Leader Churin Laksanawisit (of Phuket) with a set of preliminary proposals, including: the declaration of the border provinces as a special development zone; the promotion of financial institutions consistent with Islamic principles; the promotion of appropriate industry and tourism; the promotion of the three provinces as an international center of Islamic learning; and the establishment of Sharia law concerning family and inheritance.[19] Most of these points were drawn from the party's "Pattani Declaration," which had been used in the three Muslim majority provinces in the election campaign of 2005.[20] Many of the Democrat proposals had already been advanced by others; nevertheless, from a pre-election political standpoint it was critical for the party to reaffirm these broad and appealing policies so as to hold onto the seats it had snatched from TRT in the Muslim-majority provinces. Here, unlike in Songkhla, loyalty to the Democrats could not be taken for granted. In Songkhla the impact of the insurgency had also been considerable—Hat Yai had been bombed during 2006 and 2007 with casualties and considerable impact on the economy of the city and province—so an expression of commitment here was also politically important.

The timing of the Democrat-promoted Hat Yai meeting in mid-July was directly linked to political circumstances. Following public hearings in May, the Constitution Drafting Assembly approved the draft charter in early July and the date for a referendum was set for August 19. The constitution put a premium on preventing excessive executive power and enhancing mechanisms for review. Most significantly, it reduced considerably any chance of a single-party government by re-introducing multi-member constituencies for the lower house. This constitution favored a party like the Democrats, who would have no chance of ever gaining enough seats for a single party government, but might win enough to lead a multi-party coalition. The Democrat leadership welcomed the referendum and the new constitution, unlike the pro-Thaksin groups who continued to protest against the CNS and its anti-democratic "dictatorship."

On July 18 the National Legislative Assembly lifted the ban on political activities. A few days later Abhisit presented himself as a future national leader in a policy speech that was directly linked to the forthcoming referendum. Abhisit launched his party's "Peoples' Agenda" at a party meeting held in Bangkok on July 20 to 21. Prior to the leader's speech, party branch members and politicians were urged to support the constitution in the future referendum.[21] It was a more developed version of the program that Abhisit had announced before the September coup. Broadcast on television, it was a portent of a more media-savvy approach to Democrat campaigning. His delivery bore all the marks of careful scripting and was punctuated strategically with the repeated phrase "The time has come," and the party's slogan "The People Come First." Abhisit's "People's Agenda" comprised four key elements: 1) "Revive democracy;" 2) "Personal and educational development;" 3) "Revive the economy"; and 4) "Return peace to the south." After the referendum results of August 19 endorsed the coup-installed government's draft constitution, Abhisit told reporters that the Democrats had not campaigned and had allowed voters to exercise a free choice.[22] This was only true in a technical sense, since in the July meeting and in his speech support for the constitution was clearly expressed. In advocating the first theme of "Reviving Democracy," Abhisit affirmed the urgency of having an election as soon as possible. A referendum was essential in this process, since it expressed the people's rights.[23] Like the state agencies that promoted the referendum while simultaneously endorsing a "yes" vote, Abhisit offered Democrat supporters little choice but to vote "yes." The referendum was portrayed as the path to a constitution which would allow elections. All this needed to be done quickly to restore democracy. On the eve of the referendum he made the point even more clearly by rejecting criticism that the new constitution would weaken political parties and parliament.[24]

In the context of the starkly polarized political allegiances prevailing in the country, votes "for" and "against" the draft charter were presented as holding clear meanings. Apart from a small group of Democracy activists and intellectuals, the groups opposing the charter were aligned with pro-Thaksin and TRT networks who vigorously denounced the constitution as one imposed by dictators. During the referendum promotion period, the Democrats helped to reinforce the claims of state officials that "no" voters were being paid by the minions of Thaksin. As one Democrat supporter in Songkhla explained the matter: "If I vote 'no,' then I'll be just like the northeasterners who are selling their votes." A "no" vote was thus a tainted vote. For Songkhla residents in particular, another factor that stigmatized the "no" vote were the aggressive protests of the "United Front of Democracy against Dictatorship" in front of the Bangkok home of Prem Tinsulanonda. Among these protestors the key TRT figure and renegade southern Democrat Wira Musikaphong was prominent in denouncing Prem as the mastermind behind the September coup. In response, Songkhla's "Group Who Love Father Prem" (formed the previous year) met and planned a march on Wira's father's home in Ranot District of Songkhla. Notably, the leading figures of this group were all connected to the Democrat Party (PAO president Nawaphon Bunyamani, Mayor of Songkhla Uthit Chuchuai, and "Charlie" Nophawong na Ayutthaya).[25] At one of Hat Yai's major markets, a large banner denouncing Wira and the UFDD was displayed. Large banners were also hung on the walls of Songkhla's PAO compound pronouncing that "Father Prem is the Hero of Songkhla." It is hardly surprising, then, that "no" votes in the referendum in Songkhla were among the lowest recorded in the country.

THE BURDEN AND BLESSING OF A SOUTHERN HEARTLAND

At the referendum of August 19, just 57 percent of voters endorsed the new constitution. It was a shaky basis for the constitution's legitimacy, particularly since no minimum majority vote had been stipulated. The clear region-based differences in voting showed a highly polarized political landscape that represented alignments for and against Thaksin. Majority "no" votes were concentrated in the provinces of the northeast and the upper northern region. The Northeast had solidly rejected the draft constitution, with 63 percent voting "no." Conspicuously, the highest proportion of "yes" votes (87 percent) were concentrated in the south. On a national ranking of provinces voting in favor of the constitution, Songkhla with 90.99 percent of "yes" votes stood fourth (under the other southern provinces of Chumphon, Trang and Nakhon Si Thammarat).[26] On television talk panels on the day of the referendum, and in interviews thereafter, Democrat leaders downplayed the obvious match between the distribution of referendum votes and region-based party allegiances. This is understandable, since the Democrats were trying desperately to find ways of reaching northeastern voters and present the party and its policies as truly national. Nonetheless, the prevailing stereotype of the Democrats as the "party of the south" remained a clear obstacle in the party's efforts to refashion its image in the post-coup period. [27]

A few days after the referendum, the king endorsed the new constitution and the election date was provisionally set for December 23. Once again Abhisit's "People's Agenda" was broadcast on television. Since July Thailand's politicians have been realigning themselves into new party configurations in preparation for an election. The largest bloc of former TRT followers has rebranded itself as the "People's Power Party" under the leadership of the arch conservative and pro-Thaksin figure, Samak Sunthonwet, who has pledged to grant amnesty to the 111 TRT politicians banned by the Constitutional Court if he becomes prime minister. Other TRT splinter factions have been attempting to regroup into new alliances. Though by early October the party configuration had not yet crystallized, the critically important northeastern constituencies appeared to be again locked up by old faction bosses and their canvassing networks. Appeals to move the election date back by some politicians were opposed by Abhisit, who clearly wanted an early election while his opponents are in disarray.[28]

As for the south, widespread identification with the Democrat Party and its associated popular imagery remain strong and there is little chance (except for the in Muslim-majority provinces) that other parties will make inroads into this regional heartland in the scheduled December 2007 election, despite the introduction of multi-member constituencies under the new constitution. The young new party leader Abhisit, though a Bangkokian, is well regarded by southern voters as new party leader because he has both the blessings and the persona of his adored southern mentor, Chuan Leekpai. In Songkhla for the foreseeable future, the Democrats and their various interlinked *phuak*, though competing for territory among themselves, will continue to reproduce the party's electoral hegemony through their proven formula that mixes romantic myth in public performances with hard-nosed pragmatism at the organizational level. There still remain, of course, political rivals to the Democrats in Songkhla. The era of Thaksin gave the strongest of these rivals their best chance of undermining the Democrat ascendancy, but they failed. This time there will be no equivalent to TRT's plentiful money or marketing to boost their local political capital. Some old political war horses like Surasak Mani will return to the fray to fight the December 2007 election, contesting under any party banner that affords opportunity; but they will surely be attacked by Democrat orators once again with the charge that they lack the vital quality of *udomkan* that defines a true southerner.

NOTES

Chapter 1

1. This anti-Democrat rhyme appears to have been coined some time around the mid-1990s, during the period when the scandal broke about southern Democrat MPs benefiting illegally from transfers of land reserved for the poor. It was fused with rumors of wife-swapping among prominent Democrat MPs.
2. Chiraphon, "*Khwam niyom khong phak Prachathipat*;" Suwat, "*Wiwathanakan khwam phukphan.*"
3. McCargo, "Southern Thai Politics," 21–36.
4. Bailey, *Stratagems and Spoils*, see esp. chap. 1–3.
5. See McCargo and Ukrist, *The Thaksinization of Thailand*, esp. 70–120; Nichapha, *Branding Thai Rak Thai*; Pasuk and Baker, *Thaksin*, esp. 172–96.
6. For press opinion of Chuan's role in shaping the identity of the national party and the consequence of his impending departure from leadership, see "*Chut dotden Chuan Leekpai, Chut dotden Prachathipat, Ekkaphap thi pen nueng diao*," *Matichon Sutsapda*, January 17–23, 2003.
7. See Albritton, "Political Diversity," 233–46.
8. Few anthropologists have focused on modern election campaigns as rhetorical and symbolic displays, but see Abélès, *Quiet Days in Burgundy*; McLeod, "The Sociodrama of Presidential Politics." See also Herzfeld, *The Poetics of Manhood*, chap. 3; Loizos, *The Greek Gift*, chap. 7. For an important treatment by a political scientist, see Kertzer, *Ritual, Politics and Power*.
9. Bailey, *Strategies and Spoils*, 6.
10. Turner, *The Anthropology of Performance*, 33.
11. Cohen, *The Symbolic Construction of Community*, 11–16.
12. On the assimilation of global models into the language of Thai politics and policy, see, e.g., Nelson, "World Society in Thailand," 199–206; Orlandini, "Consuming 'Good Governance.'" For examples of the deployment of this language in election campaigns in Thailand, see Fishel, "Reciprocity and Democracy," chap. 3.
13. See Askew, *Culture and Electoral Politics*, chap. 2. On the Thai state and representations of desirable "democratic culture," see Connors, *Democracy and National Identity*, 48–83.

14. For a lucid exposition, see Douglas, *Natural Symbols*, esp. chap. 9, "Control of Symbols."

15. Murphy, *The Dialectics of Social Life*, 238. For a related rendering utilizing "culture," see Wagner, *The Invention of Culture*, 103–6.

16. Bilmes, "Rules and Rhetoric;" Kemp, "The Manipulation of Personal Relations;" O'Connor, "Merit and the Market."

17. Wattana, "Consuming Modernity in a Border Community;" Dowsey-Magog, "Popular Culture and Traditional Performance."

18. See, e.g., Bilmes, "Rules and Rhetoric," 46; Nelson, *Central Authority*, 164–65.

19. Walker, "The 'Rural Constitution.'"

20. Arghiros, *Democracy, Development and Decentralization*, 189–208; Nelson, *Analyzing Provincial Political Structures*; Niti, "Traders, Kinsmen and Trading Counterparts."

21. This is a modification of the scheme presented by F.G. Bailey in his *Stratagems and Spoils*, 35–48.

22. See Nelson, *Analyzing Provincial Political Structures*.

23. Akin, "Bangkok Slum," 245–52.

24. Withaya, "Phuak." Anthropologists have not sufficiently acknowledged the centrality of norms of friendship and other "horizontal" patterns of affiliation in Thai sociality. For rare exceptions (in addition to the work of Akhom), see Piker, "Friendship to the Death;" Foster, "Friendship in Rural Thailand."

25. Nit Tongsopit, for example, lists eleven possible meanings of *phuak* in English, incorporating both positive and negative connotations. These include "band," "group," "team," "fellow," "gang," "folk," "batch," "bloc," "people," and "multitude," in addition to *phuakphong* (friends, gang). Nit, *Photchananukrom Thai–Angkrit*, 578.

26. Akhom, *Phuk Yot*; Nithi, "*Phuk siao Phuk kloe*," *Matichon Raisapda*, December 18, 2000.

27. Nelson, "Thailand's House Elections," 315–22.

28. Hanks, "The Thai Social Order," 197–218. Note that the Thai expression for a social circle, or set, is *wongkan* or *waetwong*, not *phuak*.

29. See, e.g., Amara, *Rabop uppatham*.

30. Akin, "Persistence within Change," 45–46.

31. Observations about the commodification of patron-client relations in general were made in the mid-1970s by Akin. For standard arguments on commercialized patronage relations as the basis of political group formation and vote-canvassing networks in Thailand, see Arghiros, *Democracy, Development and Decentralization*, 6–9; Ockey, *Making Democracy*, 96–97.

32. Anyarat, "Thailand's Networks of Vote Canvassers." We might depict the actions and motivation of *all* political actors as the stark pursuit of power and "interest." Yet, the deployment of meaningful symbolic resources or "cultural capital" is critical in political relations. See Bourdieu, *Outline of a Theory of Practice*, 178.

33. Nishizaki, "The Weapon of the Strong," esp. 1–44.

34. Thamora Fishel highlights the importance of moral idioms of exchange and obligation in political discourses and symbolism in Phetburi province, though she understates the significance of the more horizontal communal and fictive kin dimensions of these exchange idioms. See Fishel, "Reciprocity and Democracy," 30–36.

35. The most detailed treatment of the region, though now out of date, remains Donner, *The Five Faces of Thailand*, 403–532.

36. Askew, "Sex and the Sacred."

37. See Tej, *The Provincial Administration of Siam*, 268–77.

38. Yongyut, "*Amnat thang kanmueang*, 83–103; Wenk, *The Restoration of Thailand*, 28.

39. For an account, albeit dated, of the Thai-speaking Muslims of Songkhla, see Burr, "Thai-speaking Muslims."

Chapter 2

1. *Phak Prachathipat*, 7–9.

2. The term *udomkan* is not prominent among those key terms in political language that scholars have identified in the period of political change leading to, and following, the overthrow of absolute monarchy in 1932. See, e.g., Nakharin, *Kan patiwat Siam*; Sombat, *Phasa thang kanmueang*. Notably, the first edition of the Royal Institute's Thai-language dictionary (1950) had no entry for "*udomkan*," though it appears by the 1970s. In

1982, one columnist commented that the word was as "strange as a late season mango," and pointed to the vague definitions given in the Royal Institute Dictionary, where *udomkan* was aligned with *udomkhati* (ideal). See Sangkhom, "*Phasa Thai khong rao 'udomkan,'*" 22–24.

3. Noranit, *Phak Prachathipat*, 23–32; Democrat Party, "*Udomkan phak.*" Not surprisingly, in the mid-1990s, a Bangkok-based Democrat Party municipal councilor who wrote a master's thesis on the topic of, "The Political Ideology of the Democrat Party" had no doubt that the party's *udomkan* could be translated as "ideology." He defined the party's *udomkan* as "a model of thinking and belief about life and society, which is a system of thinking and belief that one group accepts as right and attractive. It is a system of thinking and belief that a group adheres to as a direction for action for the Democrat Party, to work together to achieve the best." Ayut, "*Udomkan thang kanmueang,*" 10.

4. Pasuk and Baker, *Thailand: Economy and Politics*, 267–69; Wilson, *Politics*, 25, 31; Noranit, *Phak Prachathipat*, 69–70.

5. Morell and Chai-anan, *Political Conflict*, 272–76; Sangsit, "*Phak Prachathipat,*" 118.

6. Samak, who embarrassed even the military in the appointed government that succeeded Seni's, was ousted from cabinet by them in 1977. Shortly after this, he formed the conservative Prachakon Thai Party (Thai People Party), which enjoyed strong support in Bangkok for the next decade.

7. Chang Noi, "Can the Democrats Learn from Past Mistakes?," *Nation*, August 7, 2006.

8. McCargo, *Politics and the Press*, 199–214; Bukhari, *Chuan Leekpai*, 121–64.

9. *Seni Pramoj: Chiwalikhit*.

10. See Savitri Gadavanij, "Discursive Strategies for Political Survival;" *Prachathipat prasai*.

11. Kramol, *Toward a Political Party Theory*, 39.

12. See, e.g., Ockey, "Political Parties."

13. McCargo, "Thailand's Political Parties," 130–31.

14. Noranit, *Phak Prachathipat*, 8–10.

15. Suwat, "*Wiwathanakan khwam phukphan,*" 91.

16. Orathai, "Electoral Politics in Thailand," 305–7; Nelson, "Thailand's House Elections," January 6, 2001."

17. Chang Noi, "The New Political Map of Thailand," *Nation*, January 22, 2001.

18. Nithi, Sanphet, and Bancha, "*Thongthin niyom*," 62–64.

19. Suthiwong, et al., *Lokathat Thai phak Tai.* The conceptual foundations of the "world view" approach, which was popular during the 1980s, drew inspiration from a variety of Western scholarly frameworks aiming to capture the "emic" dimensions of people's perceptions of their social and natural world, including those of the American anthropologist Robert Redfield and cognitive-oriented social scientists. See Amara, *Traditional and Changing Thai World View*, 3–12.

20. Somchettana, "*Watthanatham chon.*"

21. Akhom, *Hua chueak, wua chon*, 209.

22. Author's interview with Akhom Detthongkham, December 3, 2005. See also, Jory, "Problems in Contemporary Thai Nationalist Historiography;" McCargo, "Southern Thai Politics," 29; and also appendix to the 2004 edition of Akhom, *Hua chueak, wua chon*, 275–82, which reprints local news articles highlighting reactions to his book and his mentor Suthiwong's attempts to defuse criticism.

23. The phenomenon of "cultural intimacy" and its exposure in issues of cultural coding and postures of national honor are explored lucidly by Michael Herzfeld in *Cultural Intimacy*, 1–32.

24. Akhom, *Hua chueak, wua chon*, 56.

25. Akhom interview.

26. Akhom, *Phuk Yoti.*

27. McCargo, *Southern Thai Politics*, 29.

28. Suthiwong, *Katho sanim.*

29. Suthiwong, *Southern Thai Cultural Structures*, 1–16.

30. On NGOs and civil society activists in Songkhla, see LoGerfo, "Beyond Bangkok," 234–58; Horstmann, *Class, Culture and Space*, 87–108, 124–29.

31. Charun, "*Botnam: Watthanatham thang kanmueang,*" 12.

32. Charun, "*Watthanatham thang kanmueang khong chao tai,*" 44.

33. Charun, "*Lokathat Chuan Leekpai,*" 60–73.

34. Sathaphon, "*Kho chamkat,*" 147–50.

35. Charun, "*Watthanatham thang kan mueang khong chao lumnam thalesap Songkhla.*"

36. "Athayu," *Thup na pho*, 106.

37. Author's interview with Charun Yuthong, October 26, 2003.

38. McCargo, *Southern Thai Politics*, 27–29.

39. Charun's series of ten short articles, published under the rubric of, "Party or Phuak?" appeared in *Focus Phak Tai* between September and December 2002.

40. See, e.g., Chai-anan, "*Phak niyom*," [Regionalism] *Phuchatkan Raiwan*, June 20, 1995; *Thongthin niyom lae phumiphak niyom*.

Chapter 3

1. For a discussion of the southern violence and the Democrat Party response, see Askew, *Conspiracy, Politics and a Disorderly Border*.

2. *Samila Times*, January 14–20, 2004.

3. The Si Saket by-election was held on June 1, 2003, following the death of an incumbent TRT MP. The TRT defeated the Democrats by 45,166 votes to 20,920. The Nonthaburi by-election, held on October 12, 2003, owing to the death of the sitting Chat Phatthana MP, was a bitter contest between two coalition partners. TRT won the seat convincingly with 36,966 votes, followed by Chat Phatthana with 19,274, while the Democrat candidate ran a poor third with just 8,200 votes.

4. Mongkol, "PM Seeks Bigger Majority;" Sukanya, "Southern Dilemma."

5. *Matichon Raiwan*, March 10, 2003.

6. Author's interview with Thawiwong Thirakul (Journalist ITV News Center, Hat Yai), September 10, 2003.

7. Author's interview with Sawai Phatthano, September 9, 2003.

8. Phonkrit Wassiwiwat, "*Wikhro kan mueang thongthin* [Analysis of Local Politics];" *Samila Times*, September 21–30, 2003.

9. Author's interviews with Rung-arun Dansap (deputy chief clerk, Ban Phlu Municipality), February 24, 2004, and Manop Pathumthong (campaign assistant and brother of Sunthon Pathumthong), February 9, 2005.

10. *Focus Phak Tai*, February 21–27, 2005.

11. *Focus Phak Tai*, October 25–31, 2003; Author's interview with Thammanun Selimin (Democrat Party branch chairman, Constituency 2), February 17, 2004.

12. Rungarun and Manop interviews.

13. *Nation*, January 22, 2004.

14. Author's interview with Niran Kaenyakun (former PAO councilor and aspiring TRT candidate), October 25, 2003.

15. *Focus Phak Tai*, October 25–31, 2003.

16. *Bangkok Post*, January 29, 2004.

17. Author's interview with Seri Nuanpheng (former mayor of Ban Phlu Municipality and key local TRT organizer), January 27, 2005.

18. Author's interview with Wira Musikaphong (senior TRT politician), February 20, 2004.

19. Author's interview with Seri Nuanpheng, January 27, 2005.

20. Author's interview with Thawon Senniam (Democrat MP for Constituency 4), September 29, 2003.

21. Author's interview with Khran Thawirat (former *kamnan* of Kho Hong Sub-district, *tambon* council chairman, and TRT organizer), September 11, 2003.

22. *Thai Post*, February 17, 2004; *Matichon*, February 18, 2004; *Nation*, February 20, 2004.

23. Author's interview with Suchat Intradit, February 25, 2004.

24. This was deliberate misinformation on the speaker's part, although most ordinary voters would not have known the factional alignments behind the Democrat Party leadership competition. In fact, only four of Songkhla's MPs were directly within Sanan's faction, while one was a Chuan protégé and the other three, including Phrai Phatthano, were non-aligned. Moreover, many of the southern party branch chairmen, in contrast to the majority of southern MPs, had voted for Abhisit, and the province's senior party branch chairman was particularly unhappy with Banyat's victory, which he believed had been secured by Sanan buying the votes of the northeastern party branch officials.

25. *Prachachat Thurakit*, February 26–29, 2004.

26. At least one national press journalist also noted the contrasts in the character of the two rallies. See "*Botrian 'Songkhla'* TRT *phae yap. Prakat saksi 'ngeun sue khon tai mai dai'* [The Lesson of Songkhla, TRT's Bad Loss Proclaims that 'Money Can't Buy Southern Thais']," *Prachachat Thurakit*, February 26–29, 2004.

27. *Prachachat Thurakit*, February 26–29, 2004.

28. For varieties of Democrat politicians' oratorical styles in parliamentary speeches, see Savitri Gadavanij, "Discursive Strategies for Political Survival," 156–69; 184–97.

29. Wira interview.

30. *Nation*, February 23, 2004.

31. *Nation*, February 24, 2004.

32. *Bangkok Post*, February 25, 2004.

33. *Nation*, February 24, 2004.

34. *Matichon Raiwan*, February 27, 2004.

35. *Matichon Raiwan*, February 26, 2004.

36. *Daily News*, February 25, 2004; *Matichon Raiwan*, 26 February 2004.

37. *Nation*, February 24, 2004; *Matichon Sutsapda*, February 27–March 4, 2004.

38. *Pratchachat Thurakit*, February 26–29, 2004.

39. Chiang, "*Hetphon baep Thai*," *Matichon Sutsapda* February 27–March 4, 2004.

40. *Samila Times*, February 7–21, 2004,

41. *Focus Phak Tai*, February 28–March 5, 2004.

42. *Nation Sutsapda*, March 1–7, 2004, 10–11; *Siam Rat Sapdawichan*, February 27–March 4, 2004.

43. Democrat Party, "RDI Center," http://www.democrat.or.th/rdicenter. 2004.

44. Seri interview; *Pratchachat Thurakit*, February 26–29, 2004.

45. *Matichon Sutsapda*, February 27–March 4, 2004.

46. Wira interview.

Chapter 4

1. Bailey, *Stratagems and Spoils*, 121.
2. *Chiwaprawat lae phon ngan*, appendix; Author's interview with Khreng Suwannawong (former mayor of Hat Yai), February 25, 2004.
3. For example, the town of Songkhla was dominated by Prayot Ekkuru and his *phuak* for at least two decades, while other municipalities in the country, notably Chiang Mai, Phetchaburi, and Samut Prakan had been controlled for long periods by locally prestigious *trakun*.
4. For an account of the Phetchaburi contest, see Fishel, "Reciprocity and Democracy," 132–35.
5. Nation, July 16, 2003.
6. *Focus Songkhla*, December 24–30, 2001; February 25–March 3, 2002.
7. Author's interview with Tharadon Phromsut (former opposition councilor, Hat Yai Municipality, 2002–04), September 30, 2003.
8. Official estimates of Hat Yai's population vary, depending on methods of data collection. On the basis of house certificates, the population within the municipal boundaries of Hat Yai (covering 21 sq km) was counted as 157,316 in 2002. However, according to the national census of 2000, the city's population totaled 187,920.
9. Suthiwong, Dilok, and Prasit, *Chin Thaksin*, 119–24, 237–38; Suliman, *Mueang Hat Yai*, 116–60.
10. Author's interview with Khreng Suwannawong, February 25, 2004.
11. Ibid.
12. *Chiwaprawat lae phon ngan*, 8.
13. *Matichon Raiwan*, March 10, 2003; Sombat, "Local Godfathers," 53–58; Pasuk and Sungsidh Piriyarangsan, *Corruption and Democracy*, 95–98.
14. *Chiwaprawat lae phon ngan*, Appendix.
15. Author's interview with Professor Suraphong Sothanasathian (Thammasat University), February 24, 2005.
16. Author's interview with former deputy chief clerk (*rong palat*), Hat Yai Municipality, October 13, 2003 (name withheld by request).
17. Khreng interview.

18. Suraphong, *Mueangyai*, 120–24. For similar assessments of other municipalities in Thailand, see, e.g., Chakrit and Hagensick, *Modernizing Chiangmai*, 31–40.

19. See Nelson, *Central Authority*, 25–64.

20. Watchariphon, *Phawa phunam*, 102–5.

21. Author's interview with Dr. Suchat Intradit (former speaker, Hat Yai Municipal Council), February 25, 2004; Author's interview with Chan Lilaphon (Hat Yai businessman and candidate for deputy mayor in *Thim Hat Yai Prongsai*), September 29, 2003.

22. Suraphong, *Mueang yai*, 114–16.

23. *Focus Songkhla*, January 24–30, 2000.

24. Hat Yai Municipality's former deputy-chief clerk interview. For mayoral patronage of local communities in Phetchaburi, see Fishel, "Reciprocity and Democracy," 131, 264.

25. *Focus Songkhla*, January 24–30, 2000; Author's interview with Adulsak Mukhem (former municipal counselor and *Thim Hat Yai Prongsai* candidate), October 14, 2003.

26. Author's interview with Sombun Phonloetnaphakon (hotel owner and candidate for deputy mayor in *Thim Hat Yai prongsai*), February 28, 2004.

27. See McVey, "Change and Consciousness," 109–37.

28. The family network formalized a system of regular family reunions and produced a publication detailing the membership and achievements of the "*sam thuat*" descendents in 2000.

29. *Focus Songkhla*, November 22–28, 1999; January 17–22, 2000; January 24–30, 2000.

30. *Focus Songkhla*, January 17–22, 2000.

31. Tharadon interview.

32. See Charlchai, et al., "Assessment of Flood Risk," 1–8.

33. Author's interview with Phrai Phatthano (Democrat MP and candidate for Hat Yai mayor), September 8, 2003; see also Mongkol, "Democrat MPs."

34. *Focus Phak Tai*, May 24–30, 2003.

35. *Samila Times*, August 11–20, 2003.

36. Author's interview with Thamanun Selimin (Democrat Party branch chairman, Constituency 2), February 18, 2004.

37. Phrai's comments as noted by the author who was present at the Democrat rally that followed the Prachathipat Cup games in September 2003.

38. Author's interview with Nirut Mai-on (former candidate *thim Kiattiphum* and Constituency 2 Democrat Party branch advisor), January 2, 2005; Phrai interview.

39. Author's interview with Sombun Phonloetnaphakon, February 28, 2004.

40. Author's interview with Sawai Phatthano (former Democrat Party MP for Songkhla Province), September 9, 2003.

41. Author's interview with Chan Lilaphon, September 29, 2003.

42. Author's interview with Adulsak Mukhem, October 14, 2003.

43. Phrai interview.

44. *Focus Phak Tai*, July 8–14, 2002; Author's interview with Seri Nuanpheng (former chairman of the municipal council of Tambon Ban Phlu), September 2003.

45. Author's interview with Wichan Chuaichuchai (senior editor, *Samila Times*), February 23, 2004.

46. *Samila Times*, September 21–30, 2003.

47. For e-mail comments on Phrai's candidacy, see, e.g., http://www.cityvariety.com/board/show.php?no=15

48. *Samila Times*, December 1–10, 2003.

49. *Samila Times*, December 6–12, 2003; *Focus Phak Tai*, December 6–12, 2003; Sombun interview.

50. *Samila Times*, January 31–February 6, 2004.

51. *Kanmueang Raisapda*, February 9–15, 2004.

52. *Focus Phak Tai*, December 6–12, 2003.

53. *Samila Times*, January 31–February 6, 2004.

54. Author's interview with Amnuai Phatthano (hotelier, uncle of Phrai Phatthano), February 28, 2004; *Samila Times*, January 31–February 6, 2004.

55. Author's interview with Patthama Suwannawong (daughter of Khreng Suwannawong), February 24, 2004.

56. *Kanmueang Raisapda*, February 9–15, 2004; February 23–29, 2004.

57. *Focus Phak Tai*, March 6–12, 2004.

58. Songkhla Provincial Election Commission, *Sarup kanchaisit*; see also *Matichon Raiwan*, March 2, 2004.

59. Banchet, "*Khwam tongkan.*"

Chapter 5

1. Nelson, "The Provincial Administrative Organization Elections;" Pasuk and Baker, *Thaksin*, 192; see also *Nation*, March 15, 2004.

2. *Focus Songkhla*, January 11–15, 1999.

3. *Focus Songkhla*, September 20–26, 1999.

4. *Focus Songkhla*, January 14–20, 2000.

5. Author's interview with prominent Hat Yai–based electrical contractor, February 8, 2005 (name withheld at request).

6. *Focus Phak Tai*, March 7–13, 2003.

7. *Focus Phak Tai*, November 15–21, 2004.

8. Author's interview with Nawaphon Bunyamani (deputy president, Songkhla PAO), October 21, 2003.

9. Ibid.

10. *Samila Times*, November 21–30, 2003.

11. *Focus Phak Tai*, November 15–21, 2003; *Samila Times*, November 21–30, 2003.

12. *Samila Times*, November 21–30, 2003.

13. *Focus Phak Tai*, November 22–28, 2003.

14. See, e.g., *Samila Times*, January 31–February 6, 2004.

15. *Samila Times*, March 13–19, 2004.

16. *Focus Phak Tai*, January 17–23, 2004.

17. Author's interview with Seri Pathumwan (vote canvasser for Worawit Khaothong, Khuaniang District), December 30, 2004.

18. *Focus Phak Tai*, March 6–12, 2004.

19. *Samila Times*, March 13–19, 2004.

20. *Focus Phak Tai*, March 6–12, 2004.

21. "*Phak Prachathipat miti mai song phu samak long rap luaktang pen nayok o bo cho* [The Democrat Party has declared not to officially send candidates to stand for the provincial election]," a two-sided flier distributed throughout Songkhla Province by Worawit's team, "*Rak Songkhla*."

22. Calculated from Songkhla Provincial Election Commission, *Phon kannap-khanaen*; see also *Samila Times*, March 20–26, 2004.

23. This account is based on interview transcripts and field notes taken in Khuaniang District.

24. Author's interview with Mit Kaeopradit (former Songkhla PAO candidate), December 6, 2005.

25. Author's field notes, December 2005.

26. *Krungthep Thurakit*, September 23, 2004.

27. Nelson, *Central Authority*, esp. 181–86; Nelson, *Analyzing Provincial Political Structures*.

Chapter 6

1. For commentary, see *Nation*, August 30, 2004.

2. See Supawadee and Yuwadee, "TRT Claims 5 More MPs," *Bangkok Post*, August 6, 2004; Weerayut, "Democrats in Fight;" Author's interview with Samit Chaichularat (Democrat Party branch committee member, Constituency 2), 2005.

3. *Focus Phak Tai*, November 6–12, 2004.

4. *Nation*, December 10, 2004.

5. *Nation*, January 4, 2005.

6. See, e.g., *Nation*, January 10, 2005; Tulsathit, "Opposition Leader Simply Unmarketable."

7. *Nation*, November 29, 2004.

8. See, e.g., *Nation*, January 15, 2005; January 30, 2005.

9. *Krungthep Thurakit*, November 29, 2004; *Nation*, November 29, 2004.

10. Author's interview with Wirat Kalayasiri (Democrat Party MP for Constituency 3), Songkhla, January 3, 2005.

11. *Krungthep Thurakit*, September 23, 2004.

12. *Krungthep Thurakit*, November 22, 2004.

13. Author's interview with Wichit Suwit (retiring Democrat MP for Constituency 8, Songkhla), December 30, 2004.

14. *Krungthep Thurakit*, September 23, 2004.

15. *Focus Phak Tai*, November 27–December 3, 2005; *Krungthep Thurakit*, December 10, 2004.

16. *Focus Phak Tai*, November 13–19, 2004.

17. *Krungthep Thurakit*, September 15, 2004; December 3, 2004.

18. *Krungthep Thurakit*, November 29, 2004; Author's interview with Manop Pathumthong (TRT campaign assistant and brother of Sunthon Pathumthong), February 9, 2005.

19. Author's interview with Somsri Wongsakun (personal assistant to Sunthon Patumthong), December 30, 2004.

20. Author's interview with Seri Nuanpheng, January 27, 2005.

21. Author's interview with Nirut Mai-on, January 10, 2005.

22. Author's interview with Police Sergeant Chum Monthondaeng (former bodyguard to Phrai Phatthano), December 5, 2005.

23. *Krungthep Thurakit*, September 23, 2004.

24. Author's interview with Seri Pathumwan, January 27, 2005.

25. Informants close to Worawit Khaothong (names withheld by request).

26. Author's interview with Chatchai Sirirat (nephew and parliamentary assistant to Trairong Suwankhiri), January 26, 2005.

27. Author's interview with Thip Phromphet (provincial councilor for Amphoe Thepha), October 17, 2003.

28. Author's interview with Surasak Mani, October 17, 2003.

29. *Krungthep Thurakit*, September 23, 2004; November 29, 2004; December 20, 2004.

30. Information supplied by Surasak Mani's legal advisor and campaign assistant, November 19, 2005 (name withheld by request).

31. Author's interview with Thamanun Selimin, December 30, 2004; Wichit interview.

32. Author's interview with Phuwadon Kiattisak (village headman and Democrat Party branch vice chairman, Constituency 8), January 27, 2005.

33. Author's interview with Thip Phromphet, October 17, 2003.

34. Author's interview with Abdoloh Yothet (vote canvasser for Surasak Mani), January 9, 2005.

Chapter 7

1. See McCargo and Ukrist, *The Thaksinization of Thailand*, 79–81; Ockey, "Change and Continuity," 670–72.

2. Callahan, and McCargo, "Vote Buying in Thailand's Northeast."

3. *Samila Times*, November 30–December 4, 2004.

4. Election activities were interrupted by the tsunami disaster on December 26, after which all parties suspended canvassing for a week as a sign of respect for the victims. After some speculation that the polling date would be set back, the ECT confirmed the February 6 original date, and canvassing then resumed at a frantic pace in order to make up for lost time and reach as many of the constituencies' communities as possible.

5. Author interviews with Phaisan Talamo (phuak of Police Sergeant Chum Monthondaeng), January 10, 2005, and Manop Pathumthong, February 9, 2005.

6. *Focus Phak Tai*, January 22–28, 2005.

7. Author's interview with Surasak Mani, January 9, 2005.

8. See Atthayuth and Sucheera, "Cash-For-Votes Scandal;" Pradit, "TRT Abandons South Hope."

9. This was true with the exception of rally appearances by Wanno and Wira in Thepha District in aid of Surasak's campaign on January 24.

10. Supannee, "The Unique Character of Electoral Constituencies," 6.

11. See, e.g., Morell and Chai-anan, *Political Conflict in Thailand*, 25–27.

12. Local press reporters also noted this practice and remarked on the distinctive character small rallies gave the Democrat Party. See *Samila Times*, January 25–29, 2005.
13. Author's interview with Police-Colonel Mongkon Bunchum, February 1, 2004.
14. Chang Noi, "Newin: The Lion of Songkhla;" *Nation*, January 31, 2005; *Focus Phak Tai*, January 22–28, 2005; Mongkol, "Newin in the Clear."
15. Author's interview with Chatchai Sirirat, January 26, 2005.
16. I heard the same views expressed by villagers during visits to Khuaniang and Bang Klam Districts.
17. Author's interview with Wirat Kalayasiri, January 3, 2005.
18. Author's interview with Surasak Mani, January 9, 2005.
19. Author's interview with Somdet Namphring (Democrat Party branch member and canvasser, Constituency 8), February 3, 2005.
20. Author's interview with Seri Nuanpheng, February 2, 2005.
21. Wirat interview.

Chapter 8

1. Sombat Chanthawong, *Lueaktang wikrit*, 111.
2. Daniel Arghiros, for example, seems to use the terms "canvasser" and "vote broker" interchangeably in his accounts of vote seeking in Ayutthaya. Arghiros, *Democracy, Development and Decentralization*, 96–97.
3. See Ockey, *Making Democracy*, 28–32.
4. Author's interview with Khran Thawirat, September 11, 2003.
5. Author's interview with Charan Inkhayut (*tambon* councilor of Khu Tao and Democrat supporter), January 4, 2005.
6. See Arghiros, *Democracy, Development and Decentralization*, 129–64; Sombat, *Lueaktang Wikrit*, 111–20.
7. Author's interview with Thawon Senniam, September 29, 2003.
8. Author's interview with Nirut Mai-on, January 10, 2005.
9. See, e.g., Ockey, *Making Democracy*, 36–37.
10. Callahan, *Pollwatching*, 24; Sombat, *Lueaktang wikrit*, 120–24.

11. Arghiros, *Democracy, Development and Decentralization*, 138–49; Callahan, *Pollwatching*, 24–28; Callahan and McCargo, "Vote Buying in Thailand's Northeast," 377–79.

12. See, e.g., Hicken, "The Market for Votes in Thailand."

13. To preserve individuals' anonymity, all local *hua khanaen* are referred to with fictional names.

14. See Arghiros, *Democracy, Development and Decentralization*,130–40.

15. Author's interview with Seri Pathumwan, January 2, 2005.

16. The information concerning these events was gained from interviews with Sawiang Chaisiri and corroborated by further accounts from local informants, as well as additional interviews conducted in the locality by a research assistant whose identity has been withheld at his request.

17. See Sombat, *Lueaktang wikrit*, 124 ff.

18. See, e.g., Callahan, *Pollwatching*, 20.

19. Informants' names have been withheld in order to preserve their anonymity.

20. Based on author's interviews with the following Songkhla Provincial Election Commission officials, Phaithun Chahae (Director of Songkhla PEC), January 31, 2004; Captain (rtd.) Chawalit Kalamphaheti and Police Lt.-Colonel (rtd.) Monkhon Bunchum (constituency PEC committee chairmen), February 1, 2005.

21. Author's interview with Somsri Wongsakun, February 7, 2005.

22. Author's interviews with Chatchai Sirirat, January 26, 2005; Wirat Kalayasiri, January 25, 2005; Somsri Wongsakun, February 7, 2005; Manop Pathumthong, February 9, 2005.

23. Author's interview with Surasak Mani, January 9, 2005.

24. Author's interview with Basa Walae (imam of Ban Phlu Ching, a Malay-speaking Muslim village in Tambon Thamuang, Thepha District), February 10, 2005.

25. Data source: Songkhla Provincial Election Commission Office.

26. See Callahan, *Pollwatching*, 36.

27. Ibid., 35.

28. See Orathai, "Electoral Politics in Thailand," 284–85.

Chapter 9

1. Pradit, "People Put Thaksin in Charge."
2. See *Matichon Raiwan*, February 9, 2005; February 27, 2005; Suphawadee, "Democrats to woo young."
3. *Krungthep Thurakit*, February 10, 2005.
4. Pasuk and Baker, "Thailand's 2005 Election," 8–9.
5. Askew, *Conspiracy*, 62–69; *Bangkok Post*, February 8, 2005.
6. Pradit, "People put Thaksin in charge."
7. Cited in Ibid.
8. Pradit, "Democrats ward off TRT invader."
9. Author's interview with Surasak Mani, February 8, 2005.
10. Author's interview with Seri Pathumwan, February 7, 2005.
11. Author's interview with Somsri Wongsakun, February 8, 2005.
12. Author's interview with Seri Pathumwan, February 7, 2005.

Chapter 10

1. Herzfeld, *The Poetics of Manhood*, xiv.
2. Connolly, *Identity/Difference*, 64.
3. See, e.g., Chai-anan, "*Phak niyom.*"
4. This point is well made in Chiraphon, "*Khwam niyom Khong Phak Prachathipat*," 10–15.
5. Author's field notes, February 2005.
6. *Matichon Raiwan*, March 23, 1992; Callahan, *Pollwatching*, 20.
7. Charun,"*Lokathat Chuan Leekpai*,"65–71.
8. Klin Khongmueangphet, "*Khit Chapchuai*," 99.
9. Charun,"*Lokathat Chuan Leekpai*," 62.
10. *Matichon Raiwan*, March 10, 2003.
11. Nawaphan, "*Kan sueksa choeng kan priapthiap.*"

12. This was a secret party poll for which I was unable to gain direct access. Author's interview with Niphon Bunyamani, September 4, 2003.

13. Pseudonyms are used for all personal names of party members in this account, except for Niphon Bunyamani.

14. Cited in *Focus Songkhla*, November 6–12, 2000.

15. Author's field notes (from a conversation during the celebrations to open a new seafood processing factory owned by Prapon Ekkuru, nephew of Prayot), September 2003.

16. See, e.g., Arghiros, *Democracy, Development and Decentralization*, 129–65; Fishel, "Reciprocity and Democracy," 20–31.

17. Kemp, "The Manipulation of Personal Relations," 67.

18. Fishel, "Reciprocity and Democracy," 89–118.

19. Sukanya, "Former MPs."

20. Author's interview with Sawai Phatthano, September 9, 2003.

21. See Suwat, "*Wiwathanakan khwam phukphan*," 100–1.

22. Wilson, *Politics in Thailand*, 226–28.

23. Morell and Chai-anan, *Political Conflict in Thailand*, 269; McCargo, "Thailand's Political Parties," 117.

24. Chaiwat Wiranan, "*Botbat thang kanmueang*."

25. Ockey, "Political Parties," 273.

Chapter 11

1. Fishel, "Reciprocity and Democracy," 119–61.

2. On Banhan Silpa-acha, see Nishizaki, "The Weapon of the Strong," esp. 1–44, 871–1011.

3. For a classic example of this categorization, see Suchit, "Elections and Democratization," 195–98.

4. Anek, "A Tale of Two Democracies."

5. Anyarat, "Thailand's Networks of Vote Canvassers;" Walker, "The 'Rural Constitution.'"

6. Interview with Khreng Suwannawong, February 25, 2004.

7. Leach, *Political Systems*, 14.

8. During the 2005 national elections, TRT canvassers and candidates in the northern region of Chiang Mai critiqued the Democrat Party as "the party of southerners." See Walker, "The 'Rural Constitution.'"

9. See, e.g., Chang Noi, "Can the Democrats Learn from Past Mistakes?"

10. See, e.g., the editorial essay, "A Very Poor Showing from the Democrats," *Nation*, January 10, 2005.

11. Tulsathit Taptim, "Opposition Leader Simply Unmarketable."

12. Kalan Woraphitayut, *Re-branding phak Prachathipat*.

13. Manop and Monkol Bangprapa, "Abhisit: I'm Ready to be PM."

Epilogue

1. *Bangkok Post*, February 27, 2006.

2. *Nation*, April 3, 2006.

3. *Bangkok Post*, April 10, 2006.

4. It was later revealed that the figure behind the Songkhla registration blockade was "Charlie" Nophawong Na Ayutthaya, Trairong Suwankhiri's former assistant. Since "Khun Charlie" no longer had any formal affiliation with the party, the TRT claims that Democrat politicians were involved in planning the action could not be proven.

5. *Nation*, April 24, 2006.

6. *Nation*, March 20, 2006

7. Pradit and Mongkol, "Election Official Tampered with Data."

8. *Bangkok Post*, April 20, 2006.

9 Thawon, *Khadi Prawatisat*.

10. *Thai Day*, August 7, 2006.

11. For discussion on the background and the events surrounding the September 19 coup, see Michael Montesano, "Political Contests."

12. For a brief treatment of the early statements of the coup makers, see Nelson, "Thaksin Overthrown."

13. Based on talk with a number of Songkhla Democrat politicians and party members in the days following the September coup.

14. See Democrat Party, *Kham hai kan Abhisit Vejajiva*; Democrat Party, *Kham hai kan Suthep Thueaksuban*.

15. Based on author's discussions with party members and Democrat politicians in Songkhla Province during March 2007. See also Manop, "Democrats and TRT 'Close to End'."

16. See *Matichon Raiwan*, May 5, 2007; *Khao Sot*, May 27, 2007.

17. *Bangkok Post*, May 31, 2007; *Nation*, May 31, 2007.

18. *San Prachathipat Chagwat Chaidan Tai* [Democrat Newsletter for the Southern Border Provinces] No. 1 (July) 2007.

19. Author's fieldnotes.

20. See Askew, *Conspiracy*, 63–4.

21. Leading Democrat Party members from Songkhla who attended the two-day meeting have affirmed this point with the author.

22. TITV evening news, August 20, 2007.

23. *Matichon Raiwan*, July 23, 2007.

24. *Nation*, August 18, 2007.

25. *Bangkok Post*, July 24, 2007; *Daily News*, July 25, 2007.

26. *Nation*, August 21, 2007.

27. *Matichon Raiwan*, August 23, 2007.

28. *Nation*, October 8, 2007.

SOURCES

Interviews and Field Observations

Information and viewpoints derived from interviews are indicated in the endnotes of specific chapters which provide the names and details of these individuals (where appropriate, names have been disguised). Descriptions of events, unless otherwise indicated, are drawn from the author's own observations and based on research field notes.

Newspapers

* Note on citations of news articles: Attributed news items are listed under authors' names in bibliography, otherwise they are cited in the endnotes under the title of the newspaper with relevant dates.

English Language

Bangkok Post. Various dates.

The Nation. Various dates.

Thai Language

National newspapers

Daily News. Various dates.

Khao Sot. Various dates.

Matichon Raiwan. Various dates.

Matichon Sutsapda. Various dates.

Nation Sutsapda. Various dates.

Phuchatkan Raiwan. Various dates.

Prachachat Thurakit. Various dates.

Siam Rath Sapdawichan. Various dates.

Thai Rath. Various dates.

Local/regional newspapers

Samila Times (published in Hat Yai). Various dates.

Focus Phak Tai (published in Hat Yai; entitled *Focus Songkhla* until late 2002). Various dates.

Kanmueang Raisapda (unregistered newspaper in Hat Yai; produced by opponents of Phrai Phatthano). Various dates.

Thang Thai (published in Hat Yai; commenced operation in 2004). Various dates.

Articles, Chapters, Monographs, Dissertations

Abélès, Marc. *Quiet Days in Burgundy: A Study in Local Politics*. Cambridge: Cambridge University Press, 1991.

Akhom Detthongkham. *Phuk yoti. Withi lae phalang khong kan phuk khloe phuk dong lae khanopthamniam uppatham khong phukhon sam changwat chaikhop rop thalaesap Songkhla* [Tying Bonds. Methods and strength of camaraderie bonds and patronage customs among the people of the three provinces of the Songkhla Lake basin]. Bangkok: Thailand Research Fund, 2001.

———. *Hua chueak, wua chon* [Bull Keepers and Fighting Bulls]. 2000. Reprint, Bangkok: Thailand Research Fund, 2004.

Akin Rabibhadana. "Bangkok Slum: Aspects of Social Organization." Ph.D. diss., Cornell University, Ithaca, NY, 1975.

———. "Persistence within Change: Thai Society in the Nineteenth and Twentieth Centuries." In *Sangkhom Thai nai 200 pi* [Thai Society over 200 Years], edited by Narong Phuangphit and Phonsak Chirakraisiri. Bangkok: Chao Phraya Press, 1983.

Albritton, Robert. "Political Diversity Among Muslims in Thailand." *Asian Studies Review*, vol. 23, no. 2 (1999): 233–46.

Amara Phongsaphit. *Traditional and Changing Thai World View*. Bangkok: Chulalongkorn University Social Research Institute/Southeast Asian Studies Program, 1985.

———., ed. *Rabop uppatham* [The patronage system]. Bangkok: Chulalongkorn University Press, Third Printing, 2002.

Anek Laothamatas. "A Tale of Two Democracies: Conflicting Perceptions of Elections and Democracy in Thailand." In *The Politics of Elections in Southeast Asia*, edited by R. H. Taylor. New York: Woodrow Wilson Center Press and Cambridge University Press, 1996.

Anusorn Limanee. "Thailand." In *Political Party Systems and Democratic Development in East and Southeast Asia*, edited by W. Sachsenroder and U. E. Frings. Aldershot: Ashgate, 1998.

Anyarat Chattharakul. "Thailand's Networks of Vote Canvassers: Informal Power and Money Politics." Paper presented at the 5th Euro SEAS conference, Naples, Italy, 12–15 September 2007.

Arghiros, Daniel. *Democracy, Development and Decentralization in Provincial Thailand*. Richmond/Surrey: Curzon Press, 2001.

Askew, Marc. *Culture and Electoral Politics in Southern Thailand: Electoral Campaigning, Group Formation and the Symbolic Construction of Political Allegiances in Songkhla Province*. Nonthaburi: King Prajadhipok's Institute, 1996.

———. "Sex and the Sacred: Sojourners and Visitors in the Making of the Southern Thai Borderland." In *Centering the Margin: Agency and Narrative in Southeast Asian Borderlands*, edited by Alexander Horstmann and Reed Wadley. Oxford and New York: Berghahn, 2006.

———. *Conspiracy, Politics and a Disorderly Border: The Struggle to Comprehend Insurgency in Thailand's Deep South*. Washington, D.C. and Singapore: East-West Center and ISEAS, 2007.

Athayu. *See* Charun Yuthong.

Atthayuth Butsripoom and Sucheera Pinijparakarn. "Cash-For-Votes Scandal: 'Come Get Money If We Win.'" *Nation*, January 21, 2005.

Ayut Phetchin. "*Udomkan thang kanmueang khong phak Prachathipat* [The political ideology of the Democrat Party]." Master's thesis, Chulalongkorn University, Department of Government, Bangkok, 1994.

Bailey, Frederick G. *Stratagems and Spoils: A Social Anthropology of Politics*. New York: Schocken Books, 1969.

Banchet Phrinikit. "*Khwam tongkan kanplianplaeng* [The desire to change]." *Focus Phak Tai*, March 6–12, 2004.

Bilmes, Jack. "Rules and Rhetoric: Negotiating the Social Order in a Thai Village." *Journal of Anthropological Research*, vol. 32 (1976): 44–57.

Bourdieu, Pierre. *Outline of a Theory of Practice*. London: Cambridge University Press, 1977.

Bukhari Yima. *Chuan Leekpai nai kam mue nangsuephim Thai* [Chuan Leekpai in the grip of the Thai press]. Nonthaburi: Thangdoen Press, 1998.

Burr, Angela. "Thai-speaking Muslims in Two Southern Thai Coastal Fishing Villages: Some Processes of Interaction with the Thai Host Society." In *The Muslims in Thailand*. Vol. 1, *Historical and Cultural Studies*, edited by A. D. W. Forbes. Bihar: Center for South East Asian Studies, 1988.

Callahan, William A. *Pollwatching, Elections and Civil Society in Southeast Asia*. Aldershot: Ashgate, 2000.

Callahan, William A., and Duncan McCargo. "Vote-Buying in Thailand's Northeast: The July 1995 General Election." *Asian Survey*, vol. 36, no. 4 (1996): 376–92.

Chai-anan Samudavanija. "*Phak niyom* [Regionalism]." *Phuchatkan Raiwan*, June 20, 1995.

Chaiwat Wiranan. "*Botbat thangkanmueang khong sa-kha phakkanmueang: Suksa chapho koroni phak Prachathipat* [The Political Role of Party Branches: A Case Study of the Democrat Party]." Master's thesis, Chulalongkorn University, Department of Government, Bangkok, 1992.

Chakrit Noranitipadungkan. *Elites, Power Structure and Politics in Thai Communities*. Bangkok: National Institute of Development Administration, 1970.

Chakrit Noranitipadungkan, and A. Clark Hagensick. *Modernizing Chiangmai: A Study of Community Elites in Urban Development*. Bangkok: National Institute of Development Administration, 1973.

Chang Noi. "The New Political Map of Thailand." *Nation*, January 22, 2001.

———. "Newin: The Lion of Songkhla." *Nation*, January 31, 2005.

———. "Can the Democrats Learn from past Mistakes?" *Nation*, August 7, 2006.

Charlchai Thanavut, et al. "Assessment of Flood Risk in Hat Yai Municipality, Southern Thailand, Using GIS," *Journal of Natural Disaster Science*, vol. 26, no. 1, (2004): 1–14.

Charun Yuthong. "*Botnam: Watthanatham thang kanmueang khong chao tai*. [Introduction: The political culture of southern Thai people]." *Warasan Thaksinkhadi* [Journal of Southern Thai Studies], vol. 5, no. 2 (1999): 10–12.

———. "*Watthanatham thang kanmueang khong chao tai*: *Nak prachathipatai rue nak thongthin niyom* [The Political Culture of Southern Thai People: Democratists or Localists?]." *Warasan Thaksinkhadi*, vol. 5, no. 2 (1999): 34–45.

———. "*Lokathat Chuan Leekpai: Suksa chak wathakam* [The World View of Chuan Leekpai: a Study from Discourses]." *Warasan Thaksinkhadi*, vol. 5, no. 2 (1999): 60–73.

——— [Atthayu, pseud.]. *Thup na pho* [Cleaving the cow's face—Digging up dirt]. Hat Yai: Thaledao Publishing, 2000.

———. "*Watthanatham thangkanmueang khong chao lumnam thalesap songkhla* [Political culture of the people of the Songkhla Lake basin]." Unpublished research report, Thaksin University, Songkhla, 2001.

Chiraphon Damchan. "*Khwam niyom khong phak Prachathipat nai phak tai: Sueksa koroni khet lueaktang thi 1 lae 10 changwat Nakhon Si Thammarat* [The popularity of the Democrat Party in the southern region: A case study of constituencies 1 and 10 of Nakhon Si Thammarat province]." Master's thesis, Chulalongkorn University, Bangkok, 2004.

Chiang Sao Lang. "*Hetphon baep Thai thi phak Prachathipat chana luaktang som* [The 'Thai style' reason for the Democrat Party victory in the by-election]." *Phuchatkan*, February 24, 2004.

Chiwaprawat lae phon ngan: Khreng Suwanawong [Biography and achievements of Khreng Suwanawong]. Hat Yai: privately published [no imprint details], 1992.

"*Chut dotden Chuan Leekpai, chut dotden Prachathipat, ekkaphap thi pen nung diao* [The outstanding point of Chuan Leekpai, the outstanding point of the Democrats, A single unity]." *Matichon Sutsapda*, January 17–23, 2003.

Cohen, Anthony P. *The Symbolic Construction of Community*. Florence, KY: Routledge, 1985.

Connolly, William. *Identity/Difference: Democratic Negotiations of Political Paradox*. Ithaca, NY: Cornell University Press, 1991.

Connors, Michael Kelly. *Democracy and National Identity in Thailand*. London: RoutledgeCurzon, 2003.

Democrat Party, *Kham hai kan Abhisit Vejajiva. Khadi phak Prachathipat [Statement of Abhisit Vejajiva.* The case of the Democrat Party]. Bangkok: Democrat Party, 2007

Democrat Party, *Kham hai kan Suthep Thueaksuban. Khadi phak Prachathipat* [Statement of Suthep Thueaksuban. The case of the Democrat Party]. Bangkok: Democrat Party, 2007

Democrat Party. "*Udomkan phak* [Party Ideology]." http://www.democrat.or.th/standard.htm.

Donner, Wolf. *The Five Faces of Thailand. An Economic Geography*. London: C. Hurst & Company, 1978.

Douglas, Mary. *Natural Symbols*. Harmondsworth, Middlesex: Penguin, 1973.

Dowsey-Magog, Paul. "Popular Culture and Traditional Performance: Conflicts and Challenges in Contemporary *nang talung*." In *Dynamic Diversity in Southern Thailand*, edited by Wattana Sugunassil. Chiang Mai: Prince of Songkhla University/Silkworm Books, 2005.

Fishel, Thamora Virginia. "Reciprocity and Democracy: Power, Gender, and the Provincial Middle Class in Thai Political Culture," Ph.D. diss., Cornell University, Ithaca, New York, 2001.

Foster, Brian L. "Friendship in Rural Thailand." *Ethnology*, vol. 15, no. 3 (1976): 251–67.

Hanks, Lucien. "The Thai Social Order as Entourage and Circle." In *Change and Persistence in Thai Society*, edited by G.W. Skinner and A.T. Kirsch. Ithaca: Cornell University Press, 1975.

Herzfeld, Michael. *The Poetics of Manhood. Contest and Identity in a Cretan Mountain Village*. Princeton: Princeton University Press, 1985.

———. *Cultural Intimacy: Social Poetics in the Nation State*. Routledge: New York, 1997.

Hicken, Allen D. "The Market for Votes in Thailand." Paper presented at the International Conference, "Trading Political Rights: The Comparative Politics of Vote Buying," Center for International Studies, Massachusetts Institute of Technology, Boston, 26–27 August 2002.

Horstmann, Alexander. *Class, Culture and Space: The Construction and Shaping of Communal Space in South Thailand*. Beilefeld, Transcript, 2002.

Jory, Patrick. "Problems in Contemporary Thai Nationalist Historiography." *Kyoto Review of Southeast Asia*, 3 (March 2003). http://kyotoreview.cseas.kyoto-u.ac.jp/issue/issue3/

Kalan Woraphitayut. *Re-branding phak Prachathipat: Kansang braenh thang kanmueang duai konlayut thang kan talat*. [Re-branding the Democrat Party: Building a political brand through a strategy of marketing]. Bangkok: Matichon, 2005.

Kemp, Jeremy H. "The Manipulation of Personal Relations: From Kinship to Patron-Clientage." In *Strategies and Structures in Thai Society*, edited by H. Brummelhuis and J. H. Kemp. Amsterdam: Anthropological-Sociological Center, University of Amsterdam, 1984.

Kertzer, David I. *Ritual, Politics and Power*. New Haven: Yale University Press, 1988.

Klin Khongmueangphet. "*Khit chapchuai bon watthanatham thangkanmueang khong khon tai* [Casual thoughts on the political culture of the southern Thai people]." *Warasan Thaksinkhadi* [Journal of Southern Thai Studies], vol. 5, no. 2 (1999): 96–103.

Leach, Edmund. *Political Systems of Highland Burma. A Study of Kachin Social Structure*. Boston: Beacon Press, 1964.

LoGerfo, James P. "Beyond Bangkok: The Provincial Middle Class in the 1992 Protests." In *Money and Power in Provincial Thailand*, edited by Ruth McVey. Singapore: Institute of Southeast Asian Studies, 2000.

Loizos, Peter. *The Greek Gift: Politics in a Cypriot Village*. New York: St Martin's Press, 1975.

McCargo, Duncan. "Thailand's Political Parties: Real, Authentic and Actual." In *Political Change in Thailand: Democracy and Participation*, edited by K. Hewison. London: Routledge, 1997.

———. *Politics and the Press in Thailand. Media Machinations*. Bangkok: Garuda Press, 2002.

———. "Southern Thai Politics: A Preliminary Overview." In *Dynamic Diversity in Southern Thailand*, edited by Wattana Sugunasil. Chiang Mai: Prince of Songkla University/Silkworm Books, 2005.

McCargo, Duncan, and Ukrist Pathmanand. *The Thaksinization of Thailand*. Copenhagen: Nordic Institute of Asian Studies, 2005.

McLeod, James R. "The Sociodrama of Presidential Politics: Rhetoric, Ritual and Power in the Era of Teledemocracy." *American Anthropologist*, vol. 101, no. 2 (1999): 359–73.

McVey, Ruth. "Change and Consciousness in a Southern Countryside." In *Strategies and Structures in Thai Society*, edited by Han Ten Brummelhuis and Jeremy H. Kemp. Amsterdam: Anthropological-Sociological Center, University of Amsterdam, 1984. .

Manop Thip-osod and Mongkol Bangprapa. "Abhisit: I'm ready to be PM." *Bangkok Post*, April 30, 2006.

Mongkol Bangprapa. "PM seeks Bigger Majority for Party." *Bangkok Post*, January 26, 2003.

———. "Democrat MPs Peel Away." *Bangkok Post*, August 26, 2003.

———. "Gov't Bid to Delay Direct Polls Upset." *Bangkok Post*, October 4, 2003.

———. "Newin in Clear on Cash for Votes Claims, Watchdog Says." *Bangkok Post*, February 18, 2005.

Montesano, Michael. "Political Contests in the Advent of Bangkok's 19 September Putsch." Paper presented to the Thailand Update Conference 2006, National Thai Studies Centre, Australian National University, 29 September 2006.

Morell, David, and Chai-anan Samudavanija. *Political Conflict in Thailand: Reform, Reaction Revolution*. Cambridge Massachusetts: Oelgeshlager, Gunn and Hain, 1981.

Mulder, Niels. *Everyday Life in Thailand: An Interpretation*. Bangkok: Duang Kamol, 1979.

———. *Inside Thai Society: Interpretations of Everyday Life*. Amsterdam: Pepin Press, 1996.

Nakharin Mektrairat. *Kanpatiwat Siam pho so 2475* [The Revolution in Siam 1932]. Bangkok: Amarin Wichakan Publishing, 1997.

Nawaphan Netkham. "*Kansueksa choeng kan priaptbiap khong watthanatham thang kanmueang rawang khon phak neua lae phak tai: Koroni sueksa changwat Chiang Mai lae Nakhon Si Thammarat* [A Comparative Study of Political Culture of Rural Thai People in the Northern and Southern regions: A Case Study of Chiang Mai Province and Nakhon Si Thammarat Provinces]." Master's thesis, Chiang Mai University, Chiang Mai, 2002.

Neher, Clark D. *Politics and Culture in Thailand*. Ann Arbor: Center for Political Studies, University of Michigan, 1987.

———. "Thailand in 1986: Prem, Parliament and Political Pragmatism." *Asian Survey*, vol. 27, no. 2 (1987): 219–30.

Nelson, Michael H. *Central Authority and Local Democratization in Thailand*. Bangkok: White Lotus, 1998.

———. "Thailand's House Elections of 6 January 2001: Thaksin's Landslide Victory and Narrow Escape." In *Thailand's New Politics: KPI Yearbook 2001*, edited by Michael H. Nelson. Bangkok and Nonthaburi: King Prajadhipok's Institute and White Lotus, 2002.

———. "World Society in Thailand: Globalization Confronts Thainess." In *Thai Politics: Global and Local Perspectives. KPI Yearbook No. 2*, (2002/03), edited by Michael H. Nelson. Bangkok and Nonthaburi: King Prajadhipok's Institute, 2004.

———. "The Provincial Administrative Organization Elections in Thailand on 14 March 2004: Party Politicization or Strengthening of Local Political Groups?" Paper presented at the 5th Annual Academic Conference of Political Science and Public Administration, Thammasat University, 1 December 2004.

———. *Analyzing Provincial Political Structures in Thailand: Phuak, Trakun, and Hua Khanaen*. City University of Hong Kong, Southeast Asia Research Center, Working Paper Series, no. 79, August 2005.

———. "Thaksin Overthrown: Thailand's 'Well-Intentioned' Coup." In *The Thai Challenge*, edited by Thang D. Nguyen. Singapore: ISEAS. (forthcoming)

Nichapha Siriwat. *Branding Thai Rak Thai*. Bangkok: Higher Press, 2003.

Nishizaki, Yoshinori. "The Weapon of the Strong: Identity, Community, and Domination in Provincial Thailand." Ph.D. diss., University of Washington, Seattle, 2004.

Nit Tongsopit. *New Standard Thai–English Dictionary*. Bangkok: Phraephitthaya, 1990.

Niti Pawakapan."Traders, Kinsmen and Trading Counterparts: The Rise of Local Politicians in Northwestern Thailand." *Australian Journal of Anthropology*, vol.14, no.3 (2003): 365–82.

Nithi Ieosiwong. "*Phuk siao phuk kloe* [Bonds of Camaraderie]." *Matichon Raisapda*, December 18, 2000.

Nithi Ieosiwong, Sanphet Thammathikul, and Bancha Phongphanit. "*Thongthin niyom lae phumiphak niyom nai sangkhom Thai* [Localism and regionalism in Thai society]." In *Thongthin niyom lae phumiphak niyom nai sangkhom lae kanmueang Thai* [Localism and regionalism in Thai society and politics]. Nakhon Si Thammarat: Walailak University, 1995.

Noranit Setabuth. *Phak Prachathipat: Khwam samret rue khwam lomleao* [The Democrat Party: Success or failure]. Bangkok: Thammasat University Press, 1987.

O'Connor, Richard A. "Merit and the Market: Thai Symbolizations of Self-Interest." *Journal of the Siam Society*, vol. 74 (1986): 62–80.

Ockey, James. "Political Parties, Factions and Corruption in Thailand." *Modern Asian Studies*, vol. 28, no. 2 (1994): 251–77.

———. "Change and Continuity in the Thai Political Party System." *Asian Survey*, vol. 43, no. 4. (July/August, 2003): 663–80.

———. *Making Democracy. Leadership, Class, Gender and Political Participation in Thailand.* Honolulu: University of Hawai'i Press, 2004.

Orathai Kokpol. "Electoral Politics in Thailand." In *Electoral Politics in Southeast and East Asia*, edited by A. Croissant, G. Bruns and M. John. Singapore: Friedrich Ebert Stiftung, 2002.

Orlandini, Barbara. "Consuming 'Good Governance' in Thailand." *European Journal of Development Research*, vol. 15, no. 2. (December 2003): 16–43.

Pasuk Phongpaichit and Chris Baker. *Thailand. Economy and Politics, Kuala Lumpur*: Oxford University Press, 1996.

———. *Thailand's Crisis*. Chiang Mai: Silkworm Books, 2000.

———. *Thaksin. The Business of Politics in Thailand.* Chiang Mai: Silkworm Books, 2004.

———. "Thailand's 2005 Election: Rewriting the Constitution." Paper presented at the Ninth International Conference on Thai Studies, Northern Illinois University, De Kalb, Illinois, 3–6 April 2005.

Pasuk Phongpaichit and Sungsidh Piriyarangsan. *Corruption and Democracy in Thailand.* Chiang Mai: Silkworm Books, 1994.

Phak Prachathipat: Bon senthang pratchatipathai [The Democrat Party: On the path of democracy]. Bangkok: Money Magazine, 2000.

Phonkrit Wassiwiwat. "*Wikhro kanmueang thongthin* [Analysis of local politics]." *Samila Times*, September 21–30, 2003.

Piker, Steven. "Friendship to the Death in Rural Thai Society." *Human Organization*, vol. 27 (1968): 200–4

Piya Kittaworn, et al. "Voices from the Grassroots: Southerners Tell Stories about Victims of Development." In *Dynamic Diversity in Southern Thailand*, edited by Wattana Sugunasil. Chiang Mai: Prince of Songkhla University/Silkworm Books, 2005.

Pradit Ruangdit. "TRT Abandons South Hope." *Bangkok Post*, January 24, 2005.

———. "Democrats Ward Off TRT Invader." *Bangkok Post*, February 7, 2005.

———. "People Put Thaksin in Charge, with Themselves as Monitors." *Bangkok Post*, February 19, 2005.

Pradit Ruangdit and Mongkol Bangprapa. "Election Official Tampered with Data." *Bangkok Post*, April 21, 2006.

Prachathipat prasai [Democrat speeches. Democrats live]. Bangkok: Politikpress, 2004.

RDI Center. "Results of Exit Polls, Songkhla By-election, February 22, 2004." Democrat Party. http://www.democrat.or.th.rdicenter/.

Sungsidh Piriyarangsan. "*Phak Prachathipat: Chak anurakniyom su latthi seriniyom* [The Democrat Party: From conservatism to neo-liberalism]." In *Chitsamnuk lae udomkan khong khabuankan pratchatipatai ruam-samai* [Consciousness and ideology of the Democracy movement], edited by Sungsidh Piriyarangsan and Pasuk Phongpaichit, 99–127. Bangkok: Political Economy Center, Chulalongkorn University, 1996.

San Prachathipat changwat chaidaen tai [Democrat Newsletter for the Southern border provinces], no. 1 (July) 2007.

Sangkhom Sirirat. "*Phasa Thai khong rao 'udomkan'* [Our Thai language, '*udomkan*']." *Warasan Thai* [The Thai journal], vol. 2, no. 7 (1982): 22–24.

Sathaphon Sisatchang. "*Kho chamkat thang prawattisat kap watthanatham thang kanmueang khong chao tai* [The historical limits to the political culture of southern Thai people]." *Warasan Thaksinkhadi* [Journal of southern Thai studies], vol. 5, no. 2 (1999): 147–50.

Savitri Gadavanij. "Discursive Strategies for Political Survival: A Critical Discourse Analysis of Thai No-Confidence Debates." Ph.D. diss., University of Leeds, UK, 2002.

———. "Damning with Faint Praise: The Case of No-Confidence Debates in Thailand." In *Thai Politics: Global and Local Perspectives. KPI Yearbook No. 2*, (2002/03), edited by Michael H. Nelson. Nonthaburi: King Prajadhipok's Institute, 2004.

Seni Pramoj: Chiwalikhit [Seni Pramoj: As life goes by], edited by Withaya Kaeophradai. Bangkok: Seni Pramoj Foundation, 2005.

Sombat Chanthawong. *Phasa thang kanmueang: Phathana khong naeo athibai kanmueang lae sap kanmueang nai kankhian praphet sarakhadi thang kanmueang khong Thai pho so 2475–2525* [Political language: The development of political explanation and vocabulary in Thai political feature writing, 1932–1982]. Bangkok: Sathaban Thai Khadi, Thammasat University, 1990.

———. *Lueaktang wikrit: Punha lae thang-ok* [Thai elections in crisis: Problems and solutions]. Bangkok: Kopfai Publishing, 1993.

———. "Local Godfathers in Thai Politics." In *Money and Power in Provincial Thailand*, edited by Ruth McVey. Singapore: Institute of Southeast Asian Studies, 2000.

———. "The 1997 Constitution and the Politics of Electoral Reform." In *Reforming Thai Politics*, edited by Duncan McCargo. Copenhagen: Nordic Institute of Asian Studies, 2002.

Somchettana Muni. 1994. "*Watthanatham chon thi prakot nai thongthin phak tai* [The culture of banditry in southern Thailand]." *Warasan Thaksinkhadi* [Journal of Southern Thai Studies], vol. 4, no. 1: 15–29.

Songkhla Provincial Election Commission. *Sarup kanchaisit long khanaen lueaktang samachik sapha thongthin 29 kumphaphan 2547* [Summary of the use of voting rights in elections for local assembly members]. 29 February 2004.

———. *Phon kan nap khanaen kan lueaktang samachik sapha ongkan borihan suan changwat Songkhla 14 minakhom 2547* [Results of the election for members of the Songkhla Province administrative organization]. 14 March 2004.

Suchit Bunbongkarn. "Elections and Democratization in Thailand." In *The Politics of Elections in Southeast Asia*, edited by R.H. Taylor. New York: Woodrow Wilson Center Press and Cambridge University Press, 1996.

Sukanya Lim. "Gift-bearing TRT Courts Country's Most Loyal Voters." *Nation*, January 4, 2003.

———. "Southern Dilemma." *Nation*, December 3, 2003.

Suliman Wongsuphap. *Mueang Hat Yai: Khon chin kap kansang mueang kankha nai phak tai* [Hat Yai city: The chinese and the building of a commercial city in the southern region]. Bangkok: Thailand Research Fund, 2004.

Suphannee Chalothorn. "The Unique Character of Electoral Constituencies and Their Effects on Political Behavior and Voting Turnouts." Paper Presented at the 8th International Conference on Thai Studies, Nakhon Phanom, Thailand, 9–12 January 2002.

Supawadee Susanpoolthong. "Democrats to Woo Young as Abhisit Vows Radical Change." *Bangkok Post*, February 24, 2005.

Supawadee Susanpoolthong, and Yuwadee Tunyasiri. "TRT Claims 5 More MPs." *Bangkok Post*, August 6, 2004.

Surachai Sirikrai. "General Prem Survives on a Conservative Line." *Asian Survey*, vol. 22, no. 11 (1982): 1093–1104.

Suraphong Sothanasathian. "*Mueang yai lae rupbaep thi khuan pen: Kan borihan ngan Hat Yai* [The large city and the pattern that should be adopted: The administration of Hat Yai]." Research report prepared for Prince of Songkhla University, Hat Yai, 1985.

Surin Maisrikrod. *Thailand's Two General Elections in 1992: Democracy Sustained*. Singapore: Institute of Southeast Asian Studies, 1992.

Sutthiwong Phongphaibun. *Katho sanim krit lae withichiwit chao tai ton lang* [Knocking rust off the kris and the way of life of the people of the lower south]. Bangkok: Thailand Research Fund, 2000.

———. *Southern Thai Cultural Structures and Dynamics vis-à-vis Development*. Bangkok: Thailand Research Fund, 2004.

Sutthiwong Phongphaibun, et al. *Lokathat Thai phak tai* [The world view of the southern Thais]. Songkhla: Institute for Southern Thai Studies, 1984.

Sutthiwong Phongphaibun, Dilok Wutthiphanit, and Prasit Chinnakan. *Chin Thaksin: Witti lae phalang* [The chinese of southern Thailand. Ways and power]. Bangkok: Thailand Research Fund, 1997.

Suwat Chantharasuk. "*Wiwathanakan khwam phukphan khong phak Prachathipat kap phak tai* [The evolution of the Democrat Party's identification with southern Thailand]." Master's thesis, Chiang Mai University, Chiang Mai, 1996.

Tej Bunnag. *The Provincial Administration of Siam: 1892–1915: The Ministry of the Interior Under Prince Damrong Rajanubhab*. Kuala Lumpur: Oxford University Press, 1977.

Thawon Senniam. *Khadi prawatisat. 99 wan antarai. Thammai …Ko Ko To tit khuk* [A historical case. 99 critical days. Why …the election commissioners were imprisoned]. Bangkok: T.A. Media, 2007

Thongthin niyom lae phumiphak niyom nai sangkhom lae kanmueang Thai [Localism and regionalism in Thai society and politics]. Nakhon Si Thammarat: Walailak University, 1995.

Tulsathit Taptim. "Opposition Leader Simply Unmarketable." *Nation*, January 18, 2005.

Turner, Victor. *The Anthropology of Performance*. New York: PAJ Publications, 1987.

Walker, Andrew. "The 'Rural Constitution' and the Everyday Politics of Elections in Northern Thailand." *Journal of Contemporary Asia* (forthcoming).

Watchariphon Ketphasa. "*Phawa phunam khong nayok thesamontri lae khrong-sang amnat nai thongthin Thai: Suksa chapho koroni thesaban nakhon Hat Yai* [Local Leadership of Mayors and Local Thai Power Structure: A Case Study of Hat Yai City Municipality]." Master's thesis, National Institute of Development Administration, Bangkok, 1999.

Wattana Sugunnasil. "Consuming Modernity in a Border Community." In *Dynamic Diversity in Southern Thailand*, edited by Wattana Sugunassil. Chiang Mai: Prince of Songkhla University/Silkworm Books, 2005.

Weerayut Chokchaimadon. "Democrats in Fight to Save Stronghold." *Nation*, August 13, 2004.

Wenk, Klaus. *The Restoration of Thailand Under Rama I. 1782–1809*. Tucson: University of Arizona Press, 1968.

Wilson, David A. *Politics in Thailand*. Ithaca: Cornell University Press, 1962.

Withaya Suracharithanarugse. "*Puak* [sic.]: Concept of Collective Behavior in Thai Society." In *Proceedings of the 6th International Conference on Thai Studies. Theme VII. Toward A New Frontier of Thai Studies*, 219–28. Chiang Mai: Chiang Mai University, 1996.

Yongyut Chuwaen. "*Amnat thang kanmueang nai khwam suep-nueang botbat kankha khong mueang Songkhla tang-tae klang phutthasattawat thi 22 thueng plai phutthasattawat thi 23* [Political Power in the Perpetuation of the Trading Role of Songkhla Principality, from the Middle of the 22nd Buddhist Century to the End of the 23rd Century]." In *Songkhla sueksa: Prawattisat lae borankhadi mueang songkhla* [Songkhla Studies: History and Archeology of Songkhla], edited by Phonsak Phromkaeo and Chamnong Raekphinit. Bangkok: Institute of Southern Thai Studies, 1992.

INDEX

H

I

J

K

O

P

U

V